ACHIEVING NET ZERO

DEVELOPMENTS IN CORPORATE GOVERNANCE AND RESPONSIBILITY

Series Editor: David Crowther

Recent Volumes:

DEVELOPMENTS IN CORPORATE GOVERNANCE AND
RESPONSIBILITY   VOLUME 20

ACHIEVING NET ZERO: CHALLENGES AND OPPORTUNITIES

EDITED BY

DAVID CROWTHER

Social Responsibility Research Network, UK

And

SHAHLA SEIFI

Social Responsibility Research Network, UK

United Kingdom – North America – Japan
India – Malaysia – China

Emerald Publishing Limited
Howard House, Wagon Lane, Bingley BD16 1WA, UK

First edition 2023

Reprints and permissions service
Contact: permissions@emeraldinsight.com

British Library Cataloguing in Publication Data
A catalogue record for this book is available from the British Library

ISBN: 978-1-83753-803-4 (Print)
ISBN: 978-1-83753-802-7 (Online)
ISBN: 978-1-83753-804-1 (Epub)

ISSN: 2043-0523 (Series)

Printed and bound by CPI Group (UK) Ltd, Croydon, CR0 4YY

INVESTOR IN PEOPLE

CONTENTS

LIST OF CONTRIBUTORS

Adetayo Olaniyi Adeniran	Federal University of Technology Akure, Nigeria
Onder Altuntas	Eskisehir Technical University, Turkey
Noushra Shamreen Amode	University of Mauritius, Mauritius
Georgia Beardman	Edith Cowan University, Australia
Elaine Conway	Loughborough University, UK
Prakash N. K. Deenapanray	Université Des Mascareignes, Mauritius
Jaime Yallup Farrant	Climate Justice Union, Australia
José Carlos Góis	University of Coimbra, Portugal
Sughra Ghulam	Lidl, UK
Naomi Godden	Edith Cowan University, Australia
Pratima Jeetah	University of Mauritius, Mauritius
Yousuf Kamal	University of Derby, UK
Iffet Kesimli	Kirklareli University, Turkey
James Khan	Wilman Knowledge Holder and Elder, Australia
Angus Morrison-Saunders	Edith Cowan University, Australia
Mosunmola Joseph Muraina	Ekiti State University, Nigeria
Mehran Nejati	Edith Cowan University, Australia
Josiah Chukwuma Ngonadi	Jiangsu University, China
Joe Northover	Wilman Knowledge Holder and Elder, Australia
Rabiu Olowo	Lagos State Ministry of Finance, Nigeria
Talita Panzo	University of Coimbra, Portugal
Lukman Raimi	Universiti Brunei Darussalam, Brunei
Lanre Ibrahim Ridwan	University of Lagos, Nigeria
Leonie Scoffern	Edith Cowan University, Australia
Ferhan K. Sengur	Eskisehir Technical University, Turkey
Verena Tandrayen-Ragoobur	University of Mauritius, Mauritius

PART 1

NET ZERO AND SUSTAINABILITY

STEPS ON THE JOURNEY TO NET ZERO

Elaine Conway and Yousuf Kamal

ABSTRACT

This chapter discusses the global challenge to reduce greenhouse gas (GHGs) emissions to net zero by 2050. It explains what net zero means and how it is calculated, together with some of the debate around the suitability of the target to maintain global warming levels within 'acceptable' boundaries. The chapter then presents some of the opportunities and challenges that transitioning towards net zero will pose to countries and their inhabitants, in terms of changes to policies, products, processes and behaviours that will be required to attain the target. It then discusses the need for a strategy to achieve net zero across different sectors of society and provides a few suggestions of tools and concepts that could be adopted to support the changes necessary, such as planning for change, the Sustainable Development Goals (SDGs), integrated reporting and the circular economy. The chapter concludes with a reflection on the need for the net zero target and how it is our collective responsibility to support the challenging transition to net zero for the benefit of all.

Keywords: Net zero; planning for change; strategy; Sustainable Development Goals (SDGs); integrated reporting; circular economy

INTRODUCTION

This chapter examines the net zero agenda, what it is, how it is measured and the debates that continue around the global goal of achieving net zero greenhouse gas (GHG) emissions by 2050. It also discusses some of the challenges and opportunities that arise from the transition towards net zero, from a government/national standpoint, but also at organisation and individual level. Undoubtedly, achieving net zero will necessitate a significant change across various aspects of our lives, but if we are to prevent untenable environmental disasters from

Achieving Net Zero
Developments in Corporate Governance and Responsibility, Volume 20, 3–24
Copyright © 2023 by Emerald Publishing Limited
All rights of reproduction in any form reserved
ISSN: 2043-0523/doi:10.1108/S2043-052320230000020001

threatening the viability of life on earth as we understand it, then change will be inevitable. Hence, we should look at net zero with a balanced viewpoint as to the challenges to be faced but also the positive opportunities it may bring.

The chapter proposes some ways in which organisations can transition to net zero, by considering planning for net zero within the business strategy and providing some alternative perspectives, such as the Sustainable Development Goals (SDGs), integrated reporting, and the circular economy concepts as starting points to leverage the transition process for a sustainable and far-reaching effect.

The chapter concludes with a reflection on the need for the net zero target and how it is our collective responsibility to support the challenging transition to net zero for the benefit of all.

WHAT IS NET ZERO?

Within the 2015 Paris Agreement on climate change, world leaders committed to significantly reduce greenhouse gas (GHG) emissions to contain the increase in global temperatures to 2°C below that of pre-industrial levels during this century, whilst striving to limit temperature increases to 1.5°C where possible (UNFCCC, 2016). In addition, leaders agreed to balance the emissions of GHGs within the second half of the current century, such that the total of all GHGs emanating from human activities nets off to zero (Rogelj, Geden, Cowie, & Reisinger, 2021). This has coined the term 'net zero', where countries and organisations alike are setting the goal of achieving this balance within their scope of operations. Many states in the United States, the European Union and China, amongst others, are mandating a net zero economy by 2050, including many large companies (Deutch, 2020; Fankhauser et al., 2022).

However, what does this mean in reality? Despite being a step in the right direction for reducing global temperatures and GHGs, the devil is in the detail of these national and corporate plans. For example, some plans target only carbon dioxide (CO_2) emissions, whilst others include all GHGs in their remit (Rogelj et al., 2021). Equally, there is no consensus on the scope of emissions which are included in the target: for example, some consider only those emissions which they can control directly (called Scope 1 emissions), whilst others consider their wider supply chain both up and down stream, such as raw material suppliers and the end use of their product (Scope 2 and 3 emissions) (Rogelj et al., 2021). Another grey area in many targets is whether the aim is to reduce emissions or just to offset them with other activities, such as carbon sinks (Fankhauser et al., 2022), so the target is NET zero (after the offsets), rather than zero emissions from the product/process in question.

There is also a debate about country or industry specifics (Rogelj et al., 2021). For example, should emerging economies be subject to the same targets as more highly industrialised countries, given that the latter nations are likely to be the highest polluters and have greater resources to work on reducing them? At industry level, should more highly polluting or energy-intensive industries be required to achieve net zero before less polluting or lower energy consuming ones? Some uses of energy are relatively easily convertible to decarbonised sources, such as for powering cars and other light vehicles, by converting or designing them to use electricity as their power source, and then creating the electricity from renewable sources, such as solar, wind or even nuclear (Davis et al., 2018). However, other current usages of power cannot currently be so readily converted, such as in the production of steel and cement and long-distance travel (aviation and shipping). Demand for these uses is forecast to continue well into the future, and hence until technology adapts to address these applications, their impacts on achieving net zero will need careful consideration. Some of these opportunities and challenges will be discussed in more detail later in this chapter.

These challenges are regularly the subject of international discussions at conferences such as the annual United Nations Climate Change Conference (Conference of Parties (COP)). It is critically important that countries discuss these issues together to work out the most appropriate global response. It will require substantial cooperation across nations to make the necessary changes. Clearly, it is of limited use if countries unilaterally make commitments to net zero if others increase their emissions or shift them to other countries. For example, the way in which countries depend on each other for raw materials, energy and products should be acknowledged. Many countries' demands for energy (oil and natural gas) exceed their own natural reserves and hence they rely on imports from oil- and gas-rich nations for their energy. Therefore, it is unreasonable to criticise the emissions of these fossil fuel-extracting countries which have unavoidable emissions that other countries do not have. Equally, the offshoring of manufacturing from high wage countries to lower wage countries in recent years has also shifted the inherent emissions from these manufacturing processes, which has the consequence of making the importing countries' emissions appear artificially low in comparison with the exporters', as they are still consuming the goods, just not producing them locally. The increased freight costs (and emissions) associated with this offshoring activity should also be assessed when considering the long-term viability (economic or otherwise) of such offshoring. Because of such interlinked activities worldwide, it is imperative that discussions about how to address global emissions are made at a high level across countries, so that the problem is addressed holistically and as equitably as possible.

This holistic approach is also needed to avoid unintended consequences of actions, which on the face of it reduce emissions, but then create other negative impacts. For example, whilst the shift away from fossil fuel-based power generation to sustainable sources, such as hydroelectricity is laudable, the creation of dams for hydroelectric power generation can cause significant and sometimes catastrophic damage to the environment, threatening biodiversity and huge social problems due to the diversion of water away from its natural course (Arantes, Fitzgerald, Hoeinghaus, & Winemiller, 2019; Bosshard, 2015). This has caused backlash against new hydroelectric installations across the world as there is greater awareness of the negative impacts they can have on local communities and the environment as access to water is then restricted (Schapper, Unrau, & Killoh, 2020). Growing populations, with increased water and power demands coupled with water scarcity, can instigate the construction of more hydroelectric dams. This can become particularly critical when a dam is constructed in one country which impacts the access to water in another, as has been the case in some Arab countries and is the source of conflict between Ethiopia which is constructing the Grand Ethiopian Renaissance Dam on the river Nile, which will significantly affect access to water in Egypt and Sudan (Salameh, 2021). Iran too has developed dams which have affected the quantity and quality of the water in Iraq over several years (Salameh, 2021). Aside from these geopolitical and social impacts, there is also evidence that such installations create not insignificant emissions themselves, since once a dam is constructed, there is a flooding of land to fill the reservoir, which results in an increase in GHG emissions due to the degradation of biomass from that land. These emissions are largely methane, which is a GHG which remains in the atmosphere far longer than CO_2 (Levasseur, Mercier-Blais, Prairie, Tremblay, & Turpin, 2021).

Despite remaining issues, it is generally regarded as a positive step that countries have acknowledged the need for targets to reduce the level of GHGs in the atmosphere (Rogelj et al., 2021). In many cases, there is considerable work being done to achieve them, even if that effort is not universal or being made quickly enough to be achieved by the deadline. However, there is also controversy whether achieving net zero by 2050 is sufficient to keep global temperature increases below 2°C. This is because the calculation to assess the average global temperature increase is complex. The 'temperature increase at any time is proportional to the logarithmic change in atmospheric CO_2 concentration' (Deutch, 2020, p. 2237). It is expressed as:

$$\delta T(c) \;=\; \varepsilon \ln\!\left(\frac{c}{c_0}\right)\ln(2)^{-1}$$

Where δT = change in global temperature, c = CO_2 concentration at a point in time, ln = natural logarithm and ε = the equilibrium climate sensitivity (the temperature increase from a doubling of the concentration) (Deutch, 2020).

One difficulty is that the equilibrium climate sensitivity varies significantly due to the ways in which the planet reacts to changes in its environment (Hausfather, 2021). For example, there is debate as to whether fires have a positive or negative effect on this figure. Due to this volatility, as a measure, it can vary between 1.5 and 4.5, which affects the calculation considerably, such that even if net zero were to be achieved by 2050, there is no guarantee that the earth will not increase in temperature by more than 2°C (Deutch, 2020).

The choice of a 2°C cap on average global temperatures as a target is not universally accepted in environmental and scientific circles. On the one hand, there is the sense that 2°C is unachievable and that 3°C limit should be the target, whilst on the other hand, there is concern that even if achieved, a 2°C cap is not sufficient to avoid significant environmental damage, and that the world should be aiming towards a 1.5°C limit (IPCC, 2018). In 2021, the CO_2 concentrations were approximately 416.45 parts per million by volume (ppmv) (Tiseo, 2022), which is equivalent to global temperatures rising by 1.3°C since the pre-industrial era (Hausfather, 2021). If carbon emissions do fall to net zero, then the world will still continue to warm slightly for several years, but at a much slower rate as the atmosphere adjusts to the new levels of carbon being released and absorbed. Eventually, if the carbon levels remain zero, then this warming is expected to stop (Hausfather, 2021).

Despite the variability of the calculations to underpin the global target and whether 2°C will deliver the outcomes which climate change scientists expect, net zero is the currently agreed global target. It is up to the countries themselves to work out how they will achieve their own net zero targets. First, the target itself needs to be clarified, whether it means carbon reduction only, carbon offsetting or a combination of both. Then governments will need to enlist the support of organisations and individuals to do all they can to contribute to this process, whether voluntarily or mandated by national laws.

In most cases, the initial focus is on reducing carbon where possible as this has the longest-term effect and is currently one of the quickest methods of making an impact. Where this is not possible, or the best efforts have been made to reduce carbon, then it is likely that carbon offsetting will be used to balance out the carbon emissions which are more difficult to reduce or eradicate at the current time (Fankhauser et al., 2022).

The next step after reducing the amount of carbon being released into the atmosphere is to remove residual carbon through carbon management activities (Davis et al., 2018). This is because some of the GHGs being released currently will remain in the environment for centuries (such as CO_2), whereas others, such as methane have an impact for only a few years (Fankhauser et al., 2022; Rogelj et al., 2021). At present, we have limited technologies to remove the shorter impact gases such as methane but are developing the means to remove some of the longer impacting GHGs. However, it is hoped that in time, newer technologies will be developed to achieve this process: the focus currently is to reduce the release of more GHGs into the atmosphere in the first place.

At this point, despite many countries and companies signing up to net zero, progress has been patchy. The next section will discuss some of the main opportunities and challenges faced by nations and organisations in their race to net zero.

CHALLENGES POSED BY THE NET ZERO AGENDA

Change to a net zero world is perhaps one of the most daunting tasks ever encountered by humankind. It requires a complete transformation of not only the production and consumption process but also the mindset of how people use resources for these processes. Reaching a net zero emissions level needs substantial changes across the economy. For example, in the UK context, it represents a tremendous shift in the economy that was once the largest coal consumer in the world (Hook & Sheppard, 2019). To fulfil the net zero target by 2050, there is a need for countries and their citizens to understand the urgency needed to avoid the worst impact of global warming. The 2050 target has presented substantial challenges from business to industry, from developed country to developing country and from West to East. Some of these challenges are discussed in this section.

One key sector which needs to be transformed as quickly as possible is the energy sector. This sector contributes approximately 75% of GHG emissions, and it is the single largest factor that needs to be overcome to offset the severe impact of climate change (United Nations, 2022). To reach net zero emissions by 2050, the energy sector must be decarbonised at an exceptional speed. Coal, gas and oil-fired power sources need to be rapidly replaced by renewable sources of energy such as wind or solar, and countries need to move to these alternative sources as soon as practical. This transformation would require substantial industrial modifications and will involve major cost. For example, more than 80% of UK dwellings are heated by natural gas, contributing about 15% of total UK greenhouse emissions (Hook & Sheppard, 2019). It will be a real challenge to make new houses with alternative heating systems (hydrogen could be an option but involves huge cost) or convert all the existing housing stock to renewable sources. In the United Kingdom currently, all new build properties must be built to Future Homes Standards with Energy Performance Certificate (EPC) rating A (the highest level), and legislation is under development which will require older houses to retrofit improvements to heating source and insulation levels (Hook & Sheppard, 2019).

The transport sector is another significant source of GHG emissions. For example, in the case of United Kingdom, it accounts for 28% of emissions. Whilst the sale of new petrol- and diesel-fuelled cars will cease by the end by 2030, there needs to be greater availability of affordable electric cars and more charging points to speed up consumer adoption (Harrabin, 2020). The vehicle manufacturing industry needs to transform their manufacturing process from fossil fuel to alternative sources of power, which will pose another challenge for automobile industry. Gaeta, Businge, and Gelmini (2022) argue that by 2050, renewable energies will contribute approximately 90% of the basic energy utilisation by replacing traditional fossil fuels. However, this would be a challenge for some developing countries as to what extent they can use this renewable energy for decarbonisation.

The next challenge emanates from the industrial sector. For example, steel, petrochemical and cement manufacturing still produce huge amounts of CO_2, without having any CO_2 capturing method such as re-injecting it underground, keeping it out of atmosphere or recycling it in another industrial process. This is particularly important to understand in the context of emerging markets and developing economies who are considering their development in terms of building huge infrastructure, which requires heavy industries using fossil fuels, especially to produce extreme temperature heat for industrial processes. While the use of electricity may be an alternative to fossil fuels, the electricity generation method is key. Electricity can be generated from water, wind, coal or nuclear-powered plants. Some countries, for example, the United Kingdom, have made substantial progress towards coal-free electricity and have become one of the world's biggest offshore wind users to generate electricity. Other countries around the globe are still significantly using coal to generate electricity (Gaeta et al., 2022).

Thus, this transformation of the electric grid could be a huge challenge for the rest of the world towards a net zero target.

A broad range of sophisticated technologies will be needed to achieve a net zero target, ranging from advanced nuclear power to direct CO_2 capture. Negative emission technologies would physically remove CO_2 from the atmosphere and store it in a way that would be permanent. These technologies might include afforestation and reforestation, soil carbon sequestration, biochar, bioenergy with carbon capture and storage, direct air capture, enhanced weathering and ocean alkalinisation and ocean fertilisation (Dwortzan, 2022). Innovative technologies are also required to replace heavy-industry emissions. However, challenges remain, not only how much the world would need to depend on these negative emission technologies to achieve the net zero target but also how fast it will start to capture emission at the global level. To achieve the target, these negative emission technologies need to extract CO_2 directly from the atmosphere and remove it permanently, whilst being subject to an efficient protocol of measurement, reporting and verification (Dwortzan, 2022). It is extremely doubtful that the 2050 net zero goal could be achieved without some type of stable CO_2 storing capability. Thus, building sustainable CO_2 storage facilities becomes an equally pressing issue.

Some of these carbon-reducing and storing technologies are not currently commercially available but will be key for certain industries to achieve net zero where alternatives to CO_2 emissions are not possible in the short to medium term, such as the energy, airline and long-distance shipping industries. This will require significant investment in innovation and a more future-oriented sustainable approach to conduct business. Organisations need to pursue continual investment in research and development (R&D) to develop system consistency and flexibility (Renné, 2022). The Committee for Climate Change (CCC) suggests that the cost of achieving net zero would be 1–2% of the gross domestic product (GDP) annually for the United Kingdom. However, there are various issues which would need to be addressed such as the availability of technological know-how, sources of financing, system development and maintenance and life-style change of people to support the transformation process (Gaeta et al., 2022).

Another big challenge towards the net zero target is the commitment to change from individual to corporate to government level. Whilst many people are keen to reduce carbon emissions, not everyone is committed or able to commit to doing so. This is true for the corporate sector and governments in different countries as well. In particular, it may be difficult to motivate some developing countries who believe that they are emitting less compared to other developed countries and thereby would be less interested or committed to provide efforts towards net zero emission. In case of the corporate sector, many small and medium enterprises (SMEs) are unaware of their individual impacts on climate change or how they could take pro-active action towards net zero targets. Similarly, larger corporations may need to take difficult decisions to re-design their products or processes to reduce their carbon emissions. This may well require considerable upfront investment which could impact profitability in the short term, hence acting as a disincentive to act. At individual level, there are a small percentage of people who still believe that climate crisis is science fiction and continue to deny its existence and impact on global warming at all. Achieving the 2050 net zero target requires a set of timelines, a set of strategies for every sector of economy, an understanding and assessment of where we are now and where we need to be each year until 2050. This will require coordination across all sectors of the economy and a considerable amount of time, manpower, R&D and capital investment as well. As it is a global problem, and as there are differences between have and have-nots, it is imperative that the developed nations take the lead and might also need to provide some sort of funding or technology transfer for the developing or poorer nations in their effort to achieve net zero emissions. Achieving net zero will need incentive, investment, ingenuity and unprecedented levels of cooperation from different sectors and from different geo-political governments.

This concept of cooperation and coordination is critical to the success in achieving the net zero goal and making a lasting impact globally. It will be necessary for countries to work together to manage the various trade-offs, between richer and poorer nations, manufacturing versus service economies, those who possess the raw materials, including, increasingly, access to clean water, versus those who need access to them, against the backdrop of reducing emissions. It is also vitally important that the long-term effects of projects are assessed: whilst a short-term gain to reduce CO_2 may be laudable, if the replacement product or process emits another GHG, which remains in the atmosphere far longer than CO_2, or creates significant negative environmental or social consequences, then the full impacts of the change need to be evaluated – note the example of hydroelectric dams for power generation as discussed in the 'What is net zero?' section in this chapter.

OPPORTUNITIES POSED BY THE NET ZERO AGENDA

Achieving net zero could also provide sources of opportunities. It could create a competitive advantage for those who take proactive actions first and thereby creating opportunity for their countries, businesses and people (HM Treasury, 2021). For example, developing intense decarbonisation technologies would help governments and key stakeholders not only to achieve the target but also to become leaders in such technologies. This could support greater investment to develop new decarbonising industries (Gaeta et al., 2022). Lloyds Bank (2021) has found a significant growth in new industries in the UK economy as a result of seeking ways to achieve the net zero target. Four hundred thousand jobs have already been created because of striving towards net zero, with another 2.5 million jobs likely to be created in the near future.

The UK Government's CCC has projected that the total capital required to support net zero targets up until 2050 is likely to be £1.4 trillion (Lloyds Bank, 2021). This will be invested in new infrastructure, creating new businesses and in turn, new employment opportunities. Many organisations are already considering ways to achieve net zero, by decreasing their operating costs, boosting revenues, and redesigning their capital structure, or a combination of all three activities (Allas, Bowcott, Hamilton, & Simmons, 2021). For example, in the housing sector, by building houses in compliance with net zero targets, they will offer an attractive investment. These net zero future buildings would require less time, money and energy resources than traditional dwellings. The owners or tenants of these buildings would not need to worry about blackouts, power surges or brownouts as these houses would be equipped with generators that run on fuel cells. Likewise, farming, petroleum, excavation, power, water, transport and many other manufacturing sectors could reduce their costs by reducing their own emissions (Allas et al., 2021).

Another key opportunity is the need for storage facilities for renewable energy (Rhoden et al., 2021). There will be most likely an increase in demand for the storage capabilities for hydrogen, non-natural gas and permanent CO_2 storage. As gas storage facilities will be a fundamental corner stone of upcoming power structure, getting access to these facilities would be competitive among the suppliers of gas, utilities and power-driven industries. Thus, countries or businesses need to consider securing sufficient energy storage facilities. This will open up a further avenue of profitable business for many who might consider building additional infrastructure such as power-grid, gas pipelines or link to electrolysers in addition to different gas storage facilities (Rhoden et al., 2021).

One of the most important opportunities for net zero target is that globally, many businesses have already realised the importance of achieving this target and have included it within their business strategies. This may include the development of low emission or zero emission products and services, investing in R&D and having emission reduction technologies in place. For example, achieving net zero would require substantial adjustments in engineering methods, especially in the power sensitive sector. It is likely that there will be increased demand for products of these industries and hundreds of thousands of new jobs would be created to make the industry greener and emission-free. However, some of these industries may need to be relocated based on the access to resources such as wind, hydrogen or CO_2 storage facilities (Rhoden et al., 2021).

Achieving net zero should equally provide substantial financial opportunity for business and shareholders. For example, the UK CCC estimated that around 1% of GDP will be needed to be devoted to new projects annually from now to 2050 (Fatehi, 2021). They further estimated that yearly capital investment into the decarbonisation sector will be boosted from £10bn in 2020 to £50bn by 2030 until 2050 (Fatehi, 2021). It has been further forecasted that the UK low-carbon market will increase by 11% by the next 10 years, and it will be able to provide £60bn to £170bn worth of products and services by 2030 (Fatehi, 2021). As the net zero target requires a rapid transition, it will require a radical shift of the energy sector; hence, those countries which have strengths in certain areas such as offshore wind platform installation or building CO_2 storage facilities will be able to capitalise more quickly on the new opportunities generated by new technologies and ways of working. The net zero target provides a focus for governments to plan long term and prioritise areas of greatest contribution to the target enabling lower costs and environmental benefits in the long run (HM Treasury, 2021).

Decarbonisation of transport, housing and light manufacturing needs a large amount of clean energy which can originate from water, solar, nuclear or biomass with CO_2 direct capture and storage facilities (Bataille et al., 2020). This will create further opportunity in terms of transport and energy infrastructure investment. Decreasing deforestation, expanding afforestation, and more attempts to lower emissions will also create opportunity for new businesses. Decarbonisation will provide further benefits for people as they will enjoy cleaner air, warmer homes with more efficient, fair and affordable energy prices, better protection from extreme weather conditions, more efficiency in travel, increased biodiversity and better access to green spaces (Department for Business Energy and Industrial Strategy, 2021). To achieve a net zero target by 2050, if countries and businesses take the necessary action, it should support sustainable economic growth, whilst improving air and water quality, at sustainable cost levels. However, most of these benefits will depend on how different countries and different sectors implement their strategies and how they coordinate their efforts towards achieving the target.

NET ZERO STRATEGY

To achieve net zero, countries and organisations will need to build actions into a strategy. At government level, a net zero strategy refers to a set of plans outlining policies and procedures to reduce emissions and gradually the decarbonisation of all the sectors of an economy, from agriculture to transport, from housing to airlines, from corporate to government etc. The plan should address actions in the short, medium and longer term and would need to cover every aspect of an economy. Leading private firms, non-government organisations and government organisations also need to set their own strategy for this mid-century target. For example, the UK government's net zero strategy is to reduce its emission levels to net zero in 2050, with a 78% reduction from 1990 to 2035 (Department for Business Energy and Industrial Strategy, 2021). This strategy sets out several steps to reduce emissions, to capitalise on the opportunities arising from the net zero target and to leverage more financing into the green economy. Aiming to capitalise on the benefits of net zero as well as addressing the challenges, the United Kingdom has set its net zero strategy in a way that would generate more vacancies, create new products and services with advanced and state-of-the-art technologies and become a more energy secure nation. For example, the UK government announced specific measures to end the sale of new fossil fuel–driven cars and vans by 2030, to encourage dwelling owners to move from existing gas-fired boilers to less carbon emitting heating systems and to deliver incentives for the agricultural sector to adopt less carbon-emitting cultivation methods (Department for Business Energy and Industrial Strategy, 2021).

In the construction sector, the construction and operation of net zero energy buildings could be part of strategy towards the 2050 net zero target (Hoque & Iqbal, 2015). A low carbon-constructed domestic or industrial building can considerably alleviate the ecological effects of the construction as it only gener-ates as much power as it needs on an annual basis from renewable power sources. However, all this transformation requires a robust strategy to decarbonise the existing energy systems and replace them with renewable electricity generation through wind or solar (Department for Business Energy and Industrial Strategy, 2021).

A clean and consistent energy system is the basic cornerstone of a net zero strategy for any country. Hence, a clear and definitive strategy is necessary to reduce reliance on high emissions power generation and replace it with sophisticated modern nuclear plant or renewables, bolstered by flexible storage facilities of CO_2 gases and hydrogen. This transformation process would bring high skills and highly paid job opportunities across the globe. To decarbonise industry, strategy needs to set for the smooth transformation of industrial sector by providing cleaner fuels and energy efficient resources (Department for Business Energy and Industrial Strategy, 2021).

Net zero strategies should also include plans about how GHGs could be removed from the atmosphere because even if rigorous plans were achieved for low emission products and services, it would be difficult to reduce or eliminate 100% of emissions from sectors such as the chemical industry, agriculture and livestock and aviation by 2050. For this, plans should be put forward to use CO_2 removal methods and to use negative emission technologies. HM Government (2021) suggests two approaches for this. First one is the nature-based approach such as afforestation and soil carbon sequestration, and the second one is the industrial-based approach such as direct air carbon capture and storing, bioenergy with carbon capture and storage space, wood in construction, biochar and enhanced weathering. Deutch (2020) supported this approach; that a net zero strategy should be directed to achieving an offset between lowering emissions into the atmosphere and elimination of CO_2 from the environment through innovative negative emissions technologies.

As discussed earlier, funding is a great challenge towards the achievement of net zero targets and therefore a clear strategy and budgets need to be set for funding innovation such as negative emission technologies, for developing emission-free products and services and for the removal of the CO_2 from the atmosphere. Funding from the private as well as the public sector is essential to meet the expected financial requirements to achieve the 2050 goal. A significant shift in investment in renewable energy and infrastructure needs to outweigh fossil fuel investment by no later than 2025. In this respect, developing countries need to be financially supported by the developed countries or donor agencies such as the World Bank, the United Nations (UN), International Monetary Fund (IMF) or Asian Development Bank (ADB). For example, some developing countries are dependent heavily on coal, and they have poor infrastructure for renewable energy. For these countries, a strategy needs to be established to substitute coal with natural gas and liquefied natural gas (LNG) instead of renewable energy, as direct transition to 100% renewable energy might not be possible for many developing countries such as Bangladesh.[1] An inclusive energy

---

[1]Although Bangladesh's GHG emissions per capita (excluding land use) are 0.96 tCO2e, it finds itself bearing a significant burden of the resulting climate crisis. For example, projections show that Bangladesh could have up to 13.3 million internally displaced people due to climate change by 2050 and it is one of the world's most climate vulnerable countries (Climate Transparancy, 2021).

transition plan may be needed for developing countries to direct investment appropriately and to prevent job losses. New opportunities could be created in the renewable energy sector over time for those people who previously worked in fossil fuel–based industry.

Since there are substantial international trade flows between and among developed and developing nations with differing socioeconomic and political systems, these need to be considered vis-a-vis the three decade time frame to achieve the net zero target. In this respect, Deutch (2020) noted that the net zero target might be possible for the United States and other big CO_2 emitters including Japan, Germany, South Korea, Saudi Arabia and Canada but may be more difficult for emerging economies such as India, China and Russia.

MAKING SENSE OF NET ZERO – HOW CAN ORGANISATIONS START?

The global adoption of net zero target requires a substantial reduction in emissions and removal of GHGs. To achieve this, organisations need to understand how they can contribute towards this goal. We will focus on four different areas, such as Planning for Change, SDGs, Sustainability and Integrated Reporting, and Circular Economy and Performance Economy.

Planning for Change

Planning at different levels is the most important aspect for organisations to address the challenges they face due to the 2050 target. An organisation, irrespective of being a large, medium or small enterprise, needs to embrace this reality and needs to set up their strategic plan to achieve and/or contribute towards net zero. For example, big organisations such as Rolls-Royce in the United Kingdom have started to implement their policies very successfully. In Rolls-Royce's (2021) annual report they noted the following:

> Our mission is to play a leading role in the transition to net zero; of the focus areas in our framework, climate action, adaptation and the transition to net zero are the most significant. Given the scale and nature of our business, it is the biggest potential contribution that we, as an organisation, can make to a more sustainable future and is consequently one of the greatest potential risks to our business success. Mitigating our impact on climate change and decarbonising our product portfolio is intrinsically linked to our purpose and business strategy. (Rolls-Royce, 2021, p. 34)

Like Rolls-Royce, many of the high-profile companies now disclose their strategies and achievements so far towards the net zero targets in their annual reports. For example, in 2019, 30% of the Fortune 500 companies disclosed that they already have climate goals or openly committed to reduce CO_2 by 2030, which is a substantial shift from as little as 6% in 2016 (Lu, 2021). The word/phrase 'net zero' appears 171 times in the 2021 annual report of Rolls-Royce, indicating how much priority the organisation places on this objective. This is also supported by the positive statement from the CEO of Rolls-Royce, Warren East, echoing the opportunities presented by the net zero goal:

> While challenges remain, we can look with increasing confidence to the future and the significant commercial opportunity presented by the transition to net zero. The transition to net zero power is a significant opportunity for us in Power Systems with mission critical power for data centres, power for construction and infrastructure, and marine solutions leading the demand for net zero carbon solutions. (Rolls-Royce, 2021, p. 6)

If we consider SMEs, whilst they may lack the time, know-how or financial resources of larger companies to completely eliminate their carbon footprint, many SMEs are keen to understand their sources of emission, set interim goals and then focus on implementing straightforward decarbonisation strategies before tackling longer term, more complex measures (Carbon Trust, 2022). The Carbon Trust (2022) suggested a four-step journey for SMEs to achieve net zero, including commitment, calculations, switching to green and making a reduction plan. Once commitment is done fairly and honestly then they need to calculate their emissions based on scope 1 and scope 2 (emissions arising from own operations) or scope 3 (emissions arising from the wider value/supply chain). As most SMEs are highly concerned about energy use, they can control and reduce their energy use by following this four-step process.

Sustainability and the Sustainable Development Goals (SDGs)

Another method organisations can adopt towards a net zero target would be to establish a link between 2050 net zero targets and the SDGs which are relevant to their operations. The United Nations developed 17 SDGs with the aim of addressing the critical issues facing the planet, including poverty, environmental issues and improving the quality of life for all (UN, 2015). Whilst the SDGs tackle a broader range of issues than just net zero (through the environmental goals), organisations can often find them more useful and applicable to their businesses as a way to think through their impacts on society.

Many companies are increasingly disclosing their key operations linked with one or more of the 17 SDGs and there has also been a tremendous increase in sustainability reports by the companies globally. For example, Lu (2021) noted that the number of S&P 500 companies publishing sustainability reports increased from 20% in 2011 to 90% in 2019, mainly due to stakeholder demands and the need for compliance with environmental, social and governance (ESG) goals. In the 2021 Annual Report of Rolls-Royce, there is a 17-page 'sustainability report' (pp. 34–51) which covers specifically SDG numbers 7, 8, 12, 13 and 16 and details how they are being linked with the core business operations of Rolls-Royce. This is an example of how organisations put sustainability and SDGs in the heart of their business operations. Within this sustainability report they provide many disclosures relating to net zero–related targets and achievements.

For many listed companies, it is a stock exchange requirement to publish data on sustainability actions, rather than net zero actions specifically. There are many definitions of sustainability. However, the most commonly adopted one is provided by the Brundtland Report (1987):

> Sustainability is a broad discipline, giving insights into most aspects of the human world from business to technology to environment and the social sciences. It focuses on meeting the needs of the present without compromising the ability of future generations to meet their needs.

The notion of sustainability is comprised of three pillars: economic, environmental and social – also known informally as profits, planet and people: the triple bottom-line. In 2012, the United Nations Conference on Sustainable Development provided 8 Millennium Development Goals (MDGs), which were expected to be accomplished by 2015. Later, the 17 SDGs were developed by the United Nations to succeed the MDGs (UN, 2015).

The rationale behind the SDGs is transforming the world for 2030 and since then it has been extensively used by businesses and governments around the planet. In broad terms, SDGs offer a common outline for peace and prosperity for people and the planet, considering the present needs and the potential needs for future. By providing 17 SDGs, the United Nations made an urgent call for action by all its member countries through comprehensive collaborations. Among the 17 SDGs, number 13 relates to climate change–related goals. Thus, many companies around the world are now providing some sort of disclosures about this SDG in their annual reports. Mostly, all these SDGs acknowledge that the world should be poverty-free with better health and education for all people, by reducing wealth differences and thereby stimulating economic development, at the same time overcoming climate change threats and conserving mother earth, oceans and forests. By addressing these issues, organisations can strive to be more resilient within their own environment (PWC, 2016).

Developing a resilient organisation requires the knowledge and ability to promptly respond to systematic and unsystematic risks that are frequently discussed within the umbrella of sustainability (IFAC, 2011). Broadly, the concept of sustainability also includes corporate social responsibility in addition to planet, people and profit. It requires consistent developing of business models that are resilient and that are continually transforming products, technologies and processes within a sustainable strategy. The International Federation of Accountants (IFAC) (2011) provides the following insights about a sustainable strategy:

> A sustainable strategy can lead to business resilience by enabling an organisation to create value for its shareholders while it also contributes to a sustainable society by meeting the needs of this generation without sacrificing future generations. A truly sustainable strategy is one that integrates material sustainability issues, leading to business models that enable net positive economic, environmental, and social impacts. For example, Ikea strives for resource independence by encouraging all waste be turned into resources; energy independence by being a leader in renewable energy; and becoming more energy efficient throughout its operations and supply chain. (IFAC, 2011, p. 7)

IFAC (2011) established a sustainability framework that recommends that an organisation considers four different perspectives to become sustainable. For example, the organisation needs to develop a business strategy which would be a part of their strategic discussions, objectives, goals and targets. They need to develop their internal management processes in a way that improves energy efficiency and reduces waste as quickly as possible. They need to inform and educate their financiers or primary stakeholders about how they are making profit by considering ecological and other sustainability issues and need to provide disclosures about this in their published financial reports to discharge their stewardship role. This approach considers wider stakeholders' concerns, not just those of financiers and promotes transparency against a broader set of societal expectations, including assurance to improve credibility and trust.

As stated earlier, whilst sustainability and the SDGs cover wider topics than just net zero, such as social issues and governance, often it is useful to use these broader concepts as a way to understand the full impacts that organisations have on their environment and society. There has been considerable interest in social responsibility reporting since the late 1990s when organisations were accused of violation of various social and environmental issues pertaining to working conditions, health and safety, and labour rights: especially in developing countries where the West often outsourced or manufactured their products. There has been increasing media pressure that has highlighted the need for greater social and environmental reporting, following scandals relating to child labour, poor working conditions in the supply chain and a discussion of the moral responsibilities of large corporations in particular to improve standards (Kamal & Deegan, 2013).

Hence, sustainability or social and environmental reporting now covers a wide range of issues which an organisation needs to address, depending on their specific industry and circumstances. These include employee health and safety, working conditions, human/labour rights, freedom of voice and freedom of making association, the use of child labour or forced labour (modern slavery) and product or service safety (Deegan, 2014). Environmental reporting includes how the organisation's activity affects the surrounding ecology ranging from water use, raw material use, waste management, carbon emissions and compliance with environmental regulation (Deegan, 2014).

Many elements which are covered in social and environmental or sustainability reports are measured against international standards, to provide assurance in the reliability and comparability of measures. For example, the current global guideline for sustainability reporting has been created by the Global Reporting Initiative (GRI) G4 (Global Reporting Initiative, 2013). These guidelines can help organisations to select the most appropriate metrics for their own circumstances, allowing them to develop their own roadmap to sustainability and assist in their journey to net zero.

Integrated Reporting

Another relatively recent development in the corporate reporting regime that emerged from the combination of social and environmental reporting and sustainability reporting is integrated reporting. Integrated reporting started in 2010 when the International Integrated Reporting Council (IIRC) was established through the collaboration between The Prince's Trust Accounting for Sustainability Project (A4S) and the GRI (IIRC, 2013). The primary objective was to develop a sustainability structure which is acceptable worldwide, and that considers both financial and non-financial aspects of sustainability in an 'integrated' system. It provides a value-creation model by which an organisation relies on a complete set of six categories of input capital (financial, manufactured, intellectual, natural, human, and social and relationship) which are then processed within the business model of the organisation and to provide outputs categorised using the same six capitals (IIRC, 2013). The idea is that the organisation adds or creates value across the different capitals during the transformation stage within their own business model, based on their individual organisation and industry (Conway, Robertson, & Ugiagbe-Green, 2020). In the same way as sustainability reporting, integrated reporting can assist organisations to consider a wider range of issues than just the environment, but which can support a more holistic approach to the achievement of net zero.

Integrated reporting focuses on value creation over time and is a 'concise communication about how an organisation's strategy, governance, performance and prospects, in the context of its external environment, lead to the creation of value in the short, medium and long term' (IIRC, 2013). Integrated reporting is an interesting area of the corporate reporting regime that explores corporate reporting in a revolutionary manner (see, for example, Conway et al. (2020), de Villiers, Rinaldi, and Unerman (2014), Abeysekera (2013)) and that provides a platform for effective stakeholder engagement. Researchers such as Lemma, Khan, Muttakin, and Mihret (2019) consider integrated reporting as an innovation in corporate reporting that has decision usefulness for businesses, by considering a much wider range of aspects than just the traditional measures.

Companies across the world are now modifying their annual reports to produce an integrated report. An example of one such report from a developing country, Bangladesh, is from the IDLC Finance Company for the year 2021. In their 424 page-long report, they provided a detailed discussion as to how they address all the different categories of capital and how they are being linked with their core business operations (IDLC, 2021). They also provided information about how they address the net zero 2050 target. For example, they noted, 'IDLC also aspires to measure carbon footprint of both its internal operations and loan portfolio to reduce the impact and thus reach net zero emission by 2050' (IDLC, 2021, p. 95). They also provided disclosures about how they aspire to achieve various SDGs though their business operations (IDLC, 2021, p. 108). Hence, by using the integrated report format, organisations can provide financial, social, environmental and governance information in a concise way that better caters for the needs of a wider group of stakeholders beyond the traditional providers of capital, who are traditionally the audience of the annual report (Kamal, 2022).

The Circular Economy

The final section of this chapter discusses the concept of the circular economy, which has the potential to support organisations towards the reduction of carbon emissions and therefore, could be integrated within a net zero plan. The core idea of circular economy is that we must move away from a linear economy, where we take raw materials from the environment, make them into products/services which are then disposed of, as the amount of waste that is generated from this business model is greater than the biophysical capabilities of the planet to cope with it (Larrinaga & Garcia-Torea, 2022). Instead, we should be aiming to achieve maximum usage of available products and materials in a closed loop, circular system. This can be done by reducing (waste), reusing (either in its original form or repurposed) and recycling (where alternative uses are not appropriate), but by maintaining the quality of materials as high as possible for as long as possible, so that the minimum amount possible is wasted (Taleb & Al Farooque, 2021). It can be defined as a complete system that takes into consideration issues such as climate change, biodiversity, recycling of waste by circulation of materials and by regenerating nature (Ellen MacArthur Foundation, 2022).

The core idea of a circular economy is to convert raw materials and waste in a way that produces minimum disposable waste and thereby recycling the remaining waste again and again to use as further input. To implement the circular economy, organisations may need to adopt product and process-reengineering to design circularity to its products and processes from initial production through to the end of use of the product. In addition, the energy sources used in manufacturing should be transitioned to renewables where possible. This should reduce reliance on increasingly scarce and hence expensive raw materials, mitigate against rising energy costs, uncertain supply chains and reduce business interruption risks. Whilst there may be some not insignificant initial costs to adapt to the circular economy model, which remains a drawback to some organisations, in the long run, it is anticipated that the benefits will outweigh the costs.

A fully circular economy could provide significant benefits to people, the planet and also profits, through reduced costs, a more sustainable supply chain, new job opportunities (for example, in re-engineering roles which perhaps do not currently exist) and a better environment (Conway, 2021). Some of the world's largest corporate sectors have already started to embrace the circular economy with the aim of achieving improved value creation, a more resilient organisation and the fulfilment of the organisation's social responsibility objectives. For example, the retailer, H&M, has engaged in the circular economy and provided this insight from their Head of Sustainability, Pascal Brun:

> With our size comes responsibility. The way fashion is consumed and produced today is not sustainable. We have to transform the industry we are in. Our ambition is to transform from a linear model to become circular. (Ellen MacArthur Foundation, 2022)

H&M announced its circular economy and climate-positive target by designing a road map for 'circular ecosystems' that not only contributes towards climate change and biodiversity goals but also focuses on increased customer satisfaction. H&M focuses on producing circular goods, maintaining circular supply chains and maintaining a circular customer experience through an integrated system network (Ellen MacArthur Foundation, 2022).

Renault is another forerunner of the circular economy in the motor manufacturing industry. Their objective is to expand the life of automobiles and parts, and keep raw material in use, thereby decreasing the use of fresh/new raw materials (Ellen MacArthur Foundation, 2022). For example, Renault remanufacture motor parts such as gear boxes and turbo compressors by using recycled plastic and developing another life for electrical batteries as part of their circular economy business process.

These actions together with a concerted effort to convert the power sources within manufacturing processes to renewable energy have the ability to significantly reduce carbon emissions as part of the circular economy. Hence, the concept of the circular economy is very much in line with the net zero agenda and is another way in which organisations could consider their own environmental impacts when developing their net zero strategy.

CONCLUSION

This chapter has examined the net zero agenda and how governments around the world have signed up to achieving net zero GHG emissions by 2050, in response to increasingly common environmental disasters. There is clear scientific evidence that the planet is increasing in temperature at an alarming rate as a result of those emissions, having a detrimental impact on the ecosystems of the world, which support life as we know it. By reducing the GHGs in the atmosphere, it is hoped to control this warming to an average of 2°C. There is a continuing debate about whether net zero emissions by 2050 will be sufficient to achieve this 2°C target, whether the 2°C will be enough to prevent environmental disaster, and whether we should be striving for a tougher target, more quickly. Despite these debates, net zero emission by 2050 is the target that has been agreed and it represents a substantial challenge for countries around the world in terms of the changes in the products, services, technologies, and behaviours it will require. Clearly, more developed nations, or those with greater emission-producing industries will have more of a challenge to achieve this target. Poorer nations may lack the resources to achieve the target. Hence, it will require unprecedented global cooperation to understand the unique circumstances each country may have in addressing the target.

Hence, this challenging target will need to be tackled in a variety of different ways to reduce global reliance on products and processes which create emissions of GHGs into the atmosphere. The main step is to reduce emissions in the first place where feasible. This will require re-thinking of how products are made and used and services delivered from a standpoint of their environmental impacts. It will require new ways of thinking and working and new technologies to support the re-engineering of products and processes. Clearly, it is unrealistic to assume that all industries can decarbonise or completely eradicate their GHG emissions, even by the 2050 deadline, particularly those in long-haul transportation and power generation, so there will need to be some trade-offs required and investment in carbon management activities. Even where it is possible to reduce or eradicate emissions, some GHGs remain in the environment for centuries, so we will need to remove residual carbon from the atmosphere through carbon capture and storage to slow global warming. Current carbon capture and storage technologies are insufficient to manage the carbon in the environment. Hence, new technologies will need to be developed. This will require government support through targeted policies and active investment in carbon management R&D.

At organisational level, this chapter has discussed ways in which organisations can use tools or mindsets such as planning for change, the SDGs, integrated reporting, and the concept of the circular economy to build net zero goals into their strategy. Whilst organisations operate in varying industries and situations (for example, being a market leader versus a small start-up organisation, or profit-making versus not-for-profit), every organisation, and in turn, every individual, can play a part in striving towards a net zero goal. By considering our reliance on GHGs in our personal and professional lives, we can use tools and concepts to encourage ourselves to rethink the products and services that we use, in an attempt to reduce the GHGs which are emitted through our own behaviours to help achieve the net zero goal for the benefit of our entire planet.

The level of cooperation and coordination that will be required to manage the trade-offs needed between countries and industries and to assess the true long-term impacts of moving to net zero is unprecedented. As discussed earlier, scarce resources, such as water, can be used as a political weapon by countries constructing dams for hydroelectricity generation in their own country, but which can have devastating impacts socially and environmentally on other countries further downstream below the dam. These impacts will need to be balanced and negotiated carefully to avoid conflicts and to create a future which is advantageous to all.

To conclude, the words of the renowned naturalist and environmental campaigner, Lord David Attenborough (Planet Earth II, 2016) appear the most apt to capture the essence of what net zero is aiming to achieve:

> It's surely our responsibility to do everything within our power to create a planet that provides a home not just for us, but for all life on Earth.

REFERENCES

Abeysekera, I. (2013). A template for integrated reporting. *Journal of Intellectual Capital, 14*(2), 227–245. doi:10.1108/14691931311323869

Allas, T., Bowcott, H., Hamilton, A., & Simmons, V. (2021). Opportunities for UK businesses in the net-zero transition. McKinsey & Company – Sustainability. Retrieved from https://www.mckinsey.com/business-functions/sustainability/our-insights/opportunities-for-uk-businesses-in-the-net-zero-transition

Arantes, C. C., Fitzgerald, D. B., Hoeinghaus, D. J., & Winemiller, K. O. (2019). Impacts of hydroelectric dams on fishes and fisheries in tropical rivers through the lens of functional traits. *Current Opinion in Environmental Sustainability, 37*, 28–40. doi:10.1016/j.cosust.2019.04.009

Bataille, C., Waisman, H., Briand, Y., Svensson, J., Vogt-Schilb, A., Jaramillo, M., ... Imperio, M. (2020). Net-zero deep decarbonization pathways in Latin America: Challenges and opportunities. *Energy Strategy Reviews, 30*. doi:10.1016/j.esr.2020.100510

Bosshard, P. (2015). 12 dams that changed the world. *The Guardian*.

Brundtland, G. H., & WCED. (1987). Our common future. *Environmental Conservation, 14*(4), 291–294. World Commission on Environment and Development. Retrieved from http://www.un-documents.net/our-common-future.pdf

Carbon Trust. (2022). *The journey to net zero for SMEs*. Retrieved from https://prod-drupal-files.storage.googleapis.com/documents/resource/public/ThejourneytoNetZeroforSMEsguide.pdf

Climate Transparancy. (2021). *Climate transparency report: Bangladesh's climate action and responses to Covid-19 crisis* (pp. 1–19). Retrieved from https://www.climate-transparency.org/wp-content/uploads/2021/11/Bangladesh-CP2020.pdf

Conway, E. (2021). Reporting for new business models: The challenge to support the circular economy. In A. Kumar, J. A. Garza-Reyes, & S. A. R. Kahn (Eds.), *Circular economy for the management of operations* (pp. 49–66). Abingdon; Oxford: CRC Press.

Conway, E., Robertson, F. A., & Ugiagbe-Green, I. (2020). Integrated reporting. In D. Crowther (Ed.), *The Palgrave handbook of corporate social responsibility*. London: Palgrave Macmillan.

Davis, S. J., Lewis, N. S., Shaner, M., Aggarwal, S., Arent, D., Azevedo, I. L., ... Caldeira, K. (2018). Net-zero emissions energy systems. *Science, 360*(6396). doi:10.1126/science.aas9793

de Villiers, C., Rinaldi, L., & Unerman, J. (2014). Integrated reporting: Insights, gaps and an agenda for future research. *Accounting, Auditing & Accountability Journal, 27*(7), 1042–1067. doi:10.1108/AAAJ-06-2014-1736

Deegan, C. (2014). *Financial accounting theory* (4th ed.). Sydney: McGraw Hill.

Department for Business Energy and Industrial Strategy. (2021). *Net zero strategy: Build back greener*. In *Gov.Uk* (Issue October). HM Govt. Retrieved from https://www.gov.uk/government/publications/net-zero-strategy

Deutch, J. (2020). Is net zero carbon 2050 possible? *Joule, 4*(11), 2237–2240. doi:10.1016/j.joule.2020.09.002

Dwortzan, M. (2022). Global net-zero emissions goals: Challenges and opportunities In *MIT Joint Program on the Science and Policy of Global Change*. Retrieved from https://globalchange.mit.edu/news-media/jp-news-outreach/global-net-zero-emissions-goals-challenges-and-opportunities

Ellen MacArthur Foundation. (2022). What is a circular economy? In *Circular economy introduction*. Retrieved from https://ellenmacarthurfoundation.org/topics/circular-economy-introduction/overview

Fankhauser, S., Smith, S. M., Allen, M., Axelsson, K., Hale, T., Hepburn, C., ... Wetzer, T. (2022). The meaning of net zero and how to get it right. *Nature Climate Change, 12*(1), 15–21. doi:10.1038/s41558-021-01245-w

Fatehi, K. (2021). Decarbonisation and the net zero business opportunity. In *European Association of Geoscientists & Engineers, Conference Proceedings, ProGREss'21*. 1–3. doi:10.3997/2214-4609.202159017

Gaeta, M., Businge, C. N., & Gelmini, A. (2022). Achieving net zero emissions in Italy by 2050: Challenges and opportunities. *Energies, 15*(1). doi:10.3390/en15010046

Global Reporting Initiative. (2013). *G4 sustainability reporting guidelines: Reporting principles and standard disclosures*. GRI.

Harrabin, R. (2020). Ban on new petrol and diesel cars in UK from 2030 under PM's green plan. *BBC News*. Retrieved from https://www.bbc.co.uk/news/science-environment-54981425

Hausfather, Z. (2021). Explainer: Will global warming 'stop' as soon as net-zero emissions are reached? *Carbon Brief*. Retrieved from https://www.carbonbrief.org/explainer-will-global-warming-stop-as-soon-as-net-zero-emissions-are-reached

HM Treasury. (2021). *Net zero review. Analysis exploring the key issues* (Issue October). Retrieved from https://assets.publishing.service.gov.uk/government/uploads/system/uploads/attachment_data/file/945827/Net_Zero_Review_interim_report.pdf

Hook, L., & Sheppard, D. (2019). The UK's net-zero target: What are the greatest challenges? *The Financial Times*. Retrieved from https://www.ft.com/content/2c212fa8-8d17-11e9-a1c1-51bf8f989972

Hoque, S., & Iqbal, N. (2015). Building to net zero in the developing world. *Buildings*, *5*(1), 56–68. doi: 10.3390/buildings5010056

IDLC. (2021). *Life finds a way*. Retrieved from https://web.idlc.com/uploads/financial_report/idlc-annual-report-2021-881229.pdf

IFAC. (2011). Sustainability Framework 2.0. Professional accountant as integrator. *Risk Management and Insurance Review*, *12*(1). doi:10.1111/j.1540-6296.2009.01152.x

IIRC. (2013). *The international integrated reporting <IR> framework*. International Integrated Reporting Council. Retrieved from https://www.integratedreporting.org/

IPCC. (2018). Global warming of 1.5°C. In *Global Warming of 1.5°C. An IPCC Special Report on the impacts of global warming of 1.5°C above pre-industrial levels and related global greenhouse gas emission pathways, in the context of strengthening the global response to the threat of climate change* (Vol. 2, Issue October). Retrieved from www.environmentalgraphiti.org

Kamal, Y. (2022). Stakeholders' engagement through integrated reporting practices: Evidence from dialogic accounting perspective. Paper presented in Accounting and Finance Association of Australia and New Zealand (AFAANZ) Conference held in Melbourne, Australia (July, 2022).

Kamal, Y., & Deegan, C. (2013). Corporate social and environment-related governance disclosure practices in the textile and garment industry: Evidence from a developing country. *Australian Accounting Review*, *23*(2), 117–134. doi:10.1111/j.1835-2561.2012.00205.x

Larrinaga, C., & Garcia-Torea, N. (2022). Critical perspectives on accounting an ecological critique of accounting: The circular economy and COVID-19. *Critical Perspectives on Accounting*, *82*, 1–9. doi:10.1016/j.cpa.2021.102320

Lemma, T. T., Khan, A., Muttakin, M. B., & Mihret, D. (2019). Is integrated reporting associated with corporate financing decisions? Some empirical evidence. *Asian Review of Accounting*, *27*(3), 425–443. doi:10.1108/ARA-04-2018-0101

Levasseur, A., Mercier-Blais, S., Prairie, Y. T., Tremblay, A., & Turpin, C. (2021). Improving the accuracy of electricity carbon footprint: Estimation of hydroelectric reservoir greenhouse gas emissions. *Renewable and Sustainable Energy Reviews*, *136*(April 2020), 110433. doi:10.1016/j.rser.2020.110433

Lloyds Bank. (2021). From now to net zero: A practical guide for SMEs. Retrieved from https://www.lloydsbank.com/assets/assets-business-banking/pdfs/from_now_to_net_zero.pdf

Lu, M. (2021). Visualizing the climate targets of Fortune 500 companies. *Visual Capitalist*. Retrieved from https://www.visualcapitalist.com/climate-targets-of-fortune-500-companies/

Planet Earth II. (2016). Episode 6, BBC Earth.

PWC. (2016). Navigating the SDGs: A business guide to engaging with the UN global goals. 95. Retrieved from www.pwc.com/globalgoals

Renné, D. S. (2022). Progress, opportunities and challenges of achieving net-zero emissions and 100% renewables. *Solar Compass*, *1*(March), 100007. doi:10.1016/j.solcom.2022.100007

Rhoden, I., Vögele, S., Ball, C., Kuckshinrichs, W., Simon, S., Mengis, N., … Thrän, D. (2021). *Spatial heterogeneity – Challenge and opportunity for net-zero Germany* (Issue October, pp. 1–20). Helmholtz Klima. Retrieved from https://www.netto-null.org/imperia/md/assets/net_zero/dokumente/2021_netto-null_spatial-heterogeneity.pdf

Rogelj, J., Geden, O., Cowie, A., & Reisinger, A. (2021). Net-zero emissions targets are vague: Three ways to fix. *Nature*, *591*(7850), 365–368. doi:10.1038/d41586-021-00662-3

Rolls-Royce. (2021). *Annual report 2021*. Retrieved from https://www.rolls-royce.com/~/media/Files/R/Rolls-Royce/documents/annual-report/2021/2021-full-annual-report.pdf

Salameh, M. T. B. (2021). Dam wars: Are conflicts over water looming in the Middle East? *Inside Arabia*. Retrieved from https://insidearabia.com/dam-wars-are-conflicts-over-water-looming-in-the-middle-east/

Schapper, A., Unrau, C., & Killoh, S. (2020). Social mobilization against large hydroelectric dams: A comparison of Ethiopia, Brazil, and Panama. *Sustainable Development*, *28*(2), 413–423. doi:10.1002/sd.1995

Taleb, M. A., & Al Farooque, O. (2021). Towards a circular economy for sustainable development: An application of full cost accounting to municipal waste recyclables. *Journal of Cleaner Production*, *280*, 124047. doi:10.1016/j.jclepro.2020.124047

Tiseo, I. (2022). Historic average carbon dioxide levels in the atmosphere worldwide from 1959 to 2021 (in parts per million). *Statistica*. Retrieved from https://www.statista.com/statistics/1091926/atmospheric-concentration-of-co2-historic/

UN. (2015). SDGs: Sustainable development knowledge platform. Retrieved from https://sustainabledevelopment.un.org/sdgs

UNFCCC. (2016). The Paris agreement. In *United Nations Framework Convention on Climate Change*. Retrieved from https://unfccc.int/paris_agreement/items/9485.php

United Nations. (2022). For a livable climate: Net-zero commitments must be backed by credible action. *Climate Change*. Retrieved from https://www.un.org/en/climatechange/net-zero-coalition

THE ROLE OF MANAGEMENT ACCOUNTANTS REGARDING CLIMATE CHANGE: THE CASE OF TURKEY

Iffet Kesimli

ABSTRACT

This study aims to reveal the perspectives of the management and senior accountants on the subject regarding the effects of climate change on the business world, within the framework of utilisation of tools like strategic cost management and strategic management. An electronic form was sent repeatedly to the e-mail addresses of public companies listed on the Borsa Istanbul (BIST), which were obtained from the Public Disclosure Platform (PDP), between June 2018 and June 2019. According to the data obtained from the survey of this study, it is not possible to comment that these tools are effectively utilised in Turkey. Besides, it is also early to say that top management is fully aware of the need to manage climate change. This study contributes to the literature by revealing the view of management accountants and finance experts in Turkey on climate change.

Keywords: Climate change; accountants' perception; climate change initiative; risk perception; carbon emission accounting; climate change related activities; Borsa Istanbul companies

INTRODUCTION

Uncertainty and volatility are the new normal.

Ng Boon Yew FCCA, Executive Chairman Accountancy Futures Academy.

Achieving Net Zero
Developments in Corporate Governance and Responsibility, Volume 20, 25–55
ISSN: 2043-0523/doi:10.1108/S2043-052320230000020002

It was suggested in 1827 by the French scientist Joseph Fourier that gases in the atmosphere could be responsible for trapping energy from the sun (Pierrehumbert, 2004; Peterman, 2017). It took a long time for the physics science to show an interest in greenhouse gases. Today, greenhouse gases are seen as one of the important causes of climate change. At the point reached by science, of course, a lot of new information has been reached, yet the subject is still being studied. There are many publications that deal with the technical aspects of the subject. This study aims to deal with the subject from the point of view of accounting at the level of the top management of enterprises.

As Ng Boon Yew states, uncertainty and volatility are the new normal of our era. In the foreword to the Future of Accounting Academy's report 100 Drivers of Change for the Global Accountancy Profession, Yew points out that the global panorama will be continually reshaped by a combination of market volatility, globalisation and climate innovation. Meanwhile, wealth and power changes, economic uncertainty and political transitions are also experienced (2012). These challenges are compounded by rapid advances in science and technology, demographic changes and the emergence of new business models. As witnessed social and economic environments shift. Thus, all of these coinciding phenomena will have a serious impact on businesses and the accountancy profession (Pierrehumbert, 2004; Peterman, 2017). At this point, the question arises whether accountants are ready for upcoming radical changes occurring simultaneously. Again, accountants are expected to understand how the new, reshaping future will affect the organisations they serve. According to Riva, one of the managers of Siemens Financial Services in England; energy and business data can be aggregated into financial metrics that can appeal to influential stakeholders in an organisation. Currently, most accountants act as bridges between those responsible for sustainability in the business and the management team (2015). Rapidly changing business environments will require updating some accounting and auditing standards; this will require retraining of accountants and auditors for new standards and/or changing legislation. Not only the role of financial managers but also the reporting processes will change drastically. The next generation of accountants will need to be reformed. In this chapter, the answer to the question of whether accountants are ready for radical changes will be sought within the framework of climate change, which definitely will change the needs of businesses.

CONCEPTS

Climate change is the change in climate as a result of human activities that directly or indirectly degrade the composition of the global atmosphere, in addition to natural climate change observed over comparable time periods (www.enerji.gov.tr, 2022). Just talking about weather does not mean that climate issue is addressed. The National Geographic Society emphasises the reality that weather is one of the components of climate. Climate change is the alteration of temperature and typical weather patterns in a place in the long run. These alterations may cause weather patterns to be less predictable, which in turn makes it difficult maintaining and growing crops in farming-dependent regions. Damaging weather events like hurricanes, floods, downpours and winter storms are also said to be connected to climate change (www.nationalgeographic.org, 09.04.2022). The issue of climate change can be considered a relatively new topic for the accounting community. For this reason, the concepts that are frequently used when climate change and accounting come together are discussed in detail here. Clarifying the concepts in the research is important in terms of better understanding the study and revealing its contribution to the literature. Climate change, emissions, carbon footprint, sustainability and cost analysis from different perspectives are some of them.

Climate Change Initiative

Climate Change Initiative (CCI) that seeks reinforcing the scientific, mitigation and adaptation capacities of countries and communities, which are most vulnerable to the effects of climate change, was launched by the Director-General of UNESCO, Irina Bokova, in 2009 (www.unesco.org, 17.09.2020). This initiative is not to be confused with UMass Lowell's CCI that is a university research centre informing and supporting evidence-based climate action (www.uml.edu, 09.04.2022). Among others, some climate change programmes listed by search engine are (1) US Global Change Research Program, (2) Climate Program Office, National Oceanic and Atmospheric Administration (NOAA), (3) National Extension Climate Initiative (NECI), (4) NASA Harvest (Food Security and Agriculture Program), and (5) Climate Adaptation Science Centers, United States Geological Survey (USGS).

Emission

Emission defined as an amount of a substance that is produced and sent out into the air that is harmful to the environment, especially carbon dioxide (dictionary.cambridge.org, 09.04.2022), has long been seen as a problem with vital consequences for humanity. The United Nations Framework Convention on Climate Change and the Kyoto Protocol, the aim of which is to stop the greenhouse gas accumulations in the atmosphere at a level that will prevent the human-induced danger on the climate system, are the most important steps in the historical process (Elitaş, Çonkar, & Karakoç, 2014, p. 46).

Carbon Footprint Calculation – Carbon Accounting/Budgeting

Carbon emission accounting is the calculation of the carbon footprints of the greenhouse gases released into the atmosphere, their tracking, recording and reporting, as well as the calculation of their costs to the business (Elitaş et al., 2014, p. 47). Assuming carbon accounting is part of the business's sustainability plan; (1) Green House Carbon (GHC), (2) formerly Carbon Disclosure Project (CDP®), newly named Disclosure Insight Action (CDP®), (3) Science Based Targets initiative (SBTi) and similar institutions and organisations gain importance.

Carbon footprint calculations are based on information about the buildings the enterprise powers, its flight routes, fuel consumption of vehicles like cars, vans, trucks etc., usage of public transport – buses, trains, taxis and the like. At this level, direct and indirect emissions are taken into consideration. Calculated carbon footprint may be disclosed and/or benchmarking tools may be used in order to compare and learn from similar organisations with the aim of improving it (https://sustainabletravel.org, www.carbonfootprint.com, 09.04.2022).

Preparing and Monitoring the Business for the Climate Change Initiative

The prerequisite for preparing the business for the CCI requires setting targets and preparing strategies and plans. The report prepared by the Center for Climate and Energy Solutions (C2ES) in 2006 describes the various components of the climate-related strategy, with eight steps classified into three phases. These are as follows (Hoffman, 2006, p. 5):

Phase I: Developing a climate strategy
    Step 1. Evaluating the emission profile
    Step 2. Anticipating and measuring risks and opportunities
    Step 3. Evaluating options for technological solutions
    Step 4. Setting goals and targets
Phase II: Focussing inwards
    Step 5. Developing financial mechanisms to support climate programmes
    Step 6. Engaging the organisation
Phase III: Focussing outwards
    Step 7. Formulating a policy strategy
    Step 8. Managing external relations

Strategies should be determined by following the steps mentioned above and the business should be prepared for climate change. Finance and climate change management information systems should be integrated. After the strategy is formulated and the ways to be followed are determined, climate change performance measurements should be monitored on the basis of key performance indicators (KPIs). In addition, compliance with climate change policy and legislation should be monitored.

Total Cost/Life Cycle Assessment Calculations

The theoretical foundations for carrying out environmental and economic analysis across the life cycle of a product are based on environmental Life Cycle Assessment (LCA) and Life Cycle Costing (LCC) (Miah, Koh, & Stone, 2017, p. 848). The LCA implementation consists of four phases as defined by ISO 14040 and ISO 14044: (1) goal and scope, (2) Life Cycle Inventory, (3) Life Cycle Impact Assessment and (4) interpretation. There are three different LCA methods applicable within the framework of the International Standards Organization (ISO): (1) Process LCA (P-LCA), (2) Economic-Input-Output (EIO) LCA and (3) hybrid

LCA. Life Cycle Costing (LCC) is the consideration of all costs that will arise and accrue during the life of a product, business or service (ec.europa.eu/environment, 18.09.2020). These may be: (1) The purchase price and all associated costs (transport, installation, insurance etc.), (2) Operating costs, including energy, fuel and water use, spare parts and maintenance, (3) Decommissioning, end-of-life costs such as disposal, and residual value – that is, income from the sale of the product. LCC may also cover the costs of externalities such as greenhouse gas emissions. LCC may include cost stages, estimation of costs and risk/sensitivity analysis (Miah et al., 2017, p. 848). Next to the LCA and LCC methods, Social Life Cycle Assessment (S-LCA), a four-stage method similar to LCA, that evaluates the social effects of the product throughout its life cycle, has been added (Özdemir, 2019, p. 166). The equation [Life Cycle Sustainability Assessment (LCSA)] developed to support the decision-making process in the development of a new product and assessing sustainability impacts throughout its life cycle is as follows (Özdemir, 2019, p. 178):

$$LCSA = LCA + LCC + S\text{-}LCA$$

While there is no software specifically developed for S-LCA so far [as of June 2018], there is a database of environmental LCA software based on a static input–output model used to provide industry- and country-specific forecasts of activity in product supply chains (Özdemir, 2019, p. 179).

Sustainability

In a very simple definition, sustainability means meeting our own needs (today) without compromising the ability of future generations to meet their own needs (in the future) (University of Alberta, 2013). Embedding sustainability requires integrating environmental, health and social values into the core of the business, without expecting anything in return and without sacrificing quality (Laszlo & Zhexembayeva, 2011, p. 100). Sustainability accounting, also referred to as social accounting, social and environmental accounting, corporate social reporting, corporate social responsibility reporting or non-financial reporting, is considered as a sub-branch of financial accounting that focusses on the provision of non-financial information about the firm's performance to external stakeholders (www.en.wikipedia.org, 15.09.2020). Economic, social and environmental fields form the basis of sustainability. Sustainability accounting provides a useful tool for identifying, assessing and managing social and environmental risks by identifying resource efficiency and cost savings, and linking social and environmental improvements with financial opportunities. It also allows for comparison and benchmarking of performance and identification of best practice (Constructing Excellence, 2004).

Sustainability Reporting

A sustainability report is a self-published report on the economic, environmental and social impacts of the day-to-day activities of the business or organisation. In addition to revealing the organisation's values and governance model, it also demonstrates the link between the organisation's strategy and its commitments towards a sustainable global economy. The sustainability report is the key platform where sustainability performance and positive/negative impacts are communicated. Sustainability reporting, also known by many different names like Non-financial reporting, Triple-Bottom-Line (TBL) reporting, Corporate Social Responsibility Reporting etc., is also an internal element of integrated reporting that combines financial and non-financial performance (www.globalreporting.org, 17.09.2020). Issues covered in a sustainability report would be as listed below (www.globalreporting.org, 2022):

Material Topics	Energy	Training and Education
Economic Performance	*Water and Effluents*	*Customer Privacy*
Indirect Economic Impacts	Biodiversity	Non-Discrimination
Procurement Practices	*Emissions*	*Local Communities*
Anti-Corruption	Effluent and Waste	Child Labour
Anti-Competitive Behaviour	*Materials*	*Marketing and Labelling*
Tax	Employment	Security Practices
Supplier Environmental assessment	*Occupational Health and Safety*	*Rights of Indigenous Peoples*
Supplier Social Assessment	Public Policy	Customer Health and Safety
Forced or Compulsory Labour	*Diversity and Equal Opportunity*	*Freedom of Association and Collective Bargaining*

The diversity of issues listed above shows the depth and width of sustainability. In fact none of them is new to business administration. One of my favourite topics enjoyed in classes is the stakeholders of business. As well known, there are nine stakeholders for any business entity. These are shown in Fig. 1. Not all arrows showing relationships between stakeholders are shown to avoid confusion. However, each stakeholder has bounds to all others. Furthermore, each arrow had to show two-way relations among each stakeholder, including the entity itself.

It is apparent that the Fig. 1 and list of sustainability report issues are linked; the figure displays them and the list induces the management to care for each so that the report reflects its conduct.

Managerial Accounting or Management Accounting

Although demanded and used by managers as well, financial accounting, also known as general accounting, reports on all the activities of the business and often to outside stakeholders who want information about the economic development of the business. The information contained in the reports is open to the public and therefore accessible to competitors. Management, which has the liability and responsibility to make decisions on behalf of the business, needs the information produced by the branch of accounting called managerial accounting or management accounting, which has a different perspective from financial

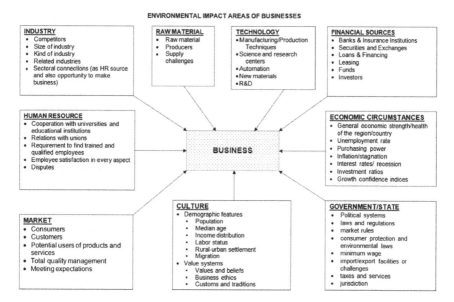

Fig. 1. Environmental Impact Areas of Business – Stakeholders.

accounting. Essentially, management accounting relies on the records kept and reports produced by financial accounting; however, far from being publicly available, this information is protected as company's secret (Bierman & Drebin, 1978, p. 5; Johnson & Gentry, 1980, p. 16). Management Accounting includes four main tasks. These are (Drebin & Bierman, 1978, p. 1) (1) Determining cost, (2) Cost control, (3) Evaluate performance, (4) Provide information for planning and specific decisions. Managerial Accounting is the identification, measurement, analysis, interpretation and presentation of financial information to management in order to achieve the objectives of the enterprise. It varies from financial accounting with the goal of assisting internal people in making well-informed business decisions (www.investopedia.com, 14.09.2020). Those who work in this field of accounting are called managerial accountants. As can be seen, despite four decades between the two definitions, there is no change in the definition of managerial accounting. However, the tools and methods managerial accountants use have diversified, changed and are enriched over time.

In fact, there are too many new concepts to count on the subject. The concepts discussed above are only a part of them. However, it is anticipated that this study will help to better understand and illustrate the diversity of tools available to management accountants and management in general.

LITERATURE

The issue of climate has, of course, been on the agenda of the world of science for a long time. When a full-text search is superficially made in peer-reviewed

journals using the terms 'climate change effects' on EbscoHost, it is seen that
there are 636 publications between 1971 and 1999, 4,005 publications between
2000 and 2009 and 16,658 publications between 2010 and 2020. When the search
is repeated in the similar way using the terms 'climate change impact' instead, it is
seen that the first publication dates back to 1911, there were no other publications
until 1971. There were 586 publications between 1971 and 1999, 5,078 between
2000 and 2009, and 21,821 between 2010 and 2020. It cannot be assumed that all
of the aforementioned publications are in the field of social sciences, and it can be
assumed that some of them appeared in both surveys. It can be predicted that
older publications are not listed in the aforementioned database. When the search
in the database was done by adding the term 'finance', publications on various
topics were reached.

Binboğa's study in which international carbon trade is handled from Turkey's
perspective (2014); study of Elitaş, Çonkar and Karakoç examining accounting
for emission rights (2014); the study of Çetintaş and Türköz, in which the role of
carbon markets in the fight against climate change is discussed (2017); Fidancı
and Yükçü's study, which deals with the philosophy of sustainability in the
management of carbon costs (2018); evaluation of Türk, Uslu and Ertaş on
environmental accounting within the framework of the law (2019) can be counted
among the publications in this group.

Some of the publications are on climate finance, which has been increasingly
used in climate change governance since the 1990s (Bracking, 2019). Consump-
tion-based carbon dioxide accounting within the framework of sustainable
development goals (SDGs) is handled by Spasier et al. (2019). Kumarasiri and
Jubb (2017) in their research based on the results of a 2009 study on Australian
companies examined the relationship between management accounting practices
regarding carbon emissions, climate change perception and accounting use, and
also whether companies consider the effects of climate change as a threat or an
opportunity. They found that accounting practices in the management of carbon
emissions remained limited. Duus-Otterstroöm (2016) worked on the distribution
of climate adaptation finance to countries and the control of these recipient
countries on the issue. Giannarakis, Zafeiriou, and Sariannidis (2017) examined
the effects of carbon performance on climate change explanations. Salk, Jonas,
and Marland (2013) emphasised that consistent and accurate accounting will
reduce carbon emissions on a local scale through flexible practices, thus
contributing to success on a global scale. Linnenluecke, Birt, Griffiths, and Walsh
(2015) argued that accounting will support the business in the climate change
adaptation process, thanks to the risk assessment function, the function of
evaluating the adaptation costs and benefits, and the function of explaining the
risks associated with the effects of climate change. The research of Ratnatunga
and Balachandran (2009), which deals with carbon business accounting, the cost
of global warming and its effects on the management accounting profession, has
the closest content to the present study. According to the authors; the existence of
carbon allocation and trading has potential implications for organisations'
business strategies, financial performance and ultimately value. Therefore,
accountants and other information providers need to consider strategies and

measures outside of traditional paradigms (Ratnatunga & Balachandran, 2009, p. 336).

RESEARCH AND FINDINGS

As stated on the website of the Ministry of Foreign Affairs, Turkey has no digitised emission limitation or reduction commitments in the Kyoto Protocol (mfa.gov.tr, 26.01.2020). However, if the strategies to be developed have the potential to make positive differences on the value of the business, it would be a proactive approach not to expect an implementation to be compulsory. The critical importance of gaining competitive advantage is clear. This situation constitutes a reasonable justification for revealing the perspectives of the management staff of the enterprises that are important for the country's economy. The aim of this study is to reveal the perspectives of accountants on the subject within the framework of the effects of climate change on the business world. For this purpose, a questionnaire form has been prepared. The survey was inspired by a report published by the Chartered Institute of Management Accountants (CIMA) in February 2010. As stated in the report, management accountants have a key role in making sustainable strategic and operational decisions. However, the Institute's researches reveal that even in activities involving finance teams in climate change-related activities, the issue is handled on an ad hoc basis. In the report it is emphasised that management accountants are equipped with tools and techniques that can enable businesses to understand the scale of the problem; they can produce workable solutions and ensure that the solutions are applied appropriately. Also, it has been stated that management accountants have an important role in providing business intelligence to support strategy and influencing decision-making, and it has been emphasised that the above-mentioned situation should change. The Institute's survey got answers from 883 management accountants who participated in international platforms (CIMA, 2010).

The Public Disclosure Platform (PDP) is an electronic system in which the notifications required to be disclosed to the public in accordance with the capital markets and exchange legislation are transmitted and announced to the public with electronic signature. In addition to Borsa Istanbul (BIST) companies, the system also lists companies whose PDP membership has expired, other PDP members and companies that are not traded. The number of companies in the aforementioned lists is not fixed values and may change over time. The questionnaire, inspired by the study conducted by CIMA, was sent electronically to the e-mail addresses of 602[1] companies, most of which are still listed on the BIST, in 2018 and 2019, at various intervals, between June 2018 and June 2019. The questionnaire was asked to be answered only by those who are senior managers in

---

[1]During the data collection phase of this study, the data of 602 companies in the above-mentioned categories were accessed, and the time and numbers stamps of messages sent are available at the researcher.

the entities or those who are directly interested in the subject. Changes in addresses and related managers during the process necessitated the constant updating of these e-mail addresses, and submissions were made to up-to-date addresses.

In addition to demographic information, 20 yes/no questions about the subject and three questions, where more than one option can be selected, were asked in the survey. The survey was answered by 49 managers.

61.2% of the respondents are male and 38.8% are female; 61.3% are in the age range of 44–68, the remaining 38.7% are in the age range of 28–43. Regarding the education levels, 63.3% of the respondents are undergraduates, 32.7% are graduates and 4.1% are associate degree graduates. While the rate of those who are single and have children is 8.2%, the rate of those who are married and have children is 67.3%; 18.4% of the respondents are single and childless, and 6.1% are married and childless. Graphic 1 and Graphic 2 display demographic data.

While 44.9% of the respondents stated that they are accountants, financial advisors, independent accountants and auditors as a profession; 28.6% of them declared that they are managers. The rate of those who state that they are finances and bankers is 10.2%, and engineers make up 6.1%.

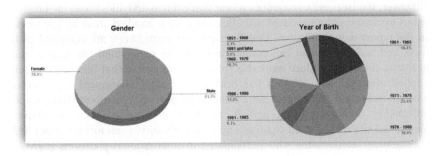

Graph 1.   Demographic Data 1.

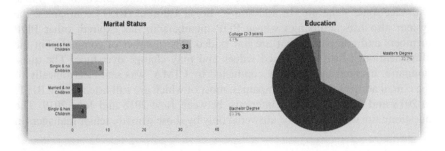

Graph 2.   Demographic Data 2.

Those who have spent more than 20 years in the profession make up 65.3% of the respondents, 20.4% of those between 10 and 19 years, while the total percentage of those with tenure of less than 10 years is 14.3. When it comes to tenure at the current company, the total percentage of those with tenure of less than 10 years is 38.7, while those with tenure of 10–19 years are 30.6%, and those with tenure of more than 20 years constitute 30.6% of the respondents. The Graphic 4 shows both tenures.

When the positions of the respondents in the institutions they work for are analysed, those who are chairman/member of the Executive Board, chairman/member of the Board of Directors and general managers constitute 20.4% of the

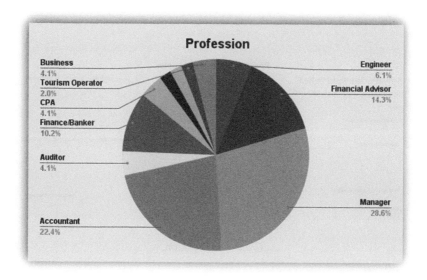

Graph 3.   Demographic Data 3.

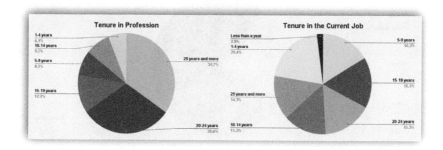

Graph 4.   Tenure.

total. While the ratio of those who are finance managers/financial affairs managers is 30.6%, managers/assistant managers and department managers make up 28.6% of the respondents.

The distribution of the current position is displayed in Graphic 5. When the department they work in is analysed, 59.2% of the respondents who work in the accounting, internal control and finance departments constitute 22.4% of the employees in the management. The 8.2% response comes from the public relations departments of the companies, as can be seen in Graphic 6.

The size of business entities is determined by a combination of qualitative and quantitative determinants. These might be the company's legal type, number of employees, number of board members, foreign trade structure, machinery, raw material processed, energy used etc. The present study tries to gauge the size and

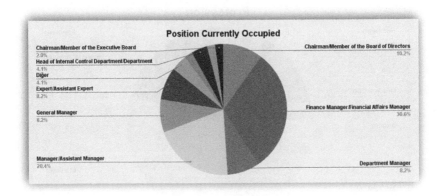

Graph 5.   Position.

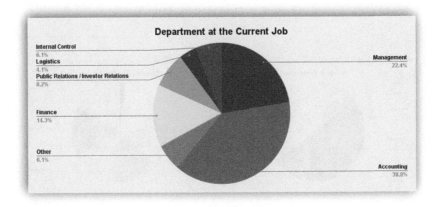

Graph 6.   Department.

impact of the entities through foreign trade and the number of employees it has. When the foreign trade levels of the businesses in which the 49 participants who participated in the survey are analysed, it comes to be that 8.2% of them are global companies and 36.7% are national companies. Companies that are national but have foreign trade make up 38.8% of the respondents, and international companies make up 16.3%.

Regarding the number of employees, it is seen that 49% of them are enterprises that are defined as large enterprises because the number of employees including the employer is more than 250. Enterprises with 50–249 employees, including the employer, are classified as medium-sized enterprises in our study, and enterprises in this group constitute 32.7% of the respondents. Micro enterprises with 1–9 employees including the employer, and small enterprises with 10–49 employees including the employer make up 18.3% of the respondents. Graphic 7 displays them in a combined way. The slices of the two pie graphs resemble each other; however, it seems that only medium size company slice coincides with 'national-has foreign trade' labeled slice on the next pie. It can be concluded from here that these might be the SMEs. Sometimes, high-tech companies with few and highly qualified employees are categorised as small, but they may be international. This is also to be taken into consideration when assessing the data.

When the sectors in which the participants' companies operate are analysed, it has been determined that the highest participation with 16.3% is from banks and special finance institutions and financial leasing and factoring companies. Companies in the paper and paper products, printing and publishing sector constitute 8.2% of the respondents. In total, respondents contribute to the research by representing 27 different sectors. While 24 of the companies, the members of which participated in the survey, operate in a single region, 11 companies operate in seven geographical regions of Turkey. Turkey is divided into seven geographical regions: Marmara, Aegean, Black Sea, Central Anatolia, Eastern Anatolia, South-eastern Anatolia and the Mediterranean regions. When the geographical regions in which the enterprises participating in the survey operate are examined, the Marmara Region alone has the highest rate with 30.6%, followed by the Aegean Region with 10.2% without combining with any other region.

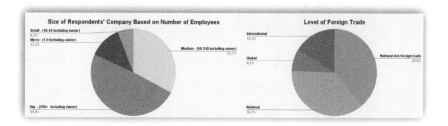

Graph 7.   Size of the Business and Level of Foreign Trade.

When the data presented so far are analysed collectively, it is possible to say that the companies listed on BIST are represented in the survey with a wide participation in terms of sector distribution, geographical distribution, different sizes and various other aspects. Therefore, it is meaningful to evaluate the responses obtained. Wherever possible, the obtained results will be compared to the data and the results of the CIMA report, which is the inspiring and motivating thing regarding the present research.

In addition to the above questions, respondents were asked whether their role in the company is related to sustainability and/or finance. The role of 95.9% of the respondents in their organisation has a relationship with finance. The rate of those whose role is related to sustainability is 83.7%.

The existence of a relationship between the role assumed in the institution and sustainability and finance is shown in Graphic 8.

In addition, questions were also asked whether climate change poses a risk to their institutions and whether adapting to climate change increases costs. A portion of 44.9% is formed by those who state that climate change poses a significant risk to their institution. A significant majority is of the opinion that adapting to climate change will increase costs – 69.4%.

Graphic 9 displays the answers of questions trying to find out whether climate change poses a significant risk to respondents' company and whether adapting to climate change would increase costs. The majority does not believe that climate change would pose a significant risk to their company. Even this alone is the proof that climate change is not well understood, and there is a long way to go no matter how short time humanity has. However, when cost is the question, they very well know that adapting to climate change would impose costs. This is very normal because respondents are mainly members of accountancy profession or they are managers, both playing with numbers all day long. The next section deals with comparisons among CIMA report and the present research's findings.

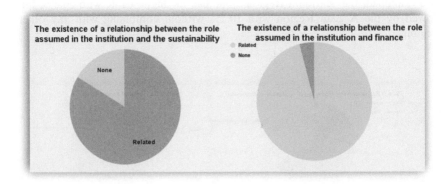

Graph 8.   Sustainability and Finance Roles of Respondents.

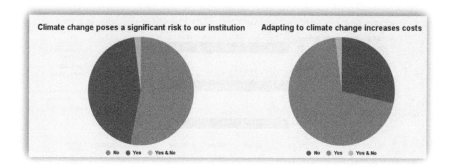

Graph 9. Risk and Cost.

COMPARISON WITH CIMA REPORT DATA

Respondents were asked whether sustainability is one of the strategic goals of their institutions. In addition, whether their businesses are well positioned to deal with climate change; whether they took the necessary measures to mitigate climate change; and whether they showed the necessary initiative to adapt to climate change. When these four questions are evaluated together as a bundle, Graph 10 comes forth.

When the CIMA report data, which is the source of inspiration, are evaluated as the equivalent of the above given four questions, the following graphic emerges. The chart (Graphic 11) is reproduced using data from the original report (CIMA, 2010, p. 3).

The total number of responses in the Turkey-related survey is 49. While stating that sustainability is not one of the strategic goals of their institutions, the only company that answered positively to the questions about measures, initiative and positioning distorts Turkish setting. Out of 49, 46 business managers who answered the questionnaire stated that sustainability is one of the strategic goals

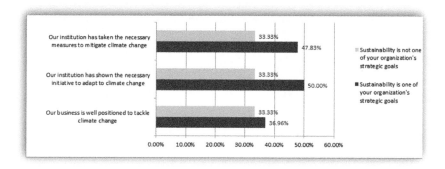

Graph 10. Measures Taken to Mitigate Climate Change – Turkey.

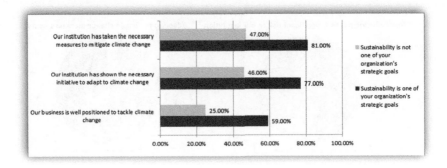

Graph 11.   Measures Taken to Mitigate Climate Change—CIMA.

of their institutions, while three businesses did not affirm this question. An enterprise's representative, who stated that sustainability is not one of the strategic goals of their institution, answered the other questions positively. When focussing on the answers of businesses that have placed sustainability among their strategic goals, it is seen that 47.83% take the necessary measures to mitigate the effects of climate change, 50% show the necessary initiative to adapt to climate change, and 36.96% position their businesses well to cope with climate change.

The graphs (Graphic 12) show the proportions of the answers given to these questions among all positive/negative answers. The ratio of respondents stating that they are well positioned against climate change is 53.1%, and the ratio of them stating that they show the necessary initiative is 49%.

Although the rate of respondents stating that they do not take the necessary initiative to encounter climate change is 51%, as can be seen from Graph 13, it is understood that those who participated in the survey from BIST companies somehow took initiative to encounter climate change. Those, who do not take any initiative, make up 34.7% of respondents.

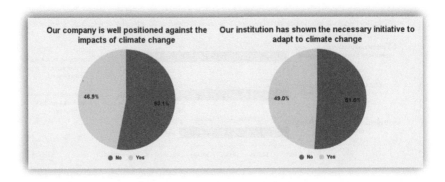

Graph 12.   Positioning and Initiative.

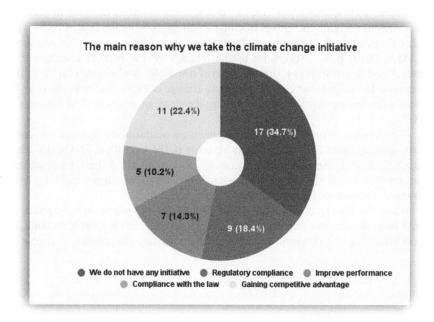

Graph 13.   Climate Change Initiative Rationale.

When evaluated together, regulatory compliance and compliance with the law are the most important motives with 28.6%; this is followed by 22.4% with the motive of gaining competitive advantage; it is understood that improving the performance is also a strong reason.

A similar result was found in the CIMA research. When the answers of all participants are evaluated; the ratio of management accountants who show compliance and performance together as the main reason for taking initiative is 44% – 42.9% in Turkish setting. The rate of those who cited competitive advantage and performance combination as a reason is 29%; the rate of those who show regulatory compliance and compliance with the law combination as a reason is 20%. The present research also revealed that regulatory compliance and compliance with the law are the most important determinants of taking CCIs. Furthermore, according to CIMA report, the total rate of those who stated that only performance or only competitive advantage was the sole and most important motive was 29%. For example, while this rate remains at 14% in Australia, competitive advantage and performance motive increases to 64% for Chinese managers (CIMA, 2010, p. 5). It might be that the considerable difference between development levels of countries or varying cultural values impact their preferences. According to the research results that form the basis of our study, the combined ratio of performance and competitive advantage is 36.7%.

According to CIMA report, the rate of respondents stating that they have taken measures to mitigate the effects of climate change is 56%; the rate of those who think that sustainability is among the strategic goals of the enterprise is one-third (CIMA, 2010, p. 3). According to the findings of the present research, it is understood from Graph 14, that the ratio of respondents who state that they take measures to mitigate the effects of climate change is 46.9% and that the ratio of those who declare sustainability is among the strategic goals of their business is 93.9%.

CIMA research revealed that management accountants are focussed on short-term thinking, with 37% of managers agreeing (CIMA, 2010, p. 7). On the other hand, 75.5% of the company executives in Turkey think that management accountants are skilled in risk management in terms of supporting long-term strategic decision-making.

While the managers who stated that climate change is not on the agenda of their institutions constitute one-fifth of the participants in the CIMA research, in Turkish setting this rate is 55.1%. While those who state that climate change is of

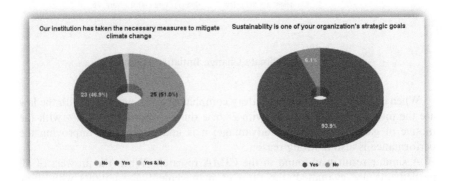

Graph 14. Measures and Strategy.

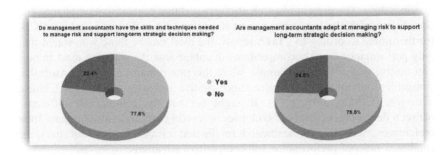

Graph 15. Skills and Dexterity of Management Accountants.

central importance for their institutions in Turkey make 20.4% of respondents, this rate is 58% in the CIMA survey (2010, p. 3). Pie charts related to this are given in Graphic 16.

The rate of those who state that climate change is integrated with the overall business strategy of their organisation is 26.5%, and the rate of those who think that their organisation is determined to mitigate the effects of climate change is 42.9% in the Turkish setting. Responses to the same questions are 33 and 56%, respectively, in the CIMA survey (2010, p. 3).

The percentage of managers, who believe that the participants in the research can do more to reduce the negative effects of the institution they represent on the environment, is 63% (CIMA, 2010, p. 3). A similar rate was also found in the research conducted within the framework of this study – 74.4%. Those who think their business is well positioned to deal with climate change make up 38% of the CIMA survey respondents (CIMA, 2010). In the Turkish setting, this rate is 36.7%.

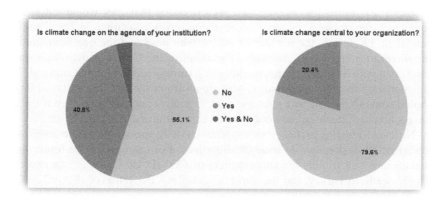

Graph 16. Agenda and Importance.

Graph 17. Integrated Strategies and Commitment.

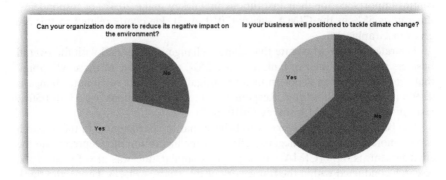

Graph 18.   Additional Measures and Positioning.

In the research conducted in Turkey, those who think that sustainability as a strategic goal in climate change management can get ahead of financial return problems accounted for 36.7%; those who declared that they would cut environmental programmes in times of economic crisis constitute 36.7%. This is consistent. Of course, the number of people who answered the questionnaire is the foremost limitation of the study. The result of the CIMA study, which was conducted with 883 participants worldwide, naturally seems more meaningful. It is understood that the participants, who are aware of the fact that sustainability should come to the fore as a strategic goal, logically concluded that even if there are economic difficulties, environmentalist expenditures should not be cut.

No event remains exclusive to any country it happens; due to the levels of globalisation, it becomes an issue of all nations. For example, in the future the human race will witness the consequences of COVID-19. Corona virus caused 98,409 deaths in Turkey, and the world death toll is 6,181,180 as of 10 April 2022.

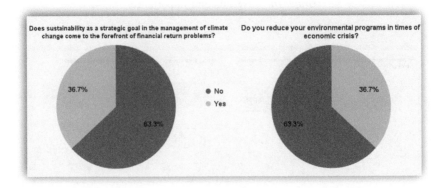

Graph 19.   Priorities.

Almost 500 million people got infected. Factories were shut down, supply chains were broken and productivity fell. Yet, new variants are continuously arising. Inman from *The Guardian* wrote in early months of the year that the world would grow 1.3% less than expected in 2020 (19.02.2020). Day-by-day increasing inter-dependency of the nations, either intentionally or unavoidably, that is, as a natural consequence of globalisation, is one of the main reasons why many factories in the aforementioned countries stopped production and orders could not be fulfilled. To draw a similarity, climate change will also have negative consequences that cannot be reversed after a while. The closest example to this is the Australian bushfires, which could not be prevented in the last three or four months of 2019. According to the news of Roach, the damage caused by the bush fires that started in September 2019 had exceeded 100 billion dollars as of January 2020 (AccuWeather, 08.01.2020). To state again, if climate change is not properly managed, it will be inevitable not to have negative impacts on the values of companies, let aside the negative consequences on economies of countries as a whole.

An answer to this question was also sought in the present research. In the survey, it was asked whether the value of the company would increase as a result of handling climate change with a proactive approach and good positioning. Out of 49 respondents, 69.4% gave the answer 'yes' to this question. What seems interesting is that 38.8% of respondents believe that a bad positioning in the face of climate change and therefore falling behind on this issue will not decrease the value of the company—Graph 20.

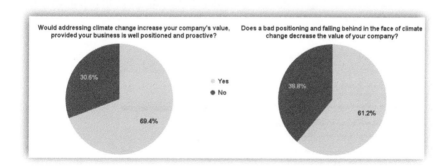

Graph 20. Impact on Company Value.

FINANCES' CONCERN WITH CLIMATE CHANGE ISSUES

CIMA research – sought to uncover the reasons why the finance function is not currently involved in climate change issues or is only involved on an ad hoc basis – asked questions about this to the participants. Since this study was inspired by the CIMA research, the same questions were asked to the participants and the answers given in Graph 21 were obtained. Noting that more than one option can be selected, the following options are presented in the survey of the study:

(1) Finance team doesn't have sufficient time to get involved in climate change initiatives; (2) Finance do not have the relevant knowledge and skills on this subject; (3) Finance is focussed more on short-term budgets and targets; (4) The climate change agenda does not fit with the role of finance; (5) The corporate responsibility team or the climate change team has not consulted with the finance team; (6) There is insufficient communication between different teams; (7) Finance team is not interested in climate change agenda, and the choice (8) Other.

Respondents were also asked whether their current position in the business is related to sustainability and/or finance. Responses to the eight options mentioned above were matched and compared with responses about sustainability and/or finance relatedness.

The majority of executives have integrated themselves into both the sustainability and finance roles. While the least popular answer in CIMA's research was 'Other', this option occupied a significant percentage in the study applied in Turkey. In CIMA's research, insufficient time, lack of skills and short-term focus were close to each other. In Turkey, the justification for insufficient time has not been popular. Lack of communication between teams, lack of climate change in the finance team's agenda and lack of skills were the most popular answers given by managers whose role was sustainability – 39.02%. The answers given to the option 'the climate change agenda does not fit with the role of finance' in Graph 21 are supported by the answers given to the 'finance team is not interested in climate change agenda'. When the two are evaluated together, the rate rises to 60.97%.

In the research conducted abroad, the sum of these two ratios was 60% (CIMA, 2010, p. 8). Percentages are calculated over the ratios of managers with a sustainability role.

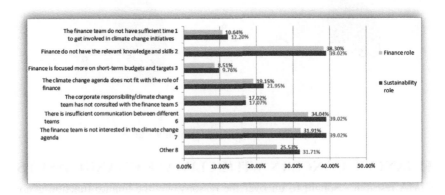

Graph 21.   Why Climate Change Is Not on the Finance Team's
Agenda–Turkey.

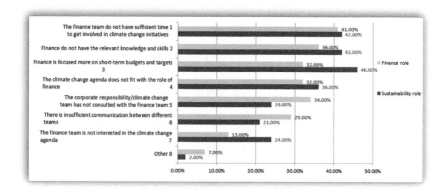

Graph 22. Why Climate Change Is Not on the Finance Team's Agenda – CIMA.

Finances in Turkey with 38.3% think that they do not have the relevant knowledge and skills on this subject, 34.4% think that communication between teams is insufficient, and 31.91% think that climate change is not the job of finances. Finances around the world with 41% think that they do not have sufficient time, and 36% think that they lack the knowledge and skills required to conceive climate change subject. On the other hand, 34% state that neither the corporate responsibility team nor the climate change team did consult with them (CIMA, 2010). These are shown in Graph 22. Valid for all questions, there is no significant difference between the distribution of the answers of the finances and the answers of those who deal with sustainability in the study conducted in Turkey.

When answers of finance role versus sustainability role holders are compared, there is a 10-point discrepancy between respondents' answers to question (5), and 11 points for the answers to question (7). Finally, in Turkish setting, regarding all questions, there are no significant differences observed between the distribution of the answers of the finances and those who deal with sustainability. However, as stated above there are some discrepancies to certain question. The only question the answers of which are closest to each other is (1) Finance team doesn't have sufficient time to get involved in CCIs.

MANAGEMENT ACCOUNTING TOOLS AND TECHNIQUES

There are management accounting tools and techniques that businesses can use to manage the environmental impact they create. In CIMA's research (2010), this question was asked and the tools and techniques were listed. Cost-benefit analysis and profitability forecasting techniques – 68% and investment appraisal – 68% are the most frequently used techniques among management accountants who contributed to this research. It is almost a constant that a group of management

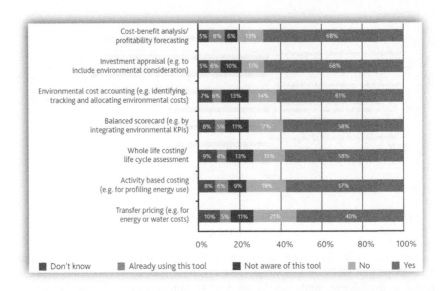

Graph 23.   Management Accounting Tools and Techniques Available.
Source: Chartered Institute of Management Accountants (CIMA) (February 2010).
*Accounting for climate change 'How management accountants can help organisations
mitigate and adapt to climate change'.* https://www.cimaglobal.com/Documents/
Thought_leadership_docs/cid_accounting_for_climate_change_feb10.pdf, p. 11.
Accessed 03 June 2018.

accountants who do not have a hint about the technique presented here are
5–10% of respondents. Those who already know and use the tools listed make up
4–8% of respondents.

The tools and techniques presented to the respondents in the study are as
follows: (1) Cost-benefit analysis/profitability forecasting, (2) Investment appraisal
(e.g. to include environmental consideration), (3) Environmental cost accounting
(e.g. identifying, tracking and allocating environmental costs), (4) Balanced
scorecard (e.g. by integrating environmental KPIs), (5) Whole life costing/LCA,
(6) Activity-based costing (e.g. for profiling energy use), (7) Transfer pricing (e.g.
for energy or water costs).

Within the framework of this study, the participants of the survey conducted in
Turkey were asked about the areas that finance would and/or should be included
in, and it was stated that they could tick more than one option. The options
presented in the survey are as follows: (1) Preparing the business case for CCIs, (2)
Carbon footprint calculation, (3) Tracking climate change performance measures/
KPIs, (4) Monitoring compliances with climate change policy and regulation, (5)
Integration of financial and climate change management information systems, (6)

Carbon accounting or budgeting, (7) Sustainability reporting (external), (8) Sustainability reporting (internal), (9) Whole costing or LCA calculations.

As listed above among nine options presented in the survey, the manager, who stated that finance should only deal with external sustainability reporting, is left alone. Maximum seven options are selected out of the nine. The manager, who stated that there are seven areas that finance should be involved in, is left alone, too. While the numbers of options chosen vary, on the average, three options have been the number of interest areas managers generally ascribe to finance. *Whole costing/LCA calculations* has been the choice of 33 out of 49 executives. This is followed by *Sustainability reporting (internal)*, the choice of 26 managers, and *Sustainability reporting (external)*, the choice of 24 managers. The least marked finance interest areas are *Preparing the business case for CCIs*, marked by six managers, and *Carbon footprint calculation* marked by seven administrators. The ratios related to this are given in Graph 24.

There is no exact equivalent for this part of the questionnaire to be compared in CIMA's research (2010). In the aforementioned research, participation in the options in the survey of the study was studied to reveal opinions of management accountants with formal roles versus ad hoc role. Graphic 25 displays and compares the two.

According to the CIMA survey, the areas that finance is, or could be, involved as undertaking its formal role in are as follows: (1) Preparing the business case for CCIs – 34%, (2) Carbon footprint calculation – 29%, (3) Tracking climate change performance measures/KPIs – 30%, (4) Monitoring compliances with climate change policy and regulation – 32%, (5) Integration of financial and climate change management information systems – 31%, (6) Carbon accounting or budgeting – 32%, (7) Sustainability reporting (external) – 30%, (8) Sustainability reporting (internal) – 36% and (9) Whole costing or LCA calculations – 38%.

As can be seen from Graphics 24 and 25, some of the preference rates of the options are quite close to each other for Turkish setting and the international one. With 32.65% *Carbon accounting or budgeting* and with the same ratio *Integration*

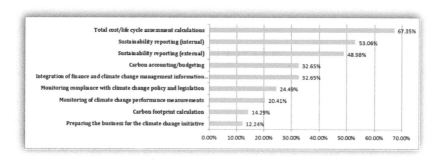

Graph 24. The Areas that Finance Is, or Could Be, Involved–Turkey.

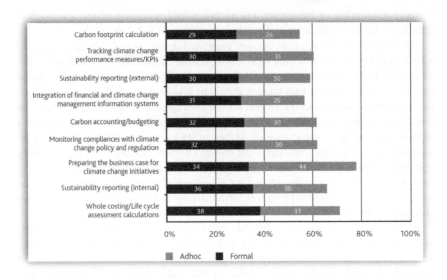

Graph 25. The Areas that Finance Is, or Could Be, Involved – CIMA.
Source: Chartered Institute of Management Accountants (CIMA) (February 2010).
Accounting for climate change 'How management accountants can help organisations
mitigate and adapt to climate change'. https://www.cimaglobal.com/Documents/
Thought_leadership_docs/cid_accounting_for_climate_change_feb10.pdf, p. 9.
Accessed 03 June 2018.

of financial and climate change management information systems are very close
with CIMA results. The rest differs a lot. It might be due to the fact that there is
no differentiation of Turkish managers regarding their formal versus ad hoc role
related to climate change. For example, the total of ad hoc climate change role
and formal role holders' answers to *Whole costing/Life cycle assessment calculations* is 71% in CIMA survey and 67.35% in the Turkish setting.

CONCLUSIONS

Ratnatunga and Balachandran emphasised that the view, that a measurable
direct correlation can be established between environmental efficiency and economic results in some enterprises, has become popular (2009, p. 342). The
instruments that will help to achieve this are strategic cost management and
strategic management accounting tools. According to the data obtained from the
survey of the study, it is not possible to say that these or similar tools are used
effectively in Turkey. It is not possible to proceed in this regard without fully
understanding the effects of the steps that businesses can take on climate change
and, therefore on environmental issues, on the financial results of the business.
For example, life cycle cost analyses are handled; it is observed that the subject is

almost exclusively handled within the framework of engineering, architecture and design, and not viewed as related to accounting. However, accounting does not only calculate the cost of a product or service until it reaches the point of sale, but it should also consider all carbon costs incurred before and after the manufacture or service performance.

Although there are similarities between the results of CIMA's research, the results of which were shared more than a decade, and the situation determined by Turkish study, there are also obvious differences. It is clear that the reporting processes, as well as the roles of financial managers, will change drastically in the near future if not changed already. It is important that those who practice the accounting profession alter their vision and improve themselves, not only in terms of adapting to the changes that will be caused by climate change but also in keeping up with various other developments in the world. This study is a situation determination for Turkey, and the deficiencies identified within the framework of the study have been revealed. In future studies, it may be suggested to propose solutions in line with the findings obtained in this study, to consider the tools and methods mentioned here and to repeat similar studies. In the short run, this study points to radical changes, need of modernisation and improvements in accounting curricula.

Net zero is beyond the scope of both CIMA's research and the present study. CIMA report does not even mention it. Since the present study is designed to duplicate CIMA research for Turkish setting, it does not handle the issue either. However, the results of both point to net zero in an implicit way. Unless management is aware of climate change issues, and start calculating the recurred costs, business side of the fight against climate change would be missing. The study is limited to in several perspectives. It focusses on the role of management accountants in managing the impacts of climate change on the business world. Therefore, such kinds of issues like actions companies take, the effects of actions accounted for, one-time large purchases of fixed assets that are to be used for revenue generation over a longer period – capital expenditures, short-term expenses that are used in running the daily operations – revenue expenditures and externalities, i.e. costs and/or benefits stemming from the production and/or consumption of goods and/or services are excluded. In future studies, integrated reports of companies can be analysed and matched with performance data, and some questionnaires may help in attaching consumer/customer attitude towards the analysed companies' products and services.

DISCUSSIONS

The most valuable and sustainable actions companies would take are those that are taken voluntarily and are resulting from internalised motives. However, mostly companies postpone the expected or desired actions until regulations make it compulsory or they sense that customers and/or consumers are about to get organised and boycott their products/services. Non-governmental organisations (NGOs) are another stakeholder group armoured with the power to force them to do so. For example, one of the issues to be covered in a sustainability report is child labour, forced labour and compulsory labour. The Trafficking Victims Protection Reauthorization Act (TVPRA) requires the United States Department of Labor's (USDOL) Bureau of International Labor Affairs (ILAB) to prepare a list of goods produced by child labour or forced labour and publish it. According to 2020 List, child labour is employed in production of 68 goods in agriculture sector, which also uses forced labour in 29 goods. Manufacturing sector employs children to produce 39 goods, and forced labour is used in the production of 20 goods. Child labour is also employed in production of 32 mining/quarrying goods, which also exploits forced labour to produce 13 goods. Both children and forced labour are the victims of pornography sector. From another perspective the numbers are as follows (www.dol.gov, 03.05.2022, 25): (1) in 22 countries child labour and in five countries forced labour are employed in production of gold, (2) bricks production uses child labour in 19 countries and forced labour in 9 countries, (3) in 18 countries child labour is employed in sugarcane production and in five countries forced labour is used, (4) coffee producers and tobacco producers in 17 countries employ child labour, (5) in 15 countries cotton producers employ child labour, and forced labour is used in eight countries, (6) in 12 countries children and in five countries forced labour are employed by cattle owners, (7) fish is another product child labour is used in 11 countries, and forced labour is used by fish producers in five countries, (8) garments in eight countries welcome child labour and seven countries use forced labour in garment production, (9) cocoa producers employ children in seven countries and (10) children are victims of pornography in seven countries. For example, according to the report, goods child labour is employed in Turkey are citrus fruits, cotton, cumin, footwear, furniture, garments, hazelnuts, peanuts, pulses and sugar beets. In cases, where the companies employing children are micro companies, it is not even considered as an illegal act, for thousands of years children worked along with their families. It is all family business, and nobody expects business owners to report about child labour. In fact a closer look at the countries that use child labour shows that these are mostly undeveloped, developing or less-developed countries. Correlation analyses would display this.

In my opinion, child labour issue is as important as climate issue. For countries that are not developed, it seems to be luxurious to bother people with these issues. Under circumstances where poverty is the foremost problem, climate is not an important issue. Same is valid for countries where purchasing power is under desired levels. The priority would not be climate or environmental issues. Fight for life would stay as the priority for near future. Child labour issue is used here in order to make an analogy with climate change issue.

The International Labour Organization (ILO) estimates that 170 million are engaged in child labour, with many making textiles and garments to satisfy the demand of consumers in Europe, the United States and beyond (https://labs.theguardian.com, 03.05.2022). Chocolate companies like Nestle, Hershey's, Mars, Archer–Daniels–Midland Company (ADM), Cadbury, Kraft, Fowler's, Crunch, Kit-Kat and Aero had been on lists in the past. Fashion brands like H&M, Forever 21, GAP, Nike, Zara, Urban Outfitters, Aldo, Primark, Adidas,

Walmart, Uniqio, Victoria's Secret, Aeropostale, and La Senza were on the lists as well. In addition to these, Apple, Disney, Philip Morris and Toys R are some other brands that were on the lists (Reddy, 2022). Among these we all remember Walmart hit the headlines. For example, 1,127 garment workers were killed in a building collapse in Bangladesh in 2013. They were making cheap and fast clothes for wealthier nations like United States (Smith, 03.05.2022). Whether any of the above-mentioned companies get impressed, from the customer pressure or not, would be a good research topic, which is beyond the scope of this chapter.

Therefore, in order to better assess the situation, cultural factors along with economic position need to be taken into consideration. Thus, it seems to be that customer pressure is something developed countries may benefit from in the short run, whereas regulations and monitoring are better tools for the rest of the countries. This does not mean that customer pressure will never work; there will be a time lag between developed and developing and/or undeveloped countries. This is why initiatives taken by managers mean a lot.

REFERENCES

Bierman, H., & Drebin, A. R., Jr. (1978). *Financial accounting.* Kent: W & J Mackay Ltd.

Binboğa, G. (2014). Uluslararası karbon ticareti ve Türkiye. *Journal of Yasar University, 9*(34), 5732–5759. doi:10.19168/jyu.90063

Bracking, S. (2019). Financialisation, climate finance, and the calculative challenges of managing environmental change. *Antipode, 51,* 709–729. doi:10.1111/anti.12510

Cambridge Dictionary. (2022). Retrieved from https://dictionary.cambridge.org/dictionary/english/emission. Accessed on September 17, 2020.

Carbon Footprint Ltd. (2022). 1-Calculate, 2-Information. Retrieved from https://www.carbonfootprint.com/. Accessed on April 9, 2022.

Çetintaş, H., & Türköz, K. (2017). İklim değişikliği ile mücadelede karbon piyasalarının rolü. *Balikesir University Journal of Social Sciences Institute, 20*(37), 147–167. Retrieved from https://search.ebscohost.com/login.aspx?direct=true&db=a9h&AN=128374020&lang=tr&site=ehost-live

Chartered Institute of Management Accountants (CIMA). (2010, February). Accounting for climate change 'How management accountants can help organisations mitigate and adapt to climate change.' Retrieved from https://www.cimaglobal.com/Documents/Thought_leadership_docs/cid_accounting_for_climate_change_feb10.pdf. Accessed on June 3, 2018.

ConstructingExcellence. (2004). Sustainability accounting. Retrieved from https://constructing excellence.org.uk/wp-content/uploads/2015/03/sus_accounting.pdf. Accessed on September 15, 2020.

Drebin, A. R., Jr., & Bierman, H. (1978). *Managerial accounting.* Kent: W & J Mackay Ltd.

Duus-Otterström, G. (2016). Allocating climate adaptation finance: Examining three ethical arguments for recipient control. *International Environmental Agreements: Politics, Law and Economics, 16*(5), 655–670. doi:10.1007/s10784-015-9288-3. Accessed on January 5, 2020.

Elitaş, C., Çonkar, M. K., & Karakoç, M. (2014). Emisyon haklarının muhasebeleştirilmesi. *World of Accounting Science, 16*(2), 45–56. Retrieved from https://search.ebscohost.com/login.aspx?direct=true&db=a9h&AN=97125888&lang=tr&site=ehost-live

Enerji Verimliliği ve Çevre Dairesi Başkanlığı – Republic of Turkey Ministry of Energy and Natural Resources. (2022). İklim Değişikliği Hakkında. Retrieved from https://enerji.gov.tr/evced-cevre-ve-iklim-iklim-degisikligi-hakkinda.Accessed on April 9, 2022.

European Commission. (2020). Environment Green Public Procurement. About GPP. Retrieved from https://ec.europa.eu/environment/gpp/lcc.htm#:~:text=Life%2Dcycle%20costing%20(LCC)%20means%20considering%20all%20the%20costs,water%20use%2C%20spares%2C%20and%20maintenance. Accessed on September 18, 2020.

Fidancı, N., & Yükçü, S. (2018). Karbon maliyetlerinin yönetiminde sürdürülebilirlik felsefesi yaklaşımı: Lisanssız elektrik üretimi örneği. *World of Accounting Science*, *20*, 230–247. Retrieved from https://search.ebscohost.com/login.aspx?direct=true&db=a9h&AN=13509675 5&lang=tr&site=ehost-live

Giannarakis, G., Zafeiriou, E., & Sariannidis, N. (2017). The impact of carbon performance on climate change disclosure. *Business Strategy and the Environment*, *26*(8), 1078–1094. doi:10.1002/bse. 1962. Accessed on January 5, 2020.

Global Reporting. Retrieved from https://www.globalreporting.org/information/sustainability-reporting/Pages/default.aspx#:~:text=What%20is%20sustainability%20reporting%3F,caused %20by%20its%20everyday%20activities. Accessed on September 17, 2020; https://www. globalreporting.org/how-to-use-the-gri-standards/gri-standards-english-language/. Accessed on April 9, 2022.

Hoffman, A. J. (2006). *Getting ahead of the curve: Corporate strategies that address climate change*. Report to the Center for Climate and Energy Solutions–C2ES. Retrieved from https://www. c2es.org/document/getting-ahead-of-the-curve-corporate-strategies-that-address-climate-change/. Accessed on September 17, 2020.

Inman, P. (2020, February 19). Coronavirus 'could cost global economy $1.1tn in lost income'. *The Guardian*. Retrieved from https://www.theguardian.com/world/2020/feb/19/coronavirus-could-cost-global-economy-1tn-in-lost-output. Accessed on February 29, 2020.

Investopedia Terms. Managerial accounting. Retrieved from https://www.investopedia.com/terms/m/ managerialaccounting.asp. Accessed on September 14, 2020.

Johnson, G. L., & Gentry, J. A. (1980). *Finney and Miller's principles of accounting*. Hoboken, NJ: Prentice-Hall Inc.

Kumarasiri, J., & Jubb, C. (2017). Framing of climate change impacts and use of management accounting practices. *Asian Academy of Management Journal of Accounting and Finance*, *13*(2), 45–68. doi:10.21315/aamjaf2017.13.2.3

Kyoto Protokolü. Türkiye Cumhuriyeti Dışişleri Bakanlığı (26 Ocak 2020). Dış Politika, Temel Dış Politika Konuları, Türkiye'nin Çevre Politikası, Uluslararası Süreçler ve Türkiye, İklim Değişikliğiyle Mücadele. Retrieved from http://www.mfa.gov.tr/kyoto-protokolu.tr.mfa. Accessed on January 26, 2020.

Laszlo, C., & Zhexembayeva, N. (2011). *Embedded sustainability: The next big competitive advantage*. Stanford, CA: Stanford University Press. Sheffield, United Kingdom, Greenleaf Publishing Ltd.

Linnenluecke, M. K., Birt, J., Griffiths, A., & Walsh, K. (2015). The role of accounting in supporting adaptation to climate change. *Accounting and Finance*, *55*(3), 607–625. doi:10.1111/acfi.12120. Accessed on September 5, 2020.

Miah, J. H., Koh, S. C. L., & Stone, D. (2017). A hybridised framework combining integrated methods for environmental Life Cycle Assessment and Life Cycle Costing. *Journal of Cleaner Production*, 846–866. doi:10.1016/j.jclepro.2017.08.187. Accessed on September 17, 2020.

National Geographic Society. Encyclopedia. Retrieved from https://www.nationalgeographic.org/ encyclopedia/climate-change/. Accessed on April 9, 2022.

Özdemir, A. (2019). Yaşam Döngüsü Değerlendirmesi ve Sürdürülebilirlik İlişkisi Bağlamında Sosyal Yaşam Döngüsü Değerlendirmesinin (S-LCA) Yeri. *Eskişehir Teknik Üniversitesi Bilim ve Teknoloji Dergisi B- Teorik Bilimler*, *7*(2), 166–183. doi:10.20290/estubtdb.517254. Retrieved from https://dergipark.org.tr/tr/download/article-file/790924. Accessed on September 18, 2020.

Peterman, K. (2017). Climate change literacy and education: History and project overview. In *The science and perspectives from the global stage* (Vol. 1), ACS symposium series. Washington, DC: American Chemical Society. Retrieved from https://pubs.acs.org/doi/pdf/10.1021/bk-2017-1247.ch001

Pierrehumbert, R. T. (2004). Warming the world. *Nature*, *432*(7018), 677. doi:10.1038/432677a

Ratnatunga, J. T. D., & Balachandran, K. R. (2009). Carbon business accounting: The impact of global warming on the cost and management accounting profession. *Journal of Accounting, Auditing and Finance*, *24*(2), 333–355. doi:10.1177/0148558X0902400208

Reddy, K. (2022). Top 28 companies that Use child labor still! Retrieved from https://content.wisestep. com/companies-use-child-labor/. Accessed on May 3, 2022.

Riva, D. (2015). Accountants can help fight climate change. Retrieved from https://economia.icaew. com/opinion/january-2015/accountants-can-help-fight-climate-change. Accessed on June 3, 2018.

Roach, J. (2020, January 8). Australia wildfire damages and losses to exceed $100 billion. *Accu-Weather*. Retrieved from https://www.accuweather.com/en/business/australia-wildfire-economic-damages-and-losses-to-reach-110-billion/657235. Accessed on February 29, 2020.

Salk, C., Jonas, M., & Marland, G. (2013). Strict accounting with flexible implementation: The first order of business in the next climate treaty. *Carbon Management*, *4*(3), 253–256. doi:10.4155/cmt.13.15

Smith, A. (2016, June 01). *Report slams Walmart for 'exploitative' conditions in Asia factories*. Retrieved from https://money.cnn.com/2016/05/31/news/companies/walmart-gap-hm-garment-workers-asia/index.html. Accessed on May 3, 2022.

Spaiser, V., Scott, K., Owen, A., & Holland, R. (2019). Consumption based accounting of CO_2 emissions in the sustainable development goals agenda. *The International Journal of Sustainable Development and World Ecology*, *26*(4), 282–289. doi:10.1080/13504509.2018.1559252

Sustainable Travel International. (2022). Blog. Retrieved from https://sustainabletravel.org/how-to-calculate-your-companys-carbon-footprint/?gclid=CjwKCAjw3cSSBhBGEiwAVII0Zz0kqlcWb RpvV1LWzojYjTxw77EeewVsKEUpe7uQW-3ADyoZOSwjpBoCm48QAvD_BwE. Accessed on April 9, 2022.

The Guardian. Retrieved from https://labs.theguardian.com/unicef-child-labour/. Accessed on May 03, 2022.

Türk, M., Uslu, A., & Ertaş, F. C. (2019). An evaluation on regulations and environmental accounting provided by Law 7153. *Journal of Accounting and Finance*, 201–209. doi:10.25095/mufad. 606015

UMass Lowell Research. Retrieved from https://www.uml.edu/research/climate-change/#:~:text=The %20Climate%20Change%20Initiative%20(CCI,%2C%20resilient%2C%20and%20equitable% 20society. Accessed on April 9, 2022.

UNESCO. (2010). Climate change initiative. Retrieved from http://www.unesco.org/new/fileadmin/ MULTIMEDIA/HQ/SC/pdf/sc_climChange_initiative_EN.pdf. Accessed on September 17, 2020.

University of Alberta. (2013). *What is sustainability*. Office of Sustainability. Retrieved from https://www. mcgill.ca/sustainability/files/sustainability/what-is-sustainability.pdf. Accessed on September 15, 2020.

US Department of Labor (USDOL) Bureau of International Labor Affairs (ILAB). (2021). 2020 list of goods produced by child labor or forced labor. Retrieved from https://www.dol.gov/sites/dolgov/ files/ILAB/child_labor_reports/tda2019/2020_TVPRA_List_Online_Final.pdf. Accessed on May 5, 2022.

Wikipedia. Sustainability accounting. Retrieved from https://en.wikipedia.org/wiki/Sustainability_ accounting#1971%E2%80%931980. Accessed on September 15, 2020.

Yew, Ng B. (2012). Association of Chartered Certified Accountants (ACCA). 100 drivers of change for the global accountancy profession. Retrieved from https://www.accaglobal.com/content/dam/ acca/global/PDF-technical/futures/pol-af-doc.pdf. Accessed on June 3, 2018.

SUSTAINABILITY RHETORIC IN MODERN TIMES

Sughra Ghulam

ABSTRACT

The turbulent phase of COVID-19 has caused uncertainty as governments fail to develop coherent strategies for cutting emissions and are struggling to match the rhetoric of sustainable activities with actions (Barbier & Burgess, 2020; Cawthorn, Kennaugh, & Ferreira, 2021). In the recent past, firms have failed in their plans to decarbonise their key sectors such as the retail sector in the United Kingdom So far, retailers' commitment to achieving net zero emissions has been an important pledge but delivery is nowhere closer to their promises (Henriques, 2020). The firms' climate targets are not going to be met by magic as serious action is needed to fulfil the promises.

Fossil fuels have led to a drastic increase in carbon emissions in the world over the last decade. Firms championing cleaner energy and low carbon technologies are needed to cut emissions. Renewable energy sources such as wind energy can help reducing the dependency of fossil fuels (Boretti, 2020; Ebhota & Jen, 2020). Wind is an indirect form of solar energy which can provide environment-friendly option in uncertain times and can provide long-term sustainability of global economy. Solar energy technologies have the potential to decrease climate change through energy-related emissions (Li, Dai, & Cui, 2020). Increasing energy demand has initiated a focus on using hydrogen from water as a substitute for oil and fossil fuels (Boretti, 2020).

The first part of the chapter discusses theoretical perspectives of sustainable development and environmental performance with regards to three main issues: energy, water and carbon emissions, whereas the later part highlights the importance of solar technology as a low-polluted alternative to fossil fuels in the retail sector. Sustainable development of energy, water and environmental precautions such as reducing carbon emissions are of interest to wider branches of industries including retail, energy and water sector, governmental policymakers, researchers, educators and society. The purpose of this chapter

Achieving Net Zero

Developments in Corporate Governance and Responsibility, Volume 20, 57–68

Copyright © 2023 by Emerald Publishing Limited

All rights of reproduction in any form reserved

ISSN: 2043-0523/doi:10.1108/S2043-052320230000020003

is to increase the debate of the key issues of sustainable development regarding environment, energy and water in the modern times.

Keywords: Sustainability; energy; emissions; environment; solar; deforestation

INTRODUCTION

In the world of dwindling social interactions, concentrated bottleneck environmental issues, conventional energy resources and increasing technological advancements, present energy system is also changing drastically (Kudria et al., 2021). We are at a point where pandemic-related services are still normalising their activities back to where they were before pandemic. In these uncertain times, there is a need to utilise novel sources of energy that can play a prominent role as being a game changer source of power (Kudria et al., 2021; Vaka, Walvekar, Rasheed, & Khalid, 2020).

The world is planning to hit the net zero emissions by 2050. The question remains whether sustainability rhetoric will become reality or will be a vessel devoid of real actions and making the loudest noise with vague plans. The firms are embracing the idea of decarbonisation and trying to phase out fossil fuels in various factors (Millot, Krook-Riekkola, & Maïzi, 2020). Excessive use of crops and trees to increase energy supply can lead to the competition for the land for food production resulting in loss of animal diversity and loss of plants. Environmental groups are calling for the firms to increase the debate of fierce bio-resources and the rules of renewable energy: The energy that is provided through bio-resources that can cause a knock-on effect on biodiversity or global food production (Obrist, Kannan, Schmidt, & Kober, 2021).

Energy is important to sustain life on earth, to be able to travel, communicate and fulfil basic needs of life. The rapid increase in global population requires sustainable energy resources as the increasing demand conflicts with constrained global fossil fuels. Among many sustainable energy resources, solar energy is promising because of various reasons such as high capacity, universality, environmental friendliness, and inexhaustible supply. Therefore, it remains a great challenge to utilise solar energy in a more convenient, clean and economic way (Hosseini & Wahid, 2020; Strauch, Dordi, & Carter, 2020).

It is argued that rapid development of technologies such as hydrogen or clean electricity is needed to minimise the need of using crops and trees for the energy generation (Kudria et al., 2021; Marchenko & Solomin, 2015). Energy demand in the world is increasing at a fast pace. Therefore, there is a need for adopting new technologies and strategies related to renewable energy sources. In this regard, solar energy is a cost-effective way of converting energy from sunlight into electricity, providing thermal or electrical energy for variety of purposes such as generating electricity, providing light or heating water for industrial, commercial or domestic use. The increasing energy demands are likely to force us to find clean energy sources. Renewable energy resources have opened new ways for the harvesting of the light energy emerging through nanomaterials. It can be used through photocatalytic, photothermal and photovoltaic way (Barber, 2020).

ENVIRONMENTAL CONCERNS OF THE PLANET

In many ways, global environment is changing because of various reasons such as noise pollution, toxic air, global warming, waste disposals, loss of biodiversity, deforestation, ozone layer depletion and overpopulation that pose a major risk to health and well-being of the livings. Climate change is one of the major issues of the planet and there is a need for collective action at the national and international level to highlight this issue (Lambin et al., 2018; Temper, Demaria, Scheidel, Del Bene, & Martinez-Alier, 2018).

Gradually, climate change has become a prominent feature in the modern literature and is of interest to both practitioners and researchers and governments. It is a budding concept that companies incorporate into their business model to do good for the society as well as for the planet. It is a process which aims to be responsible for the company's actions and encourages a good impact with the help of its activities on the consumers, employees, stakeholders, environment and communities. Former British Chancellor of Exchequer, Gordon Brown, is the well-known proponent of developmental corporate responsibility. He argued,

> Now we need to move towards a challenging measure of corporate responsibility, where we judge results not just by the input but by its outcome; the difference we make to the world in which we live. (Horrigan, 2010, p. 229)

Human beings rely on respective ecosystems for food, habitation and natural environment functioning in healthy relationship, clean air and extreme weather mitigation. Governments set out sweeping plans to become successful in achieving net zero emissions to cope with global warming. Brussels has become the world's largest mover on achieving net zero emissions (Audretsch, Cunningham, Kuratko, Lehmann, & Menter, 2019).

Gases in the atmosphere play a critical role to trap enough solar radiation to keep the temperature of the earth changing. International, social and geopolitical conflicts and relations play an important role in making policies to clean the environment. Humans continue to reduce the biological diversity of living things by cutting trees. The loss of biodiversity has its price, not only by addition of chemicals that are very difficult for the nature to handle and recycle but also results in pollution and habitat loss (Walden et al., 2017; Williams et al., 2020).

There are some factors that affect water availability which can affect climate change. It may include temperature, rainfall, evaporation rates, vegetation types and water runoff. Increased agriculture irrigation and population growth need more water resources. Plants need water for photosynthesis, reproduction and growth. The processes of temperature control and carbon dioxide fixation require plants to transpire enormous amount of water. The minimum soil moisture essential for crop growth varies. Vegetative cover, temperature, rainfall patterns, high levels of soil organic matter, active soil biota and water runoff affect percolation of rainfall into soil used by plants (Dolan et al., 2021; Dunning, Black, & Allan, 2018).

The increasing demands on the global water supply threaten the supply for food and production and biodiversity and other human needs. Water scarcity is increasing globally on many regions with more than one billion people without the facility of clean drinking water. Most of the diseases in the developing countries are transferred through drinking polluted water. Water is essential for maintaining productive environment for the human population as well as for microbes, animals and plants worldwide. With increasing population, demand for water and food consumption has increased rapidly threatening human food supply and water scarcity, severely reducing biodiversity in both terrestrial and aquatic ecosystems (Pimental & Goodman, 2004; Rosa, Chiarelli, Rulli, Dell'Angelo, & D'Odorico, 2020).

Investments in renewable energy resources and environmentally and socially responsible activities may help governments or firms to develop new capabilities, resources and competencies which can be seen in firm's culture, human resource, technologies and structure (Li et al., 2020; Singh, Chen, Del Giudice, & El-Kassar, 2019). Firms and society depend on each other for their well-being, fast financial growth and their cooperation can be beneficial for the firms in the long run (Hajian & Kashani, 2021; Nyame-Asiamah & Ghulam, 2019). Companies doing socially good can improve their reputation and customer loyalty which can reduce the risk of consumer boycotts or becoming the target of lawsuits, which can attract socially concerned consumers and investors (Deswanto & Siregar, 2018; Porter & Kramer, 2002).

Environmental and social dimensions require effective management of different types of economic capital that firms need to acquire a long-term perspective of corporate social responsibility not only in management but also in decision-making processes. Such decision-making can guarantee cash flow sufficient to create liquidity which can produce persistent returns for the shareholders (Anser, Yousaf, Majid, & Yasir, 2020; Pham, Thanh, Tučková, & Thuy, 2020).

Environmental management practices (EMPs) play a key role to enhance firms' performance (Montabon, Sroufe, & Narasimhan, 2007; Orlitzky, Schmidt, & Rynes, 2003). Montabon et al. (2007) investigated the relationship between EMPs and financial performance and found a strong positive correlation between corporate environmental performance and corporate financial performance. Another relationship of eco-friendly performance and financial performance was found by Flammer (2015) who focussed on the impact of eco-friendly programmes and found that the stock market reacted positively to the announcement of eco-friendly activities.

In the study of environmental and sustainable activities, Ameer and Othman (2012) investigated the impact of ecosystems and environmental performance, ethical standards, diversity and community on financial performance. The population for the study consisted of 100 top sustainable global companies in 2008 from developed countries and emerging markets for the period from 2006 to 2010. They argued if companies that use a set of responsible practices show better performance as compared to those firms that do not agree with these types of practices. Hypotheses were formulated on the basis that firms that correspond to a set of responsibilities under higher sustainable practices have better financial performance as compared to those firms that do not engage in sustainable practices. The results of the analysis demonstrated that there was a correlative causality between financial performance and practices of sustainable activities of the firms.

As a result of external pressures, firms adopt different green strategies and practices to create value and long-term benefits. Lozano, Lukman, Lozano, Huisingh, and Lambrechts (2013) focussed on heavily polluted industries and highlighted pressures from different groups of stakeholders such as government, communities, customers and competitors. Zhu and Sarkis (2007) argue that both non-market and market pressures play a role of moderating variables between performance and environmental practice. His study focussed on sustainable activities and their related pressures from the stakeholders. Forced pressure improves environmental practices such as green purchasing and investment recovery whereas competitors' pressure improves economic performance (Zhu & Sarkis, 2007). Therefore, firms adopt social and environmental practices because of stakeholder and social pressures.

AN OVERVIEW OF ENERGY RESOURCES

The increase in global energy utilisation is playing an important role in growing renewable and sustainable global transmission of energy. Increasing trend has been seen for the demands of the clean energy. Therefore, solar energy plays pivotal role as a type of clean energy for protecting environment and for the development of the economy. Several approaches towards converting sunlight into energy are discussed. Increasing global pressure and predicted energy and food production indicates that there is a need to fully explore the potential use of solar energy. It is a powerful transformation of heat derived through sunlight and can be used for various purposes from cooking, heating and generating electricity to reducing carbon emissions, enhancing the water released from clouds in the form of rain, sleet or snow over extra-tropical cyclones causing serious rainfalls or landslides, keeping extreme temperatures under control, preventing extreme humidity and ice crystals below freezing temperatures and causing regional changes in the environment (Qazi et al., 2019; Rosa et al., 2020).

Mostly, the Sun's energy penetrates through atmosphere of the earth to the surface. The incoming solar radiation reaches the earth in cloud-free areas. The ultimate source of the earth's energy is solar radiation built up through complex form of energy and utilised by living things. Significant use of fossil energy is required for irrigation. The modern world has a greater dependency on the usage of energy in different forms such as irrigation technologies (Sivaram, 2018; Zhang, Fu, Wang, & Zhang, 2019).

Environmental changes including pollution have caused different diseases such as malaria caused by polluted water and tuberculosis because of polluted air, lung cancer, heart diseases, stroke and acute respiratory problems. Natural diversity of species is required to maintain agriculture, forests and productive environment for the humans. The continuous loss of vegetation and forests and accumulation of carbon dioxide, nitrous oxide in the atmosphere and methane gas have affected the global climate change. Moreover, decreased natural resources, overcrowding, garbage disposal, ozone layer destruction, public health issues and global warming have caused environmental crisis (Kumar, Meena, & Verma, 2017; Xu et al., 2020).

The planet Earth is becoming hotter than ever and is on the verge of global crisis. Exhausting gases from industrial and vehicles, nitrates, heavy metals and plastic are toxic and they cause pollution. Air pollution is caused by factories, industries, variable pollutants and gases combined with fossil fuels (Yousefi et al., 2019). Ozone is a protective layer of metal revolving around earth's surface to protect it from harmful radiation. The chloroform contamination in chloro-fluorocarbons (CFCs) affects the ozone layer by reaching the atmosphere and creating a hole in it. Therefore, ozone layer destruction is another important environmental issue needed to be addressed (Mohammadiha, Malakooti, & Esfahanian, 2018; Yousefi et al., 2019).

Global warming caused by ecological changes is attributed to human activities leading to greenhouse gas (GHG) emissions. Global warming increases the temperature of the oceans, whereas abnormal patterns of the environment cause heavy snowfall and desertification. Harmful rainfalls can occur due to contami-nation of the atmosphere through burning fossil fuels, plants releasing nitrogen oxide and carbon oxide into the atmosphere leading it to acid rains that can affect animals, aquatic species and other inhabitants (Haque et al., 2019; Kumar et al., 2017).

The coalition of businesses such as BP, Shell and the state council of China, as well as other global institutions advocate for the development of alternative energy resources such as hydrogen or electricity. The use of oils and trees from crops have long been controversial as scientists, campaigners and environmen-talists think that these types of activities can have environmental impacts (Murta, De Freitas, Ferreira, & Peixoto, 2021; Sun & Li, 2020).

UNITED NATIONS' STANCE ON ENERGY RESOURCES

The challenges of energy security and cost of energy are becoming even more present for governments across the world. As a result, governments are changing their approaches to electricity generation, and countries are seeking for diversi-fication in their energy generation mixes towards clean conventional plans and renewable sources. The exploitation of renewable sources is an important agenda for European Union (EU) environmental and global energy policy goals. In a communication entitled 'A policy framework for climate and energy in the period from 2020 to 2030', the EU proposes to increase the share of renewable energy to at least 27% of EU energy consumption by 2030 through decarbonising the economy by 80%–95% by 2050 (Crabtree, Zappalá, & Hogg, 2015).

GHG concentrations, ocean heat levels and sea level rises set new records in 2021 and reached to a critical point, according to a UN food and agricultural report. Plastic pollution has become pervasive in agricultural soils posing a threat to people's health, food security and the environment. A new UN environmental report in 2021 intensified the role of the nations to adopt new climate strategies and nature-based solutions as low-cost options to reduce climate risks, protect and restore biodiversity, and create benefits for economies as well as communities.

RENEWABLE GREEN RESOURCES

According to the British government's projections, solar power is expected to become the second cheapest form of electricity in the United Kingdom within few years (Malik & Ayop, 2020). A recent report by the Department of Business, Energy and Industrial Strategy compares the costs of future energy projects and found that solar could beat conventional gas systems. The development of solar power technologies is one of the key solutions of increasing demand of energy worldwide. Rapid growth within the field of solar technologies is facing many challenges such as low-performing balance of systems, low solar cell efficiencies, lack of financing mechanisms and high upfront costs, shortage of skilled manpower and inadequate infrastructure (Kabir, Kumar, Kumar, Adelodun, & Kim, 2018). Solar energy utilisation will minimise the fossil fuels consumption resulting in reducing its ecological footprints. It would be the best option for the future energy demands in terms of its cost effectiveness, easy accessibility, efficiency, and capacity compared to other renewable energy sources (Bulfin, Ackermann, Furler, & Steinfeld, 2021; Kannan & Vakeesan, 2016).

The history has witnessed various civilisations such as people of Oceania, Europe, China and ancient Egypt worshipping the Sun for its power (Ball, 2012). The world has started to realise the power of the Sun but is yet to fully appreciate its influence on our lives and its use and place in technology as a source of energy. Recently, a lot of political manoeuvring can be seen in realising that there is a need for an alternative fossil fuel. Therefore, solar energy has arrived as an important source of energy as well as an intrinsic part of technology (Ball, 2012; Bulfin et al., 2021).

Excessive consumption of plastic productions and resources generate a global waste crisis and GHGs. Forests are the natural source of cleaning carbon dioxide, producing fresh oxygen and regulating temperature, whereas deforestation means removing green cover for commercial, residential and industrial purposes. Reducing deforestation is vital to mitigate climate change and to preserve the integrity of complex ecosystems. Governments are carving out decarbonisation plans of the transport sector, trying to introduce more renewable energy sources into wind, solar, geothermal energies and biogases (Ebadi & Hisoriev, 2018).

With the shrinking supply of fossil fuels worldwide, there is a need for the clean and affordable renewable energy resources to meet the growing demands. The dependency of the distribution networks on the renewable energy sources such as photovoltaic and concentrated solar power is promoted due to environmental and financial problems with conventional plants based on fossil fuels. Solar energy sources constitute appropriate commercial options for large and small power plants (Moukhtar, El Dein, Elbaset, & Mitani, 2021).

Renewable energy resources are becoming a popular choice because of their convenient environmental impact and various advantages. Among them, wind emerges as one of the most plausible energy sources in modern power generation. Large-scale energy sources are associated with fluctuations in power and voltage due to intermittent nature. The large-scale integration of wind energy is becoming more efficient and feasible when a proper storage system is added to acquire proper discharging or energy charging. For this reason, pump hydroelectric energy storage is performing better for wind integration (Carew, Warnock, Bayindir, Hossain, & Rakin, 2020).

In an era where many countries are looking for sustainable, carbon-free and affordable renewable energy as an answer to risks of climate change, it is important to discuss the relationship between life and land, in advance of the development of renewable energy sources to make the bumpy ride smoother for the sustainable future. The general commitments to reduce emissions of GHGs are leading to predict a promising future for wind and solar energy (Esteban, Diez, López, & Negro, 2011).

Wind energy has become the fastest and strongest growing renewable energy technology worldwide. Offshore wind has many advantages over onshore in terms of public perception and technology. Turbulence is generally lower and wind speed is higher in the offshore wind as compared to onshore environment. In the United Kingdom, The Crown Estate has now held three rounds of bidding for the award of wind farm site developments rights in UK waters (Crabtree et al., 2015; Moukhtar et al., 2021).

The Olympic Games have also pledged net zero carbon emissions and launched a carbon offsetting programme (Gold & Gold, 2021). The recent Olympic Games have also raised some concerns from environmental advocates about the event's sustainability. The social, ecological and economic sustainability of the games have declined in the recent past. The deterioration in sustainability comes despite the international Olympic Committee's efforts to minimise the environmental impact of the event. There were efforts to make medals from the donated electronics, podiums were recycled plastic and waste was to be recycled (Gold & Gold, 2021; Müller et al., 2021).

The global outbreak of coronavirus has double-folded effect on every part of human and environment life. The pandemic situation has in fact improved the air quality in different cities across the world, reduced water pollution and noise, lessened GHG emissions, minimised pressure on the tourist destinations which may help with restoring the ecological systems. There is also a negative impact on the environment in terms of medical waste, haphazard use and disposal of disinfectant gloves, masks, continuously endangering the environment (Rume & Islam, 2020).

CONCLUSION

The world is flooded with sustainability policies and net zero emissions targets, but it seems lacking the delivery of those targets (Cawthorn et al., 2021; Haque et al., 2019). GHG emissions continue to rise, and the planet is on the path to increasing global warming which is expected to be worse by the end of the century. Therefore, people are sceptical of high sustainability claims and governments are looking for the ways to deliver those promises. Shifting climate seems brutally apparent in Arctic Sea ice, Himalayan glaciers, wildfires and floodwaters. Scientists have warned that warming climate will lead to more weather extremes (Cawthorn et al., 2021; Haque et al., 2019).

Recently, G20 environment ministers have pledged to acquire new climate targets despite disintegrating views on phasing out coal, removing subsidies for fossil fuels from various countries such as China, Russia, India and Saudi Arabia (Hook, 2021). There is a risk of climate populism and climate politics when it comes to implementing commitments to climate change (Stephens, 2021). The gritty international and national politics will decide ultimately how much is needed to be done to limit global warming. The United States and China are segmenting their power politics to save the planet by decarbonising and drive to net zero and their efforts to grow richer from technological leap accompanied with greening economies (Hook, 2021; Stephens, 2021).

Present inconsistency between increasing rhetoric on the international level and policy inaction at the ground levels can create confusions. In the United Kingdom, soaring promises from banning polluting vehicles in the car industry to heating homes with hydrogen and wind poses the question whether these promises are going to be enough for net zero emissions. Governments will have to seriously investigate the ideas and costs for green mechanisms, practical and fair climate strategies, and credentials, which have missed the mark so far (Kudria et al., 2021; Vaka et al., 2020).

It seems easy for the elite to swap sport utility vehicles (SUVs) for electric models but for the majority, the practical business of decarbonisation, insulating businesses and homes, scrapping polluting vehicles and ripping out fossil fuels will be a challenge. To meet the targets for eliminating the fossil fuels will not go beyond discussion at international forums, provided it combines with mobilisation of resources and setting the practical strategies (Fawzy, Osman, Doran, & Rooney, 2020; Stephens, 2021).

Executives are feeling the heat of being under pressure by shareholders to solve the green problems and to do more to tackle methane pollution, reduce carbon emissions and find other ways to improve their environmental performance with an eye on a net zero future (Carew et al., 2020). New reforms can promise to transform the world from worst polluters into net zero pioneer. The question is whether wind and solar is going to be enough or firms will have to see innovative ways to renew energy to fulfil demands.

REFERENCES

Ameer, R., & Othman, R. (2012). Sustainability practices and corporate financial performance: A study based on the top global corporations. *Journal of Business Ethics, 108*(1), 61–79.

Anser, M. K., Yousaf, Z., Majid, A., & Yasir, M. (2020). Does corporate social responsibility commitment and participation predict environmental and social performance? *Corporate Social Responsibility and Environmental Management, 27*(6), 2578–2587.

Audretsch, D. B., Cunningham, J. A., Kuratko, D. F., Lehmann, E. E., & Menter, M. (2019). Entrepreneurial ecosystems: Economic, technological, and societal impacts. *The Journal of Technology Transfer, 44*(2), 313–325.

Ball, J. (2012). Tough love for renewable energy: Making wind and solar power affordable. *Foreign Affairs, 91*, 122–133.

Barber, J. (2020). Solar-driven water-splitting provides a solution to the energy problem underpinning climate change. *Biochemical Society Transactions, 48*(6), 2865–2874.

Barbier, E. B., & Burgess, J. C. (2020). Sustainability and development after COVID-19. *World Development, 135*, 105082.

Boretti, A. (2020). Production of hydrogen for export from wind and solar energy, natural gas, and coal in Australia. *International Journal of Hydrogen Energy, 45*(7), 3899–3904.

Bulfin, B., Ackermann, S., Furler, P., & Steinfeld, A. (2021). Thermodynamic comparison of solar methane reforming via catalytic and redox cycle routes. *Solar Energy, 215*, 169–178.

Carew, N., Warnock, W., Bayindir, R., Hossain, E., & Rakin, A. S. (2020). Analysis of pumped hydroelectric energy storage for large-scale wind energy integration. *The International Journal of Electrical Engineering Education.* 0020720920928456.

Cawthorn, D. M., Kennaugh, A., & Ferreira, S. M. (2021). The future of sustainability in the context of COVID-19. *Ambio, 50*(4), 812–821.

Crabtree, C. J., Zappalá, D., & Hogg, S. I. (2015). Wind energy: UK experiences and offshore operational challenges. *Proceedings of the Institution of Mechanical Engineers, Part A: Journal of Power and Energy, 229*(7), 727–746.

Deswanto, R. B., & Siregar, S. V. (2018). The associations between environmental disclosures with financial performance, environmental performance, and firm value. *Social Responsibility Journal, 14*(1), 180–193.

Dolan, F., Lamontagne, J., Link, R., Hejazi, M., Reed, P., & Edmonds, J. (2021). Evaluating the economic impact of water scarcity in a changing world. *Nature Communications, 12*(1), 1–10.

Dunning, C. M., Black, E., & Allan, R. P. (2018). Later wet seasons with more intense rainfall over Africa under future climate change. *Journal of Climate, 31*(23), 9719–9738.

Ebadi, A. G., & Hisoriev, H. (2018). Physicochemical characterization of sediments from Tajan river basin in the northern Iran. *Toxicological and Environmental Chemistry, 100*, 540–549.

Ebhota, W. S., & Jen, T. C. (2020). Fossil fuels environmental challenges and the role of solar photovoltaic technology advances in fast tracking hybrid renewable energy system. *International Journal of Precision Engineering and Manufacturing-Green Technology, 7*(1), 97–117.

Esteban, M. D., Diez, J. J., López, J. S., & Negro, V. (2011). Why offshore wind energy? *Renewable Energy, 36*(2), 444–450.

Fawzy, S., Osman, A. I., Doran, J., & Rooney, D. W. (2020). Strategies for mitigation of climate change: A review. *Environmental Chemistry Letters, 18*, 1–26.

Flammer, C. (2015). Does corporate social responsibility lead to superior financial performance? A regression discontinuity approach. *Management Science, 61*(11), 2549–2568.

Gold, J. R., & Gold, M. M. (2021). Olympic legacies and the sustainability agenda. *Nature Sustainability, 4*(4), 290–291.

Hajian, M., & Kashani, S. J. (2021). Evolution of the concept of sustainability. From Brundtland Report to sustainable development goals In C. M. Hussain & J. F. Velasco-Muñoz (Eds.), *Sustainable resource management* (pp. 1–24). Elsevier.

Haque, U., Da Silva, P. F., Devoli, G., Pilz, J., Zhao, B., Khaloua, A., . . . Yamamoto, T. (2019). The human cost of global warming: Deadly landslides and their triggers (1995–2014). *Science of the Total Environment, 682*, 673–684.

Henriques, M. (2020). Will Covid-19 have a lasting impact on the environment. *BBC News.*

Hook, L. (2021). Fraught G20 meeting on new climate targets highlights divisions. *Financial Times.* Retrieved from ft.com

Horrigan, B. (2010). *Corporate social responsibility in the 21st century: Debates, models and practices across government, law and business* (p. 229). Cheltenham: Edward Elgar Publishing.

Hosseini, S. E., & Wahid, M. A. (2020). Hydrogen from solar energy, a clean energy carrier from a sustainable source of energy. *International Journal of Energy Research, 44*(6), 4110–4131.

Kabir, E., Kumar, P., Kumar, S., Adelodun, A. A., & Kim, K. H. (2018). Solar energy: Potential and future prospects. *Renewable and Sustainable Energy Reviews, 82*, 894–900.

Kannan, N., & Vakeesan, D. (2016). Solar energy for future world: A review. *Renewable and Sustainable Energy Reviews, 62*, 1092–1105.

Kudria, S., Ivanchenko, I., Tuchynskyi, B., Petrenko, K., Karmazin, O., & Riepkin, O. (2021). Resource potential for wind-hydrogen power in Ukraine. *International Journal of Hydrogen Energy, 46*(1), 157–168.

Kumar, S., Meena, H. M., & Verma, K. (2017). Water pollution in India: Its impact on the human health: Causes and remedies. *International Journal of Applied Environmental Sciences, 12*(2), 275–279.

Lambin, E. F., Gibbs, H. K., Heilmayr, R., Carlson, K. M., Fleck, L. C., Garrett, R. D., ... Nolte, C. (2018). The role of supply-chain initiatives in reducing deforestation. *Nature Climate Change, 8*(2), 109–116.

Li, Y., Dai, J., & Cui, L. (2020). The impact of digital technologies on economic and environmental performance in the context of industry 4.0: A moderated mediation model. *International Journal of Production Economics, 229*, 107777.

Lozano, R., Lukman, R., Lozano, F. J., Huisingh, D., & Lambrechts, W. (2013). Declarations for sustainability in higher education: Becoming better leaders, through addressing the university system. *Journal of Cleaner Production, 48*, 10–19.

Malik, S. A., & Ayop, A. R. (2020). Solar energy technology: Knowledge, awareness, and acceptance of B40 households in one district of Malaysia towards government initiatives. *Technology in Society, 63*, 101416.

Marchenko, O. V., & Solomin, S. V. (2015). The future energy: Hydrogen versus electricity. *International Journal of Hydrogen Energy, 40*(10), 3801–3805.

Millot, A., Krook-Riekkola, A., & Maïzi, N. (2020). Guiding the future energy transition to net-zero emissions: Lessons from exploring the differences between France and Sweden. *Energy Policy, 139*, 111358.

Mohammadiha, A., Malakooti, H., & Esfahanian, V. (2018). Development of reduction scenarios for criteria air pollutants emission in Tehran Traffic Sector, Iran. *Science of the Total Environment, 622–623*, 17–28.

Montabon, F., Sroufe, R., & Narasimhan, R. (2007). An examination of corporate reporting, environmental management practices and firm performance. *Journal of Operations Management, 25*(5), 998–1014.

Moukhtar, I., El Dein, A. Z., Elbaset, A. A., & Mitani, Y. (2021). Economic study of solar energy systems. In *Solar energy: Technologies, design, modeling, and economics* (pp. 113–133). Springer, Cham.

Müller, M., Wolfe, S. D., Gaffney, C., Gogishvili, D., Hug, M., & Leick, A. (2021). An evaluation of the sustainability of the Olympic Games. *Nature Sustainability, 4*(4), 340–348.

Murta, A. L. S., De Freitas, M. A. V., Ferreira, C. G., & Peixoto, M. M. D. C. L. (2021). The use of palm oil biodiesel blends in locomotives: An economic, social and environmental analysis. *Renewable Energy, 164*, 521–530.

Nyame-Asiamah, F., & Ghulam, S. (2019). The relationship between CSR activity and sales growth in the UK retailing sector. *Social Responsibility Journal, 16*(3), 387–401.

Obrist, M. D., Kannan, R., Schmidt, T. J., & Kober, T. (2021). Decarbonization pathways of the Swiss cement industry towards net zero emissions. *Journal of Cleaner Production, 288*, 125413.

Orlitzky, M., Schmidt, F. L., & Rynes, S. L. (2003). Corporate social and financial performance: A meta-analysis. *Organization Studies, 24*(3), 403–441.

Pham, N. T., Thanh, T. V., Tučková, Z., & Thuy, V. T. N. (2020). The role of green human resource management in driving hotel's environmental performance: Interaction and mediation analysis. *International Journal of Hospitality Management, 88*, 102392.

Pimental, D., & Goodman, R. M. (2004). Economic impact of insects. In *Encyclopedia of plant and crop science* (pp. 407–409). New York, NY: Marcel Dekker.

Porter, M. E., & Kramer, M. R. (2002). The competitive advantage of corporate philanthropy. *Harvard Business Review, 80*(12), 56–133.

Qazi, A., Hussain, F., Rahim, N. A., Hardaker, G., Alghazzawi, D., Shaban, K., & Haruna, K. (2019). Towards sustainable energy: A systematic review of renewable energy sources, technologies, and public opinions. *IEEE Access, 7*, 63837–63851.

Rosa, L., Chiarelli, D. D., Rulli, M. C., Dell'Angelo, J., & D'Odorico, P. (2020). Global agricultural economic water scarcity. *Science Advances, 6*(18), eaaz6031.

Rume, T., & Islam, S. D. U. (2020). Environmental effects of COVID-19 pandemic and potential strategies of sustainability. *Heliyon, 6*(9), e04965.

Singh, S. K., Chen, J., Del Giudice, M., & El-Kassar, A. N. (2019). Environmental ethics, environmental performance, and competitive advantage: Role of environmental training. *Technological Forecasting and Social Change, 146*, 203–211.

Sivaram, V. (2018). *Taming the sun: Innovations to harness solar energy and power the planet.* Cambridge, MA: MIT Press.

Stephens, P. (2021). Climate change is a global threat demanding national solutions. *Financial Times.* Retrieved from ft.com

Strauch, Y., Dordi, T., & Carter, A. (2020). Constraining fossil fuels based on 2 C carbon budgets: The rapid adoption of a transformative concept in politics and finance. *Climatic Change, 160*(2), 181–201.

Sun, P., & Li, J. (2020, August). Analysis on the restriction of oil use to environmental protection. In *IOP Conference Series: Earth and Environmental Science* (Vol. 558, No. 2 p. 022049). IOP Publishing.

Temper, L., Demaria, F., Scheidel, A., Del Bene, D., & Martinez-Alier, J. (2018). The Global Environmental Justice Atlas (EJAtlas): Ecological distribution conflicts as forces for sustainability. *Sustainability Science, 13*(3), 573–584.

Vaka, M., Walvekar, R., Rasheed, A. K., & Khalid, M. (2020). A review on Malaysia's solar energy pathway towards carbon-neutral Malaysia beyond Covid'19 pandemic. *Journal of Cleaner Production,* 122834.

Walden, L. L., Harper, R. J., Sochacki, S. J., Montagu, K. D., Wocheslander, R., Clarke, M., ... Smith, A. P. (2017). Mitigation of carbon using Atriplex nummularia revegetation. *Ecological Engineering, 106*, 253–262.

Williams, B. A., Grantham, H. S., Watson, J. E., Alvarez, S. J., Simmonds, J. S., Rogéliz, C. A., ... Walschburger, T. (2020). Minimising the loss of biodiversity and ecosystem services in an intact landscape under risk of rapid agricultural development. *Environmental Research Letters, 15*(1), 014001.

Xu, R., Yu, P., Abramson, M. J., Johnston, F. H., Samet, J. M., Bell, M. L., ... Guo, Y. (2020). Wildfires, global climate change, and human health. *New England Journal of Medicine, 383*(22), 2173–2181.

Yousefi, M., Kafash, A., Valizadegan, N., Ilanloo, S. S., Rajabizadeh, M., Malekoutikhah, S., ... Ashrafi, S. (2019). Climate change is a major problem for biodiversity conservation: A systematic review of recent studies in Iran. *Contemporary Problems Ecology, 12*, 394–403.

Zhang, B., Fu, Z., Wang, J., & Zhang, L. (2019). Farmers' adoption of water-saving irrigation technology alleviates water scarcity in metropolis suburbs: A case study of Beijing, China. *Agricultural Water Management, 212*, 349–357.

Zhu, Q., & Sarkis, J. (2007). The moderating effects of institutional pressures on emergent green supply chain practices and performance. *International Journal of Production Research, 45*(18–19), 4333–4355.

PART 2

REGIONAL STUDIES

GOING BEYOND THE COVID-19 PANDEMIC: CLIMATE CHANGE REMAINS THE BIGGEST THREAT FOR SMALL ISLAND DEVELOPING STATES

Verena Tandrayen-Ragoobur

ABSTRACT

Climate change and the COVID-19 pandemic are complex and have multi-faceted effects on countries in an unpredictable and unprecedented manner. While both COVID-19 and the climate crisis share similarities, they also have some notable differences. Being both systemic in nature with knock-on and cascading effects that propagate due to high connectedness of countries, COVID-19, however, presents imminent and directly visible dangers, while the risks from climate change are gradual, cumulative and often distributed dangers. Climate change has more significant medium and long-term impacts which are likely to worsen over time. There is no vaccine for climate change compared to COVID-19. In addition, those most affected by extreme climatic conditions have usually contributed the least to the root causes of the crisis. This is in fact the case of island economies. The chapter thus investigates into the vulnerability and resilience of 38 Small Islands Developing States (SIDs) to both shocks. Adopting a comprehensive conceptual framework and data on various indices from the literature and global databases, we assess the COVID-19 and climate change vulnerabilities of SIDs on multiple fronts. The results first reveal a higher vulnerability across all dimensions for the Pacific islands compared to the other islands in the sample. There is also evidence of a weak correlation between climate change risk and the COVID-19 pandemic confirming our premise that there are marked differences between these two shocks and their impacts on island communities.

Achieving Net Zero
Developments in Corporate Governance and Responsibility, Volume 20, 71–94
Copyright © 2023 by Emerald Publishing Limited
All rights of reproduction in any form reserved
ISSN: 2043-0523/doi:10.1108/S2043-052320230000020004

Keywords: Climate change; COVID-19 pandemic; shocks; small islands; vulnerability; resilience

INTRODUCTION

Small Island Developing States (SIDs) shared common traits in terms of vulnerability and resilience to economic, social, health and climate shocks. Owing to their insularity, geographic remoteness, small size, high dependence on agriculture and fishing activities and weak adaptive capacity to changing shocks, small islands face a number of challenges and their population are the most vulnerable. Their heavy reliance on international trade and imports of basic foodstuffs as well as high rates of diet-related non-communicable diseases are making them more vulnerable to shocks and stresses. Tourist-dependent SIDs, in particular, have seen their economic and social development severely affected by COVID-19 and the accompanying health containment measures and travel restrictions. Whilst some small islands have been spared by high rates of COVID-19 infections and deaths, with sea borders being an advantage for containing the virus (Nanau, 2020), repercussions of the pandemic have been mostly felt in terms of economic and social effects especially on fragile small economies. Sea boundedness can also be a disadvantage as many SIDs are highly dependent on connection with other countries. The pandemic has shown how risks rise significantly with composite events, that is rather than addressing and recovering from one shock at a time, several extreme events have been occurring in rapid sequence and overwhelm their capacities to respond. Many SIDs are facing a range of sustainability challenges in terms of food security due to heavy reliance on imports (Cheng et al., 2021; Connell et al., 2020; Foley et al., 2022) and growing tourism industry with important negative environmental and social impacts (Foley et al., 2022; Tyllianakis et al., 2019).

These inherent characteristics make them most vulnerable to climate change amongst other shocks (IPCC, 2007; Kelman, 2006; Nurse et al., 2014; Robinson, 2020; Scandurra, Romano, Ronghi, & Carfora, 2018). The effects of climate change include increased sea surface temperature, accelerated sea level rise, ocean acidification, increased intensity and frequency of cyclones, change in rainfall patterns, and alterations in ocean currents and circulations amongst others (Brander, 2009; FAO, 2018; IPCC, 2007). Vulnerability of SIDS to these climate change impacts impedes considerably their sustainable development process (Roberts, 2021). COVID-19 and climate change both cause global disruption that transcends borders and affect millions of people. Both crises are risk multipliers that exacerbate inequalities and pose health threats of global magnitude (Harper & Vinke, 2020). Climate change and loss of biodiversity further intensify the risk of future pandemics. The compound risks of climate and COVID-19 crises are being accompanied by unseen levels of inequality, food insecurity, impoverishment, environmental degradation and climate destabilisation leading to economic uncertainty and mounting public health threats. The pandemic has intensified inequalities within and among countries where the poorest and most vulnerable people have a greater risk of being infected by the virus and endure the most of the economic fallout (UN, 2021). The pandemic has also signalled out the deeply rooted problems of societies in terms of structural inequalities, insufficient social protection, weak public health systems and inadequate health coverage, environmental degradation and climate change (UN, 2021). These threats are questioning countries' current business paradigm, in particular, small island economies which need to rethink their economic model to promote sustainable and inclusive development.

The implications of climate change on SIDS are increasingly being studied ranging from its effects on ocean fisheries (Monnereau & Oxenford, 2017), fresh water access (Karnauskas et al., 2018) and storm frequency to tourism and migration, mortality, crimes, conflicts and sustainable pathways (Petzold & Magnan, 2019; Saxena, Qui, & Robinson, 2018; Seetanah & Fauzel, 2018) and livelihoods of communities (Nunn & Kumar, 2018). Studies on SIDS (Betzold & Mohamed, 2017a, 2017b; Cowburn, Moritz, Grimsditch, & Solandt, 2019; Kelman et al., 2019; Orlowksa, 2018; Ramlall, 2014; Ratter, Petzold, & Sinane, 2016; Sultan, 2017; Tandrayen-Ragoobur, 2021) assess only one dimension of vulnerability at a time, which therefore highlights an urgency for a more holistic assessment of the vulnerability and resilience of small island economies to shocks. Current studies on a systemic assessment of SIDS' vulnerability and resilience situation to climate change can be recently traced to the study of Thomas, Baptiste, Martyr-Koller, Pringle, and Rhiney (2020) which attempts to unpack the factors that explain the patterns of hazards, exposure, vulnerability, adaptation planning and implementation and climate justice among a group of SIDs via an extensive review of the literature on climate change and SIDs. Studies on the vulnerability of SIDs to COVID-19 are by Foley et al. (2022) which focus on challenges and opportunities for climate actions across a group of small islands. Other empirical analysis on the impact of the pandemic on small islands have focussed mainly on the tourism industry (Becker, 2021; Coke-Hamilton, 2020; Connell, 2021; Gounder, 2020; Gu, Slusarczyk, Hajizada, Kovalyova, & Sakhbieva, 2021; Tandrayen-Ragoobur, Tengur, & Fauzel, 2022). None of these studies links the intertwined vulnerabilities of SIDs to both climate change and the COVID-19 pandemic. Ebi et al. (2021) adopt a different perspective by analysing the interactions between the two threats. Their analysis, however, focusses mainly on the similarities between the two shocks rather than on their differences which can have important implications on the vulnerabilities and resilience of countries.

This chapter argues that while the COVID-19 pandemic and climate change tend to share many similar attributes, there are important differences between them. The similarities can be seen by the fact that they are both systemic in nature, both are non-stationary in that past probabilities and distributions of occurrences are highly dynamic and difficult for future projections, they are both non-linear with the socio-economic impacts growing disproportionally and are risk multipliers, exacerbating existing vulnerabilities as well as being regressive as to impacting the most vulnerable populations. Conversely, while COVID-19 showed immediate dangers to our survival, climate change risks generate more gradual and growing threats. The timescales of both the occurrence and the resolution of pandemics and climate hazards are also different. The former are measured in weeks, months and years while the latter are measured in years, decades and centuries (McKinsey Quarterly, 2020). Further, pandemic is a case of contagion risk while climate change presents a case of accumulation risk (McKinsey Quarterly, 2020). Hence, climate change poses an existential and long-term threat while the coronavirus presents an immediate crisis. Climate change is an even greater and more global challenge. In 2021, the Emergency Event Database recorded 432 disastrous events related to natural hazards across the globe compared to an average of 357 annual catastrophic events for the period 2001 to 2020. These accounted to 10,492 deaths and affected 101.8 million people and caused around USD 252.1 billion of economic losses (Global Natural Disaster Assessment Report, 2022). While COVID-19 is more a short- and medium-term shock that has been brought under control by extensive immunity via vaccinations and sanitary health precautions, climate change manifests as short-term shocks but with long-term trends and remains a major threat for small islands, in particular.

This study thus attempts to fill a gap in the literature by focussing on the vulnerability of SIDs to climate change and COVID-19 pandemic and at the same time showing that while the virus has been contained, the climate crisis continues to persist and poses a greater threat to SIDs' populations. The objective of the chapter is to extend on Ebi et al. (2021) conceptual framework, to assess the vulnerabilities and resilience of SIDs to the combined and differential impacts of the pandemic and climate change. Rather than focussing solely on the similarities between the two shocks in line with Ebi et al. (2021), we go one step further by assessing the differences between them and their implications on the vulnerabilities and resilience of SIDs. Their model is further extended to incorporate other dimensions of vulnerabilities as well as the resilience component. Finally, we add the differences in the degree of risks and severity along with the varied impacts of the pandemic and climate change. Understanding the compound vulnerabilities of small nations, in particular, will help in dealing with the mounting threats of climate change in the medium and longer term. The COVID-19 and climate change differential impacts are assessed using data for 38 small island developing states on the Inform Risk Index from the Disaster Risk Management Knowledge Centre from 2012 to 2020 and information from the Emergency Events Database (EM-DAT) from the Centre for Research on the Epidemiology of Disasters (CRED). The data cover information on hazards and exposure, vulnerability and lack of coping capacity to COVID-19 and climate change.

The structure of the chapter is as follows: Section 'Hazards, Exposure and Vulnerability: Literature Survey and Conceptual Framework' reviews the existing literature on climate change vulnerability and sets out the conceptual framework. Section 'Data and Methodology' explains the data and methodology used. Section 'Situational Analysis of Climate Change and COVID-19 Pandemic on SIDs' discusses the results and we conclude with relevant policy options in Section 'Findings and Discussions'.

HAZARDS, EXPOSURE AND VULNERABILITY: LITERATURE SURVEY AND CONCEPTUAL FRAMEWORK

The severity of the impacts of economic, social, health and environmental shocks is contingent on the level of exposure and vulnerability of the population to these stresses. Various terms are used in the vulnerability literature namely hazards, threats shocks, stresses, risks, exposure, sensitivity, adjustment, adaptation and resilience to name a few. Risk is perceived as the interaction between hazards and the vulnerability and exposure of both human and natural systems (Thomas et al., 2020). It is the conditional probability and magnitude of harm or loss associated with exposure to a stress (Kasperson, Kasperson, Turner, Hsieh, & Schiller, 2002). Hazard is the threat of a stress or perturbation to a system. It has many origins: environmental, socio-economic, physical, health-related and political. It is a potentially damaging physical event or human activity, which may lead to the loss of life or injury, property damage, social and economic disruptions and environmental degradation (UN/ISDR, 2004). Exposure relates to the people and systems exposed to the hazard while sensitivity implies the extent to which people are likely to experience harm and the magnitude of that harm because of exposure to stresses (Kasperson et al., 2002). Vulnerability is the degree to which a person or the system is likely to experience harm due to exposure to shocks or disturbances and the ability to absorb these perturbations without driving the system into a different state is resilience (Kasperson et al., 2002). Lastly, responsiveness to these shocks occurs via adjustment and adaptation. The former indicates a system response to stress, which tends to be minor and short-term while adaptation requires fundamental changes that alter the system itself.

It is clear that vulnerability pertains to an undesirable outcome (e.g. vulnerability to poverty, vulnerability to food insecurity or vulnerability to natural hazards) and that such vulnerability is due to 'exposure to hazards', which cause 'perturbations' (Alwang, Siegel, & Jorgensen, 2001, p. 6). Vulnerability can arise from micro (household) to meso (regional) and macro levels (countries). Hence, vulnerability is composed of two facets namely an external side and an internal side (Bohle, 2001; Chambers, 2009; De Leon, 2006). The external side to vulnerability represents risks, shocks and stresses that households, communities and individuals face. The internal side to vulnerability is linked to defenceless implying the lack of coping capacity to these shocks. Brown (2017) distinguishes between natural or innate vulnerability and situational vulnerability. The former relates to situations whereby certain groups of people are in permanent risks, while situational vulnerability refers to particular circumstances that can lead to vulnerability.

Though various studies have analysed several aspects of vulnerabilities, there is limited research which addresses vulnerability at the intra-country and inter-country levels (Robinson, 2020). Comparing different dimensions of vulnerability across countries with more or less similar characteristics may provide important information on their adaptation strategies and resilience. Vulnerability being a function of exposure, sensitivity to hazards and adaptive capacity (Allison et al., 2009; Robinson, 2020) encompasses many dimensions in terms of economic vulnerability (Atkins, Mazzi, & Ramlogan, 1998; Briguglio, 1997); environmental vulnerability (Pantin, 1997); social vulnerability (UNEP, 1998) and biophysical vulnerability (IPCC, 1991). This chapter adds to the above dimensions by adapting Ebi et al. (2021) conceptual framework to analyse the vulnerabilities of climate change and COVID-19 in different forms and their adaptation and resilience to these shocks. Our first extension on Ebi et al. (2021) is the integration of three additional forms of vulnerabilities in terms of bio-physical vulnerability, governance/institutional vulnerability and cultural vulnerability. Second, we broaden the perspective by including the adaptation and resilience of SIDS to the two shocks, which connect with the achievement of sustainable and inclusive development. Lastly, we postulate that though both COVID-19 and climate change are important shocks, the latter poses a greater risk than the former and tops up the list of priorities, for all countries and in particular small islands. While countries have gradually recovered from the pandemic with vaccinations and induced restrictions on mobility, the climate crisis continues to persist as there is no vaccine for climate change. The risks, severity and impacts of climate change tend to be more significant and long term relative to the effects of COVID-19. This element is added to Ebi et al. (2021) which considered uncertainty and risk levels of both shocks to be similar. Whilst pandemics are a case of contagion risk, climate hazards present a case of accu-mulation risk with greater long-term impacts. The risks from climate change are gradual, cumulative and often distributed dangers that manifest themselves in degrees and over time. To the level of risks and uncertainty, we thus add the diverging impacts as for COVID-19, the effects have been contained. This is not the case for climate change.

Within the above framework, environment vulnerability is key to SIDS which are among the most impacted countries to climate change, considering their natural environment, geographical and climatological characteristics (Collymore, 2007). The impacts of intense cyclones on communities are worse where marine and shoreline ecosystems have been degraded by human actions like pollution, over-exploitation, habitat degradation and modification. Environment vulnera-bility includes both climatic and human-caused actions. Biophysical vulnerability is another dimension central to small islands' vulnerability and is explained in terms of weather systems, coastal systems, terrestrial systems and human systems (Hilhorst & Bankoff, 2004; Macchi et al., 2008). Changing weather patterns, rising air temperatures, high rainfall patterns, extreme weather events such as cyclones and storms, accelerated sea level rise (Ragoonaden, Seewoobaduth, & Cheenacunnan, 2017; Sumner et al., 2021), atmospheric pollutants and growing population and development (Bhagooli & Mattan-Moorgawa, 2014) lead to considerable consequences on the coastal ecosystem, the biodiversity and fish stocks, amongst others. These two types of vulnerabilities are highly connected where the ultimate effects of hazards are viewed in terms of the amount of damage caused.

Further, economic vulnerability is analysed in terms of the likelihood that a country's economic development is hindered by the happening of exogenous unforeseen shocks (Guillaumont, 2008, 2009). SIDS are more exposed to both internal and external shocks, like social conflicts, extreme events and climate changes than other nations. Current empirical evidences on economic vulnerability reveal that small islands have high degrees of economic openness and export concentration. These create greater exposure to exogenous shocks, which are detriment to economic development. Moreover, other economic sectors that sustain their development, namely tourism, agriculture and fisheries are perceived as the most vulnerable sectors in this changing climate (Paul, 2021; Robinson, 2020). The other dimension of vulnerability is associated with social vulnerability arising when there is a limited coping capacity and resilience to recovery (Bohle, Downing, & Watts, 1994). Low-income and socio-cultural stratification result in a higher degree of social vulnerability (Massmann & Wehrhahn, 2014). Certain factors like poverty, inequality, access to resources and social status are likely to determine the social vulnerability of communities and individuals to hazards (including non-climate hazards). These are generic characteristics while other specific factors that are peculiar to certain shocks are situation of dwellings and living in low-lying coastal areas, amongst others. The social vulnerability consequences range from water-borne diseases, resettlement to effects on basic needs.

Extending on the traditional forms of vulnerability analysed in the literature, three forms of vulnerabilities are considered in the conceptual framework (See Fig. 1) in connection to the COVID-19 pandemic and climate change. First, cultural vulnerability is highly connected with social vulnerability as low risk perception, limited participation of communities and non-inclusion of local knowledge and practices in managing shocks directly influence the coping capacity of the population, thus increasing their social and cultural

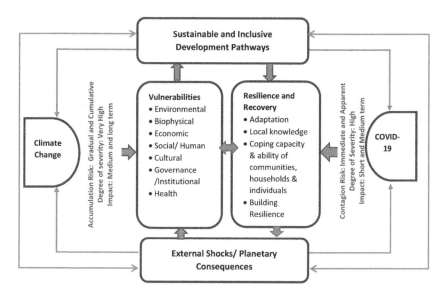

Fig. 1. Conceptual Framework. *Source:* Adapted from Ebi et al. (2021).

vulnerabilities. Social vulnerability is modelled in terms of the use of local knowledge and practices, traditional coping mechanisms, community participation, risk perception and public awareness on climate change amongst other stresses. The socio-cultural status of communities is linked to their religious beliefs, financial capacities, educational levels, human behaviour, customs and traditions and past experiences of hazards and risks (Papathoma-Köhle, Thaler, & Fuchs, 2022; Wachinger, Renn, Begg, & Kuhlicke, 2013).

The second addition to the Ebi et al. (2021) framework is institutional vulnerability to shocks, which has not been thoroughly investigated. The institutional dimension has been largely neglected focussing mainly on social and physical vulnerabilities (Papathoma-Köhle et al., 2022) and more so in connection to the COVID-19 and climate change shocks. Institutional vulnerability indicates the context and the process by which formal institutions (that is regulations, laws, constitutions, bureaucracy etc.) and governance are either too weak to provide protection, safety and human security against stresses. Countries with good governance and functional institutions face less impact from shocks in terms of deaths, monetary damage and they may have a higher speed of recovery (Jongman et al., 2015; Wu et al., 2019). Good institutions help nations to invest in adaptation and mitigation strategies, enable a fast reaction to crises and provide support to households and communities during the recovery phase. Institutions thus play a key role in building resilient societies (Birkmann, Welle, Solecki, Lwasa, & Garschagen, 2016; Thaler et al., 2019) at all phases of the disaster or shock circle, namely, in mitigation (land use planning regulations, risk transfer mechanisms), preparedness (accountability, early warning systems), response (priorities, treatment of vulnerable groups) and rehabilitation (resources and allocation, insurance and compensation) (Papathoma-Köhle & Thaler, 2018). Institutions played a key role in containing the COVID-19 pandemic. The response of appropriate bodies to prevent the spread of the virus and mitigate the impact of the pandemic on the most vulnerable segments of the population is contingent on a good institutional framework. Compared to the COVID-19 pandemic, the institutional framework plays a more important role in addressing climate change. The capacity of society to mitigate and adapt to climate change crisis depends on a wide range of factors with complex institutional arrangements in terms of production strategies, land and water governance, social support systems, availability of climate information, household and gender dynamic and interaction with external actors, amongst others. To prevent climate actions from being undermined, institutions need a coordinated approach to tackle corruption, bribery, fraud and nepotism which are common issues that halt the execution of projects that cut GHG emissions and build resilience to climate change.

Other than institutional vulnerability, health vulnerability is integrated in the framework. SIDS are deemed as the front lines, experiencing a range of severe and long-term risks from extreme weather conditions to increased risk of communicable and non-communicable diseases. Their fragile and climate non-resilient health care systems coupled with the lack of effective and affordable health services have posed major challenges to the lives and livelihoods of islanders, especially. A large part of the SIDs' populations tend to be highly geographically dispersed, living in precarious environmental and social conditions and exposed to mounting extreme weather events, hence making it difficult for them to access health services. Pandemic-induced mobility restrictions have further worsened health access. Climate change being a potent risk multiplier can also contribute to pandemics (Jordan, 2019; Winston, 2020). Rising temperatures, for instance, can create favourable conditions for the spread of certain infectious, mosquito-borne disease like dengue fever and malaria. Disappearing habitats can also force various animal species to migrate, thus increasing the likelihood of spillover pathogens between them. Conversely, measures that mitigate environmental risks like reducing pollution, shortening and localising supply chains and substituting animal proteins by plant proteins may help mitigate the risk of pandemics.

Over and above the vulnerability dimension, resilience is key within the development literature and this dimension is added in the above conceptual framework. A system is resilient when it is less vulnerable to shocks over time, and can recover from them (OECD, 2014). Vulnerability and resilience are complementary and complex concepts that need to be assessed when managing local consequences of global shocks (Briguglio, 2014; Robinson, 2020; Scanderra et al., 2018; Tiernan et al., 2019). Resilience to shocks is crucial for SIDs, in terms of the capacity and ability of communities, households or individuals to prevent, mitigate or cope with risk, and recover from these shocks. While SIDS are dealing with a combination of vulnerabilities, the notion of adaptation and resilience becomes necessary. Nonetheless, SIDS are considered to have very little climate change resilience (Paul, 2021).

The next extension to Ebi et al. (2021) model is that despite the fact that both pandemics and climate risks are physical shocks, their associated risks, severity and impacts differ. COVID-19 and climate change are trans-boundary threats that have widespread consequences on communities and especially the most vulnerable ones. They are both systemic threats with risks permeating within a highly interdependent and connected system (Renn et al., 2020; Schweizer, 2021). Their cascading effects across different countries have further exacerbated pre-existing vulnerabilities. Similarly, they are both stationary where it becomes difficult to forecast their occurrence and non-linear where the socio-economic effects rise exponentially once certain thresholds are met and overburdened like the health system. They are both risk multipliers and regressive in nature whereby they exacerbate existing vulnerabilities and affect disproportionately the more vulnerable segments of society. They cannot be considered in isolation as the population, governments and policymakers need to be prepared and build their long-term resilience to face both threats. Nonetheless, there are key divergences like the risks from climate change are gradual and cumulative while the pandemic presents imminent risks. In addition, the timescales of both the occurrence and resolution of climate hazards and pandemics are different. The contagion nature of pandemics produce correlated events on a global scale which can affect the entire system at once while climate hazards present a case for accumulation risk that give rise to an increased likelihood of severe, simultaneous but not directly correlated events that can reinforce one another. We further argue that while climate change manifests as short-term shocks but with long-term trends, COVID-19 is expected to be a short- and medium-term shock that has been brought under control by extensive immunity via vaccinations and sanitary health precautions. Based on these premises, this chapter probes into the different dimensions of vulnerabilities of SIDs and assesses the similarities and divergences of both shocks.

DATA AND METHODOLOGY

Data Source

Data are collected for 38 SIDs from the Disaster Risk Management Knowledge Centre, Inter-Agency Standing Committee Reference Group on Risk, Early Warning and Preparedness and the European Commission at https:// drmkc.jrc.ec.europa.eu/inform-index. The INFORM Risk Index is based on risk concepts over three dimensions namely hazards and exposure, vulnerability and lack of coping capacity. The INFORM Risk Index was also adapted in the midst of COVID-19 pandemic by measuring risks faced by countries from the health and humanitarian impacts of COVID-19 that have in turn overwhelmed their current national response capacity. The INFORM COVID-19 Risk Index shows the vulnerability of nations to the health, social and economic impacts of the pandemic. Data on COVID-19 confirmed cases, deaths, and vaccination rates are also downloaded from https://ourworldindata.org/.

Data from the Emergency Events Database – Université Catholique de Louvain (UCL) – CRED, D. Guha-Sapir (EM-DAT), on number of people affected and number of death resulting from disasters, number of natural hazards and costs of damages are also used. Data are gathered on the Climate Risk Index from Munich RE. Germanwatch – https://www.germanwatch.org/en/3657. The Global Climate Risk Index 2021 assesses and ranks the extent to which countries have been impacted by climate-related extreme weather events like storms, floods and heatwaves, amongst others. The most recent data available are for 2019 and for the period 2000–2019 and ranks countries on fatalities per 100,000 inhabitants, losses in million and losses per unit of GDP.

Methodology

The Inform Risk Index splits the vulnerability in three components, namely, hazards and exposure; fragility of the socio-economic system and lack of coping capacity. Physical exposure and physical vulnerability are factored in the hazards and exposure dimension. It is measured in terms of natural and human hazards. Natural hazards are split into six components, namely, earthquake, flood, tsunami, tropical cyclone, drought and epidemic while human hazards are current conflict intensity and projected conflict risk. Natural and human-induced hazards are aggregated by using the geometric mean, giving equal weights to each dimension. This chapter uses the index of natural hazards as a measure of environmental and physical vulnerability. The second dimension of the index encompasses socio-economic vulnerability in terms of development and deprivation, which has a weightage of 50%, inequality with a weightage of 25%, aid dependency of 25%. Vulnerable groups are also factored in the computation of socio-economic vulnerability. The two categories in terms of socio-economic vulnerability and vulnerable groups are aggregated through the geometric mean. This dimension represents economic, social and political vulnerabilities of communities. In this study, the index is used as a measure of socio-economic vulnerability. Lastly, the coping capacity dimension includes information on the ability of the country to cope with shocks and the effort of the government to contribute to the reduction of disaster risk. It is aggregated by a geometric mean of two categories, namely, institutional and infrastructure. The overall inform risk is a multiplicative equation as follows:

$$\text{Risk} = \text{Hazard and Exposure}^{1/3} \times \text{Vulnerability}^{1/3} \times \text{Lack of coping capacity}^{1/3}$$

The different indicators used to measure overall exposure and vulnerability to climate change and the COVID-19 pandemic are summarised in Table 1 (See Appendix 1). One limitation of the indicators is the unavailability of information to measure cultural vulnerability and two aspects of biophysical vulnerability in terms of coastal system (for instance, coral bleaching, acidification of surface waters or degraded coastal fisheries) and terrestrial system (in terms of degradation of mangroves and sea grass, and degradation and salinisation of groundwater, amongst others).

SITUATIONAL ANALYSIS OF CLIMATE CHANGE AND COVID-19 PANDEMIC ON SIDS

First, the vulnerability of SIDs is analysed in relation to their exposure to climate change, natural hazards and number of people affected by disasters, and second, their vulnerability to the pandemic is assessed in terms of the number of COVID-19 cases versus number of COVID-19 deaths.

Climate Change, Natural Hazards and Disasters

We first probe into the climate change shocks faced by the small islands under study. The data assess the Natural Hazard Index for the group of 38 islands (see Fig. 2). Countries like Haiti, Papua New Guinea and Dominican Republic top up the list with a high exposure index of 7.0 for Haiti and 6.7 for the two other islands. The value of the index ranges from 0 to 10, where 10 is highest risk or highest contribution to risk. They are followed by Solomon Islands, Cuba, Vanuatu, Belize, Jamaica, Tonga and Dominica, with all of them having an index exceeding the value of 5, showing high vulnerability to natural hazards.

To evaluate climate change vulnerability further, we consider the total number of people affected by natural disasters over the last three years per 1,000

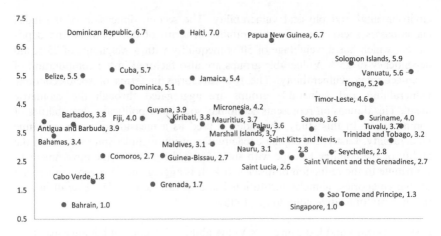

Fig. 2.   Exposure to Natural Hazards Across 38 Small Islands. *Source:*
Adapted from the Inform Natural Hazard Index, 2022.

inhabitants. It can be observed that Haiti, Sao Tome and Principe, Fiji, Guyana, Timor-Leste, Comoros and Tonga have high rates (see Fig. 3). Haiti is in fact exposed to a wide spectrum of natural disasters like droughts, floods, hurricanes, earthquakes and landslides. Whilst many Caribbean countries are exposed to the same threats, the potential destruction and loss of life and livelihoods tend to be the highest in Haiti due to their fragile social, economic and environmental conditions and pre-existing vulnerabilities across communities.

COVID-19 Situation Across Small Island Developing States

The next shock under study is the COVID-19 pandemic. The cumulative confirmed COVID-19 cases per million are analysed in relation to total deaths per million. The data on cumulative cases and deaths are computed since the first registered COVID-19 cases till July 2022. It can be observed that islands like Seychelles, Maldives, Bahrain, Palau and Barbados have had the highest number of cases followed by high fatality rates. Irrespective of regions that is Caribbean, Pacific, Atlantic, Indian Ocean and South China Sea (AIS), small islands have not escaped the COVID-19 pandemic despite their remoteness and sea bound-edness. In fact, these nations are high tourist destinations which have opened their borders with the gradual removal of travel restrictions among other sanitary containment measures and have thus witnessed a rise in the number of COVID-19 cases. Countries with low number of cases and COVID-19 death rates are Haiti, Guinea-Bissau and Papua New Guinea (See Fig. 4).

FINDINGS AND DISCUSSIONS

Using the indicators in Table 1, this chapter investigates into the different vulnerability dimensions of the 38 small islands in relation to the COVID-19

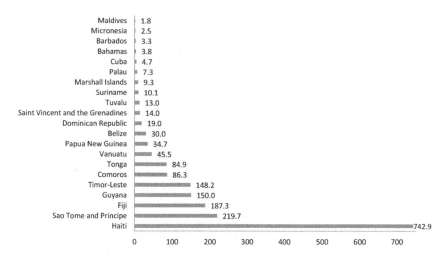

Fig. 3. Total Number of People Affected by Natural Disasters Over the Last Three Years per 1,000 People Across Small Islands. *Source:* Adapted from the Inform Natural Hazard Index, 2022. Data is available for only a limited number of small islands.

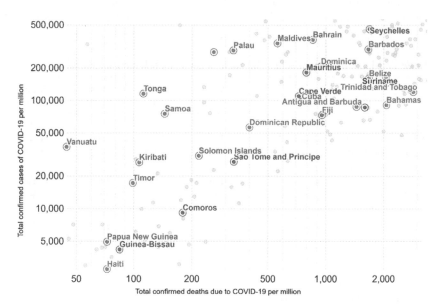

Fig. 4. Total Confirmed COVID-19 Cases Versus Death per Million, July 2022. *Source:* Data from Johns Hopkins CSSE COVID-19 Data.

pandemic and climate change. The islands are grouped into three regions namely the Caribbean comprising of 16 countries, Pacific with 13 islands and the Atlantic, Indian Ocean and South China Sea (AIS) covering nine nations. The mean of the different vulnerability dimensions is computed for each group of countries and for the overall sample (See Table 2).

The values of the indicators for environmental vulnerability in terms of the INFORM Natural Hazard Index (INHI) and Recent Shocks (RS) are highest for the Pacific followed by the Caribbean. The Pacific group tends to be most vulnerable compared to the other groups with the mean value of the INHI at 4.4 while that of the RS is 5.6; these are well beyond the overall average of 3.8 and 3.4, respectively, for the sample of 38 islands. The islands of the Pacific are very vulnerable to large-scale disasters like cyclones. Climate change is making these disasters more frequent and intense (Ober & Bakumenko, 2020). In 2020, they had to face a new challenge: weathering a Category 5 cyclone, the highest measurement on the cyclone intensity scale, while at the same time facing the paralysing conditions and economic uncertainty caused by the COVID-19 pandemic (Ober & Bakumenko, 2020). Four Pacific islands highly hit by high-intensity cyclones are Solomon Islands, Vanuatu, Fiji and Tonga. Every year, small island developing states, including the Pacific islands, make up two-thirds of those countries that suffer the highest relative losses from natural disasters such as floods, storms and droughts (WHO, 2021). Sea level rise and mounting weather disasters are reducing access to fresh water, degrading reefs and beaches and taking the land where homes once stood, exacerbating the

Table 2. Mean of Vulnerability Indicators for the 38 Island Economies.

	Mean Overall	Mean AIS	Mean Pacific	Mean Caribbean
Environmental Vulnerability				
INFORM Natural Hazard Index (INHI)	3.821	2.233	**4.438**	4.213
Recent Shocks (RS)	3.458	2.244	**5.615**	2.388
Socio-Economic Vulnerability				
Socio-Economic Vulnerability	4.053	3.633	**5.092**	3.444
Vulnerable Groups	2.863	2.278	**4.254**	2.063
Institutional Vulnerability				
INFORM Institutional Index	5.405	5.189	**5.708**	5.281
Health Vulnerability				
Access to Health Care Index	4.611	4.111	**5.354**	4.288
Health Conditions	2.424	1.689	**4.523**	1.131
COVID-19 Vulnerability Index				
Health Capacity Specific to COVID-19	5.418	5.022	**6.415**	4.831
COVID-19 Lack of Coping Strategy	5.418	5.022	**6.415**	4.831
COVID-19 Hazard and Exposure Index	4.118	**5.189**	4.369	3.313
COVID-19 Vulnerability Index	4.547	4.011	4.446	**4.931**

Source: Author's Computation, 2022.

socio-economic vulnerabilities of communities. These islands have the smallest carbon footprint but bear the biggest burden from climate change.

The analysis probes further into the other dimensions of vulnerability of SIDs namely socio-economic vulnerability, institutional vulnerability and health vulnerability. In terms of socio-economic vulnerability, the index for the Pacific region is the highest with a mean value of 5.1 on the Socio-economic Vulnerability Index and an average value of 4.3 for the vulnerable group measure. The Human Development Index (HDI) which is part of the computation of the Socio-economic Vulnerability Index for SIDS is a vital indicator of well-being for the population and success in human development also acts as a driver of productive capacity and economic growth. In 2019, Palau, Bahamas, Barbados and Mauritius were included in the group of countries with very high human development with HDI scores above 0.80, while 14 SIDs were in the high human development category (ranked between 0.70 and 0.79). Most high-income SIDS are the Caribbean while lower middle–income SIDS are mainly in the Pacific, Atlantic and the Indian Ocean, with the exception of Mauritius, Seychelles, Palau and Nauru. It can be seen from the data that the Socio-economic Vulnerability Index as well as the index for vulnerable groups tend to be smaller for the Caribbean where most countries are within the high-income category. The next dimension of vulnerability is the Institutional Vulnerability Index which proves to be the highest amongst Pacific SIDS with a value of 5.7 compared to an average value of 5.4 for the sample. One of the distinct features of Pacific island economies is the lack of appropriate institutions that promote growth and development (Prasad, 2008). Over the recent years there have been various projects targeted towards the reinforcement of the foundations of good governance and the promotion of government accountability and transparency in the implementation of effective policies.

Next, in terms of the Health Vulnerability Index, the values of the access to health index as well as the health conditions measures are much higher for the Pacific islands with a mean value of 5.3 and 4.5, respectively. Similar to the other indicators, the mean for this group of small islands exceed the overall mean for the sample of small islands under study. In fact, as countries develop economically, changes in food consumption habits and other factors contribute to a rise in diseases such as cancer, diabetes and cardiovascular diseases amongst others. The prevalence of these non-communicable diseases (NCDs) tend to be high across SIDs, which share a disproportionately high burden of the risk factors, morbidity and premature mortality caused by NCDs. NCDs are a leading cause of premature mortality, with 52% of people with NCDs in SIDS dying prematurely (aged 30–69 years). In the Pacific, NCDs account for approximately 70% of mortalities (WHO, 2021). Unhealthy diets and physical inactivity across the Pacific islands account for eight of the world's 10 most obese nations, and seven of the 10 with the highest rates of diabetes (WHO, 2021). In terms of health systems, SIDS tend to be under-resourced and many health services are still struggling to transition to a chronic care model. The health workforce capacity also fails to respond to NCDs conditions. Further, due to their small market size, remoteness and high transport costs along with lack of economies of scale for negotiating prices of drugs and poor medical technology result in high and variable prices of medication (WHO, 2021). According to the 2019 Global Health Security Index, a measure of the health system's readiness to manage an event like a global pandemic, the large majority of SIDS fall into the 'Least prepared' category (WHO, 2021).

Lastly, from the COVID-19 Vulnerability Index, the extreme vulnerability of the Pacific region is noted in terms of their lack of coping strategy to the pandemic as well as their limited health capacity specific to COVID-19. COVID-19 has made in difficult for authorities to implement recovery and relief measures especially for the most affected communities. However, the mean value of the COVID-19 Hazard and Exposure Index tends to be high for the AIS region whereas the average value of the COVID-19 Vulnerability Index peaks for the Caribbean region. The Caribbean region has not only been battling the ongoing pandemic with its many complications and variants but has also been tackling compounding hazards of droughts, heavy rains, storms and ensuing floods and landslides.

The correlation between the different vulnerability dimensions are further analysed via the Pearson correlation coefficient. It measures the linear relationship between two variables and concentrates on the strength and the direction of this association. It ranges between -1 and 1, whereby a value of ±1 indicates a perfect degree of association between the two variables. As the coefficient approaches the value of 0, the relationship between the two variables gets weaker. A positive sign of the coefficient implies a positive relationship while a negative sign postulates a negative link. To ensure the robustness of our results and relax the assumption of a linear link, the Spearman rank correlation is also applied. The latter is a non-parametric test used to measure the monotonic association between two variables. Monotonicity is 'less restrictive' than the linear relationship.

Table 3 shows both the Pearson correlation coefficient and Spearman rank correlation for three COVID-19 indicators in relation to recent climate shocks faced by the small islands for the overall sample and by region. An index value less than 0.3 may imply weak correlation, while a value between 0.31 and 0.5 denotes moderate association and a value higher than 0.5 means high correlation. Both the Pearson correlation coefficient and the Spearman rank correlation reveal moderate association (the coefficients are greater than 0.3) between COVID-19 Vulnerability Index and RS for the overall sample of countries and a similar result is obtained with the COVID-19 lack of coping strategy indicators. There seems to be a weak association between COVID-19 Hazard and Exposure Index and shocks, as it should be noted that all countries, irrespective of size, have been exposed by the pandemic. This supports our premise that there are key differences between the two physical shocks. The risks associated with the COVID-19 pandemic and climate hazards along with their severity and impacts differ in varied ways. The global climate crisis is far lengthier and far more disruptive that what countries and, in particular, SIDS have currently experienced with the coronavirus. The risks from climate change are gradual and cumulative manifesting themselves in varied degrees and intensities over time. This accumulation of risks amplifies over time, leading to more severe and

Table 3. Pearson Correlation Coefficient and Spearman Rank Correlation for COVID-19 Indicators and Recent Climate Shocks.

	COVID-19 Vulnerability Index	COVID-19 Lack of Coping Strategy	COVID-19 Hazard and Exposure Index
Pearson Correlation Coefficient			
Recent Climate Shocks			
Overall Sample of 38 Countries	0.349	0.416	0.132
Regions			
Caribbean	0.303	0.471	0.184
Pacific	0.340	0.305	0.198
AIS	0.511	0.615	0.514
Spearman Rank Correlation			
Recent Climate Shocks			
Overall Sample of 38 Countries	0.393	0.369	0.015
Regions			
Caribbean	0.254	0.346	0.119
Pacific	0.225	0.351	0.467
AIS	0.701	0.631	0.433

Source: Author's Computation, 2022.

disastrous threats happening at the same time and reinforcing one another. This therefore has important implications of the mitigation actions of SIDS. Besides these differences between the COVID-19 shock and the climate change crisis, it should be noted that climate change in itself is a risk multiplier which is likely to contribute to pandemics. Most of the root causes of climate change increase the risk of pandemics. Loss of habitat due to deforestation or other man-made activities forces animals to migrate and potentially contact other animals or people and serve as a source for spillover of infections from animals to people.

From a region-wise perspective, the data reveal that the AIS region has a higher level of association between the different COVID-19 indicators and RS, relative to the Caribbean and the Pacific regions. The Pearson correlation coefficient and the Spearman rank correlation exceed 0.5 confirming a stronger association between COVID-19 and RS. It can be argued that for the AIS region, there are greater similarities between the two shocks in terms of their systemic effects cascading to different economic sectors and activities, as well as their non-linearity reflected in the disproportionate socio-economic impacts of both threats which overburdened existing services. They affect to a large extent the most vulnerable segments of the population, exacerbating existing inequalities and vulnerabilities.

CONCLUSION AND POLICY IMPLICATIONS

This chapter extends on Ebi et al. (2021) conceptual framework to analyse the vulnerabilities of 38 small islands across the Caribbean, Pacific and the AIS region to the COVID-19 pandemic and climate change. Data from global databases are used to analyse the different dimensions of vulnerability of these island economies. Vulnerabilities are assessed in terms of environmental, bio-physical, social, economic, cultural, institutional and health vulnerabilities. These different dimensions are measured by specific comparable indicators for the group of islands under study. The findings indicate that though the two shocks have similarities, they tend to have marked differences. This is confirmed by our results which reveal a weak association between COVID-19 and climate change shocks/exposure to natural hazards. The Pearson correlation coefficients are in the low range of 0.132–0.349 for the overall sample while the Spearman rank correlation coefficients are as low as 0.015–0.393. While the similarities between the two shocks tend to be robust for the AIS region, there are also some notable differences between pandemics and climate hazards for the other regions with low correlation coefficients.

Understanding the similarities, the differences and the broader relationships between pandemics and climate risk is a critical first step in order to derive practical implications that inform actions of SIDS. This will also provide more information on how to mitigate the climate and pandemic risks and be better prepared and resilient to future shocks. Building a safer and more resilient environment with anticipatory actions ahead of extreme weather events can save countless lives. Systems that have been set up in advance and which build on existing local capacity are better suited to deal with systemic shocks like climate change and COVID-19. It is, however, vital to account for the differentiated needs and impacts of shocks on the population and also on the most vulnerable segments of society. Vulnerabilities and needs must be recognised and addressed by involving different stakeholders and finding solutions together to face the rising risks of changing climate and pandemics. Collective efforts at all levels that is locally, regionally and internationally and across all sectors are needed to tackle climate change and pandemic in order to build more resilient societies and economies. More important is to differentiate between the impacts of pandemics and climate change as the latter tend to be more prolonged with important multiplier effects. One limitation of the study however rests on the inability to measure resilience of SIDS to these shocks due to non-availability of data. Future work could concentrate on qualitative data based on interviews or focus group discussions with key stakeholders across small islands to gather information on their adaptation and mitigation strategies to shocks.

REFERENCES

Allison, E. H., Perry, A. L., Badjeck, M. C., Neil Adger, W., Brown, K., Conway, D., & Dulvy, N. K. (2009). Vulnerability of national economies to the impacts of climate change on fisheries. *Fish and Fisheries*, *10*(2), 173–196. doi:10.1111/j.1467-2979.2008.00310.x

Alwang, J., Siegel, P. B., & Jorgensen, S. L. (2001). *Vulnerability: A view from different disciplines* (Social protection Discussion Paper No. 0115). Washington, DC: World Bank. Retrieved from http://siteresources.worldbank.org/SOCIALPROTECTION/Resources/SP-Discussion-papers/Social-Risk-Management-DP/0115.pdf

Atkins, J., Mazzi, S., & Ramlogan, C. (1998). A study on the vulnerability of developing and island states: A composite index. Issued by the Commonwealth Secretariat, August 1998.

Becker, H. (2021). The impact of the COVID-19 global pandemic on the Cuban tourism industry and recommendations for Cuba's response. *Multidisciplinary Business Review, 14*(1), 71–83.

Betzold, C., & Mohamed, I. (2017a). Seawalls as a response to coastal erosion and flooding: A case study from Grande Comore, Comoros (West Indian Ocean). *Regional Environmental Change, 17*(4), 1077–1087. doi:10.1007/s10113-016-1044-x

Betzold, C., & Mohamed, I. (2017b). Seawalls as a response to coastal erosion and flooding: A case study from Grande Comore, Comoros (West Indian Ocean). *Regional Environmental Change, 17*(4), 1077–1087.

Bhagooli, R. Mattan-Moorgawa, S., (2014) Training manual coastal and marine environment for engineers. University of Mauritius, 117–134.

Birkmann, J., Welle, T., Solecki, W., Lwasa, S., & Garschagen, M. (2016). Boost resilience of small and mid-sized cities. *Nature, 537*(7622), 605–608.

Bohle, H.-G. (2001). Vulnerability and criticality: Perspectives from social geography. In *Newsletter of the international human dimensions programme on global environmental change.* Walter-Flex-Str. 3, D - 53113 Bonn, Germany.

Bohle, H. G., Downing, T. E., & Watts, M. J. (1994). Climate change and social vulnerability: Toward a sociology and geography of food insecurity. *Global Environmental Change, 4*(1), 37–48.

Brander, K. (2009). Impacts of climate change on marine ecosystems and fisheries. *Journal of the Marine Biological Association of India, 51*(1), 1–13. doi:10.1007/s10584-012-0541-2

Briguglio, L. (1997, December). *Alternative economic vulnerability indices for developing countries, Report prepared for the expert group on vulnerability index.* United Nations Department of Economic and Social Affairs-UN(DESA).

Briguglio, L. (2014). A vulnerability and resilience framework for small states. In D. Bynoe-Lewis (Ed.), *Building the resilience of small states: A revised framework* (pp. 1–102). London: Commonwealth Secretariat.

Brown, K. (2017). *Vulnerability and young people.* Bristol: Policy Press.

Chambers, R. (2009). *Climate vulnerability and capacity analysis.* Brighton: Institute of Development Studies University of Sussex.

Cheng, Y. D., Farmer, J. R., Dickinson, S. L., Robeson, S. M., Fischer, B. C., & Reynolds, H. L. (2021). Climate change impacts and urban green space adaptation efforts: Evidence from US municipal parks and recreation departments. *Urban Climate, 39*, 100962.

Coke-Hamilton, P. (2020). Impact of COVID-19 on tourism in small island developing states. Retrieved from https://unctad.org/en/pages/newsdetails.aspx?OriginalVersionID=2441

Collymore, J. (2007). Disaster impacts on the Caribbean. In *International perspectives on natural disasters: Occurrence, mitigation, and consequences* (pp. 303–322). Dordrecht: Springer. doi:10.1007/978-1-4020-2851-9_16

Connell, J., Lowitt, K., Saint Ville, A., & Hickey, G. M. (2020). Food security and sovereignty in Small Island developing states: Contemporary crises and challenges. In J. Connell & K. Lowitt (Eds.), *Food security in Small Island states* (pp. 1–23). Singapore: Springer.

Connell, J. (2021). COVID-19 and tourism in Pacific SIDS: Lessons from Fiji, Vanuatu and Samoa? *The Round Table, 110*(1), 149–158.

Cowburn, B., Moritz, C., Grimsditch, G., & Solandt, J. L. (2019). Evidence of coral bleaching avoidance, resistance and recovery in the Maldives during the 2016 mass-bleaching event. *Marine Ecology Progress Series, 626*, 53–67. doi:10.3354/meps13044

De Leon, J. V. (2006). *Vulnerability: A conceptual and methodological review* (p. 84). Bonn: United Nations University. Institute for Environment and Human Security.

Ebi, K. L., Bowen, K. J., Calkins, J., Chen, M., Huq, S., Nalau, J., ... Rosenzweig, C. (2021). Interactions between two existential threats: COVID-19 and climate change. *Climate Risk Management, 34*, 100363.

FAO. (2018). *The state of world fisheries and aquaculture 2018 – Meeting the sustainable development goals, Rome.* ISBN 978-92-5-130562-1.

Foley, A. M., Moncada, S., Mycoo, M., Nunn, P., Tandrayen-Ragoobur, V., & Evans, C. (2022). Small Island Developing States in a post-pandemic world: Challenges and opportunities for climate action. *Wiley Interdisciplinary Reviews: Climate Change, 13*(3), e769.

Селевые потоки: катастрофы, риск, прогноз, защита

Gounder, R. (2020). Economic vulnerabilities and livelihoods: Impact of COVID-19 in Fiji and Vanuatu. *Oceania, 90*, 107–113.

Guillaumont, P. (2008). *Adapting aid allocation criteria to development goals. An essay for the 2008 development cooperation forum, UN ECOSOC, May 2008*, Ferdi Working Paper.

Guillaumont, P. (2009). *An economic vulnerability index: Its design and use for international development policy.* No 200907, Working Papers. CERDI.

Gu, S., Ślusarczyk, B., Hajizada, S., Kovalyova, I., & Sakhbieva, A. (2021). Impact of the COVID-19 pandemic on online consumer purchasing behavior. *Journal of Theoretical and Applied Electronic Commerce Research, 16*(6), 2263–2281.

Harper, A., & Vinke, K. (2020). *COVID-19, displacement and climate change.* UNHCR. Retrieved from https://www.unhcr.org/2020-unhcr-annual-consultations-with-ngos/COVID-19_Displacement_Climate-Change-Factsheet-June-2020.pdf

Hilhorst, D., & Bankoff, G. G. (2004). Introduction: Mapping vulnerability. *Mapping Vulnerability: Disasters, Development and People*, 1–9.

IPCC. (1991). The seven steps to the vulnerability assessment of coastal areas to sea-level rise – Guidelines for case studies. *IPCC Report, 24.*

IPCC. (2007). Summary for policymakers. In S. Solomon, D. Qin, M. Manning, Z. Chen, M. Marquis, K. B. Avery, ... H. L. Miller (Eds.). *Climate change 2007: The physical science basis. Contribution of Working Group I to the Fourth Assessment Report of the Intergovernmental Panel on Climate Change* (pp. 1–18). Cambridge: Cambridge University Press.

Jordan, J. C. (2019). Deconstructing resilience: Why gender and power matter in responding to climate stress in Bangladesh. *Climate and Development, 11*(2), 167–179.

Jongman, B., Winsemius, H. C., Aerts, J. C. J. H., de Perez, E. C., van Aalst, M. K., Kron, W., & Ward, P. J. (2015). Declining vulnerability to river floods and the global benefits of adaptation. *Proceedings of the National Academy of Sciences, 112*(18), E2271–E2280.

Karnauskas, K. B., Schleussner, C. F., Donnelly, J. P., & Anchukaitis, K. J. (2018). Freshwater stress on small island developing states: Population projections and aridity changes at 1.5 and 2°C. *Regional Environmental Change, 18*, 2273–2282.

Kasperson, J. X., Kasperson, R. E., Turner, B. L., II, Hsieh, W., & Schiller, A. (2002). Vulnerability to global environmental change. In A. Diekmann, T. Dietz, C. C. Jaeger, & E. A. Rosa (Eds.), *The human dimensions of global environmental change.* Cambridge, MA: MIT Press (forthcoming).

Kelman, I. (2006). Island security and disaster diplomacy in the context of climate change. *Les Cahiers de la Sécurité, 63*(1), 61–94.

Kelman, I., Orlowska, J., Upadhyay, H., Stojanov, R., Webersik, C., Simonelli, A. C., ... Němec, D. (2019). Does climate change influence people's migration decisions in Maldives? *Climatic Change, 153*(1), 285–299. doi:10.1007/s10584-019-02376-y

Macchi, M., Oviedo, G., Gotheil, S., Kross, K., Boedhihartono, A., Wolfangel, C., & Howell, M. (2008). *Indigenous and traditional peoples and climate change.* IUCN Issues Paper. Retrieved from http://cmsdata.iucn.org/downloads/indigenous_peoples_climate_change.pdf

Massmann, F., & Wehrhahn, R. (2014). Qualitative social vulnerability assessments to natural hazards: Examples from coastal Thailand. *Revista de Gestão Costeira Integrada [Journal of Integrated Coastal Zone Management], 14*(1), 3–13.

Monnereau, I., & Oxenford, H. A. (2017). Impacts of climate change on fisheries in the coastal and marine environments of Caribbean Small Island Developing States (SIDS). *Caribbean Marine Climate Change Report Card: Science Review, 2017*, 124–154.

Nanau, G. (2020). Pacific Islands' leadership responses and lessons from the COVID-19 pandemic. In *Developmental leadership programme: Opinions University of the South Pacific (USP) Suva, Fiji.*

Nunn, P., & Kumar, R. (2018). Understanding climate-human interactions in Small Island Developing States (SIDS) implications for future livelihood sustainability. *International Journal of Climate Change Strategies and Management, 10*(2), 245–271.

Nurse, L. A., McLean, R. F., Agard, J., Briguglio, L. P., Duvat-Magnan, V., Pelesikoti, N., ... Webb, A. (2014). In V. Barros, C. Field, D. Dokken, M. Mastrandrea, K. Mach, T. Bilir, ... Mastrandrea (Eds.), *Small islands.* Cambridge: Cambridge University Press.

Orlowska, J. (2018). Effects of climate change on children in the Maldives. Malé, Maldives. Retrieved from http://saruna.mnu.edu.mv/jspui/handle/123456789/5520

Ober, K., & Bakumenko, S. (2020). A new vulnerability: COVID-19 and tropical cyclone Harold create the perfect storm in the Pacific. United Nations Office for the Coordination of Humanitarian Affairs, Reliefweb, *3*.

OECD. (2014). Guidelines for resilience systems analysis. OECD Publishing. Retrieved from https://www.oecd.org/dac/Resilience%20Systems%20Analysis%20FINAL.pdf

Pantin, D. A. (1997, November). *Alternative ecological vulnerability indices for developing countries with special reference to small island developing states (SIDS).* report for the United Nations Department of Economic and Social Affairs, Sustainable Economic Development Unit, University of the West Indies, Trinidad.

Papathoma-Köhle, M., Schlögl, M., Dosser, L., Roesch, F., Borga, M., Erlicher, M., ... & Fuchs, S. (2022). Physical vulnerability to dynamic flooding: Vulnerability curves and vulnerability indices. *Journal of Hydrology, 607*, 127501.

Papathoma-Köhle, M. A. R. I. A., & Thaler, T. (2018). *Institutional vulnerability* (pp. 98–124). Cambridge: Cambridge University Press.

Papathoma-Köhle, M., Thaler, T., & Fuchs, S. (2021). An institutional approach to vulnerability: Evidence from natural hazard management in Europe. *Environmental Research Letters, 16*(4), 044056.

Paul, S. (2021) Macroeconomic trends, vulnerability, and resilience capability in Small Island Developing States.

Prasad, N. (2008). Growth and social development in the Pacific Island countries. *International Journal of Social Economics, 35*(12), 930–950.

Petzold, J., & Magnan, A. K. (2019). Climate change: Thinking small islands beyond Small Island Developing States (SIDS). *Climatic Change, 152*(1), 145–165.

Ragoonaden, S., Seewoobaduth, J., & Cheenacunnan, I. (2017). Recent acceleration of Sea level rise in Mauritius and Rodrigues. *Western Indian Ocean Journal of Marine Science*, 51–65.

Ramlall, I. (2014). Gauging the impact of climate change on food crops production in Mauritius. *International Journal of Climate Change Strategies and Management, 6*(3). doi:10.1108/IJCCSM-12-2012-0079

Ratter, B. M., Petzold, J., & Sinane, K. (2016). Considering the locals: Coastal construction and destruction in times of climate change on Anjouan, Comoros. In *Natural resources forum* (Vol. 40(3), pp. 112–126). Oxford: Blackwell Publishing Ltd. doi:10.1111/1477-8947.12102

Renn, O., Kröger, W., Laubichler, M., Lucas, K., Schanze, J., Scholz, R. W., & Schweizer, P.-J. (2020). Systemic risks from different perspectives. *Risk Analysis*. doi: 10.1111/risa.13657

Roberts, J. L. (2021). Climate change and heatwaves. *Shaping the Future of Small Islands: Roadmap for Sustainable Development*, 233–248.

Robinson, S. A. (2020). Climate change adaptation in SIDS: A systematic review of the literature pre and post the IPCC Fifth Assessment Report. *Wiley Interdisciplinary Reviews: Climate Change, 11*(4), 5–21. doi:10.3763/ehaz.2001.0306

Saxena, A., Qui, K., & Robinson, S. A. (2018). Knowledge, attitudes and practices of climate adaptation actors towards resilience and transformation in a 1.5 C world. *Environmental Science & Policy, 80*, 152–159.

Scandurra, G., Romano, A. A., Ronghi, M., & Carfora, A. (2018). On the vulnerability of Small Island Developing States: A dynamic analysis. *Ecological Indicators, 84*, 382–392. doi:10.1016/j.ecolind.2017.09.016

Schweizer, P.-J. (2021). Systemic risks–concepts and challenges for risk governance. *Journal of Risk Research, 24*(1), 78–93.

Seetanah, B., & Fauzel, S. (2018). Investigating the impact of climate change on the tourism sector: Evidence from a sample of island economies. *Tourism Review, 74*(2), 194–203.

Sultan, R. (2017). *Assessing the climate change-migration Nexus through the Lens of migrants: The case of the Republic of Mauritius.* Geneva: IOM.

Sumner, P. D., Rughooputh, S. D., Boojhawon, R., Dhurmea, K., Hedding, D. W., le Roux, J., & Nel, W. (2021). Erosion studies on Mauritius: Overview and research opportunities. *South African Geographical Journal, 103*(1), 65–81. doi:10.1080/03736245.2020.1795915

Tandrayen-Ragoobur, V. (2021). Social and economic vulnerability to climate change: A gender dimension for Indian Ocean Islands. *Small Island Developing States: Vulnerability and Resilience Under Climate Change*, 185–210.

Tandrayen-Ragoobur, V., Tengur, N. D., & Fauzel, S. (2022). COVID-19 and Mauritius' tourism industry: An island perspective. *Journal of Policy Research in Tourism, Leisure and Events*, 1–17.

Thaler, T., Attems, M.-S., Bonnefond, M., Clarke, D., Gatien-Tournat, A., Gralepois, M., ... Fuchs, S. (2019). Drivers and barriers of adaptation initiatives – How societal transformation affects natural hazard management and risk mitigation in Europe. *Science of the Total Environment*, *650*, 1073–1082.

Thomas, A., Baptiste, A., Martyr-Koller, R., Pringle, P., & Rhiney, K. (2020). Climate change and small island developing states. *Annual Review of Environment and Resources*, *45*(6), 1–6.

Tiernan, A., Drennan, L., Nalau, J., Onyango, E., Morrissey, L., & Mackey, B. (2019). A review of themes in disaster resilience literature and international practice since 2012. *Policy Design and Practice*, *2*(1), 53–74.

Tyllianakis, E., Grilli, G., Gibson, D., Ferrini, S., Conejo-Watt, H., & Luisetti, T. (2019). Policy options to achieve culturally-aware and environmentally-sustainable tourism in Fiji. *Marine Pollution Bulletin*, *148*, 107–115.

UNEP. (1998). Human development report 1998. UNDP Report (p. 228). Oxford University Press.

UN/ISDR. (2004). Glossary. Basic terms of disaster risk reduction. Retrieved from http://www.unisdr. org/unisdr/eng/library/lib-terminology-eng%20home.htm

United Nations Office for Disaster Risk Reduction. (2022). Global assessment report on disaster risk reduction 2022: Our world at risk: Transforming governance for a resilient future. Geneva.

UN. (2021). *The sustainable development goals Report 2021*.

Wachinger, G., Renn, O., Begg, C., & Kuhlcke, C. (2013). The risk perception paradox—Implications for governance and communication of natural hazards. *Risk Analysis*, *33*(6), 1049–1065.

Winston, A. (2020). Is the COVID-19 outbreak a black swan or the new normal. *MIT Sloan Management Review*, *16*, 154–173.

World Health Organization. (2021). *Health and climate change global survey report*. World Health Organization: Geneva.

Wu, C., Ji, C., Shi, B., Wang, Y., Gao, J., Yang, Y., & Mu, J. (2019). The impact of climate change and human activities on streamflow and sediment load in the Pearl River basin. *International Journal of Sediment Research*, *34*(4), 307–321.

APPENDIX

Table 1. Indicators Measuring Climate Change and COVID-19 Vulnerabilities.

		Dimensions		
Environmental and Physical Vulnerability	Socio-Economic Vulnerability	Governance and Institutional Vulnerability	Health Vulnerability	COVID-19 Vulnerability
Exposure to Earthquakes	Human Development Index	Disaster Risk Management	Physicians Density per 10,000 people	Air transport, passengers carried
Exposure to Tsunamis	Multidimensional Poverty Index	Corruption Perception Index	Hospital Beds	Number of tourists arrivals
Exposure to Floods	Gender Inequality Index	Government Effectiveness Index	Proportion of population with access to three doses of diphtheria-tetanus-pertussis (DTP3) (%)	Point of entry
Exposure to Droughts	Income Gini Coefficient		Proportion of population with access to measles-containing-vaccine second-dose (MCV2) (%)	Access to Cities
Exposure to Tropical Cyclones	Total public Aid (M US$)		Proportion of population with access to pneumococcal conjugate 3rd dose (PCV3) (%)	Road density
Exposure to Epidemics	Public Aid per capita (US$)		Per capita public and private expenditure on health care	Adult literacy rate
Total affected by natural disasters last three years (1,000 people)	Net ODA received (% of GNI)		Maternal Mortality ratio	Mobile cellular subscriptions
Natural Disasters % of total population	Volume of remittances (in USD) as a proportion of GDP (%)		Estimated number of people living with HIV – Adult (>15) rate	Internet users
			Number of new HIV infections per 1,000 uninfected population	Demographic and Co-morbidities – Proportion of the population at increased risk of COVID-19 disease
			Incidence of Tuberculosis	People using at least basic sanitation services (%)

Table 1. (*Continued*)

		Dimensions		
Environmental and Physical Vulnerability	Socio-Economic Vulnerability	Governance and Institutional Vulnerability	Health Vulnerability	COVID-19 Vulnerability
			Malaria incidence per 1,000 population at risk	People using at least basic drinking water services (%)
			People need interventions against neglected tropical diseases (% of total population)	Hygiene – People practicing open defecation (%)
				Population Density (people per sq. km of land area)
				Population Living in Urban Areas (%)
				Population living in slums (% of urban population)
				Household Size – household population divided by number of households in a country
Combined Index Used				
(1) INFORM Natural Hazard Index	(1) INFORM Socio-Economic Vulnerability Index	(1) INFORM Institutional Index	(1) Access To Health Care Index	(1) INFORM COVID-19 Hazard & Exposure
(2) Recent Shocks Index			(2) Health Conditions	(2) INFORM COVID-19 Vulnerability Index
			(3) Health capacity specific to COVID-19	

Source: Author's Computation from Different Sources.

WASTE MANAGEMENT AND SUSTAINABILITY: A CASE STUDY IN ANGOLA

Talita Panzo and José Carlos Góis

ABSTRACT

The success of waste management depends on public awareness of environmental issues and the ability of the local government to provide facilities. Many countries have serious problems of financial resources and infrastructure for waste management. As there is a lack of awareness of the population on the importance of waste management, municipal governments only adopt remediation actions to manage waste collection service.

In Angola, during the last decade, the government has been committed to the reconstruction and development of the country, creating infrastructure for the provision of essential services and publishing legal tools to respond to environmental issues. In 2012 the government approved the Strategic Plan for the Management of Municipal Solid Waste (PESGRU). The strategic plan was designed for a time horizon until 2025. Due to the economic crisis that hit the country, the implementation of the plan suffered several setbacks and the deadlines established for the different programmes are being compromised.

A study carried out in 2020 on waste management in Angola, with four of the main provinces as a stage, through the analysis of official documents, direct observation and face-to-face interviews with those in charge of waste management, revealed a lack of funding for the implementation of PESGRU and low assistance from the Ministry of the Environment and the central government and showed the unsustainability of the waste management model in light of the principles recommended by international good practices.

Keywords: Waste management; municipalities; indicators; sustainability; financial resources; environment awareness; education

Achieving Net Zero
Developments in Corporate Governance and Responsibility, Volume 20, 95–108
Copyright © 2023 by Emerald Publishing Limited
All rights of reproduction in any form reserved
ISSN: 2043-0523/doi:10.1108/S2043-052320230000020005

INTRODUCTION

All human activity leads to the production of waste and if the waste management process is inadequate, there will be contamination of soil, water and air. With the economic development and the globalisation of markets, we are witnessing an increasing commercialisation of products, encouraged by consumption habits and, consequently, an increase in waste production. With population concentration in urban areas, urban disorder and lack of viable road infrastructure, waste management is a major problem, and people living in these areas are exposed to serious health risks. The situation is equally alarming in rural areas where there is a dearth of waste management strategies, especially in underdeveloped and developing countries. In 2012, the World Bank project estimated that an annual production of municipal solid waste (MSW) should be approximately 1.3 million tons for urban settlements and that such number should double by the end of 2025 (Hoornweg & Bhada-Tata, 2012).

This situation has been arousing concern in different sectors of society that are trying to alert and raise awareness among the population and the authorities about the environmental effects and the repercussions on health. Proposals to solve the problem have been very diverse and contextualised for each country, depending on its economic, geographical, political and educational characteristics. However, it cannot be said that the problem is under control or in the process of being solved, with the threat to health and the environment remaining. Therefore, the search for ways to correctly manage waste from a social, environmental and economic point of view is essential.

Waste management basically includes the activities of collection, transport, storage, sorting, treatment, recovery and disposal of waste, as well as soil decontamination operations, including the supervision of these operations and the monitoring of disposal sites after closure.

In the early 1980s, negative environmental impacts increased society's concern, namely the greenhouse effect, the loss of biodiversity and acid rain. At the end of the same decade, other factors were incorporated as threats to the planet, namely, the worsening of global climate change, the reduction of the ozone layer, toxic waste, pollution of surface and underground waters, energy waste and desertification. A period of reforms aimed at human activity that is compatible with development and environmental conservation then began. From 1990 onwards, progress was made in establishing regulations and funding aimed at improving environmental quality. Schools now include full diplomas in environmental specialities. At the 1992 Eco-92 on Environment and Development, held in Rio de Janeiro in 1992, the governments of most participating countries expressed strong support for environmental protection and sustainable development, and called for the implementation of the provisions of the United Nations Framework Convention on Climate Change (UNFCCC) through the adoption and enforcement of national laws, regulations, standards and policies establishing high levels of environmental protection. With the Kyoto Protocol that came into force in 2005, industrialised countries committed themselves to reducing, during the period from 2008 to 2012, total GHG emissions by at least 5% compared to

1990 levels (Agenda 21/un.org, 2022). More recently, the Paris Agreement under the UNFCCC set out measures to reduce carbon dioxide emissions from 2020. The central objective of the agreement is to strengthen the global response to the threat of climate change and to strengthen the capacity of countries to deal with the impacts of climate change (Sustainable development goals/un.org, 2022). These international commitments are based on the conviction that the main way to deal with environmental issues is through global, national and local solutions that promote sustainable development, where not only economic but also social and environmental aspects are considered.

Although society is increasingly aware of its responsibility towards environmental issues and is committed to this goal, accepting its responsibility in defending and protecting the environment, the countries' priorities are different in this respect and depend heavily on the economic development and cultural behaviour of the population. In September 2015 world leaders adopted the 2030 Agenda for Sustainable Development and its 17 goals that cut across disciplines, sectors and institutional mandates, acknowledging the integrated nature of the many challenges that humanity faces – from gender inequality to inadequate infrastructure, from youth unemployment to environmental degradation (UNEP, 2022).

The economic sustainability of waste management systems and the environmental education of populations are considered essential factors to ensure the implementation and sustainability of waste management plans. To avoid economic losses and the potential negative consequences at the social and environmental level, Urban Waste Management Plans (UWMPs) emerged as an essential tool for the desired sustainability. UWMPs must present the strategic axes of the waste management policy, the goals to be achieved, the technological infrastructures, the waste collection and treatment systems, as well as the management system financing model.

In the recent past, when people talked about sustainable waste management, they thought of recycling. Today the aim is to minimise the amount of waste and keep as many materials as possible in the resource cycle, seeking to reduce the negative impacts of consumption. Efforts have been made to move from a linear economy to a circular economy with no waste (or minimal waste) or where waste becomes a resource. The circular economy is considered essential to building a sustainable waste service and for a green economy. Life cycle assessment (LCA) has been a widely followed tool for understanding the ecological footprint of any waste management process and treatment.

Waste management is an integrated process based primarily on the economic status of each country (Srivastava, Krishna, & Sonkar, 2014). Waste management comprises many steps. Monitoring of waste production is a primary step. Various waste container monitoring technologies, such as geographic information systems (GIS), radio frequency identification (RFID) systems, ultrasonic sensors and international mobile/general packet radio service system (GSM/GPRS) are proposed to improve waste collection in containers and trucks (Hassan, Jameel, & Sekeroğlu, 2016). However, these state-of-the-art techniques are mostly not possible in poor countries due to their high cost. Waste disposal in landfills is the most commonly adopted route worldwide due to its convenience of execution. In terms of waste recovery, composting is the most economical process for organic waste recovery. When infrastructure capable of treating specific waste already exists, strategic plans and goals are created, as is the case of construction and demolition waste and health waste.

In developed countries, incineration and packaging recycling are the most common processes for municipal waste recovery, the latter being supported by the separate waste collection. Energy production from biogas generated by waste degradation in landfills or biodigesters or by waste incineration is a reality in countries with greater economic power and with human resources and qualified structures to monitor these more advanced technologies. Several criteria are adopted to monitor the performance of services from a social point of view and their economic and environmental sustainability. For the analysis of alternative proposals for waste management, the LCA is commonly adopted.

In order to manage MSW and the integration of various processes, there are several techniques and tools to evaluate this integration and the quality of solid waste management (Melaré, Gonzalez, & Faceli, 2017). Some evaluations are based on mathematical tests, usually applied where data on waste management are available, such as the life cycle evaluation methodologies (Coelho & Lange, 2018; Nabavi-Pelesaraei, Bayat, Hosseinzadeh-Bandbafha, Afrasyabi, & Berrada, 2017), material flow analysis (Duygan & Meylan, 2015) and multi-criteria decision analysis (Vucijak, Kurtagic, & Silajdzic, 2016). The use of sus-tainability indicators is also common. Studies conducted by Zurbrügg, Gfrerer, Ashadi, Brenner, and Küper (2012) in Indonesia, by Căilean and Teodosiu (2016) in Romania and by Rigamonti, Sterpi, and Grosso (2016) in the Lombardy region (Italia) showed the relevance of this methodology.

In order to assess waste management sustainability in a municipality in the Northeast of Brazil, Pereira and Fernandino (2019) adopted a sustainability indicator matrix proposed by Santiago and Dias (2012) organised into five dimensions: political, economic, environmental, cultural and social to evaluate integrated solid waste management quality. The indicators presented three possible responses that indicated a favourable, alert and unfavourable stage in relation to the sustainability of MSW management. Each of them presented an associated numerical value, therefore allowing to conduct a quantitative analysis from qualitative data. This approach allowed comparisons of different municipal contexts based on their performance on the indicator matrix. The final score of each dimension was given by adding the scores in each indicator. The average level of sustainability of MSW management (LS) was calculated from the ratio of scores, according to Eq. (1). Levels of sustainability scores were categorised into four intervals as shown in Table 1.

$$\overline{LS} = \frac{\sum \text{scores obtained in the evaluation}}{\sum \text{maximum scores in each dimension}} \times 10 \qquad (1)$$

According Pereira and Fernandino (2019) the application of the model to a municipality in the Northeast of Brazil revealed some problems due to the lack of

Table 1. Sustainability level Classification.

Sustainability Interval	Level of Sustainability
$0 \leq \overline{LS} \leq 1.0$	Unsustainable
$1.0 \leq \overline{LS} \leq 4.0$	Low sustainability
$4.0 \leq \overline{LS} \leq 8.0$	Medium sustainability
$8.0 \leq \overline{LS} \leq 10.0$	High sustainability

responses that were representative of reality or because they were not sufficiently comprehensive for the methodology to be used as a model. Some indicators could not be assessed due to lack of information, and other indicators had to be restructured in order to cover a greater variability of the realities encountered. Although this methodology can be easily applied by technicians and municipal managers who have access to information on waste management services, the huge information gap on this subject in developing countries is a problem and a huge challenge.

In other countries classified as developing, such as India and China, where waste management is considered inefficient and compliance is variable and limited and where the priority is to move from reliance on dumpsites, which offer no environmental protection, to landfills and to implement waste segregation at source and the construction of specialised waste treatment facilities to separate recyclable materials (Kumar & Agrawal, 2019; Kumar et al., 2017), studies on quality and sustained waste management services are still difficult to conduct.

In developed countries, represented by EU countries, waste-related indicators are used to measure and track trends in waste generation and certain aspects of waste management as: municipal waste generation and treatment, by treatment method; recycling rate of e-waste; recycling rate of packaging waste by type of packaging; material prices for recyclates; recovery rate of construction and demolition waste (ec.europa.eu, 2022). Through the various directives, EU countries have been under pressure to adopt sustainable waste management practices. Although municipal waste only constitutes about 10% of the total waste produced, due to its heterogeneous composition, environmentally sound management is a major challenge. For this reason, the way municipal waste is managed gives a good indication of the quality of the overall waste management system. In Portugal, member of the EU since 1986, to assess the quality of municipal waste collection service, several indicators are established and the waste collection service is divided into two levels: High-level service, performed by entities that collected recyclable waste, and low-level service, performed by entities that collected unsorted waste. The indicators for both levels include 17 points: (1) ease of access to unsorted waste collection services, (2) ease of access to sorted waste collection services, (3) ratio of average waste management services tax to average disposable income per household, (4) percentage of washed containers to total containers, (5) percentage of complaints and suggestions to the number of responses by waste management service, (6) ratio between income and expenditure associated with waste management service, (7) percentage of recyclable waste collected and waste sent to recycling companies, (8) rate of recyclable waste sent for mechanical biological treatment (MBT), (9) rate of waste sent for MBT and diverted from landfill, (10) potential landfill capacity, (11) renewal of vehicles used for waste collection, expressed by the accumulated average distance per vehicle, (12) productivity of the fleet used for waste collection, expressed by the ratio of the total amount of waste collected and capacity of the fleet used, (13) ratio of human resources per total amount of waste collected, (14) ratio of energy consumption per total amount of waste collected, (15) quality of landfill leachates after treatment, (16) CO_2 emissions associated with vehicles used in waste collection per total amount of recyclable waste collected, (17) CO_2 emissions associated with vehicles used in waste collection per total amount of unsorted waste collected (ERSAR, 2021). Based on the above indicators, the entity that assesses the quality of municipal waste service (ERSAR) produces a report classifying each indicator in five ranges, from the worst to the best performance.

In developed countries, waste management costs are supported through the sale of materials for recycling, organic compost or electricity and the fees charged to households and companies according to the amount and nature of the waste, based on benchmarks set by the government or the regulatory authority. On the other hand, in developing countries, no fee is charged to waste producers, and waste management costs are essentially supported by the State.

In African countries after the end of the colonial era, the population migrated to urban centres and the waste management services deteriorated. The problem of municipal waste management was aggravated due to the inability to collect all municipal waste, particularly in peri-urban communities, where roads are in poor conditions and urban planning is chaotic.

A research study conducted in East Africa shown that the urban waste collection service is carried out either by the municipality or by private operators hired by the municipality. Industries and shopping centres contract with private operators to collect waste on their premises, while community markets and hospitals mainly rely on municipal collection service. When waste containers are too far apart, communities dump waste indiscriminately and some disposal points are often overflowing with uncollected waste. Communities without waste collection services resort to incineration, burial and use of waste as animal feed. Dumpsites are the most common method of waste disposal (Okot-Okumu, 2012). Dumpsites pose a real danger to workers, waste pickers and stray animals visiting the sites. Most workers do not wear proper personal protective equipment and waste pickers do not follow any health and safety regulations (Oteng-Ababio, Arguello, & Gabbay, 2013). Environmental policy-making remains a function of central government, with local governments implementing policies and legislation; however central government funding is very low and local revenues are negligible. Political interference caused by personal interests has also hampered opportunities to implement decrees or regulations (Godfrey et al., 2019). The low standard of living, high degree of illiteracy and low GDP have been factors that negatively influence the willingness of population to participate in public management issues. The combination of all these factors together with the weaknesses of the urban council has led in some cases to the accumulation of waste in the neighbourhoods, and to environmental degradation generating epidemics of diseases such as cholera and diarrhoea (Tomita, Cuadros, Bruns, Tanser, & Slotow, 2020).

Angola, which is our case of study, became independent in November 1975. After independence, years of civil war followed until 2002 (Dulley & Sampaio, 2020). During the civil war period there was a marked deterioration of sanitation in urban areas due to the rural exodus, caused by the flow of people seeking shelter in the cities and looking for better conditions for their survival. At that time, there was no adequate infrastructure for the treatment of urban waste throughout the country. Only in 2007, the first landfill was built in Angola, located in Luanda province, which is the capital. In 2012, Presidential Decree 196/12 of 30 August was approved, which defined the Strategic Plan for Municipal Waste Management (PESGRU, 2012).

Ten years after the publication of PESGRU, it is important to know which infrastructures were built, the degree of implementation of the plan and its social, economic and environmental sustainability. It is also pertinent to know what measures are being implemented for the management of non-municipal waste.

MATERIALS AND METHODS

Angola has around 25 million inhabitants, most of whom live in urban areas (62.3%) (INE, 2016). After independence, Angola had several periods of civil war that ended in 2002, which cost a significant number of human lives, weakened infrastructure and delayed the development of institutional capacities. Over the past decade, the government has been committed to the reconstruction and development of the country and the creation of infrastructure to provide essential services. However, after years of strong growth, the economy entered a period of slowdown, mainly caused by the fall in oil prices in 2017, which have been the mainstay of the Angolan economy. In fact, after years of successive deceleration, inflation accelerated, reaching 18.6% in 2018 and many projects that were started and had an established goal were interrupted (Impala, 2019).

Angola is a unitary country with two levels of sub-national governments, composed of 18 provinces and 162 municipalities. Municipalities are further divided into 532 communes for administrative purposes. Governors of the provinces are appointed by the executive, and municipal administrators are appointed by the governors of the province in which the municipality is located. Municipalities are independent budget units since 2007 (following the imple-mentation of the Local Administration Law 02/07). Major recent legislation texts include the Decree 08/08 modifying local financial arrangements through the introduction of the Fund for Municipal Management Support and the Decree 09/08 aiming to provide technical support to municipalities in order to comply with their new functions. The provinces are responsible for the promotion and orientation of socio-economic development, provincial planning, social support, education (alphabetisation, primary education), healthcare, environment protection etc. They also play a role in the execution of decisions made by central authorities regarding regional/local matters, and supervise public institutes and companies of provincial/local importance. Municipalities are responsible for municipal and urban planning, agriculture and rural development, primary healthcare, municipal police, sanitation etc. (OECD, 2016).

For this study were selected the fourth higher provinces in population according 2014 census. According to the available data, the highest population density (INE, 2016), and the highest MSW production in Angola (PESGRU, 2012) are in the provinces of Luanda, Benguela, Huíla and Huambo. According to INE (2016), the population of the province of Luanda in 2014 was 6,945,386 inhabitants. The population in the other three provinces is 2,231,385, 2,497,422 and 2,019,555, respectively (INE, 2016). Together, these provinces have 54% of the population.

After the end of the civil war, Luanda province experienced strong economic growth, with manufacturing, trade and services as its main economic activities. Among the products produced in Luanda are food products, beverages, textiles, construction materials, plastic products, cigarettes and shoes, as well as the paper, furniture, textile, metallurgical and cement industries. Oil is refined in the country's only refinery located in Luanda. The port of Luanda allows the exportation of coffee, cotton, sugar, diamonds, iron and salt. Currently, the capital suffers from heavy traffic, lack of water and energy. One of the biggest difficulties is the excessive production of urban waste. Before the construction of Mulenvos landfill in 2007, in Cazenga municipality, in Luanda province, the waste was disposed in several dumpsites in the city (PESGRU, 2012).

The research methodology designed in this study was the collection and analysis of official documents, direct observation, complemented with photographic records and interviews with the high level responsible of waste management in each province. The study was carried out before COVID-19 during the second semester of 2019 and the first trimester of 2020.

The aim was to analyse the problem of solid urban waste management, to assess the behaviour, knowledge and perception of the population on the subject of waste management, to relate the deficiencies in waste removal to the quality of life of the population, to listen to the entities responsible for implementing the measures and strategies and to analyse social, economic and environmental sustainability.

RESULTS AND DISCUSSION

For many years, Decree 5/98 of 19 June was the only legal instrument to address to environmental issues in Angola. With economic and population growth, waste production increased sharply and waste management became an issue. Thus, in 2012, the government of Angola approved the Strategic Plan for Solid Urban Waste Management (PESGRU, 2012), through Presidential Decree 196/2012 of 30 August, and the Waste Management Regulation, through Presidential Decree 190/12 of 24 August, establishing several strategic axes and programmes for the mobilisation of society in a sustainable financing framework capable of making a qualitative leap in the management of MSW and creating conditions for the management of other wastes regarded as hazardous or of high production.

Presidential Decree 190/12 of 24 August covers all activities, industrial or otherwise, that cause waste that may directly affect the environment and establishes the preparation of a waste management plan that ensures sustainable environmental management practices, across the various types of waste, which prevents or reduces the production of waste and its hazardousness and attempts to promote its recovery.

The PESGRU was designed for a time horizon of up to 2025 and is aligned with the Millennium Development Goals (2015 and 2020) and the 'Angola 2025 – a country of the future' programme. The objectives, goals and monitoring procedures were established for each strategic axis. The purpose of training human resources and improving the environmental awareness of the population, as well as the legal framework and financial support for the implementation of waste management, are described in this legal document.

With the implementation of PESGRU, the government intended to address environmental and public health problems. The main objectives were to increase the waste producer's responsibility, encouraging them to follow an environmental protection strategy to achieve environmental objectives, contributing to the minimisation of environmental impacts, improving the quality of public health and providing business opportunities in this area. The programme was developed following the waste management hierarchy, following in order of priority the following principles: waste prevention, reuse, recycling, recovery and disposal. At the same time, it aimed to create criteria for environmental protection and equity throughout the territory.

However, about 10 years after PESGRU and Waste Management Regulation were published, the deadlines set for many of the programmes have been compromised, and many infrastructures remain unbuilt or are not even planned, and others that were under construction have been stopped. The recent economic crisis has forced the government to request financial intervention from the IMF, and has accentuated the inability of the state administrative services to fulfil the contracts with the urban waste collection operators and aggravated the ineptitude of the municipal governments to implement fees and, consequently, generate sufficient revenue to maintain the contracts with private operators.

Container overflow in more densely populated areas and waste burning are frequent scenarios in many urban areas of the provinces studied (Fig. 1). According to ELISAL (2019), which is the public company for sanitation and cleaning in Luanda, only 2 of the 10 waste transfer stations built in Luanda province after PESGRU were operational in 2019. The inoperability of the waste transfer stations to receive the waste collected in the neighbourhoods means that the capacity of the existing containers is often exhausted, leading residents to indiscriminately dispose of waste in the streets, uninhabited houses, empty lots and drainage ditches, forming monstrous rubbish dumpsites that contribute to the development of endemic diseases such as malaria, malaria and cholera.

Fig. 1.   Overcrowded Garbage Containers and Burning of Waste in Urban
Area of Luanda.

All the collected municipal waste transported to the Mulenvos landfill is disposed of without any sorting, which leads to the foreseen lifetime of the landfill being seriously compromised. In addition, Luanda province is heavily industrialised, especially the municipality of Viana, and industrial waste is also sent to landfill. Although the landfill in Luanda was built according to good construction practices, the biogas collection network is inoperative and biogas is being released directly into the atmosphere, contrary to what good practices recommend in order to avoid an increase in GHG emissions. Based on the Intergovernmental Panel on Climate Change (IPCC) Guidelines and the GHG Emissions Protocol, more than 2 million Mg CO2eq were produced in 2017 at the Mulenvos landfill with the anaerobic decomposition of MSW, with about 19,085,454 Mg of MSW being deposited in the landfill in that year (Maria, Góis, & Leitão, 2020).

The high rate of road congestion caused by the high number of vehicles, the poor condition of the roads and the informal street commerce make it extremely difficult to comply with the schedules and frequency of the collection and cleaning services. The waste collection service is provided by ELISAL and private companies contracted by the municipalities, and the cost is borne entirely by the provincial government. The public company ELISAL is responsible for landfill operation and monitoring of garbage trucks with a central GPS system installed at the Mulenvos landfill, but this control system was inoperative when this study was carried out.

Benguela province with 10 municipalities has no landfills, only uncontrolled landfills and dumpsites. The four most populated municipalities with the largest number of businesses, located on the coast of the province, produce about 550 tons of waste daily, an estimated 0.5 kg of waste per day per inhabitant. At the dumpsites, it is common to see local community residents looking for food and materials for sale, living with worms, flies, rats and cockroaches (Fig. 2). In addition to waste disposal by private operators hired by the municipality, it is frequent to see people with vans depositing waste in dumpsites.

With the economic and financial crisis in 2017, the Benguela provincial government unilaterally broke the contract with private waste operators due to financial incapacity. Door-to-door collection was the model found by the municipalities to mitigate the problem, which led to the end of the activities of the

Fig. 2.   Local Communities and Pickers Searching Materials for Sale in
Benguela.

large private operators, replacing them with micro-enterprises. Industrial, hospital and agricultural waste is not treated and is frequently incinerated in an uncontrolled way; other times it is disposed of in dumpsites, which poses a threat to public health. To mitigate this public health problem, the provincial government has been removing the piles of waste scattered around the province and depositing them in uncontrolled landfills, but these do not have any sealing of the bottom of the cells and are not subject to any plan to control the impact on soil and water.

The province of Huambo, located in the central region of the country, has an uncontrolled landfill and several dumpsites for the disposal of waste from 11 municipalities. The construction of a landfill was planned for 2014, but the works were interrupted due to financial difficulties and since then collection operators have been depositing waste around the unfinished landfill.

In Huambo municipality there have been various initiatives to collect waste and clean up the city with the participation of military and police forces, students, churches, youth associations and the general population. Information campaigns have also been carried out through the media on how to treat waste and specifying the collection schedule.

The province of Huila situated in the southern region of the country has 14 municipalities, and although it is considered to be the richest in the southern region of Angola, it does not have any landfill, only dumpsites. Waste collection is carried out by private operators in partnership with municipal administrations. As in other provinces, families living near the dumpsites survive by collecting glass bottles and other materials for sale. The maintenance of the waste collection vehicles, the intense traffic and the lack of passable roads are pointed out among the difficulties in the collection service. The irregularity of collection is pointed out by the population as the cause of the accumulation of waste next to the few existing containers.

CONCLUSIONS

A significant effort has been made by the Angolan government to regulate MSW management, establishing strategies and objectives to be achieved by 2025. Despite the various programmes for the implementation of the MSW strategic plan published in 2012, the established deadlines are compromised due to the economic crisis in 2017 and the inability of the administrative services to manage contracts with private operators and the incapability of the municipality to implement taxes and generate enough revenue to maintain the waste collection service.

Due to the low economic and environmental level of people, the acceptance of fee to pay for the waste collection service will be difficult due to the low quality of this service provided and the inability to increase the collection area.

From this study emerges the lack of funding needed to implement PESGRU and the poor assistance provided by the National Ministry of Environment and the National Directorate of Environmental Education to educate people about the health problems caused by waste and create livelihood opportunities for poor communities as waste pickers.

The sustainability of waste management in Angola is compromised if the government does not give financial priority to waste management, creating the minimum necessary infrastructure, encouraging partnerships and sharing responsibilities with the population and companies in complying with good practices and bearing the costs of services. For this challenge to succeed, the population must be made aware of the social, economic and environmental importance that waste management represents for the development and well-being of society and, at the same time, mechanisms must be created to evaluate the performance of the services provided.

REFERENCES

Agenda 21/un.org. (2022). Agenda 21. Retrieved from https://sustainabledevelopment.un.org/outcomedocuments/agenda21/. Accessed on August 8, 2022.

Căilean, D., & Teodosiu, C. (2016). An assessment of the Romanian solid waste management system based on sustainable development indicators. *Sustainable Production and Consumption, 8*, 45–56. doi:10.1016/j.spc.2016.07.004

Coelho, L., & Lange, L. (2018). Applying life cycle assessment to support environmentally sustainable waste management strategies in Brazil. *Resources, Conservation and Recycling, 128*, 438–450. doi:10.1016/j.resconrec.2016.09.026

Dulley, I., & Sampaio, L. (2020). Accusation and legitimacy in the civil war in Angola. *Vibrant: Virtual Brazilian Anthropology, 17*. doi:10.1590/1809-43412020v17a355

Duygan, M., & Meylan, G. (2015). Strategic management of WEEE in Switzerland—Combining material flow analysis with structural analysis. *Resources, Conservation and Recycling, 103*, 98–109. doi:10.1016/j.resconrec.2015.06.005

ec.europa.eu. (2022). Waste-retalet indicators. eurostat. Retrieved from https://ec.europa.eu/eurostat/web/waste/data/indicators. Accessed on August 5, 2022.

ELISAL. (2019). *Produção de resíduos sólidos na província de Luanda (amostragem de três meses de recolha)*. Luanda: Empresa de Limpeza e Saneamento de Luanda.

ERSAR. (2021). *Guia de Avaliação da Qualidade dos Serviços de Águas e Resíduos Prestados aos Utilizadores: 3ª geração do sistema de avaliação.* Série Guias Técnicos 22. Versão de 31.01.2021. LNEC and ERSAR.

Godfrey, L., Ahmed, M., Gebremedhin, K., Katima, J., Oelofse, S., Osibanjo, O., ... Yonli, A. (2019). Solid waste management in Africa: Governance failure or development opportunity? In N. Edomah (Ed.), *Regional development in Africa.* doi:10.5772/intechopen.86974

Hassan, S., Jameel, N., & Sekeroğlu, B. (2016). Smart solid waste monitoring and collection system. *International Journal of Advanced Research in Computer Science and Software Engineering, 6*(10), 7–12. Retrieved from www.ijarcsse.com

Hoornweg, D., & Bhada-Tata, P. (2012). *What a waste: A global review of solid waste management.* Urban Development Series; Knowledge Papers No. 15. World Bank, Washington DC. Retrieved from https://openknowledge.worldbank.org/handle/10986/17388

Impala. (2019, March 4). Press conference by Joana Pedro, technician from the Department of Financial Statistics of the Angolan INE. Retrieved from https://www.impala.pt/noticias

INE. (2016). *Resultados definitivos do recenseamento geral da população e da habitação de Angola 2014.* Luanda: Instituto Nacional de Estatística.

Kumar, A., & Agrawal, A. (2019). Recent trends in solid waste management status, challenges, and potential for the future Indian cities – A review. *Current Research in Environmental Sustainability, 2,* 100011. doi:10.1016/j.crsust.2020.100011

Kumar, S., Smith, S., Fowler, G., Velis, C., Kumar, S. J., Arya, S., ... Cheeseman, C. (2017). Challenges and opportunities associated with waste management in India. *Royal Society Open Science, 4*(3). doi:10.1098/rsos.160764

Maria, C., Góis, J., & Leitão, A. (2020). Challenges and perspectives of greenhouse gases emissions form municipal solid waste management in Angola. *Energy Reports, 6*(1), 364–369. doi:10.1016/j.egyr.2019.08.074

Melaré, A., Gonzalez, S., & Faceli, K. (2017). Technologies and decision support systems to aid solid-waste management: A systematic review. *Waste Management, 59,* 567–584. doi:10.1016/j.wasman.2016.10.045

Nabavi-Pelesaraei, A., Bayat, R., Hosseinzadeh-Bandbafha, H., Afrasyabi, H., & Berrada, A. (2017). Prognostication of energy use and environmental impacts for recycle system of municipal solid waste management. *Journal of Cleaner Production, 154,* 602–613. doi:10.1016/j.jclepro.2017.04.033

OECD. (2016). Angola: Unitary country. Retrieved from https://www.oecd.org>regional>profile-Angola. Accessed on August 7, 2022.

Okot-Okumu, J. (2012). Solid waste management in African cities – East Africa. In L. F. Marmolejo Rebellon (Ed.), *Waste management – An integrated vision.* doi:10.5772/50241

Oteng-Ababio, M., Arguello, J., & Gabbay, O. (2013). Solid waste management in African cities: Sorting the facts from the fads in Accra, Ghana. *Habitat International, 39,* 96–104. doi:10.1016/j.habitatint.2012.10.010

Pereira, T., & Fernandino, G. (2019). Evaluation of solid waste management sustainability of a coastal municipality from the Northeastern Brazil. *Ocean & Coastal Management, 179.* doi:10.1016/j.ocecoaman.2019.104839

PESGRU. (2012, August). Plano Estratégico para a Gestão de Resíduos Urbanos. Decreto-lei n.o 196/12, Diário da República, I Série, n.o 168, Angola.

Rigamonti, L., Sterpi, I., & Grosso, M. (2016). Integrated municipal waste management systems: An indicator to assess their environmental and economic sustainability. *Ecological Indicators, 60,* 1–7. doi:10.1016/j.ecolind.2015.06.022

Santiago, L. S., & Dias, S. M. F. (2012). Matriz de indicadores de sustentabilidade para a gestão de resíduos sólidos urbanos. *Engenharia Sanitária e Ambiental, 17*(2), 203–212. doi:10.1590/S1413-41522012000200010

Srivastava, R., Krishna, V., & Sonkar, I. (2014). Characterization and management of municipal solid waste: A case study of Varanasi city, India. *International Journal Current Research and Academic Revue, 2,* 10–16.

Sustainable development goals/un.org. (2022). Goal 13. Take urgent action to combat climate change and its impact. Retrieved from https://www.un.org/sustainabledevelopment/climate-change/. Accessed on August 8, 2022.

Tomita, A., Cuadros, D., Bruns, J., Tanser, F., & Slotow, R. (2020). Exposure to waste sites and their impact on health: A panel and geospatial analysis of nationally representative data from South Africa, 2008–2015. *The Lancet Planetary Health*. doi:10.1016/S2542-5196(20)30101-7

UNEP. (2022). *Sustainable development goals*. UN Environment Programme. Retrieved from https://www.unep.org/evaluation-office/our-evaluation-approach/sustainable-development-goals. Accessed on August 5, 2022.

Vucijak, B., Kurtagic, S., & Silajdzic, I. (2016). Multicriteria decision making in selecting best solid waste management scenario: A municipal case study from Bosnia and Herzegovina. *Journal of Cleaner Production, 130*, 166–174. doi:10.1016/j.jclepro.2015.11.030

Zurbrügg, C., Gfrerer, M., Ashadi, H., Brenner, W., & Küper, D. (2012). Determinants of sustainability in solid waste management – The Gianyar waste recovery project in Indonesia. *Journal of Waste Management, 32*, 2126–2133. doi:10.1016/j.wasman.2012.01.011

A CASE STUDY OF THE INTER-STAKEHOLDER PARTICIPATORY STRUCTURE IN THE SOLID WASTE GOVERNANCE OF THE SMALL ISLAND DEVELOPING STATE OF MAURITIUS

Noushra Shamreen Amode, Prakash N. K. Deenapanray and Pratima Jeetah

ABSTRACT

Purpose: *The chapter aims to evaluate the efficacy of stakeholder participation in the solid waste management system of Mauritius in view of providing a possible mechanism to attain the goals of a sustainable waste management framework.*

Methodology: *The study employs qualitative indicators, namely, User Inclusivity and Producer Inclusivity of the Wasteaware Benchmark Indicators. Secondary data are used to conduct a critical and comprehensive analysis of the sub-indicators falling under each of the two main indicators to determine the overall compliance level with respect to stakeholder engagement of the waste management sector of Mauritius.*

Findings: *The results of the study show a LOW/MEDIUM compliance level for both User Inclusivity and Provider Inclusivity indicators, which indicates that improvement is required in the stakeholder engagement mechanism in Mauritius. The main weaknesses identified comprise of lack of an adequate legal framework with clear definition of waste types with regards to segregation, especially for non-hazardous wastes, low efficiency of sustainable*

Achieving Net Zero
Developments in Corporate Governance and Responsibility, Volume 20, 109–150
ISSN: 2043-0523/doi:10.1108/S2043-052320230000020006

waste management awareness campaigns and lack of inclusion of the informal sector. The main strengths identified consist of a proper bidding mechanism in place and a good level of equity in the provision of waste management services with respect to comingled waste collection. Suggested improvement areas include a revamping of the existing legal framework related to waste management to cater for higher inclusivity of all stakeholders together with including sustainable waste management topics in the formal education curriculum.

Originality: *The User Inclusivity and Producer Inclusivity indicators were previously applied only to cities to measure the level of stakeholder participation, but this study has demonstrated that these indicators can also be adopted on a nation-wide level to evaluate stakeholder engagement. The use of these indicators together with secondary data presents a less time-consuming method to assess stakeholder participation in the waste sector, which can be particularly useful for Small Island Developing States.*

Keywords: Stakeholder participation; solid waste governance; sustainable waste management; evaluation indicators; small island developing states; inclusivity in waste management

INTRODUCTION

The soaring amount of Municipal Solid Waste (MSW) being generated is causing increased apprehension in both developing and developed countries due to a lack of effective and sustainable waste management and disposal strategies. In fact, global waste generation is projected to experience a 70% annual increase from 2016 to 2050 due to high population growth rates and urbanisation (World Bank Group, 2019). The mismanagement of MSW might pose severe environmental and societal constraints which might impede sustainable development, especially in Small Island Developing States (SIDS) whereby waste generation per capita is on average 48% higher than the global mean (UNEP, 2019).

Waste management is in fact one of the priority areas identified to be addressed by SIDS during the Third International Conference On Small Island Developing States (UNDESA, 2014) since the fragility of ecosystems, the scarcity of resources and the quasi-isolation from economic poles (Beerachee, 2012) render the task of managing solid waste sustainably even more difficult. Together with these aforementioned constraints, it has been highlighted that development of sustainable waste management strategies are extremely challenging for SIDS and often fail due to the lack of stakeholder engagement and participation (Agamuthu & Herat, 2014; Fuldauer, Ives, Adshead, Thacker, & Hall, 2019). In effect, several studies have pointed out that only technical aspects are not sufficient to give rise to an adequate solid waste management system which fulfils its goals of ensuring sanitation sustainably, especially in developing nations like SIDS (Joseph, 2006; Turcott Cervantes et al., 2021; Wilson, Velis, & Rodic, 2013). Successful implementation of a sustainable solid waste management system requires accounting for solid waste governance factors which includes engagement of stakeholders (waste generators (households, industries and agriculture), waste processors (formal and informal recyclers) and government institutions (regulators, waste managers and urban planners)) (Joseph, 2006) from all social sectors (Ezeah, Fazakerley, & Roberts, 2013; Turcott Cervantes et al., 2021; UN, 1992). In the case of Mauritius, it has been shown that social acceptability is a prominent determinant for waste-to-energy technologies revealing the necessity for broad stakeholder engagements in developing sustainable solid waste management strategies (Neehaul, Jeetah, & Deenapanray, 2020).

In the SIDS of Mauritius as well, the Ministry of Environment, Solid Waste Management and Climate Change, which is the lead governmental stakeholder for solid waste management, aims to implement more sustainable waste management strategies (Ministry of Environment, Solid Waste Management and Climate Change, 2022a). The Ministry recognises the need for participatory approaches to promote the involvement of stakeholders to achieve this goal as highlighted in the previous Solid Waste Management Strategy 2011–2015 (PAGE, 2017) as well as in the new waste management strategy that is being developed (Ministry of Environment, Solid Waste Management and Climate Change, 2020a). However, there have been limited studies undertaken to date to evaluate the effectiveness of stakeholder engagement in the Solid Waste management framework of Mauritius. One such study was undertaken by the United Nations Human Settlements Programme (UN-HABITAT) in 2010, but it involved only one urban location, namely the Municipality of Curepipe. The study employed the indicators of User Inclusivity and Provider Inclusivity and noted a 'LOW' compliance level for both criteria. However, no in-depth analysis was made to provide insight on the different sub-indicators used to come to the value of 'LOW' compliance, and the study did not incorporate rural areas, which represents more than 50% of the total population of Mauritius (The World Bank Group, 2022b). Matter-of-factly, the study has left out four Municipalities and seven District Councils, which represented around 93% of the population of Mauritius in 2009 (Central Statistics Office, 2010). Fig. 1 depicts the Municipal and District Councils of Mauritius.

Also, the UN-HABITAT (2010) study was undertaken more than a decade ago which makes the outcomes outdated, and, hence, might not reflect the current waste management situation in the island. The User Inclusivity and Provider Inclusivity indicators can also be utilised on the online Wasteaware platform of the University of Leeds, which includes an in-built database to calculate the values for the two indicators for different cities around the world (University of Leeds, n.d). The database shows a LOW-MEDIUM compliance level for User and Producer inclusivity (University of Leeds, n.d) for the Municipality of Curepipe. However, this database contains data which date back to the year 2009, which might not be representative of the current situation in the whole island of Mauritius, and similar to the data of the UN-HABITAT (2010) study, it covers only one Municipality.

Therefore, this study intends to provide a thorough analysis of the same two indicators (User Inclusivity and Provider Inclusivity) of the Wasteaware Benchmark Indicators as described by Wilson et al. (2015) by extending the scope of the

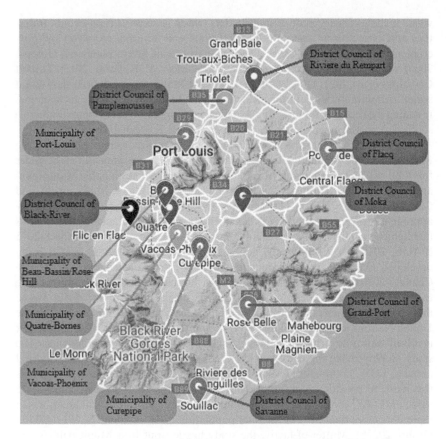

Fig. 1.   Locations of Municipalities and District Councils of Mauritius.
Source: Local Government Service Commission (2020).

analysis to the whole island – i.e. Five Municipal Councils and seven District Councils – to produce a more accurate insight into the current stakeholder participatory structure of Mauritius.

The study seeks to produce a detailed examination of the existing stakeholder participation structure through the identification of potential gaps in order to evaluate the effectiveness of this feature in the Solid Waste Management System of the Island of Mauritius, and, thereafter, to suggest possible improvement areas to curb the identified lacunae in view of providing a possible mechanism to attain the goals of a sustainable waste management framework.

OVERVIEW OF THE STUDY AREA

The Island of Mauritius is an African SIDS with a population of 1,219,187 (Statistics Mauritius, 2021a). Mauritius is classified as an Upper-Middle-Income economy by the World Bank (The World Bank Group, 2022a) and a developing nation (UNDP Mauritius, 2022).

Mauritius generates around 509,094 tonnes of waste (Statistics Mauritius, 2020a), most of which comprise organic waste (about 54% of the total amount of MSW (Ministry of Environment, Solid Waste Management and Climate Change, 2020a)). Fig. 2 shows the composition of the MSW generated in Mauritius. A new solid waste characterisation exercise was completed in 2022, but the results are not available in the public domain.

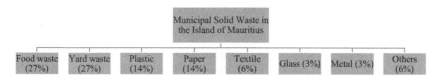

Fig. 2. Composition of Municipal Solid Waste in Mauritius. *Source:* Ministry of Environment, Solid Waste Management and Climate Change (2020a).

Mauritius is facing increasing challenges related to solid waste management with its sole sanitary landfill approaching saturation (Ministry of Environment, Solid Waste Management and Climate Change, 2022a). In fact, the waste generation per capita in Mauritius has increased by 946% in a span of 22 years (Mohee, Rughoonundun, & Peryagh, 2009; Statistics Mauritius, 2021b). Fig. 3 represents the waste generation amount per capita for years 1998–2020. The decrease in 2020 is probably related to the extended shut-down of socio-economic activities due to the COVID-19 pandemic. The main reasons given for this staggering increase are improved standard of living, progress in economic development, including tourism (Foolmaun, Chamilall, & Munhurrun, 2011; Government of Mauritius, 2011; Kothari, Kumar, Panwar, & Tyagi, 2014; Mohee et al., 2015).

As mentioned earlier, the Ministry of Environment, Solid Waste Management and Climate Change (2022a) of the Republic of Mauritius plans to develop and implement more sustainable waste management strategies which focus on waste recovery and recycling (Ministry of Environment, Solid Waste Management and Climate Change, 2022a) in order to curb the current waste management problems. The rationale underpinning solid waste management going forward is the creation of a circular waste economy that would reduce the residual volume of landfilled waste while simultaneously providing sustainable development dividends, including green jobs creation through small-and-medium enterprises. However, as of now, while the Ministry of Environment, Solid Waste Management and Climate Change (2022a) acknowledges that landfilling is not

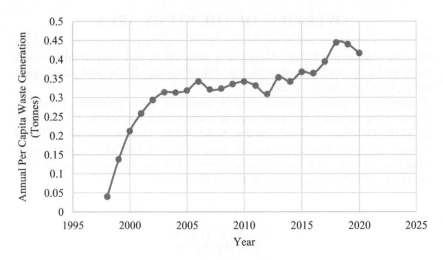

Fig. 3.   Waste Generation per Capita for the Island of Mauritius From 1998
to 2020. *Source:* UNEP (2016), Central Statistics Office, Republic of Mauritius (2008,
    2009), Statistics Mauritius (1998, 1999, 2000, 2001, 2002, 2003, 2004, 2006, 2008,
2010, 2011, 2012a, 2012b, 2013, 2014, 2015, 2016, 2017, 2018a, 2018b, 2020a, 2020b,
                         2021b), Beerachee (2012).

a sustainable solid waste management option, it is still being employed as the
main waste management method and the Government is currently undertaking
the vertical expansion of the existing landfill as a 'knee jerk' solution to tackle the
increasing amount of solid waste being generated (Central Procurement Board,
2021; Ministry of Environment, Solid Waste Management and Climate Change,
2020a).

Stakeholders of the Solid Waste Management Governance Framework of Mauritius

Fig. 4 represents the different stakeholders of the solid waste management system
of Mauritius together with the waste flows.

In Fig. 4, the solid lines represent the waste flows from the point of generation
to final treatment/disposal and the broken lines show the stakeholders involved in
each stage of the waste management process. Further details are provided in the
subsequent sections.

Generators

In Mauritius, the main waste generators are households, hotels, commercial
entities, industries and the construction sector (Mohee, 2002; Statistics Mauritius,
2020a). In 2020, around 93.5% of the total waste landfilled in Mauritius consisted
of domestic and commercial wastes (Statistics Mauritius, 2020a).

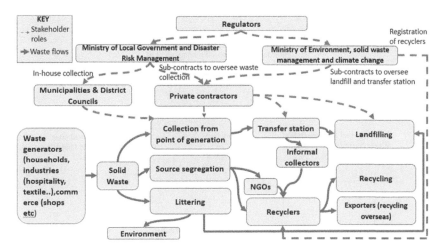

Fig. 4. Waste Flows (Solid Lines) and Stakeholder Roles (Broken Lines) in the Solid Waste Management System of Mauritius. *Source:* PAGE (2017) (for waste flows) and Author's own elaboration for stakeholder roles).

Regulators

The primary regulator for the sound management of solid waste is the Ministry of Environment, Solid Waste Management and Climate Change (Ministry of Environment, Solid Waste Management and Climate Change, 2020a). The Solid Waste Management Division (SWMD) of the Ministry has the responsibility to oversee solid waste management (Kowlesser, 2012). The creation of the SWMD in 1989 marked the birth of a Solid Waste Management Governance framework in Mauritius (Kowlesser, 2012).

The SWMD has four major functions as summarised in Fig. 5.

The SWMD ensures the adequate management of solid waste by means of the provision of waste carrier licences for the collection of solid waste. The SWMD also has oversight of the management of the Mare Chicose landfill, which is privately operated under contractual agreement with the Ministry of Environment, Solid Waste Management and Climate Change. It is pointed out that the collection, transport and disposal of waste at landfill is carried out by the Municipal and District Councils operating under the Ministry of Local Government and Disaster Risk Management (Ministry of Environment, Solid Waste Management and Climate Change, 2020a). The overall waste governance is, therefore, currently split between two ministries.

Previously, the Waste Carrier's Licencing Unit fell under the aegis of the Ministry of Local Government and Disaster Risk Management. However, in order to promote coherent organisational structure and adequate utilisation of human resources, the responsibility for this Unit was transferred to the Solid

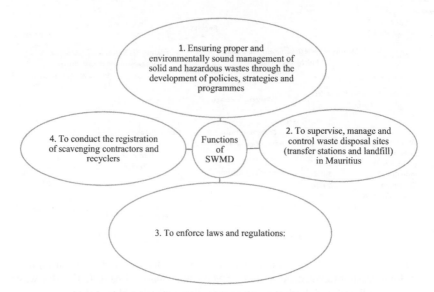

Fig. 5.   Functions of Solid Waste Management Division of the Ministry of
Environment, Solid Waste Management and Climate Change of the Republic of
Mauritius. *Source:* Ministry of Environment, Solid Waste Management and Climate
Change (2020a).

Waste Management Division of the Ministry of Environment, Solid Waste
Management and Climate Change in February 2021 (Ministry Of Local
Government And Disaster Risk Management, 2021).

The 12 local authorities (Municipal (5) and District Councils (7) (UNIDO,
2016)), which operate under the Ministry of Local Government and Disaster
Risk Management, undertake waste collection around the Island (Ministry of
Environment, Solid Waste Management and Climate Change, 2020a). The local
authorities carry out the waste collection either in-house or through the con-
tracting of third parties (public–private partnerships) or both (Ministry of
Environment, Solid Waste Management and Climate Change, 2020a). A
curb-side waste collection system is adopted throughout the Island, which
essentially involves door-to-door waste collection at least once per week
(Foolmaun et al., 2011).

Once collected, the waste is transported to the six transfer stations located in
strategic areas of Mauritius to enable waste transfer optimisation to the sole
landfill of the island located at St. Hubert. Fig. 6 shows the locations of the
transfer stations and the landfill in Mauritius.

The Waste Management and Resource Recovery Act 2023 which provides the
legal framework for solid waste management in Mauritius, provides a list of
governmental bodies forming part of the solid waste management framework of
Mauritius. This law specifies the setting up of a National Waste Management
Coordination Committee chaired by the Minister responsible for of solid waste

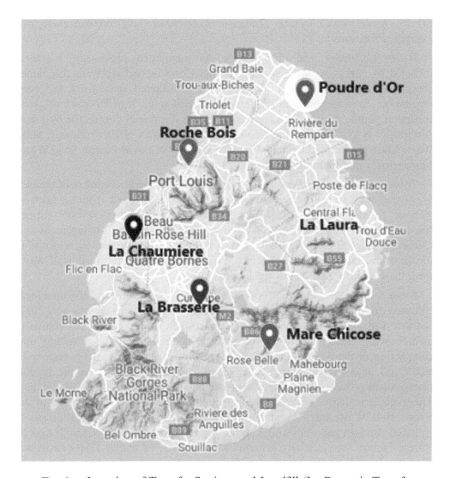

Fig. 6. Location of Transfer Stations and Landfill (La Brasserie Transfer Station (Designed Capacity: 150–300 T/day); La Chaumiere Transfer Station (Designed Capacity: 350–450 T/day); Roche Bois Transfer Station (Designed Capacity: 300–400 T/day); Poudre d'Or Transfer Station (Designed Capacity: 150–180 T/day); La Laura Transfer Station (Designed Capacity: 100–150 T/day). *Source:* Ministry of Environment, Solid Waste Management and Climate Change (2020a).

and hazardous waste. Its main goal is to promote the achievement of a circular economy though reduction of waste, conservation of resources and material recovery (Waste Management and Resource Recovery Act 2023, 2023).

Private Operators (Collectors; Transporters; Operators of Transfer Stations and Landfill; Processors)

Waste Collectors and Transporters. As mentioned previously, waste is collected by either the Municipal or District Councils or by private companies contracted by these local authorities. The contracted scavengers are only responsible to transport the waste to the designated transfer stations from collection points. A list of the registered private companies contracted by Local Authorities is available on the webpage of the Ministry of Environment, Solid Waste Management and Climate Change (Ministry of Environment, Solid Waste Management and Climate Change, 2020a).

Transfer Station Operators and Transporters. The operation and maintenance of the transfer stations and subsequent transportation of waste from the transfer stations to the landfill are activities conducted by other private entities sub-contracted by the Ministry of Environment, Solid Waste Management and Climate Change (2020a). Table 1 shows the different private entities responsible for the management of the different transfer stations and the transport of waste from these transfer stations to the landfill.

Landfill Operator. The landfill is managed by a Joint Venture between a local company (Sotravic Ltd) and a German company (Eneotech) (Kowlesser, 2012; Sotravic Ltd, n.d). The main activities undertaken by the contracted company include waste reception from the transfer stations, tipping, levelling and compaction of the waste into the cells, and, thereafter, covering the waste with either soil or a biodegradable layer (Sotravic Ltd, n.d). Part of the landfill management process also includes adequate handling of leachate and landfill gas. The leachate is firstly collected into leachate ponds and then carted away to the Roche Bois Wastewater Treatment Plant (Sotravic Ltd, n.d). Landfill gas is collected through gas wells and is either redirected towards the Landfill Gas to Energy facility for electricity generation or is flared to reduce GHG emissions (Sotravic Ltd, 2020; Sotravic Ltd, n.d).

Table 1. Private Entities Contracted by Government for Management of the Transfer Stations.

Transfer Station	Private Company Contracted for Its Management
La Chaumiere	Sotravic Ltd was the previous contractor, in May 2022 a bidding process has been launched again and currently the contract has not yet been awarded to a new company
La Brasserie	Sotravic Ltd
Roche-Bois	GV Square Deal Multipurpose Cooperative Society Ltd.
Poudre d'Or	Maxi Clean Co. Ltd
La Laura	Compagnie Régionale de Services et de L'Environnement Ltée

Source: Ministry of Environment, Solid Waste Management and Climate Change (2020a, 2022b), Central Procurement Board (2020), Republic of Mauritius, Seventh National Assembly (2021).

Processors. Although waste recovery is not a significant waste management activity in Mauritius, a small percentage (about 5%) of the recyclable wastes is collected through a public–private partnership by the 36 registered recyclers (Ministry of Environment, Solid Waste Management and Climate Change, 2019). In order to encourage resource recovery and recycling in Mauritius, the Government has announced the implementation of some economic instruments like the provision of a tipping fee of MUR 300 per ton of waste collected from transfer stations for the purpose of recycling, the allocation of MUR 2000 per ton of used tyres recycled or exported for recycling, and increasing the incentive for plastic bottle recycling from MUR 5/kg to MUR 15/kg (Ministry of Environment, Soild Waste Management and Climate Change, 2019).

The Government also plans to erect civic amenity centres to increase the rate of recycling in the island. The first civic amenity centre has been set up at the La Chaumiere transfer station, which together with the incentives for recycling pre-sorted wastes of different classes, aims at reducing the illegal dumping of wastes, such as electronic and electrical waste, bulk waste, used oils and construction waste that are not collected alongside MSW (Bhurtun, 2020; Ministry of Environment, Solid Waste Management and Climate Change, 2020a; PNQ, 2020). The civic amenity centre comprises of designated containers where the pre-sorted waste can be deposited by the public for recyclers to collect (Bhurtun, 2020; PNQ, 2020; Tengur, 2020). Agreements have been signed with six recycling companies to cater for waste recycling from the civic amenity centre at La Chaumiere (Bhurtun, 2020). The Government plans to set up civic amenity centres at the remaining four transfer stations and an additional five unspecified locations (Ministry of Environment, Solid Waste Management and Climate Change, 2022a; PNQ, 2020).

Non-Governmental Organisations (NGOs)

An additional group of stakeholders which supports the implementation of sound waste management in Mauritius is NGOs. Two main NGOs, namely Eco Mode Society and Eternal Bliss Life Foundation, are affiliated with the Ministry of Environment, Solid Waste Management and Climate Change for the purpose of waste management. The former is mainly involved in raising awareness with respect to the 3Rs (reduce-reuse-recycle), and the latter is engaged in the collection of wastes around Mauritius for recycling and reusing purposes (Ministry of Environment, Solid Waste Management and Climate Change, 2020a).

Another NGO which has been very active in the promotion of recycling in Mauritius is Mission Verte, which was shouldered by the GEF-SGP to distribute dedicated bins for the collection of source-segregated wastes around the island (Ministry Of Environment And National Development Unit, 2010).

Informal Waste Collectors

The informal sector, which consists of informal waste pickers, also forms part of the processor stakeholder category. These informal waste collectors are mainly involved in the collection of waste for recycling or reuse purposes at no or very low cost (PAGE, 2017). The informal waste pickers operate mainly at transfer stations and in industrial zones (PAGE, 2017). Some of them can also be seen collecting recyclables, mainly in the form of PET bottles, from municipal bins and from littered waste. In addition to plastics, the other types of wastes collected comprise of metal, paper and wood (PAGE, 2017).

METHODOLOGY

The methodology used for this study is based on Wilson et al. (2015) and on Lai, Hensley, Krutli, and Stauffacher (2016). The study consists of use of the Wasteaware Benchmark Indicators developed by Wilson et al. (2015) to measure the degree of inclusivity, which is described as the extent to which stakeholders are engaged and their level of influence on the solid waste management system (Wilson et al., 2015). The inclusivity is further broken down into two different aspects, namely (1) User Inclusivity (related to waste generators) and (2) Provider Inclusivity (related to regulators and processors), in order to gauge the involvement of the different groups of stakeholders involved in the solid waste management process.

The Wasteaware Benchmark Indicators have been selected for this study since as well as being relevant for both developed and developing countries (Turcott Cervantes, López, Cuartas, & Lobo García de Cortázar, 2018), the indicators allow the use of existing data for the evaluation process and the need for primary data collection is eliminated (Wilson et al., 2015). The indicators that were used in the present study, and a description thereof are listed in Table 2.

To evaluate each of the indicators described in Table 2, a secondary data collection process was undertaken based on the methodology of Lai et al. (2016). The data collection process involves document analysis in three different phases as outlined below:

In the first phase, a comprehensive analysis of different pieces of legislation of the Republic of Mauritius (Environment Protection Act, 2002, 2002; Local Government Act (Dumping and Waste Carriers) Regulations 2021, 2021; Local Government Act (Registration of Recycler and Exporter) Regulations 2013, 2013; Local Government Act (Registration of Scavenging Contractors) Regulations 2004, 2004; The Local Government Act 2011, 2011; The Public-Private Partnership Act 2004, 2005) is undertaken in order to determine which ones are related to waste management. All of the legislations which are found to have some form of relationship with waste are then scrutinised to determine the type of regulations available and the aspects of waste management that the existing legislations cover.

In the second phase, other national documents (Ministry of Environment & Sustainable Development Mauritius Environment Outlook Report 2011

Table 2. Indicators Chosen and Their Description.

A. Indicators for Measuring Degree of User Inclusivity	Description of Indicator
A1. Equity of Service Provision	Measures the level to which every member of the society, regardless of income level, receives an adequate solid waste management service which safeguards the environment and public health, is up to the level to meet the needs of the citizens and is affordable
A2. The right to be heard	Gauges whether there is a legal obligation for authorities to involve and consult citizens during the decision-making process to implement matters that will directly impact them
A3. Level of Public Involvement	Determines if there is proof of involvement of the public during decision-making, planning and undertaking of solid waste management measures
A4. Public Feedback Mechanisms	Determines whether there is a public feedback mechanism in place on solid waste management services and evaluates the use of such a mechanism
A5. Public Education and Awareness	Evaluates if adequate sensitisation campaigns are implemented comprehensively and whether these campaigns are culturally appropriate. This indicator emphasises the level of activity/level to which awareness programmes are being deployed.
A6. Effectiveness in achieving change in behaviour	Assesses whether the public and businesses are changing their behaviour with respect to waste management and waste handling modus operandi. This indicator emphasises on the effectiveness of the awareness programmes deployed

B. Indicators for Measuring Degree of Provider Inclusivity	Description of Indicator
B1. Legal framework	Analyses the extent to which regulatory instruments are present and implemented locally and nationally to enable the provision of a stable solid waste management service by both the public and private sectors
B2. Representation of the private sector	Gauges whether there is active participation of the private sector through organisations or structures in solid waste management planning taking place in different decorum (e.g. committees, forums, steering groups, task force)
B3. Role of the informal and community sector	Evaluates whether the formal solid waste management system recognises and acknowledges of the role of the informal and community sectors
B4. The balance of public vs. private sector interests in delivering services	Determines if there is a system of checks and balances in place to ensure that waste management services are being provided by the public and private sectors in a way that is not considerably disadvantageous to either party and which leads to shared benefits
B5. Bid processes	Measures the level to which the bidding process is open, transparent and accountable.

Source: Adapted from Wilson et al. (2015).

(Government of Mauritius, 2011); Mauritius Strategy for Implementation
National Assessment Report 2010 (Ministry of Environment And National
Development Unit, 2010), Annual Report 2019/2020 (Ministry of
Environment, Solid Waste Management and Climate Change, 2020b); Strategy
and Action Plan on Resource Recovery and Recycling (Ministry of Environment,
Solid Waste Management and Climate Change, 2022a); Annual Report Finan-
cial Year 2020–2021 (Ministry of Environment, Solid Waste Management and
Climate Change, 2022c); La Gestion Des Dechets (Ministry Of Environment,
Soild Waste Management And Climate Change, 2019); Plastic Free Mauritius:
Defining the Roadmap: Recycling of Plastic Wastes – Session 5 (Ministry of
Environment, Solid Waste Management and Climate Change, 2021b); Budget
2021–2022: Appendix C: Special and Other Extra Budgetary Funds (Ministry of
Finance, Economic Planning and Development, 2021); Budget 2022–2023:
Appendix C: Special and Other Extra Budgetary Funds (Ministry of Finance,
Economic Planning and Development, 2022); Annual Report On Performance
(Ministry of Local Government And Disaster Risk Management, 2021);
Republic of Mauritius: Industrial Waste Assessment: Opportunities for Industrial
Symbiosis (PAGE, 2017); Legal Review For The Implementation Of Sustainable
Public Procurement In Mauritius (Procurement Policy Office, 2011); PNQ Solid
Waste Management Strategy (Private Notice Question (PNQ), 2020); CSR Guide
(Mauritius Revenue Authority, 2021); Solid Waste Management in Mauritius
(Kowlesser, 2012); Public Opening of Bids on: Friday 18 June 2021 Project:
Procurement of Landfill Works for Vertical Expansion of the Mare Chicose
Landfill and Operation and Post Closure Management of Cells (Central
Procurement Board, 2021); Projects Currently at advertising stage as at
28.12.20 (Central Procurement Board, 2020); Overview of Wastes Management
in Mauritius (Beerachee, 2012) related to action plans and waste management
strategies or other strategies, which encompass solid waste are examined to
obtain a broad overview of the existing waste management system in Mauritius.
Annual reports and guidelines from different Ministries are studied to obtain a
more in-depth insight on the regulatory framework, the measures being undertaken in line with the different policies and strategies and the extent to which
these measures have been successfully or unsuccessfully implemented.

   The third phase consists of a review of press articles (Bhurtun, 2020;
Dowarkasing, 2019; Edouard, 2021; Government Information Service, 2015,
2021a, 2021b; Le Mauricien Ltd, 2019a, 2019b; LEXPRESS.MU, 2007; Mauritius
Broadcasting Corporation, 2022a, 2022b; Moorlan, 2022; Samoisy, 2015), scientific publications (Foolmaun et al., 2011; Gooding, 2016; Mohee, 2002; Mohee
et al., 2009, 2015) and other publications by formal bodies like the UNEP amongst
others (Africa Solid Waste Management: DATA BOOK 2019 (African Clean
Cities Platform, 2019); MAURITIUS Multi-Annual Indicative Programme
2021–2027 (European Commission, 2021); UNDP Mauritius: Annual Report
2021 Building Forward Better (UNDP Mauritius, 2022); Industrial Waste
Assessment In The Republic Of Mauritius – Opportunities For Industrial Symbiosis; Inclusive and Sustainable Industrial Development Working Paper Series
WP 15 (UNIDO, 2016); Solid Waste Management In The World's Cities Water

And Sanitation In The World's Cities 2010 (United Nations Human Settlements Programme, 2010); Mauritius: Port Louis Urban Profile (United Nations Human Settlements Programme, 2011); Mauritius: Black River Urban Profile (United Nations Human Settlements Programme, 2012); Wasteaware Cities Indicators (University of Leeds, n.d); Rapports Sur La Discrimination, La Ségrégation Et Le Droit À Un Logement Adéquate. Nations Unies Droit de l'Homme, procedures Speciales (Ahnee et al., 2021); EUBeach clean up à Maurice (Delegation of the European Union to the Republic of Mauritius and to the Republic of Seychelles, 2020) in order to avoid missing any additional information and to obtain a more holistic overview of the waste management system in Mauritius.

As it can be noted from the above description, all data are collected from formal sources in order to ensure data quality.

Each criterion mentioned in Table 2 is then assigned a score (between 0 and 20) as per the User Manual for Wasteaware ISWM Benchmark Indicators by Wilson et al. (2015).

RESULTS AND DISCUSSIONS

Table 3 shows the scores for each indicator for user inclusivity. The combined score amounts to 29%, which represents a Low/medium compliance level for user inclusivity as per the methodology of Wilson et al. (2015).

The A1 indicator has been provided a score of Medium compliance since the waste collection system in Mauritius is well structured with the Ministry of Local Government and Disaster Risk Management (Municipal and District Councils) ensuring island-wide waste collection (Ministry of Environment, Solid Waste Management and Climate Change, 2019). Foolmaun et al. (2011) specified that the waste collection system in Mauritius is fairly good. The UN Habitat (2010) has also reported that the parallel waste collection system for both commercial entities and households in Mauritius for the city of Curepipe as a case study has a 100% coverage, and almost all of the waste generated is disposed in the sole environmentally sound landfill of Mare Chicose (United Nations Human Settlements Programme, 2010). Further, the Government of Mauritius (2011) reports that waste collection services are provided to 100% and 96% of the population of urban and rural regions, respectively. More recently, the Ministry of Environment, Solid Waste Management and Climate Change of the Republic Mauritius (2022b) has published its Annual Report for the Financial year 2020–2021, wherein it has been stipulated that the waste collection coverage is 100% in Mauritius.

However, a higher rating has not been provided since some regions are still not covered by waste collection services. The regions in question comprise the state-owned lands of Mauritius which are illegally occupied by economically vulnerable people commonly known as 'squatters' (Government Information Service, 2015; United Nations Human Settlements Programme, 2011, 2012), who are unable to afford adequate housing due to lack of means. These squatter

Table 3. Scores for User Inclusivity Sub-Indicators.

A. Indicators for Measuring Degree of User Inclusivity	Score				
	0 (No Compliance)	5 (Low Compliance)	10 (Medium Compliance)	15 (Medium/ High Compliance)	20 (High Compliance)
A1. Equity of Service Provision			10		
A2. The right to be heard	0				
A3. Level of Public Involvement		5			
A4. Public Feedback Mechanisms			10		
A5. Public Education and Awareness			10		
A6. Effectiveness in achieving change in behaviour	0				
Cumulated score for Indicator 'User Inclusivity'			29% => LOW/MEDIUM		

Source: Authors' elaboration.

settlements within underprivileged communities are mostly found in the South-Western coastal regions and in the outskirts of the capital of Mauritius, Port-Louis (Gooding, 2016). Unhygienic conditions are highly prevalent in such areas (Government Information Service, 2015) and one of the main reasons is that the people are not offered adequate waste collection services (Ahnee et al., 2021; Samoisy, 2015; United Nations Human Settlements Programme, 2011), which justifies the fact that in spite of having figures showing high waste collection rates for Mauritius, the equity of service provision is lacking for a small number of destitute citizens. Since these regions are unlawfully occupied, there is non-provision or lack of public utility services (Ahnee et al., 2021; United Nations Human Settlements Programme, 2011). However, even if waste collection services were to be provided, access to most of the state-lands inhabited by squatters is very limited and might not accommodate the waste collection lorries due to poor infrastructure and due to the fact that most of these settlements are found on mountain slopes (United Nations Human Settlements Programme, 2011).

Another reason for not giving a higher score for indicator A1 is the lack of provision of effective waste services with regards to recycling. In effect, it has been reported that there is a lack of recycling bin provision in Mauritius, which makes the recycling process inconvenient for Mauritians who complain that the existing recycling bins are always full (Jankee, 2021). The lack of provision of sufficient recycling bins demonstrates that some citizens are able to recycle their wastes, while others are unable to do so in spite of being keen to source-segregate and recycle. This shows a lack of equity in waste services provision for recycling. This weakness highlights the incongruence between the waste generators and the authorities responsible for waste collection, who in spite of wanting to promote recycling in the country (Ministry of Environment, Solid Waste Management and Climate Change, 2022a), is not providing equal services to everyone in view of achieving the desired goal of sustainable waste management and a circular waste economy.

A score of Medium compliance has been judged fair in this case despite the above-mentioned issues since the occupation of the state-owned lands is informal (though illegal the occupation is deserving of human rights considerations) and the issue in this case is deeper than the non-provision of waste collection services: it is more related to the provision of adequate housing to these disadvantaged members of the Mauritian society, which is a significant challenge that the Government of Mauritius faces as evidenced by the study of Gooding (2016). Further, with regards to the provision of recycling services, the Government is planning the scaling up of civic amenity centres in different locations across the island to curb the weakness. Nonetheless, while the civic amenity centres are expected to bring about improvement in the recycling sector, there are still issues pertaining to access: the civic amenity centres are located in remote areas, quite far from residential locations, which implies that people without private transportation (which comprise mostly of those who are at the low rungs of the socioeconomic ladder) will still be deprived of access to recycling services.

A plausible temporary remedial measure to cater for the issue of lack of hygiene due to inadequate provision of waste collection services in squatter settlements might be to provide a door-to-door waste collection service through the use of hand or bicycle carts by the informal sector (Wilson et al., 2015). This measure was in fact undertaken successfully for informal settlements through the Tam Tam Mobile programme in 2015 by the UN-HABITAT (United Nations Human Settlements Programme, 2019). Other regions around the world which employ hand-driven carts to collect waste from informal settlements include Kenya (Gutberlet et al., 2016), Dominican Republic (Perdue, 2016) and South Africa (Republic of South Africa Department of Human Settlements, 2019).

As far as the weakness in the provision of recycling services is concerned, an improvement area might be to provide more bins dedicated for the collection of recyclables at different locations island-wide. Studies have demonstrated that increasing the immediate accessibility of recycling bins increases their use (Rosenthal & Linder, 2021), thus having more bins in locations which are more easily accessible to the citizens might improve recycling behaviour in Mauritius as well.

A rating of 'No Compliance' has been provided to the A2 indicator since there is no legislation or regulatory framework in place which specifies that all stakeholders outside the governmental structure can participate in policy development for the solid waste management system. The EPA (Environment Protection Act, 2002) of the Republic of Mauritius specifies consultation only with governmental bodies chosen by the Minister. The EPA stipulates the availability of 'Public Comment' only for the case of Environmental Impact Assessments (EIAs), which have to be submitted for undertakings listed in Part B of the Fifth Schedule of the

EPA, including the setting up of landfills and transfer stations and the incineration of waste (MSW, quarantine waste, medical and clinical wastes)
(Environment Protection Act, 2002). However, this does not fulfil the requirements of indicator A2 that covers the existence of clear legal instruments ensuring
the active participation and consultation of citizens in decisions regarding solid
waste management. To curb this issue, a probable measure might be the
amendment of Section 21 of the the Waste Management and Resource Recovery
Act 2023, wherein instead of stating that public consultations `may' be carried
out, the Act should make it an obligation for authorities to consult and involve
members of the society during the decision-making process related to solid waste
management. An example of this is Section 19 (Public consultation) in the
Climate Change Act 2020 (Republic of Mauritius, 2020) that was proclaimed in
April 2022. Another example of implementation of 'The right to be heard'
through laws is the Waste (England and Wales) Regulations 2011 of the United
Kingdom which promotes active participation of the public for matters regarding
solid waste management (Government Digital Service, 2021).

The indicator A3 has been judged as having a 'Low Compliance' level since
there is some evidence of stakeholder participation at some stages of
decision-making even if it is not a legal requirement as mentioned earlier. An
evidence of stakeholder participation at planning stage is the organisation of *Les
Assises de L'Environnement* in December 2019 which had the aim of consulting
several stakeholders of the Mauritian society, including the private sector, the
youth, journalists, the civil society, NGOs and academics, in order to prepare the
Environment Masterplan 2020–2030 (that is yet to be finalised), which also
incorporates issues related to solid waste management (European Commission,
2021; Ministry of Environment, Solid Waste Management and Climate Change,
2020a). Higher compliance rating has not been provided since there is no proof of
stakeholder consultation at other stages of the planning, implementation and
monitoring and evaluation process of the waste management strategy. Also, there
is currently no mechanism in place to ensure that stakeholders meet regularly for
consultations and there are no processes for public participation as discussed
above. Examples to demonstrate the lack of public participation are the failed
attempts made by the Mauritian government to divert waste from the landfill
which included the setting up of a waste-to-energy incineration facility in 2008
(LEXPRESS.MU, 2007; Neehaul et al., 2020), and, more recently, in 2019, a
waste processing facility for the treatment of contaminated hazardous waste
through incineration (Dowarkasing, 2019). Both projects could not be implemented due to large public outcry, whereby inhabitants of these regions and
NGOs conducted demonstrations to vent out their opposition for such projects as
they feared the environmental impacts from waste incineration would be detrimental to them. Adequate inclusion of all stakeholders at different stages of these
two projects might have avoided such strong public opposition (Neehaul et al.,
2020).

An improvement area for increasing the level of public involvement might be
to implement existing public participation models which have been employed in
other regions of the world (Squires, 2006). An example of this is the IAP2

spectrum of Public Participation (IAP2 International Federation, 2018). The IAP2 spectrum of Public Participation has been applied for waste management purposes in City of Kamloops, Canada (City of Kamloops, 2021), and in Arizona in the United States (Maricopa Association of Governments, 2021).

As far as the indicator A4 is concerned, a 'Medium compliance' rating has been provided since there is evidence of a feedback mechanism in place for solid waste management services in Mauritius (Ministry of Environment, Solid Waste Management and Climate Change, 2020). There is a reasonable degree of accessibility to the feedback mechanism through the webpage of the Government of Mauritius [Link to form: https://govmu.org/EN/Pages/viewalleservices.aspx] and the Ministry of Environment, Solid Waste Management and Climate Change provides a hotline, an email address, a postal address and a telephone number for lodging complaints. Anyone with an internet connection can have access to the information and even if a member of the public does not have a home internet connection, there are free WiFi zones available island-wide (Mauritius Telecom, 2021). The SWMD is in a position to receive grievances through the contact details provided, but the dedicated bodies responsible to attend to these complaints is the Pollution Prevention and Control Division of the Ministry of Environment, Solid Waste Management and Climate Change and the Police de l'Environnement (Ministry of Environment, Waste Management and Climate Change, 2020; Statistics Mauritius, 2020a). The effectiveness of the contact mechanism can be evidenced by the fact that the Ministry received about 382 complaints in 2020, out of which 7.1% were related to solid waste management (Statistics Mauritius, 2020a). It should, however, be noted that the Ministry of Environment, Solid Waste Management and Climate Change does not really specify whether the contact details provided on its website in relation to solid waste can specifically be used for the provision of feedbacks as well as flagging of complaints or grievances. An adequate feedback form is, however, present on the webpage of the Ministry of Local Government and Disaster Risk Management [Link to feedback form: https://localgovernment.govmu.org/Pages/feedback. aspx], which is the main body responsible for waste collection in Mauritius. In this case as well, it has not been specified for which purpose the online link can be employed. It is a general feedback form which can cover any topic relevant to the Local Government services, including waste collection.

A Medium/High compliance rating has not been provided since there is a drawback related to the accessibility of the contact details and feedback mechanism as it requires some level of knowledge on internet navigation, which might be an issue for the elderly or those who do not have access to or lack the skills to use digital devices. A higher compliance rating has also not been assigned in this case since there is no evidence that the feedback mechanisms in place account for the public's opinions on decisions undertaken related to solid waste management (Wilson et al., 2015) since the mechanisms in place seem to be mostly related to complaints rather that provision of opinions on all aspects of the solid waste management decision-making process.

An improvement area with regards to the feedback process might be to indicate clearly the availability of a feedback mechanism and the items that it covers on the webpages of the Ministry of Environment, Solid Waste Management and Climate Change and of the Ministry of Local Government and Disaster Risk Management. For a higher score, clear information should be provided to members of the public that the mechanism also caters for opinions on solid waste management undertakings and provisions should be made to ensure a higher level of accessibility for all social groups, for example by communication through the TV, newspapers or the radio and social media platforms. Moreover, to cater for the use of face-to-face feedback mechanisms should not be overlooked, especially for disadvantaged groups that might not have access to technology or that might not have the skills required to use online mechanisms. In this view, Mauritius might implement the 'citizen report card' method deployed by the World Bank in Morocco to obtain feedback from the public for waste related services (Kaza, Yao, & Markgraf, 2016). It is pointed out that the EPA makes provision for establishing a National Network for Sustainable Development (NNSD) that may be used as coordination mechanism for public feedback. However, this is no information available in the public domain regarding the operation and outcomes of the NNSD meetings. The 10th sitting of the NNSD took place in January 2022 (Mauritius Broadcasting Corporation, 2022a), which implies a very low meeting frequency of around one sitting every two years on average since the proclamation of the EPA in 2002.

With regards to the indicator A5, which measures the degree of deployment of public awareness-raising programmes related to solid waste, a 'Medium compliance' score has been provided since there is a specific department, namely, the Information and Education Division of the Ministry of Environment, Solid Waste Management and Climate Change for this purpose (Ministry of Environment, Solid Waste Management and Climate Change, 2020a). The Information and Education Division has been involved in promotion of waste sorting, composting, recycling and cleaning in primary, secondary and tertiary educational institutions (Ministry of Environment, Solid Waste Management and Climate Change, 2020a).

The mass media through TV, radio, brochures is also used as a means to raise awareness with regards to solid waste management (Ministry of Environment, Solid Waste Management and Climate Change, 2020a). One prominent public education campaign entitled 'Ou Zet Salte Dimoun Li Koz Ou' was conducted in the year 2021. It also comprised the launching of a dedicated WhatsApp number for reporting littering (Ministry of Environment, Solid Waste Management and Climate Change, 2021a). Another sensitisation programme launched through the collaboration of the Ministry of Environment, the Ministry of Tourism, the *Mauritius Tourism Promotion Authority* (MTPA) and Association of Hoteliers and Restaurants in Mauritius (AHRIM), together with the local authorities, the European Union delegation as well as the National Youth Environment Council in the year 2021 consisted of the 'Clean up and Awareness Campaign' (Government Information Service, 2021a). This awareness programme ran from July 2021 to October 2021 and covered beach clean-ups in addition to the education of citizens on the environmental impacts of waste through the setting up of signboards in designated locations (Government Information Service, 2021a).

Beside the resource persons from the Information and Education Division, the registered NGOs that were introduced above are also involved in education campaigns (Ministry of Environment, Solid Waste Management and Climate Change, 2020a).

Further, through the National Environment and Climate Change Fund (EPA, 2002; Republic of Mauritius, 2020), there is a dedicated budged allocated for the purpose of public education on environmental issues, which also covers solid waste management. The budgetary allocation to the National Environment and Climate Change Fund for the financial years 2021–2022 and 2022–2023 amounted to MUR 3,283 million (Ministry of Finance, Economic Planning and Development, 2021) and MUR 2,462 Million (Ministry of Finance, Economic Planning and Development, 2022), respectively.

For the A5 indicator, a higher score has not been provided since the Ministry of Environment, Solid Waste Management and Climate Change itself reports that there is insufficient awareness and education campaigns related to solid waste management through a SWOT analysis published in its Annual Report for the Financial Year 2020–2021 (Ministry of Environment, Solid Waste Management and Climate Change, 2022c). In the Financial Year 2019–2020, only 60 sensitisation campaigns were conducted which targeted a mere 100,000 persons, representing less than 10% of the total population (Ministry of Environment, Solid Waste Management and Climate Change, 2020b). It should also be noted that this indicator does not cater for the effectiveness of the education programmes deployed, which is measured by indicator A6.

A possible means of remediating the weaknesses with regards to the lack of awareness raising campaigns might be through collaboration with the private sector. The Government might conduct dedicated training with stakeholders from the private sector on sustainable waste management. In this way, a larger amount of people might have access to education related to waste management since the private sector comprises of the majority of the working force of Mauritius (Statistics Mauritius, 2021b). An example of such a programme has been implemented in Turkey through the collaboration of the Ministry of Environment and Urbanization of the Republic of Turkey, the UNDP and the International Solid Waste Association (ISWA) Turkey (UNDP, 2021).

Another way of promoting awareness through public–private partnerships might be through Corporate Social Responsibility (CSR). Several private companies conduct awareness raising programmes related to sustainable waste management aimed at the civil society as part of their CSR frameworks. Examples include the Coca-Cola company which has implemented awareness programmes to promote recycling in several regions worldwide including Greece, the United Kingdom and Netherlands amongst others (The Coca-Cola Company, 2018) and in the Mauritian context, Emtel Ltd has collaborated with the NGO Mission Verte to raise awareness related to waste recycling (Emtel Ltd, 2021). To further increase awareness-raising related to sustainable waste management, the existing CSR legal framework of Mauritius that already caters for priority areas of intervention like environment and sustainable development, as well as educational support and training (Mauritius Revenue Authority, 2021) can be used as a tool. In this regard, a possible recommendation to encourage more actions related to these two priority areas might be to consider amending the existing legal framework related to CSR to include economic incentives such as a reduced amount of money to be contributed to the National Social Inclusion Foundation by a company in case the company proves that awareness raising programmes related to waste management has been deployed to a significant number of target groups, including employees or other groups like the vulnerable social groups falling under the Charter of the National Social Inclusion Foundation (National Social Inclusion Foundation, n.d).

Indicator A6 has been provided with a rating of 'No Compliance' since there is lack of evidence showing the effectiveness of the sensitisation programmes deployed with respect to waste management. In fact, there is evidence for the lack of environmental awareness, especially with regards to the issue of illegal dumping of waste. In 2021, local media reports show that despite COVID-19 restrictions which prevented people from picnicking on beaches, a total of 158.6 kg of waste was collected from the Blue-Bay public beach out of which 48.7 kg comprised of cans and 18.7 kg consisted of beer bottles (Edouard, 2021). The Delegation of the European Union to the Republic of Mauritius reports that the EU Beach Clean Up campaign it organised in Mauritius resulted in 200 kg of waste being collected in less than 2 hours (Delegation of the European Union in Mauritius, 2020). Waste dumping has also been reported on roads, in fields, in drains, in cemeteries and even at tourist attractions like the Rochester Falls (Wai Choon, 2021). In effect, during the *Assises de L'Environnement*, the Ministry of Environment, Solid Waste Management and Climate Change (2019) also conceded that there is a lack of civic sense due to drawbacks related to awareness-raising to alter mentality and perception about solid waste. Additionally, the Ministry reports a low level of recycling due to a lack of source segregation by waste generators (Ministry of Environment, Solid Waste Management and Climate Change, 2021b), which shows that the awareness campaigns on waste segregation and recycling conducted by the Information and Education Division (Ministry of Environment, Solid Waste Management and Climate Change, 2020a) have failed to bring about behavioural change, and to instill a sense of responsibility amongst the waste generators.

A way to curb the problem of lack of effectiveness related to awareness on solid waste is to include education on sustainable consumption and production and integrated waste management in the school curriculum at both primary and secondary levels (Hasan, 2004). While the Information and Education Division of the Ministry of Environment, Solid Waste Management and Climate Change is involved in the provision of sensitisation campaigns in schools, this does not form part of the formal school curriculum (Jankee, 2021). In effect, studies have shown that sustainable waste management behaviours like waste sorting are less likely to be adopted by young people in developing countries (Sarbassov et al., 2019; Singhirunnusorn, Donlakorn, & Kaewhanin, 2017; Statistics South Africa, 2018). For this reason, formal education of young people on sustainable solid waste management through the school system might be an efficient way to increase the number of people reached for awareness campaigns, as well as to enhance the efficacy of such campaigns (Debrah, Vidal, & Dinis, 2021; Hasan, 2004; Olsen et al., 2020). To enable the deployment of such a measure, the Government needs to firstly train teachers on the issue so that they are able to deliver appropriate education to the students using adequate pedagogical tools (Debrah et al., 2021). Implementation of such awareness-raising programmes in the school curriculum has proved to be efficient in several regions worldwide including the United States (Hasan, 2004), Poland (Grodzinska-Jurczak, Bartosiewicz, Twardowska, & Ballantyne, 2010) and Germany (Stockert & Bogner, 2020).

Another possible method that the Government can employ to improve the efficiency of the awareness programmes deployed is by training some residents of communities, like women, youth and senior citizen groups to deliver the sensitisation campaign amongst the members of their communities instead of using an 'outsider'. In so doing, it might be easier to persuade the waste generators to adopt sustainable waste management behaviours since they will already be familiar with the communicators (United Nations ESCAP, 2015).

Comparing the overall rating of 29% for User Inclusivity with the scores obtained in previous studies, it is noted that the situation has not improved significantly over the past decade. In effect, the User Inclusivity as per the UN-HABITAT (2010) study is at a LOW compliance level while the rating for User Inclusivity as per the online Wasteaware Platform of the University of Leeds shows a LOW-MEDIUM compliance level with a score of 21% (2009 data for the City of Curepipe only). The ratings from both studies are lower than the rating found in this study, demonstrating some level of improvement, albeit the overall rating remains at a LOW/MEDIUM level. Also, the two previous studies (UN-HABITAT, 2010; University of Leeds, n.d) used data for only 1 urban location, which might not be very representative of the entire dynamics of stakeholder participation in the waste management system in Mauritius.

Table 4 shows the scores for the different indicators for Provider Inclusivity. The combined score amounts to 40%, which represents a LOW/MEDIUM compliance level for Producer Inclusivity.

The indicator B1 has been evaluated at 'Medium Compliance' since while there are laws in place related to ensuring the provision of waste collection services, the enunciation of inclusion and participation of the different types of private stakeholders lacks robustness. Table 5 shows the relevant regulations in place in Mauritius related to the issue of stakeholder engagement.

As per the existing legislation, the responsibility for all non-hazardous waste collection is mainly for the Local Government. The Local Government can outsource the waste collection process through public–private partnerships according to the above-mentioned regulations, but there is a lack or absence of regulations for community-based organisations or organised informal sector participation. In fact, the informal sector is primarily involved in the collection and recycling of recyclable materials, but there is an absence of laws or policies for supporting the informal sector (African Clean Cities Platform, 2019; PAGE, 2017). There is currently no record on the number of workers involved in

Table 4. Scores for Producer Inclusivity Sub-Indicators.

B. Indicators for Measuring Degree of Provider Inclusivity	Score				
	0 (No Compliance)	5 (Low Compliance)	10 (Medium Compliance)	15 (Medium/ High Compliance)	20 (High Compliance)
B1. Legal framework			10		
B2. Representation of the private sector			10		
B3. Role of the informal and community sector	0				
B4. The balance of public vs. private sector interests in delivering services		5			
B5. Bid processes				15	
Cumulated score for Provider Inclusivity			40% => LOW/MEDIUM		

Source: Authors' elaboration.

informal waste collection and no regulations are in place to ensure health and safety of these workers (PAGE, 2017).

While the Waste Management and Resource Recovery Act 2023 has attempted to provide definitions for different types of waste, there is a lack of granularity and clarity with respect to the definition of non-hazardous waste. As per this piece of legislation, all waste that is not classified as hazardous waste is de facto non-hazardous waste, with only some sub-categories specified under the more general term of 'solid waste'. In fact, the law mentions that the term 'solid waste' does not englobe hazardous waste, but also mentions that the term 'solid waste' includes industrial waste. This might bring about some degree of per-plexity since industrial waste might also be hazardous in nature. Also, it is only when clear definitions of waste types are provided that other regulations in line with sustainable waste management (e.g. with respect to waste sorting and extended producer responsibility) can be properly implemented with clear allo-cation of institutional responsibilities. The Waste Management and Resource Recovery Act 2023 does make provision for responsibility allocation with regards to institutions and waste generators. One of such duty for both stakeholders is the segregation and separate storage of waste. However, the legislation in question does not specify the waste groups according to which the waste should be segregated. For instance, as per the law, a 'waste generator' is anyone who produces waste and an 'institution' is any public or private body, agency or entity, which implies that waste generators and institutions may generate any type of waste. The law does not specify whether the waste generators and insti-tutions should segregate waste as per the definitions of solid waste, household waste, commercial waste, industrial waste and hazardous waste provided in the legislation or whether waste should be segregated into other types of classification (for example, organic, plastic, paper etc) in line with plausible recovery and

Table 5. Current and Past Legislations Related to Stakeholder Engagement in the Solid Waste Management in Mauritius.

Regulatory Provisions for Solid Waste Management in Mauritius	Main Aspects Covered by the Law
1. Local Government Act (Dumping and Waste Carriers) Regulations 2021 (Revoked in 2023)	− Relates to regulations on disposal and transfer and transport of solid waste − Mentions the existing transfer stations and the disposal site in Mauritius − Provides the format for the application form for a waste carrier license − Provides the cost associated with possession of a waste carrier license − Lists the types of wastes that are allowed to be disposed at the landfill
2. Local Government Act (Registration of Scavenging Contractors) Regulations 2004 (Revoked in 2023)	− Gives regulations to follow for a scavenging contractor to register himself − Gives the format of the application form for registration of scavenging contractors
3. Local Government Act (Registration of Recycler and Exporter) Regulations 2013 (Revoked in 2023)	− Gives regulations for registration of recyclers and exporters of waste and mentions clearly that unless one is registered under this Act, one shall not recyle, dismantle or export waste − Gives the different categories of waste that are relevant to this Act − Gives formats of registration forms for recyling, dismantling and exporting − Gives formats of annual reports for recyling/dismantling and exporting waste
4. Environment Protection (Standards for hazardous wastes) Regulations 2001 (Revoked in 2023)	− Gives definition of hazardous wastes − Contains provisions for storage, transport and treatment and disposal of hazardous wastes − Includes formats for hazardous waste inventory and consignment note for hazardous wastes
5. The Public-Private Partnership Act 2004	− Aims to provide a regulatory framework in relation to public-private procurement − Covers public-private partnership (PPP) agreements, including those of the waste sector − Makes a few provisions related to the bidding process and compensation of private parties by the Government in relation to PPP
6. Environment Protection (Extended Producer Responsibility for Electrical and Electronic Equipment) Regulations 202X'	− Currently being drafted and not finalised yet, only draft version available − At consumer level: makes provision for the sorting of e-waste and their disposal to designated collection points, through take-back mechanisms or through collection exercises − At producer level: defines the duties of producers of electrical and electronic equipment mainly in terms of financial incentives involved in the sound management of e-waste, primarily through collaboration with a Producer Responsibility Organisation (PRO) which is defined as an NGO mandated to implement the collective Extended Producer Responsibility Scheme

Table 5. (*Continued*)

Regulatory Provisions for Solid Waste Management in Mauritius	Main Aspects Covered by the Law
	− At distributor level: regulations specify that distributors should take back e-waste from consumers, provide information to customers on the take back program, provide a collection point for e-waste if they are a retailer whose premises cover at least 400 m2, contact a PRO for the collection of e-wastes from their premises and finally the law prohibits distributors from transferring e-waste to unauthorized entities
7. Waste Management and Resource Recovery Act 2023	− Encompasses the provisions in the revoked pieces of legislations mentioned above (1–4) − Provides definitions for different types of wastes (waste, solid waste, household waste, commercial waste, industrial waste, hazardous waste) − Attempts to provide definitions for different stakeholders involved in the solid waste management system of Mauritius − Provides duties for stakeholders involved in waste management (duties of waste generators, duties of local authorities, duties of institutions)

Source: Authors' elaboration.

recycling activities. Therefore, a major improvement area with regards to indicator B1 would be to have more clear legal definitions for different types of hazardous and non-hazardous waste, and, thereafter, including clauses pertaining to the clear enunciation of the responsibilities of different stakeholders with regards to waste segregation and storage within an integrated waste management framework.

Further, even though the provision of comingled waste collection services can be considered as being relatively stable with quasi 100% of waste collected (Ministry of Environment, Waste Management and Climate Change of the Republic Mauritius, 2022b), the weakness of the regulatory framework with respect to sustainable solid waste management is highlighted by the fact that it does not cater for the provision of a stable service in line with the strategies of the Ministry with regards to solid waste recovery and recycling. This lack of regulatory framework can be attested by the inefficiency of public–private partnerships for recycling whereby despite the provision of a fee of MUR 300 per tonne of waste taken from transfer stations for recycling purposes, no private recycler has approached the Ministry of Environment, Solid Waste Management and Climate Change to make use of this incentive (Ministry of Environment, Solid Waste Management and Climate Change, 2020b). This can be due to inefficient communication amongst the different stakeholders. It might also be that the financial incentive is not sufficient with respect to the amount of waste that can be collected for recycling from transfer stations. Also, since source segregation is not implemented in Mauritius, the wastes found at transfer stations are mainly comingled and this is a disincentive for waste recovery. The financial incentive might work only if recyclers are able to collect a consequential amount (scale of economies) of uncontaminated, source-segregated recyclable wastes from transfer stations, and this can be possible only when there is a regulatory framework covering source segregation for different types of waste generators, which is not yet the case for Mauritius. Nevertheless, the scaling up of civic amenity centres in the future might contribute to overcoming the barrier of recovering uncontaminated waste.

To address the above-mentioned issues, the Government might further improve on the Waste Management and Resource Recovery Act 2023 by including provisions to include the informal sector and community-based organizations as well as comprehensive definitions for different waste types that might enable better implementation of waste segregation and sorting by the different stakeholders.

As far as indicator B2 is concerned, a 'Medium Compliance' rating has been provided since there is evidence of private sector participation in waste management planning forums, committees, task force or steering group. As discussed earlier, the private sector is active at all stages of the solid waste value chain, including generation, collection, transportation, recovery and recycling, and disposal. Transfer stations and the landfill are also operated by private companies. While the waste value chain is largely formalised, there is still an informal sector that is not included in the decision-making process as was discussed earlier. For instance, the formal private sector participated in *Les Assises de L'Environnement* (European Commission, 2021; Ministry of Environment, Solid Waste Management and Climate Change, 2020a). The informal sector that plays a pivotal role in the collection of recyclable wastes in Mauritius is not included in discussions regarding solid waste management (African Clean Cities Platform, 2019; PAGE, 2017). More recently, the Ministry of Environment, Solid Waste Management and Climate Change (2021b) organised a consultative workshop on plastic pollution which included plastic waste management. However, this workshop also excluded the participation of the informal sector and only NGOs, registered recyclers, academics and representatives of the UNDP and the Head of the European Delegation to Mauritius were invited (Government Information Service, 2021b; Ministry of Environment, Solid Waste Management and Climate Change, 2021b).

While the Government of Mauritius seems to be heading in the right direction with regards to the representation of the private sector in waste management committees or forums, the exclusion of the informal sector or other stakeholders such as community-based organisations might not bring the desired outcomes in view of the policies and strategies that are planned to be implemented, especially with respect to waste recovery and recycling (African Clean Cities Platform, 2019; PAGE, 2017). The improvement areas for indicator B2 will be similar to those of indicator B3 since the weakness of B2 is mostly linked to the informal sector.

For the indicator B3, 'No compliance' has been judged a fair rating due to the afore-mentioned reasons. There is an absolute lack of acknowledgement of the informal sector in the provision of waste-related services in spite of the existence of informal waste collectors who collect waste primarily for reuse or recycling (African Clean Cities Platform, 2019; PAGE, 2017). There is no legal structure or policy pertaining to the safety (PAGE, 2017) or remuneration of such waste pickers. It is not clear whether the regulation on minimum wage (The National Wage Consultative Council Act, 2021) applies to the informal waste collection sector. Also, the informal sector is excluded from participation in waste management forums, committees and consultation workshops, and there is no evidence of recognition of the role of informal waste collectors in the recent strategies and policies being implemented by the Ministry of Environment, Solid Waste Management and Climate Change (Ministry of Environment, Solid Waste Management and Climate Change, 2019, 2021b, 2022a). Additionally, no formal mechanism is in place for engagement of community-based organisations or the community in general. It is usually assumed that the views of NGOs reflect the views of the community, which might not be true in all cases. There are 35 Citizen Advice Bureaus (CABs) across Mauritius to involve citizens to some extent, but it is mainly a form of grievance mechanism rather than a platform to actively engage the community in waste-related issues (National Development Unit, n.d).

A first improvement area with respect to indicator B3 (and by extension indicator B2) might be the formal recognition of waste-picking activities (Medina, 2008) followed by the implementation of a legal framework to accommodate informal waste collectors in terms of safety and working conditions. This primary step will make it possible for the informal sector to be included in public–private partnerships in terms of formal agreements or contracts for waste collection and reduce the economic vulnerability of the informal waste pickers (Medina, 2008). Such an approach will also be useful to extend solid waste collection to informal communities as highlighted above. Such measures have already been implemented successfully in Brazil (Medina, 2008).

Another step is to include the informal sector in the process of policymaking and decision-taking. To ensure that the inclusion of the informal sector is smooth and to prevent potential conflict with other stakeholders like registered recyclers (since the informal sector is mostly involved in the collection of recyclables in Mauritius (PAGE, 2017)), an awareness raising campaign should be conducted amongst the other stakeholders to outline the advantages of formally including the informal waste pickers (Buch, Marseille, Williams, Aggarwal, & Sharma, 2021). The sensitisation campaign should focus on the identification of differentiated but complementary roles to achieve the goals of a sustainable waste management system (Buch et al., 2021). For instance, in Mauritius, different groups of 'informal' waste pickers might be engaged in formal agreements with the Government or directly with the registered recyclers to collect dry recyclable wastes.

A further potential measure to implement to improve the rating for indicator B3 might be to encourage informal waste pickers to form cooperative societies in order to strengthen their negotiation power with respect to other stakeholders in the solid waste management sector (International Labour Organization, 2019). The Government might help these cooperatives through financial support (Gerdes & Gunsilius, 2010), the provision of adequate equipment (Medina, 2008) and the provision of relevant trainings (Buch et al., 2021). Such types of actions have already been applied in several countries including Brazil, Argentina, India, Uruguay and Colombia (Medina, 2008).

An additional improvement area for indicator B3 might be to diversify the role of the existing Citizen Advice Bureaus to include community engagement in waste related issues. This would ensure that the views and participation of the citizens are formally recognised by the Government.

The indicator B4 has been provided with a 'Low Compliance' level score since there is not enough checks and balances in place to ensure the provision of waste management services in a way which is mutually beneficial to both the public and private sectors (Wilson et al., 2015). In Mauritius, the public sector is often disadvantaged relative to the private sector due to the lack of penalties and measures in place resulting in significant financial losses to the Government in the waste management sector (Ministry of Environment, Solid Waste Management and Climate Change, 2022c). This is evidenced by the fact that there was an over claim of MUR 10.9 Million by the contractor operating the Mare Chicose landfill due to a lack of control over payments to contractors managing the landfills and transfer stations (Ministry of Environment, Solid Waste Management and Climate Change, 2022c). In response to this issue, the Ministry of Environment, Solid Waste Management and Climate Change has started to implement remedial measures in terms of regular site visits and plans to set up CCTV cameras at the landfill (Ministry of Environment, Solid Waste Management and Climate Change, 2022c). Also, irregularities have been observed in the management of the landfill that have resulted in the deduction of around MUR 14 million from payment due and the matter has been reported to the police (Ministry of Environment, Solid Waste Management and Climate Change, 2022c). This situation may suggest that there is insufficient flexibility with respect to changing conditions within a long-term agreement, and the risk of inadequate provision of waste management services.

There is also evidence of the public sector failing in its duties with respect to remuneration of private contractors. For instance, in 2022, the Municipality of Beau-Bassin Rose-Hill owed an amount of MUR 3,833,333.31 for cleaning activities conducted by the private company Securiclean (Mauritius) Ltd (Moorlan, 2022).

These cases show that there is a lack of robust solid waste management system combining the strengths of both the public and private sector in Mauritius (Wilson et al., 2015) despite the waste collection coverage claimed to be 100% (Ministry of Environment, Waste Management and Climate Change of the Republic Mauritius, 2022b).

A possible way to curb the above-mentioned issue with respect to indicator B4 is by amending the legislations to include clear penalties in case of infringement of contracts for private operators involved in the waste management system of Mauritius alongside existing contractual clauses. Also, the public sector should implement a more robust due-diligence programme for the private waste contractors. One example might be to hire independent third parties to conduct regular ethical audits for the private contractors as specified in the OECD Principles for Integrity in Public Procurement (OEDC, 2009).

As far as indicator B5 is concerned, a 'Medium/High' compliance rating has been considered reasonable for the solid waste management system of Mauritius since the bidding process is fairly transparent. The solicitation of bids as well as the award of contacts together with the bid prices of all bidders is posted online (Environment, Solid Waste Management and Climate Change of the Republic Mauritius, 2020a). There is little evidence of lack of accountability or transparency since the bidding process is fairly robust as it is regulated by the Public Procurement Act which is based on the UNCITRAL Model Law on Public Procurement, and the World Bank Procurement rules (Procurement Policy Office, 2011). Nonetheless, a 'High Compliance' rating has not been provided to indicator B5 since in 2019 there was a case involving conflict of interest for the allocation of the contract for the operation of the La Brasserie and Laura Transfer stations to the private operator overseeing the management of the Mare Chicose landfill at the time of facts (Independent Review Panel, 2019a, 2019b; Le Mauricien Ltd, 2019a, 2019b). However, it should be noted that the contract related to the La Brasserie Transfer Station was cancelled by the Independent Review Panel of the Procurement Police Office (2019b) that led to the annulment of the previous procurement procedure and the undertaking of a fresh bidding process (Independent Review Panel, 2019b; Le Mauricien Ltd, 2019b). The other case was dismissed on the grounds that the applicant was one day late to file the application for review to the Independent Review Panel. This was in spite of the respondent (the Ministry in this case) delaying in issuing its decisions to the applicant (Independent Review Panel, 2019a). These two cases demonstrate that the bidding process in Mauritius is fairly open, transparent and has a mechanism of accountability since the matters were reported in detail in local media, and all the decisions of the Independent Review Panel of the Procurement Police Office can be consulted online (Independent Review Panel, 2019a, 2019b; Le Mauricien Ltd, 2019b). This assessment is used to justify the 'Medium/High' compliance score.

A possible room for improvement related to indicator B5 might be to consider the possibilities of conflict of interests of the bidders during the procurement process. In this view, a due diligence analysis on the ethical conduct of the bidders might be undertaken and the results of such an analysis might be a factor to be considered in the allocation of contract. The due diligence programme might be based on the guidelines of the OECD Principles for Integrity in Public Procurement which includes selecting tenderers based on pre-defined criteria encompassing provision of proof of anti-corruption policies and procedures by the tenderers (OECD, 2009). This will ensure more transparency and will avoid embarrassing situations for all parties involved.

When the overall rating of 40% for Provider Inclusivity is compared with the scores obtained in previous studies, it can be deduced that similar to User Inclusivity, there has been only slight improvement over the last decade. This can be demonstrated by the fact that UN-HABITAT (2010) study showed a LOW compliance level while the rating as per the online Wasteaware Platfom of the University of Leeds shows a LOW-MEDIUM compliance level with a score of 35% (2009 data for the City of Curepipe only). The ratings from both the UN-HABITAT study (2010) and the Wasteware Platform of the University of Leeds are lower than the actual rating found in this study, which demonstrates some level of improvement. Similar to the case of User Inclusivity, it should be noted that the previous two studies (UN-HABITAT, 2010; University of Leeds, n.d) used data for only one urban location that might not be an accurate depiction of the stakeholder involvement in the island-wide solid waste management governance.

CONCLUSION

In an attempt to scrutinise the existing gaps in the stakeholder participatory structure in the waste management governance of the Island of Mauritius, the different existing laws and regulations, national policies and strategies and other secondary data were reviewed to inform an assessment of the two Wasteaware Benchmark Indicators, namely User Inclusivity and Provider Inclusivity. It has been found that User Inclusivity demonstrates a LOW-MEDIUM compliance level, which shows no major improvement as compared to previous studies conducted by the UN-HABITAT (2010) and the University of Leeds (n.d) which used data from only one urban location from the year 2009. For Provider Inclusivity, which has also been assigned a LOW-MEDIUM compliance level in this study, it can be noted that there has been an amelioration as compared to the study conducted by the UN-HABITAT (2010), however, the overall compliance level is the same as the outcome of the Wasteaware Platform of the University of Leeds (n.d) even if the figure has slightly improved from 35% to 40%.

The outcomes of the case study demonstrate that the main drawback related to both User and Producer Inclusivity is the lack of an adequate legal framework. For User Inclusivity, the lack of regulations impacts mainly the Right of Citizens to participate in solid waste management related decisions that have a direct impact on them. The existing regulations comprise public consultation only for Environmental Impact Assessments related to a limited number of solid waste management undertakings that are not related to the policy and strategic planning process For Producer Inclusivity, it can be deduced that while there are regulations in place which ensure the sound management of solid waste to some extent, the existing legal structure does not allow for the implementation of a sustainable solid waste management strategy in line with the sustainable development goals, especially in terms of waste recovery and recycling to develop a circular waste economy. While there is a single piece of legislation which governs waste management, it has some shortcomings with regards to the provision of clear definitions of different waste types, especially for non-hazardous wastes. The lack of a legislative framework with regards to the health and safety and working conditions of informal waste pickers is also a factor having a significant impact on the rating of Producer Inclusivity for Mauritius. It has been noted that the informal waste sector is not acknowledged in the waste management framework of Mauritius, and there is a complete disregard of informal waste pickers during stakeholder consultative workshops or forums on waste management. This is, even though the informal waste pickers are an important link in the recovery of waste that underpins the re-cycling value chain. Further, the Producer Inclusivity criterion demonstrates a lack of robust solid waste management system combining the strengths of both the public and private sector in Mauritius even if the waste collection coverage is said to be 100%. This is due to a lack of a strong monitoring system to evaluate the quality of the services being provided by the private sector, which can possibly be remedied through the implementation of a more robust due-diligence programme for the private waste contractors, which could include ethical on-site audits conducted by independent third parties.

To cater for the shortcomings related to stakeholder participation and engagement in existing laws, it is suggested that a revamping of the existing legal framework is required to include clear definitions of non-hazardous wastes which will enable clear allocation of responsibilities to all stakeholders in line with the sustainable and integrated waste management strategy planning to be implemented by the Government. The revamp should also cater for the informal sector as well as public participation at the different stages of a waste management policy or strategic planning cycle and project formulation. This can be done through the use of the existing Citizens Advice Bureau.

Another significant limitation of the stakeholder participatory structure with regards to User Inclusivity is the lack of efficient sensitisation campaigns to promote stakeholder engagement for addressing the problem of littering, and to promote the adoption of sustainable behaviours such as waste sorting at source in order to facilitate waste recovery for a circular economy. It is suggested that the Government should include sustainable waste management in the formal school curricula so as to instill a civic sense and shape the mindset of the population towards sustainability starting from a young age. It has also been suggested that the Government could train people from community-based organisations, to deploy training since they live in close proximity with citizens at the grass-roots level. Another proposition has been to encourage private companies to integrate sustainable consumption and production, including sustainable waste management in their CSR activities starting with their employees and extending to the local communities that they support.

The study also shows that the criteria of equity of service provision, public feedback mechanisms and public education and awareness (in terms of level of activity, not effectiveness to achieve actual sensitisation) have the highest compliance ratings for the User Inclusivity indicator. The facts that comingled waste collection services virtually cover the whole Island, feedback forms and contact details are present online and are accessible to anyone with an internet connection, and several actions are implemented through a dedicated budget for raising awareness on sustainable waste management have supported the higher rating for each of the three aforementioned criteria for User Inclusivity. However, potential improvements include using informal waste pickers to hand-pick waste in informal settlements or putting in place the enabling conditions for informal dwellers to drop off their waste in the nearest public bins. Increasing the number of source-separated collection bins island-wide, diversification of the communication channels to increase the accessibility of the feedback mechanism for all stakeholders and adoption of 'Train the Trainer' schemes to increase the level of activity and the number of people reached for waste sensitisation campaigns have also been proposed.

Regarding Producer Inclusivity, the highest rating is observed for the bidding process, which is open, transparent and provides a fair level of accountability. An improvement area could be the inclusion of due diligence on the ethical disposition of bidders during the procurement process.

The overall deduction from the study is that while Mauritius has implemented some measures to engage stakeholders in solid waste management governance, there is much scope for improvements. One example is the inclusion of the informal sector in the decision-making process. Further, the existing legal structure should be improved to support the implementation of a sustainable solid waste management strategy through clear, definitions and standards related to non-hazardous wastes that comprise the bulk of all solid waste, and clauses on stakeholder engagement at different stages of intergrated waste management policy planning processes and decision-making.

REFERENCES

African Clean Cities Platform. (2019). Africa solid waste management: Data BOOK 2019 [online]. Retrieved from https://africancleancities.org/assets/data/JICA_databook_EN_web_20191218. pdf. Accessed on June 25, 2022.

Agamuthu, P., & Herat, S. (2014). Sustainable waste management in Small Island Developing States (SIDS). *Waste Management & Research, 32*(8), 681–682.

Ahnee, D., Antoine, A., Chowree, C., Ducasse, M., Hosseny, S., Lamusse, F., . . . Philippe, I. (2021). *Rapports Sur La Discrimination, La Ségrégation Et Le Droit À Un Logement Adéquate*. Nations Unies Droit de l'Homme, procedures Speciales [online]. Retrieved from https://www.ohchr.org/Documents/Issues/Housing/SubmissionsCFIhousingdiscrimin/DAL_DrwaAEnnLakaz_KRN_Mauritius.docx. Accessed on May 05, 2022.

Beerachee, B. (2012). *Overview of wastes management in Mauritius* [online]. Seoul: Solid Waste Management Division, Ministry of Local Government and Outer Islands, Mauritius. Retrieved from http://webcache.googleusercontent.com/search?q=cache:veiFcj8y4KgJ:www.uncrd.or.jp/content/documents/04_BEERACHEE-Mauritius.pdf+&cd=1&hl=en&ct=clnk&gl=mu. Accessed on January 22, 2022.

Beerachee. (n.d.). Theme: Solid waste management [online]. Retrieved from https://environment. govmu.org/Documents/human%20development%20report/Presentation_post%20assises_16.12. 20.pdf?csf=1&e=O1ORWS. Accessed on January 20, 2022.

Bhurtun, A. (2020). À La Chaumière: Un Civic Amenity Centre pour faciliter le recyclage des déchets [online]. Retrieved from https://ionnews.mu/video-a-la-chaumiere-un-civic-amenity-centre-pour-faciliter-le-recyclage-des-dechets/. Accessed on February 02, 2022.

Buch, R., Marseille, A., Williams, M., Aggarwal, R., & Sharma, A. (2021). From waste pickers to producers: An inclusive circular economy solution through development of cooperatives in waste management. *Sustainability, 13,* 8925. doi:10.3390/su13168925

Central Procurement Board. (2020). Projects currently at advertising stage as at 28.12.20 [online]. Retrieved from https://cpb.govmu.org/Documents/Project%20Status/Project%20Status%2028. 12.20-Website.xlsx?csf=1&e=MLBVhC. Accessed on February 01, 2022.

Central Procurement Board. (2021). Public opening of bids on: Friday 18 June 2021 project: Procurement of landfill works for vertical expansion of the Mare Chicose landfill and operation and Post closure management of cells [online]. Retrieved from https://cpb.govmu.org/Documents/pub_openings/ N27_CPB90_19_Vertical_Expansion.pdf#search=vertical. Accessed on March 05, 2022.

Central Statistics Office. (2008). *Mauritius in figures* [online]. Republic of Mauritius, Ministry of Finance & Economic Development. Retrieved from https://statsmauritius.govmu.org/ Documents/Statistics/By_Subject/Other/MIF/MIF_Yr08.pdf. Accessed on January 18, 2022.

Central Statistics Office. (2009). *Mauritius in figures* [online]. Republic of Mauritius, Ministry of Finance & Economic Development. Retrieved from https://statsmauritius.govmu.org/ Documents/Statistics/By_Subject/Other/MIF/MIF_Yr09.pdf. Accessed on January 18, 2022.

Central Statistics Office. (2010). *Digest of demographic Statistics 2009* [online]. Republic of Mauritius, Ministry of Finance & Economic Development. Retrieved from https://statsmauritius.govmu. org/Documents/Statistics/Digests/Demography/Digest_Demo_Yr09.pdf. Accessed on August 02, 2022.

City of Kamloops. (2021). *Let's talk organics: Community engagement summary report* [online]. Retrieved from https://letstalk.kamloops.ca/19131/widgets/75999/documents/61459. Accessed on December 05, 2022.

Debrah, J. K., Vidal, D. G., & Dinis, M. A. P. (2021). Raising awareness on solid waste management through formal education for sustainability: A developing countries evidence review. *Recycling, 6,* 6. doi:10.3390/recycling6010006

Delegation of the European Union to the Republic of Mauritius and to the Republic of Seychelles. (2020). *EUBeach clean up à Maurice: Plus de 200 kilos de déchets divers collectés en moins de deux heures et lancement d'une campagne de sensibilisation* [online]. Retrieved from https://eeas. europa.eu/delegations/mauritius_lt/86054/EUBeach%20clean%20up%20%C3%A0%20Maurice %20:%20Plus%20de%20200%20kilos%20de%20d%C3%A9chets%20divers%20collect%C3% A9s%20en%20moins%20de%20deux%20heures%20et%20lancement%20d'une%20campagne% 20de%20sensibilisation. Accessed on March 01, 2022.

Dowarkasing, M. S. (2019). *Environmental issues: Veolia – making Mauritius a hub for treating contaminated waste?* [online]. Mauritius: La Sentinelle Ltd. Retrieved from https://www. lexpress.mu/node/356369. Accessed on May 12, 2022.

Edouard, O. (2021). Environnement: des plages de déchets... [online]. L'express.mu (La Sentinelle Ltd). Retrieved from https://www.lexpress.mu/article/399716/environnement-plages-dechets. Accessed on March 01, 2022.

Emtel Ltd. (2021). Our sustainability commitment [online]. Retrieved from https://www.emtel.com/ corporate-social-responsibility. Accessed on December 05, 2022.

Environment Protection Act. (2002). Environment protection Act, Act 19 of 2002 – 5 September 2002 (unless otherwise indicated) [online]. Retrieved from https://environment.govmu.org/ Documents/Legislations/A.%20Acts/1(i)Consolidated%20Environment%20Protection%20Act %202002.pdf. Accessed on February 10, 2022.

Environment Protection (Standards for hazardous wastes) Regulations. (2001). Government Notice No157 of 2001 [online]. Retrieved from https://environment.govmu.org/Documents/SWMD/ standards%20for%20Hazardous%20Waste%20Regulations%202001.pdf. Accessed on August 10, 2022.

Environment protection (extended producer responsibility for electrical and electronic equipment) regulations 202X. (DRAFT MODE) [online]. Retrieved from https://www.mcci.org/media/ 278758/draft-epr-regulations-on-eee_280920.pdf?utm_medium=email&utm_campaign=Draft

%20Extender%20Producer%20Responsibility%20EPR%20Regulations&utm_content=Draft%
20Extender%20Producer%20Responsibility%20EPR%20Regulations+CID_18b0c14fcd237ab9
ebd6d9506d1369d0&utm_source=Email%20marketing%20software&utm_term=draft. Accessed
on January 22, 2022.

European Commission. (2021). Mauritius multi-annual indicative Programme 2021 – 2027 [online].
Retrieved from https://ec.europa.eu/international-partnerships/system/files/mip-2021-c2021-
9085-mauritius-annex_en.pdf. Accessed on May 28, 2022.

Ezeah, C., Fazakerley, J. A., & Roberts, C. L. (2013). Emerging trends in informal sector recycling in
developing and transition countries. *Waste Management. 33*, 2509–2519. doi:10.1016/j.
wasman.2013.06.020

Foolmaun, R. K., Chamilall, D. S., & Munhurrun, G. (2011). Overview of non-hazardous solid waste
in the small island state of Mauritius. *Resources, Conservation and Recycling, 55*(11), 966–972.
doi:10.1016/j.resconrec.2011.05.004

Fuldauer, L. I., Ives, M. C., Adshead, D., Thacker, S., & Hall, J. W. (2019). Participatory planning of the
future of waste management in small island developing states to deliver on the Sustainable Development Goals. *Journal of Cleaner Production, 223*, 147–162. doi:10.1016/j.jclepro.2019.02.269

Gerdes, & Gunsilius. (2010). *The waste experts: Enabling conditions for informal sector integration in
solid waste management*. Deutsche Gesellschaft für Technische Zusammenarbeit (GTZ) GmbH
[online]. Retrieved from https://www.giz.de/en/downloads/gtz2010-waste-experts-conditions-is-
integration.pdf. Accessed on June 25, 2022.

Gooding, T. (2016). Low-income housing provision in Mauritius: Improving social justice and place
quality. *Habitat International, 53*, pg 502–516. doi:10.1016/j.habitatint.2015.12.018

Government Digital Service. (2021). Consultation outcome: Summary of responses and government
response [online]. Retrieved from https://www.gov.uk/government/consultations/waste-manag
ement-plan-for-england/outcome/summary-of-responses-and-government-response. Accessed
on November 15, 2022.

Government Information Service. (2015). Residential squatting is being addressed with rigour and
humanity, says Vice-Prime Minister Soodhun [online]. Retrieved from http://www.govmu.org/
English/News/Pages/Residential-squatting-is-being-addressed-with-rigour-and-humanity,-says-
Vice-Prime-Minister-Soodhun-.aspx. Accessed on June 10, 2022.

Government Information Service. (2021a). Keeping Mauritius clean is the responsibility of each citi-
zen, states Minister Ramano [online]. Retrieved from https://govmu.org/EN/newsgov/
SitePages/Keeping-Mauritius-clean-is-the-responsibility-of-each-citizen,-states-Minister-
Ramano.aspx. Accessed on June 18, 2022.

Government Information Service. (2021b). Plastic-Free Mauritius: Raising awareness on the policies to
control plastic pollution [online]. Retrieved from https://gis.govmu.org/News/SitePages/Plastic-
Free-Mauritius–Raising-awareness-on-the-policies-to-control-plastic-pollution.aspx. Accessed
on June 23, 2022.

Government of Mauritius. (2011). *Ministry of environment & sustainable development Mauritius environment Outlook report 2011* [online]. Retrieved from https://wedocs.unep.org/bitstream/handle/20.
500.11822/8593/-Mauritius%20Environment%20Outlook%20Report%20-2011Mauritius-
Environment-Outlook-2011.PDF?sequence=3&isAllowed=y. Accessed on June 16, 2022.

Grodzinska-Jurczak, M., Bartosiewicz, A., Twardowska, A., & Ballantyne, R. (2010). Evaluating the
impact of a school waste education Programme upon students', parents' and teachers' environmental knowledge, attitudes and behaviour. *Environmental Knowledge, Attitudes and
Behaviour, International Research in Geographical and Environmental Education, 12*(2),
106–122. doi:10.1080/10382040308667521

Gutberlet, J., Kain, J.-H., Nyakinya, B., Oloko, M., Zapata, P., & Campos, M. J. Z. (2016). Bridging
weak links of solid waste management in informal settlements. *The Journal of Environment &
Development, 0*(0), 1–26. doi:10.1177/1070496516672263

Hasan, S. E. (2004). Public awareness is key to successful waste management. *Journal of Environmental
Science and Health – Part A: Toxic/Hazardous Substances & Environmental Engineering,
A39*(2), 483–492. doi:10.1081/ESE-120027539

IAP2 International Federation. (2018). IAP2 spectrum of public participation [online]. Retrieved from https://www.iap2.org/resource/resmgr/pillars/Spectrum_8.5x11_Print.pdf.   Accessed   on December 05, 2022.

Independent Review Panel. (2019a). In the Matter of Compagnie Regionale de Services et de l'environnement Ltee v/s Ministry of Social Security, National Solidarity, and Environment and Sustainable Development (Environment and Sustainable Development Division) (Solid Waste Management Division) (Cause No. 16/19/IRP) [online]. Retrieved from https://ppo.govmu.org/ Pages/Independent%20Review%20Panel/Decisions-2019.aspx. https://ppo.govmu.org/ Documents/IndependantReviewPanel/Decisions%202019/IRP%2020-19.pdf.   Accessed   on June 25, 2022.

Independent Review Panel. (2019b). In the Matter of Compagnie Regionale de Services et de l'environnement Ltee (CRSE Ltee) v/s Ministry of Social Security, National Solidarity, and Environment and Sustainable Development (Environment and Sustainable Development Division) (Solid Waste Management Division) (Cause No. 19/19/IRP) [online]. Retrieved from https://ppo.govmu.org/Pages/Independent%20Review%20Panel/Decisions-2019.aspx. https://ppo. govmu.org/Documents/IndependantReviewPanel/Decisions%202019/IRP%2019-19.pdf.   Accessed on June 25, 2022.

International Labour Organization. (2019). *Waste pickers' cooperatives and social and solidarity economy organizations* [online]. Retrieved from https://www.ilo.org/global/topics/cooperatives/ publications/WCMS_715845/lang–en/index.htm#:~:text=12-,Waste%20pickers'%20cooperati ves%20and%20social%20and%20solidarity%20economy%20organizations,reducing%20the% 20amount%20of%20landfill. Accessed on June 25, 2022.

Jankee, K. (2021). Enhancement of polyethylene terephthalate bottles recycling in Mauritius through the creation of a mobile application. *European Journal of Sustainable Development*, *10*(3), 27. doi:10.14207/ejsd.2021.v10n3p27

Joseph, K. (2006). Stakeholder participation for sustainable solid waste management. *Habitat International*, *30*, 863–871.

Kaza, S., Yao, L., & Markgraf, C. (2016). Five ways to increase citizen participation in local waste services. World Bank [online]. Retrieved from https://blogs.worldbank.org/sustainablecities/ five-ways-increase-citizen-participation-local-waste-services. Accessed on June 23, 2022.

Kothari, R., Kumar, V., Panwar, N. L., & Tyagi, V. V. (2014). Municipal solid-waste management strategies for renewable energy options. In L. Wang (Ed.), *Sustainable bioenergy production* (p. 267). Boca Raton, FL: CRC Press, Taylor & Francis. Retrieved from https://www.taylorfrancis.com/ books/mono/10.1201/b16764/sustainable-bioenergy-production-lijun-wang?refId=44d83aee-e4e8-4 54c-b024-96db573e26f5&context=ubx

Kowlesser, P. (2012). *Solid waste management in Mauritius*. Solid Waste Management Division Ministry of Local Government and Outer Islands, Mauritius [online]. Retrieved from https:// globalmethane.org/documents/events_land_120910_17.pdf. Accessed on January 10, 2022.

Lai, A., Hensley, J., Krutli, P., & Stauffacher, M. (2016). *Solid waste management in the Seychelles* [online]. Retrieved from http://www.cycad.ch/fileadmin/pdf/lh/cs_2016_report.pdf. Accessed on January 20, 2022.

Le Mauricien Ltd. (2019a). Mare-Chicose Saga : Sotravic essuie un revers à l'IRP avec un contrat de Rs 97,4 M [online]. Retrieved from https://www.lemauricien.com/actualites/societe/mare-chicose-saga-sotravic-essuie-un-revers-a-lirp-avec-un-contrat-de-rs-974-m/304109/.   Accessed on June 25, 2022.

Le Mauricien Ltd. (2019b). Transport de déchet: l'IRP annule un contrat de plus de Rs 100 M pour Sotravic [online]. Retrieved from https://www.lemauricien.com/actualites/societe/transport-de-dechet-lirp-annule-un-contrat-de-plus-de-rs-100-m-pour-sotravic/311223/. Accessed on June 25, 2022.

LEXPRESS.MU. (2007). Les déchets de la discorde [online]. Mauritius, La Sentinelle Ltd. Retrieved from https://www.lexpress.mu/article/les-d%C3%A9chets-de-la-discorde. Accessed on May 12, 2022.

Local Government Act (Dumping and Waste Carriers) Regulations 2021. (2021). Government Notice No. 193 of 2021 THE LOCAL GOVERNMENT ACT regulations made by the minister under section 162B of the local Government Act [online]. Retrieved from https://environment.govmu.

org/Documents/SWMD/Dumping%20and%20Waste%20Carriers%20Regulations%202021. pdf. Accessed on June 23, 2022.

Local Government Act (Registration of Recycler and Exporter) Regulations 2013. (2013). Local Government (registration of recycler and exporter) regulations 2013 GN No. 248 of 2013 Government Gazette of Mauritius No. 92 of 19 October 2013 THE LOCAL GOVERNMENT ACT regulations made by the minister under section162(2) of the local Government Act [online]. Retrieved from https://environment.govmu.org/Documents/SWMD/Registration%20of%20Recycler%20and%20Exporter%20Regulations%202013.pdf. Accessed on June 23, 2022.

Local Government Act (Registration of Scavenging Contractors) Regulations 2004. (2004). THE LOCAL GOVERNMENT ACT regulations made by the minister under section 156A (3) of the local Government Act [online]. Retrieved from https://environment.govmu.org/Documents/SWMD/reg%20of%20scavenging.pdf. Accessed on June 23, 2022.

Local Government Service Commission. (2020). *Annual report 2019–20* [online]. Retrieved from https://lgsc.govmu.org/Lists/AnnualReports/Attachments/5/LGSC%20Annual%20Report%202019-20%20final%2029.10.pdf. Accessed on February 20, 2023.

Maricopa Association of Governments. (2021). Public participation plan [online]. Retrieved from https://azmag.gov/Portals/0/Documents/Communications/MAG_PPP_English_2021_04_02. pdf. Accessed on December 05, 2022.

Mauritius Broadcasting Corporation. (2022a). Le National Network for Sustainable Development Committee présidé par le ministre de l'Environnement [online]. Retrieved from https://mbcradio.tv/article/le-national-network-sustainable-development-committee-pr%C3%A9sid%C3%A9-par-le-ministre-de. Accessed on July 20, 2022.

Mauritius Broadcasting Corporation. (2022b). Le Journal Télévisé – Février 10, 2022 [online]. Retrieved from https://mbcradio.tv/article/le-journal-t%C3%A9l%C3%A9vis%C3%A9-%E2%80%93-f%C3%A9vrier-10-2022. Accessed on February 13, 2022.

Mauritius Revenue Authority. (2021). CSR Guide [online]. Retrieved from https://www.mra.mu/download/CSRGuide.pdf. Accessed on June 15, 2022.

Mauritius Telecom. (2021). Wi-fi Mauritius [online]. Retrieved from http://www.wifimauritius.mu/. Accessed on June 19, 2022.

Medina, M. (2008). *The informal recycling sector in developing countries.* The World Bank [online]. Retrieved from https://documents1.worldbank.org/curated/en/227581468156575228/pdf/472210BRI0Box31ing1sectors01PUBLIC1.pdf. Accessed on June 24, 2022.

Ministry Of Environment And National Development Unit. (2010). *Mauritius strategy for implementation national assessment report 2010* [online]. Retrieved from https://sustainabledevelopment.un.org/content/documents/1255Mauritius-MSI-NAR2010.pdf. Accessed on February 02, 2022.

Ministry Of Environment, Soild Waste Management And Climate Change. (2019). La Gestion Des Dechets [online]. Retrieved from https://environment.govmu.org/Documents/Assises/final%20solid%20waste%20moe%202019%201112.pdf. Accessed on February 21, 2021.

Ministry of Environment, Solid Waste Management and Climate Change. (2019). LA GESTION DES DECHETS [online]. Retrieved from https://environment.govmu.org/Documents/Assises/final%20solid%20waste%20moe%202019%201112.pdf. Accessed on February 28, 2022.

Ministry Of Local Government And Disaster Risk Management. (2021). *Annual report on performance* [online]. Retrieved from https://localgovernment.govmu.org/MyDocument/Annual%20Report%20on%20Performance%20FY%202021-2021%20MOLGDRM%20Final.pdf. Accessed on February 02, 2022.

Ministry of Environment, Solid Waste Management and Climate Change. (2020a). Ministry of environment, solid waste management and climate change [online]. Retrieved from https://environment.govmu.org/Pages/Index.aspx. Accessed on June 26, 2022.

Ministry of Environment, Solid Waste Management and Climate Change. (2020b). *Annual report 2019/2020* [online]. Retrieved from https://environment.govmu.org/Lists/AnnualReports/Attachments/4/ANNUAL%20REPORT%202019-2020.pdf. Accessed on January 25, 2022.

Ministry of Environment, Solid Waste Management and Climate Change. (2020b). *Annual report 2019/ 2020* [online]. Retrieved from https://environment.govmu.org/Lists/AnnualReports/ Attachments/4/ANNUAL%20REPORT%202019-2020.pdf. Accessed on March 30, 2022.

Ministry of Environment, Solid Waste Management and Climate Change. (2021a). Ou Zet Salté Dimoun Li Koz Ou [online]. Retrieved from https://environment.govmu.org/Documents/ events/Poster%20-%20Ou%20Zet%20Salt%C3%A9%20Dimoun%20Li%20Koz%20Ou.pdf? csf=1&e=c59t7W. https://environment.govmu.org/SitePages/VideoGallery.aspx. Accessed on June 22, 2022.

Ministry of Environment, Solid Waste Management and Climate Change. (2021b). Plastic free Mauritius: Defining the roadmap: Recycling of plastic wastes – Session 5 [online]. Retrieved from https://environment.govmu.org/Documents/Plastic%20free/Day%202%20-%2019% 20October%202021/4.%20Plenary%20Session/Plenary%20Session%205%20-%20Recycling% 20of%20Plastic%20Wastes%20(including%20LDPE,%20HDPE,%20PP).pdf. Accessed on June 25, 2022.

Ministry of Environment, Solid Waste Management and Climate Change. (2022a). Strategy and action plan on resource recovery and recycling [online]. Retrieved from https://environment.govmu. org/Documents/SWMD/Brief%20on%20SW%20Strategy_06.01.22%20(2)%20(1).pdf. Accessed on May 05, 2022.

Ministry of Environment, Solid Waste Management and Climate Change. (2022b). Press notice operation and maintenance of La Chaumiere transfer station and transportation of wastes from La Chaumiere transfer station to Mare Chicose LandfillCPB/67/2021 [online]. Retrieved from https://publicnotice.govmu.org/publicnotice/?p=10141. Accessed on February 20, 2023.

Ministry of Environment, Solid Waste Management and Climate Change. (2022c). *Annual report financial year 2020–21* [online]. Retrieved from https://environment.govmu.org/Documents/ SWMD/FINAL%20ANNUAL%20REPORT%202021.pdf. Accessed on June 23, 2022.

Ministry of Finance, Economic Planning and Development. (2021). Budget 2021–2022: Appendix C: Special and other Extra budgetary Funds [online]. Retrieved from https://mof.govmu.org/ Pages/budget_2021_22/Estimates-2021-2022-%26-Indicative-Estimates-2022-2023-and-2024-2025.aspx. Accessed on June 25, 2022.

Ministry of Finance, Economic Planning and Development. (2022). Budget 2022–2023: Appendix C: Special and other Extra budgetary Funds [online]. Retrieved from https://budgetmof.govmu. org/documents/V_C2022_23AppendixC.pdf. Accessed on June 25, 2022.

Mohee, R. (2002). Assessing the recovery potential of solid waste in Mauritius. *36*(1), 33–43. doi:10. 1016/s0921-3449(02)00011-3

Mohee, R., Rughoonundun, H., & Peryagh, C. (2009). *Report for the waste management in Papua New Guinea: Activity 4 deliverable: Synthesis and evaluation of the collected data.*

Mohee, R., Mauthoor, S., Bundhoo, Z. M. A., Soomaroo, G., Soobhany, N., & Gunasee, S. (2015). Current status of solid waste management in small island developing states: A review. *Waste Management, 43*, 539–549.

Moorlan, S. (2022). Dettes: la municipalité de BB-RH condamnée à payer Rs 3,8 m à CIM finance [online]. Retrieved from https://www.lexpress.mu/article/409392/dettes-municipalite-bb-rh-condamnee-payer-rs-38-m-cim-finance. Accessed on June 25, 2022.

National Development Unit. (n.d). Citizens Advice Bureau [online]. Retrieved from https://ndu. govmu.org/Pages/CAB/Citizens-Advice-Bureau.aspx. Accessed on August 10, 2022.

National Social Inclusion Foundation. (n.d). National CORPORATE SOCIAL RESPONSIBILITY (CSR) FOUNDATION: Our charter [online]. Retrieved from https://www.nsif.mu/wp-content/ uploads/2019/08/Charter-of-the-National-Social-Inclusion-Foundation-.pdf. Accessed on July 28, 2022.

Neehaul, N., Jeetah, P., & Deenapanray, P. (2020). Energy recovery from municipal solid waste in Mauritius: Opportunities and challenges. *Environmental Development, 33*, 100489.

OECD. (2009). *OECD Principles for integrity in public procurement* [online]. Retrieved from https:// www.oecd.org/gov/ethics/48994520.pdf. Accessed on August 06, 2022.

Olsen, S. K., Miller, B. G., Miller, B. G., Eitel, K. B., Cohn, T. C., Olsen, S. K., & Miller, B. G. (2020). Assessing teachers' environmental citizenship based on an adventure learning workshop: A case study from a social-ecological systems perspective. *Journal of Science Teacher Education, 31*, 869–893.

PAGE. (2017). *Republic of Mauritius: Industrial waste assessment Opportunities for industrial Symbiosis* [online]. Retrieved from https://www.greengrowthknowledge.org/sites/default/files/downloads/policy-database/MAURITIUS%29%20Industrial%20Waste%20Assessment%20-%20Opportunities%20for%20Industrial%20Symbiosis.pdf. Accessed on February 25, 2022.

Partnership For Action On Green Economy (PAGE). (2017). *Republic of Mauritius: Industrial waste assessment: Opportunities for industrial symbiosis* [online]. United Nations Industrial Development Organisation. Retrieved from https://govmu.org/EN/infoservices/business/Documents/FINALREPORT-INDUSTRIALWASTEASSESSMENT.PDF. Accessed on February 20, 2023.

Perdue, B. (2016). *Solid waste management in Santo Domingo, Dominican Republic* [online]. Retrieved from https://www.strausscenter.org/news/solid-waste-management-in-santo-domingo-dominican-republic/. Accessed on November 15, 2022.

Private Notice Question (PNQ). (2020). PNQ solid waste management strategy [online]. Retrieved from https://www.maurice-info.mu/wp-content/uploads/2020/07/PNQ-Solid-Waste-Management-Strategy.pdf. Accessed on February 02, 2022.

Procurement Policy Office. (2011). *Legal review for the implementation of sustainable public procurement in Mauritius* [online]. Retrieved from https://www.oneplanetnetwork.org/sites/default/files/legal_review_mauritius.pdf. Accessed on June 25, 2022.

Republic of Mauritius. (2020). The Climate Change Act 2020, Government Gazette of Mauritius No. 145 of 28 November 2020.

Republic of Mauritius, Seventh National Assembly. (2021). *Parliamentary debates, first session* [online]. Retrieved from https://www.maurice-info.mu/wp-content/uploads/2021/06/hansard-22-juin-2021.pdf. Accessed on February 20, 2023.

Republic of South Africa Department of Human Settlements. (2019). Section M: Solid waste management, the neighbourhood planning and design Guide [online]. Retrieved from https://www.hssonline.gov.za/docs/SECTION%20M_SOLID%20WASTE%20MANAGEMENT.pdf. Accessed on November 15, 2022.

Rosenthal, S., & Linder, N. (2021). Effects of bin proximity and informational prompts on recycling and contamination. *Resources, Conservation and Recycling, 168.* doi:10.1016/j.resconrec.2021.105430

Samoisy, L. (2015). Entre Rêve et Désillusion. 5-Plus Dimanche [online]. Retrieved from https://www.5plus.mu/node/899. Accessed on May 05, 2022.

Sarbassov, Y., Sagalova, T., Tursunov, O., Venetis, C., Xenarios, S., & Inglezakis, V. (2019). Survey on household solid waste sorting at source in developing economies: A case study of Nur-Sultan City in Kazakhstan. *Sustainability, 11,* 6496.

Singhirunnusorn, W., Donlakorn, K., & Kaewhanin, W. (2017). Household recycling behaviours and attitudes toward waste bank project: Mahasarakham Municipality. *Journal of Asian Behavioural Studies, 2,* 17.

Sotravic Ltd. (2020). Power generation [online]. Retrieved from https://www.sotravic.net/energy/power-generation.html. Accessed on January 10, 2020.

Sotravic Ltd. (n.d). Mare Chicose sanitary landfill [online]. Retrieved from https://globalmethane.org/documents/events_land_120910_24.pdf. Accessed on February 01, 2022.

Squires. (2006). *Public participation in solid waste management in Small Island Developing States* [online]. Retrieved from https://www.nswai.org/docs/PUBLIC%20PARTICIPATION%20IN%20SOLID%20WASTE%20MANAGEMENT%20IN%20SMALL%20ISLAND%20DEVELOPING%20STATES.pdf. Accessed on December 23, 2022.

Statistics Mauritius. (1998). Population and Vital Statistics, Republic of Mauritius – Year 1998 [online]. Retrieved from https://statsmauritius.govmu.org/Documents/Statistics/ESI/1999/EI0296/ESI_0296_0002.pdf. Accessed on February 20, 2023.

Statistics Mauritius. (1999). Population and Vital Statistics, Republic of Mauritius – Year 1999 [online]. Retrieved from https://statsmauritius.govmu.org/Documents/Statistics/ESI/2000/EI0318/ESI_0318_0003.pdf. Accessed on February 20, 2023.

Statistics Mauritius. (2000). Population and Vital Statistics, Republic of Mauritius – Year 2000 [online]. Retrieved from https://statsmauritius.govmu.org/Documents/Statistics/ESI/2001/EI0345/ESI%200345%20001.pdf. Accessed on February 20, 2023.

Statistics Mauritius. (2001). Population and Vital Statistics, Republic of Mauritius – Year 2001 [online]. Retrieved from https://statsmauritius.govmu.org/Documents/Statistics/ESI/2002/ EI0371/ESI%200371%20002.pdf. Accessed on February 20, 2023.

Statistics Mauritius. (2002). Population and Vital Statistics, Republic of Mauritius – Year 2002 [online]. Retrieved from https://statsmauritius.govmu.org/Documents/Statistics/ESI/2003/ EI0405/ESI%200405%200001.pdf. Accessed on February 20, 2023.

Statistics Mauritius. (2003). Population and Vital Statistics, Republic of Mauritius – Year 2003 [online]. Retrieved from https://statsmauritius.govmu.org/Documents/Statistics/ESI/2004/ EI0444/ESI%200444.pdf. Accessed on February 20, 2023.

Statistics Mauritius. (2004). Population and Vital Statistics Year 2004 [online]. Retrieved from https:// statsmauritius.govmu.org/Documents/Statistics/ESI/2005/EI0490/ESI%200490.pdf.   Accessed on February 20, 2023.

Statistics Mauritius. (2006). Population and Vital Statistics, Republic of Mauritius, Year 2006 [online]. Retrieved from https://statsmauritius.govmu.org/Documents/Statistics/ESI/2007/EI0617/vital. pdf. Accessed on February 20, 2023.

Statistics Mauritius. (2008). Population and Vital Statistics, Republic of Mauritius, Year 2008 [online]. Retrieved from https://statsmauritius.govmu.org/Documents/Statistics/ESI/2009/EI0748/Pop_ Vital_Yr08.pdf. Accessed on February 20, 2023.

Statistics Mauritius. (2010). Population and Vital Statistics Republic of Mauritius, Year 2010 [online]. Retrieved from https://statsmauritius.govmu.org/Documents/Statistics/ESI/2011/EI0880/vital. pdf. Accessed on February 20, 2023.

Statistics Mauritius. (2011). *Mauritius in figures* [online]. Republic of Mauritius, Ministry of Finance & Economic Development. Retrieved from https://wedocs.unep.org/rest/bitstreams/15664/ retrieve. Accessed on January 18, 2022.

Statistics Mauritius. (2012a). *Mauritius in figures* [online]. Republic of Mauritius, Ministry of Finance & Economic Development. Retrieved from https://statsmauritius.govmu.org/Documents/ Statistics/By_Subject/Other/MIF/MIF_Yr12.pdf. Accessed on January 20, 2022.

Statistics Mauritius. (2012b). Population and Vital Statistics Republic of Mauritius, Year 2012 [online]. Retrieved from https://statsmauritius.govmu.org/Documents/Statistics/ESI/2013/EI1018/ Amended%20FINAL%20_ESI%202012.pdf. Accessed on February 20, 2023.

Statistics Mauritius. (2013). Environment Statistics – 2013 [online]. Republic of Mauritius, Ministry of Finance, Economic Planning and Development. Retrieved from https://statsmauritius.govmu. org/Documents/Statistics/Digests/Environment/Digest_Env_Yr13.pdf. Accessed on February 20, 2023.

Statistics Mauritius. (2014). Population and Vital Statistics Republic of Mauritius, Year 2016 [online]. Retrieved from https://statsmauritius.govmu.org/Documents/Statistics/ESI/2015/EI1161/ population.pdf. Accessed on February 20, 2023.

Statistics Mauritius. (2015). Environment Statistics – 2015 [online]. Republic of Mauritius, Ministry of Finance, Economic Planning and Development. Retrieved from https://statsmauritius.govmu. org/Documents/Statistics/Digests/Environment/Digest_Env_Yr15.pdf. Accessed on February 20, 2023.

Statistics Mauritius. (2016). Population and Vital Statistics Republic of Mauritius, Year 2016 [online]. Retrieved from https://statsmauritius.govmu.org/Documents/Statistics/ESI/2017/EI1299/Pop_ and_Vital_Stats_2016.pdf. Accessed on February 20, 2023.

Statistics Mauritius. (2017). Environment Statistics – 2017 [online]. Republic of Mauritius, Ministry of Finance, Economic Planning and Development. Retrieved from https://statsmauritius.govmu. org/Documents/Statistics/Digests/Environment/Digest_Env_Yr17.pdf. Accessed on February 20, 2023.

Statistics Mauritius. (2018a). Environment Statistics – 2018 [online]. Republic of Mauritius, Ministry of Finance, Economic Planning and Development. Retrieved from https://statsmauritius. govmu.org/Documents/Statistics/Digests/Environment/Digest_Env_Yr18.pdf.   Accessed   on January 08, 2020.

Statistics Mauritius. (2018b). Population and Vital Statistics Republic of Mauritius, Year 2018[online]. Retrieved from https://statsmauritius.govmu.org/Documents/Statistics/ESI/2019/EI1436/Pop_ Vital_Yr18.pdf. Accessed on February 20, 2023.

Statistics Mauritius. (2020a). Environment Statistics – 2020 [online]. Retrieved from https://statsmauritius.govmu.org/Documents/Statistics/ESI/2021/EI1601/Env_Stats_Yr20_%20280721.pdf. Accessed on May 10, 2022.

Statistics Mauritius. (2020b). Population and Vital Statistics Republic of Mauritius, Year 2020 [online]. Retrieved from https://statsmauritius.govmu.org/Documents/Statistics/ESI/2021/EI1572/Pop_Vital_Yr20_150321.pdf. Accessed on June 24, 2022.

Statistics Mauritius. (2021a). Population and Vital Statistics Republic of Mauritius, Year 2021[online]. Retrieved from https://statsmauritius.govmu.org/Documents/Statistics/ESI/2022/EI1636/Pop_Vital_Yr21_110322.pdf. Accessed on June 20, 2022.

Statistics Mauritius. (2021b). Annual digest of statistics 2020 [online]. Retrieved from https://statsmauritius.govmu.org/Documents/Statistics/By_Subject/Other/MIF/MIF_Yr20_300821.xlsx. Accessed on June 12, 2022.

Statistics South Africa. (2018). *Environment in-depth analysis of the general household survey 2002–2016 report; Statistics South Africa: Pretoria, South Africa* (Vol. IX). ISBN 9780621460841

Stockert, A., & Bogner, F. (2020). Cognitive learning about waste management: How relevance and interest influence long-term knowledge. *Education Sciences, 10*, 102. doi:10.3390/educsci10040102

Tengur, S. (2020). Civic Amenity Centre. Association for the Protection of the Environment and Consumers [online]. Retrieved from http://apec.mu/2020/10/17/civic-amenity-centre/. Accessed on February 02, 2022.

The Coca-Cola Company. (2018). Progress against a world without waste [online]. Retrieved from https://www.coca-colacompany.com/news/progress-against-a-world-without-waste. Accessed on December 05, 2022.

The Local Government Act 2011. (2011). The Local Government Act 2011 Act 36/2011 Proclaimed by [Proclamation No. 23 of 2011] w.e.f 15th December 2011 [online]. Retrieved from http://brdc.mu/wp-content/uploads/2015/11/LGA-2015-Updated.pdf. Accessed on February 28, 2022.

The National Wage Consultative Council Act. (2021). Regulations made by the Minister under sections 8 and 23 of the National Wage Consultative Council Act. Government Notice No. 18 of 2021 [online]. Retrieved from https://labour.govmu.org/Documents/NWCC/18_NNW_Amendment.pdf. Accessed on August 10, 2022.

The Public-Private Partnership Act 2004. (2005, March 1). Act 37/2004 Proclaimed by [Proclamation No. 8 of 2005] w.e.f [online]. Retrieved from https://bot.govmu.org/Documents/The%20PPP%20Act%202004_03Nov2020.pdf. Accessed on June 23, 2022.

The World Bank Group. (2022a). The World Bank in Mauritius [online]. Retrieved from https://www.worldbank.org/en/country/mauritius/overview. Accessed on June 26, 2022.

The World Bank Group. (2022b). Urban population (% of total population) – Mauritius [online]. Retrieved from https://data.worldbank.org/indicator/SP.URB.TOTL.IN.ZS?locations=MU. Accessed on June 25, 2022.

Turcott Cervantes, D. E., López, M. A., Cuartas, H. M., & Lobo García de Cortázar, A. (2018). Using indicators as a tool to evaluate municipal solid waste management: A critical review. *Waste Management, 80*, 51–63. doi:10.1016/j.wasman.2018.08.046

Turcott Cervantes, D. E., Romero, E. O., Berriel, M. C. H., Martínez, A. L., Salas, M. C. M., & Lobo, A. Assessment of some governance aspects in waste management systems: A case study in Mexican Municipalities. *Journal of Cleaner Production, 278*. doi: 10.1016/j.jclepro.2020.123320

UN – United Nations. (1992). *Agenda 21, United Nations Conference on Environment & Development*. Rio de Janeiro, Brazil [online]. Retrieved from https://sustainabledevelopment.un.org/content/documents/Agenda21.pdf. Accessed on May 28, 2022.

UNDP. (2021). Harnessing the role of private sector in inclusive and sustainable waste management [online]. Retrieved from https://www.undp.org/policy-centre/istanbul/news/harnessing-role-private-sector-inclusive-and-sustainable-waste-management. Accessed on December 05, 2022.

UNDP Mauritius. (2022). *UNDP Mauritius: Annual report 2021 building forward better* [online]. Retrieved from https://www.undp.org/sites/g/files/zskgke326/files/2022-06/UNDP_Mauritius_Annual_Report_2021.pdf. Accessed on June 25, 2021.

UNEP. (2016). Green economy Fiscal policy analysis – Mauritius [online]. Retrieved from https://
www.greengrowthknowledge.org/sites/default/files/downloads/resource/Green%20Economy%
20Fiscal%20Policy%20Analysis_Mauritius.pdf. Accessed on February 20, 2023.

UNIDO. (2016). *Industrial waste assessment in the Republic of Mauritius – Opportunities for industrial symbiosis.* Inclusive and Sustainable Industrial Development. Working Paper Series WP 15 | 2016 [online]. Retrieved from https://www.un-page.org/files/public/mauritius_industrial_waste_assessment.pdf. Accessed on January 22, 2022.

United Nations Department of Economic and Social Affairs, Division for Sustainable Development (UN DESA). (2014). In: *Partnerships briefs for Small Island developing states: Water and sanitation, food security and waste management, UN conference on Small Island Developing States, 1-4 Septermber 2014, Apia, Samoa* [online]. UN DESA. Retrieved from https://sustainabledevelopment.un.org/content/documents/1369SIDS_BRIEFS_WaterAndSanitation.pdf. Accessed on January 22, 2020.

United Nations Environment Program (UNEP). (2019). *SIDS waste management Outlook* [online]. Retrieved from https://www.unenvironment.org/ietc/node/44. Accessed on January 15, 2022.

United Nations ESCAP. (2015). *Valuing waste, transforming Cities* [online]. Retrieved from https://www.unescap.org/sites/default/files/Full%20Report%20%20.pdf. Accessed on June 23, 2022.

United Nations Human Settlements Programme. (2010). *Solid waste management in the world's cities water and sanitation in the world's cities 2010.* UN-Habitat [online]. Retrieved from https://unhabitat.org/sites/default/files/2021/02/solid_waste_management_in_the_worlds_cities_water_and_sanitation_in_the_worlds_cities_2010.pdf. Accessed on May 5, 2022.

United Nations Human Settlements Programme. (2011). *Mauritius: Port Louis urban profile.* UN-Habitat [online]. Retrieved from https://mirror.unhabitat.org/pmss/getElectronicVersion.aspx?nr=3384&alt=1. Accessed on May 06, 2022.

United Nations Human Settlements Programme. (2012). *Mauritius: Black River urban profile.* UN-Habitat [online]. Retrieved from https://mirror.unhabitat.org/pmss/getElectronicVersion.asp?nr=3367&alt=1. Accessed on May 06, 2022.

United Nations Human Settlements Programme. (2019). How one man from the slums of Yaoundé turned waste into a business [online]. Retrieved from https://unhabitat.org/news/16-jul-2019/how-one-man-from-the-slums-of-yaounde-turned-waste-into-a-business.   Accessed   on November 15, 2022.

University of Leeds. (n.d). Wasteaware cities indicators [online]. Retrieved from http://wabi.wasteaware.org/. Accessed on June 24, 2022.

Wai Choon, C. (2021). *[Dossier] Maurice... Poubelle à ciel ouvert* [online]. Retrieved from https://lexpress.mu/article/387319/dossier-maurice-poubelle-ciel-ouvert. Accessed on August 11, 2022.

Wilson, D. C., Rodic, L., Cowing, M. J., Velis, C. A., Whiteman, A. D., Scheinberg, A., ... Oelz, B. (2015). 'Wasteaware' benchmark indicators for integrated sustainable waste management in cities. *Waste Management, 35,* 329–342. doi:10.1016/j.wasman.2014.10.006. Supplementary material. Retrieved from https://eprints.whiterose.ac.uk/85319/9/Wilson_et_al_Supplementary_information_Wasteaware_ISWM_Benchmark_Indicators_User_Manual_FINAL.pdf

Wilson, D. C., Velis, C. A., & Rodic, L. (2013). Integrated sustainable waste management in developing countries. *Proceedings of the ICE – Waste and Resource Management, 166,* 52–68. doi:10.1680/warm.12.00005

World Bank Group. (2019). Solid waste management [online]. Retrieved from https://www.worldbank.org/en/topic/urbandevelopment/brief/solid-waste-management. Accessed on January 09, 2022.

PART 3

SECTORAL STUDIES

DETERMINING THE NEXUS OF ENERGY EFFICIENCY AND SUSTAINABLE DEVELOPMENT IN NIGERIA: TIME SERIES ANALYSIS

Lukman Raimi, Lanre Ibrahim Ridwan and Rabiu Olowo

ABSTRACT

The study investigates the effects of energy resource efficiency on the triple themes of sustainable development (economic, social and environmental dimensions). We adopt a quantitative research method, and the required macroeconomic data were extracted from World Development Indicators for a period of 30 years (1991–2020). The extracted data were analysed using correlation analysis and linear regression. Ultimately, the estimations from the three models produced mixed results. Energy resource efficiency (EFF) exerts a significant positive effect on economic sustainability (ECS), a significant negative effect on social sustainability (SOS) and a significant negative effect on environmental sustainability (EVS). However, claims on government (COG) exerted an insignificant negative effect on ECS, an insignificant negative effect on SOS and a significant positive effect on environmental sustainability (EVS). In practical terms, the findings are consistent with previous empirical studies, and they also validate X-efficiency theory (XET) and resource curse theory (RCT). The study concludes with implications, limitations and further research directions.

Keywords: Energy efficiency; economic sustainability; social sustainability; environmental sustainability; resources; sustainable development; Nigeria

Achieving Net Zero
Developments in Corporate Governance and Responsibility, Volume 20, 153–176
Copyright © 2023 by Emerald Publishing Limited
All rights of reproduction in any form reserved
ISSN: 2043-0523/doi:10.1108/S2043-052320230000020007

INTRODUCTION

Energy in the form of fossil fuels and nuclear and hydroelectric power, among others, is indispensable for quality living. Additionally, energy efficiency through access to affordable and safe energy services is expedient across the globe to lift the bottom billions of people who constitute nearly one-third of humanity out of the energy poverty trap (Byrne & Taminiau, 2016). Furthermore, energy resources and their optimal utilisation have a direct relationship with sustainable development (SD) because energy is the life wire of the productive effectiveness and efficiency of industry, commerce, agriculture and the functionality of administrative offices in different sectors of the economy (Oyedepo, 2012). From the perspective of energy economics, energy efficiency has a high propensity to stimulate a development process that is environmentally, economically and socially sustainable (Ayres, Turton, & Casten, 2007; Raimi & Olowo, 2021). Most developed countries are known to have attained energy efficiency in consumption and production, but developing countries arguably still contend with energy inefficiency. Intergovernmental agencies, UN member governments and other critical stakeholders have made energy efficiency and depletion of energy resources front-burner issues because of the effect on biodiversity extinction, climate change forest destruction, global heating, population health and natural disasters (Ibrahim & Alola, 2020). At the firm level, the need to minimise the effect of energy consumption on housing/built environments and manufacturing plants where large amounts of energy are used is imperative (Ingrao, Messineo, Beltramo, Yigitcanlar, & Ioppolo, 2018). The volume of energy consumption/usage has a significant negative effect on the health of human beings and the natural environment (Forsberg & Von Malmborg, 2004; Ioppolo, Cucurachi, Salomone, Shi, & Yigitcanlar, 2019). The richer have higher energy consumption and access to cleaner energy options, and vice versa; hence, energy consumption per capita is an important indicator for measuring the standard of living of citizens (Kerimray, De Miglio, Rojas-Solórzano, & Ó Gallachóir, 2018; Oyedepo, 2012). Therefore, energy issues and SD overlap, and both are receiving growing attention in applied research, professional summits and policymaking circles in developed and developing countries because of their importance (Kaygusuz, 2012; Kok & Benli, 2017; Oparaocha & Dutta, 2011; Oyedepo, 2014). In particular, energy consumption is the cornerstone of SD because most energy policies across the globe have energy efficiency as their core objective, while other energy objectives merely complement and are reinforced (Ganda & Ngwakwe, 2014). In Africa and Southeast Asia, it has been reported that citizens face endemic poor access to clean energy as a result of the unreliable supply of energy products and services, including high disruption costs, which both negatively impact production efficiency and competitiveness (Emodi & Yusuf, 2015). Nigeria's case is a paradox because it is blessed with an abundance of energy resources of different types, yet citizens are neck-deep in widespread energy poverty that manifests in the forms of poor access to clean energy, unreliable supply of energy products and services and unstable energy supply to household and industrial users, leading to high disruption costs (Emodi, Emodi, Murthy, &

Emodi, 2017). Moreover, it has been reported that approximately 40% of the population has access to the grid electricity supply, but 70% of citizens in rural areas depend on firewood (Eleri, Ugwu, & Onuvae, 2012).

High dependence on firewood by marginalised groups in Nigeria poses serious livelihood hazards to homes and communities, as the smoke inhalation death of almost 79,000 Nigerians was reported in 2011 (Eleri & Onuvae, 2011). Additionally, the World Health Organization reported that the smoke-inhalation deaths caused by the use of firewood by women have increased to 98,000 (Emodi & Boo, 2015). For optimal and efficient energy resource development and utilisation, Emodi et al. (2017) prescribed to policymakers the use of the long-range energy alternative planning (LEAP) model for managing Nigeria's future energy demand, supply and associated GHG emissions from 2010 to 2040. The significance of energy for SD in the Nigerian economy has been clearly articulated in the National Energy Policy and the Renewable Energy Master Plan Final Draft (Energy Commission of Nigeria, 2003, 2005).

According to Raimi (2010) and Raimi and Olowo (2021), all critical sectors of the Nigerian economy require energy resources to different degrees. The telecommunication sector requires energy resources for the continuous functioning of the base stations and network interconnectivity of telecommunication facilities. The financial industry needs energy resources for the activation of ATM facilities, Visa Cards, Online banking, Money transfers, Automated Cheques clearing, Online Stock Trading, Forex trading, Financial Security monitoring and supervision. Without energy resources, transport and communication services cannot be effectively and efficiently provided. In the educational sector (e.g. primary schools, secondary schools, colleges of education, polytechnics, universities and research institutes), energy resources are required to keep educational infrastructure, amenities, sensitive teaching gadgets, audio-visual aids, equipment and ICT facilities running. In the manufacturing sector, energy resources such as gas, petrol, diesel, engine oil, lubricating oil, uranium, tar sand, biomass, etc. are required to facilitate the activation of large machines, plants and industrial installation for optimal capacity utilisation and production. In the informal sector of the economy dominated by small and cottage businesses owned by artisans, petty traders, mechanics, tailors, hairdressers, bricklayers, plumbers, etc., energy resources are required to operate their equipment and gadgets for maximum service delivery to customers.

For the health sector, 24 hours of energy resources are inevitable for the efficient operation of hospital laboratories, surgery theatres, pharmaceutical plants, sickbays and other hospital infrastructural facilities. Furthermore, the agricultural sector needs diverse energy sources to activate tractors, harvesters, agric processing equipment/plants, feed mills, poultry farms, animal rearing projects and irrigation stations. It is also necessary to enhance the wellbeing of farmers and other settlers in plantations and mechanised farming communities. In the defence sector of the economy, the military, police and other security agencies need stable, reliable, regular and adequate energy to run security installations. Gas, diesel, petrol and engine oil are required for the maintenance of armoured tanks, aircraft, surveillance helicopters, patrol vehicles, submarines, warships and for general the wellbeing of military officers.

At the household level, diverse energy and power sources are needed for good health, quality of life, self-esteem and longevity. These four benefits can only be achieved through a reliable, stable, effective and efficient supply of energy for the activation of fans, fridges, air conditioners, pressing iron, washing machines, cooking stoves, taps, radio, television, etc. At the international level, energy security, energy adequacy, energy stability, optimisation of energy potentials and energy sustainability are parameters for assessing the level of development in a country and good governance (Raimi, 2010).

There is a growing concern about the nexus of energy efficiency and sus-tainability across the globe, and the significance of the issue has encouraged multidisciplinary research efforts aimed at improving energy efficiency (Kluczek, 2019). The issue of energy efficiency is vital because it is believed that attaining energy efficiency has the potential to promote SD that can be measured in terms of environmental, social and wider macroeconomic benefits (Goodacre, Sharples, & Smith, 2002). Moreover, for decades, environmental economists, ecologists and greens have consistently called on governments and energy companies across the globe to reduce the consumption of fossil fuels and the output of so-called greenhouse gases (GHGs) because of their devastating effects on the planet and the people (Ayres et al., 2007). Additionally, Sorrell (2010) had long opined that the actualisation of higher levels of energy efficiency is predicated to enhancing the contribution of energy to productivity to economic growth; improved energy efficiency needs to be complemented by an ethic of sufficiency and radical reduction on carbon emissions globally. Therefore, the themes of sustainability are intricately tied to energy efficiency. Undoubtedly, energy efficiency is an important aspect of the sustainability debate and agenda (Hanley, McGregor, Swales, & Turner, 2009). The important question is as follows: Does energy efficiency through reduction of energy utilisation rebound or backfire effects on the triple themes of SD?

Based on the foregoing, this study empirically determines the effects of energy resource efficiency (EEF) on the triple themes of SD (economic, social and environmental dimensions) in the developing context of Nigeria. In specific terms, the study provides answers to three research questions (RQs): *RQ1*: What is the effect of EEF on economic sustainability (ECS)? *RQ2*: What is the effect of EEF on social sustainability? *RQ3*: What is the effect of EEF on environmental sustainability?

RESEARCH CONTEXT AND ECONOMIC SNAPSHOTS

Nigeria is a country with 36 states and a federal capital territory. It is an oil-dependent economy with a population of over 200 million citizens (Ibrahim & Olasinde, 2020; Kalu, 2020). It has a country area of 92,377 (1,000 ha), a land area of 91,077 (1,000 ha), an agricultural area of 68796.8521 (1,000 ha) and a forest area of 22280.1479 (1,000 ha), which places it in a vantage position to exploit different energy resources (FAO, 2021). Regarding economic growth indices, Nigeria, as of 2020, has a nominal GDP of $432.29 billion and GNI per capita of $5,000 (World Development Indicators database, 2021). Although Nigeria has humongous reserves of renewable energy resources, they are not well exploited and harnessed. Attention is more focussed on renewable electricity, which accounts for an insignificant fraction of the total public sector energy investments. Worse still, there is either no databank on renewable energy investments in Nigeria, or it is inaccessible (Akuru & Okoro, 2014). Even foreign exchange accruing to the nation from the sale of gas, coal, hydro, biomass and solar radiation has not been utilised for economic growth and development. Several scholars have warned and are still warning that oil-dependent public finance is unsustainable and could lead Nigeria into endemic rent dependency, underdevelopment and failed states (Adedoyin, 2019; Agu, 2011). At present, oil-dependent developing countries in Africa and the Middle East with weak wealth creation capacity are experiencing hard realities in their public finances, and the future looks very bleak in the face of dwindling oil revenues generated from rents effortlessly (Andersson & Djeflat, 2012; Raimi & Aljadani, 2020).

LITERATURE REVIEW

In this section, we review conceptual, policy-focussed, theoretical and empirical papers to identify gaps and derive richer insights into the problem being investigated.

Theoretical Framework

The key concepts that underpin this study are EEF and SD. The term energy efficiency within the purview of this study refers to a chain of integrated practices required to improve the use and management of the various energy sources for the purpose of reaching the same optimal results – or better outcomes in terms of lower energy consumption (Salvia & Schneider, 2019). There are three commonly used indicators for measuring energy efficiency, namely, monetary-based, thermodynamic-based and physical-based indicators (Zhang & Kim, 2014). Among the three indicators, monetary-based and physical-based indicators are the commonly used macrolevel measurements for energy research and writing energy policies (Ang & Choi, 2002; Zhang & Kim, 2014). Moreover, Zhang and Kim (2014) noted that other widely used indicators for evaluating energy efficiency and the level of CO_2 emissions include energy intensity (energy/GDP), carbon intensity (carbon/GDP) and the carbon factor (carbon/energy).

The term SD refers to a development strategy that addresses the socioeconomic and environmental needs of the present generation and, by design, would not endanger or compromise the needs of the upcoming generations (Adebakin & Raimi, 2012; Nagesha & Subrahmanya, 2006). A development process becomes sustainable when it integrates economic and social development with environmental protection (Mohammad, 2010). Every nation struggles to attain a sustainable energy system. A nation is described as having a sustainable energy system, when the unitisation process of the energy resources is cost-efficient, reliable, environmentally friendly and has the propensity to promote economic development, climate change mitigation, equitable access to energy by the populace, including job creation and generation of income (Oyedepo, 2012).

The current global agenda is to forge a link between EEF and three themes of SD (economic, social and environmental sustainability (EVS)). Economic sustainability refers to an integrated approach of safeguarding and sustaining human and material resources for creating long-term sustainable values through optimal use, recovery and recycling (University of Gävle, 2018b). Social sustainability, on the other hand, refers to the maintenance and improvement of the wellbeing of current and future generations through access to basic social services such as healthcare, education, transportation, housing and recreation, including security (Glasson & Wood, 2009; McKenzie, 2004; Michael & Peacock, 2011).

Environmental or ecological sustainability refers to the productive conservation of the waters, the soil and the ecosystem and the reduction of externalities impacting the natural environment and humanity (University of Gävle, 2018a). The negative effects of economic and social sustainability (SOS) lead to EVS threats that have been identified to include climate change, widespread deforestation, ocean acidification, biodiversity loss, habitat destruction and air pollution (Byrne & Taminiau, 2016). When the three aspects of SD aligned in the utilisation and management of energy resources, energy efficiency was achieved. There is no single index that comprehensively measures SD, but there is a consensus that it has social (SOC), economic (ECS) and environmental (EVS) dimensions (Bizikova & Denton, 2016). However, Kluczek (2019) proposed three energy efficiency measures using the triple themes of SD. He stated that EVS is measured by the level of energy intensity (total energy consumption and/or consumption of electricity energy) and GHG emissions. Economic sustainability is the total energy cost/production and net benefits (reduced energy cost over the expected life of new equipment). Social sustainability is measured by the full-time equivalent number of jobs created per unit of energy consumed and full-time equivalent jobs created yearly per unit of energy saved. Therefore, EEF can only be attained at the firm and national levels when energy resources are used in ways that are environmentally, economically and socially sustainable. To achieve a more enduring energy efficiency, Riti and Shu (2016) argue in favour of the transition from traditional fossil fuel consumption to renewable energy sources because an empirical investigation found that renewable energy consumption impacts environmental degradation due to high pollution emissions generated by fossil fuel consumption.

X-efficiency theory (XET) and resource curse theory (RCT) jointly provide a logical explanation for EFF in relation to SD (ECS, SOC and EVS). Leibenstein's theory of X-efficiency, which was postulated in 1966, states that X-efficiency is achieved in the economy when resources are optimally utilised such that a given set of inputs, when transformed, produce maximum outputs. In other words, the theory provides an explanation for the gap between ideal allocative efficiency and actually existing efficiency on the one hand and an attack on the fundamental economic assumption in microeconomics that firms minimise costs to attain allocative efficiency (Perelman, 2011).

To achieve X-efficiency in the economy, there is a need for efficient utilisation of factor inputs by economic agents in a manner that averts X-inefficiency, which means underutilisation of resources or less than full efficiency leads to the attainment of less than maximum output (Raimi & Olowo, 2021). Inefficient utilisation of economic resources is associated with eight (8) elements: (1) inefficient labour utilisation, (2) inefficient capital utilisation, (3) inefficient time sequence, (4) inefficient employee cooperation, (5) inefficient information flow, (6) inefficient bargaining effectiveness, (7) inefficient credit availability utilisation and (8) inefficient heuristic procedures (Leibenstein, 1979).

Several empirical studies have designed measures of inefficiency, leveraging Leibenstein's theory of X-efficiency (Button & Weyman-Jones, 1994). To strengthen XET, this research also adopts RCT to explain why governments of many resource-rich countries fail to productively and efficiently utilise their natural resource wealth to respond to public welfare needs and develop infrastructural facilities for citizens in most developing economies (Mukund, 2016; Tadjoeddin, 2007). The RCT also explains the rationale for the negative growth and development outcomes associated with oil-led development. Specifically, oil-rich nations manifest an inverse relationship between high levels of natural resource dependence and growth rates (Karl, 2007; Lashitew & Werker, 2020).

Empirical studies by Blomqvist (2010) found that there is a negative relationship between resource abundance and economic growth and a positive relationship between resource abundance and internal conflicts, leading to the phenomena of rentierism and Dutch disease (Blomqvist, 2010). Moreover, energy efficiency has been found to impact EVS in particular (Centobelli, Cerchione, & Esposito, 2018) and enhance progression towards SD (Forsberg & Von Malmborg, 2004).

The combination of XET and RST provides a stronger theory for explaining the cause–effect relationship between EFF and SD in Nigeria. Logically, it is presumed that a high level of X-efficiency without the manifestation of the resource curse phenomenon in the economy would significantly and positively impact the three dimensions of SD. Both theories find relevance in energy resource-abundant countries or nations with diverse energy resources.

Energy resources are classified as primary and secondary. Primary energy resources are those provided by nature, while secondary energy resources are those created from primary energy resources through industrial transformation and conversion (Smart Energy Education, 2016). The transformation process where inefficient energy resource utilisation and conversion occur is depicted in Fig. 1.

The plausible causes of energy resource inefficiency (subject to empirical verification) could be associated with any of the eight inefficient elements explicated by XET. These inefficiencies occur in the Nigerian energy sector during the transformation of primary energy resources into secondary energy resources and have been linked to energy production and gas flaring. From Table 1, Nigeria's

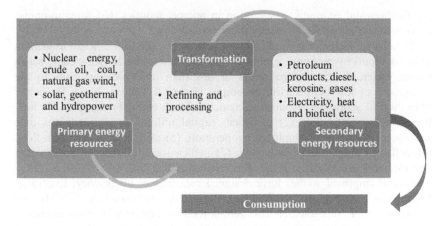

Fig. 1.   Energy Sources Transformation. *Source:* Author's configuration
adapter from Demirel (2016).

Table 1. Oil Production – Top 10 Flaring Countries (1000 Barrels per Day kb/d).

Category	2012	2013	2014	2015	2016	2017	2018	2019	2020
Russia	9,922	10,054	10,107	10,253	10,551	10,580	10,759	10847.00	9865.00
Iraq	2,983	3,054	3,368	4,045	4,444	4,454	4,613	4741.00	4102.00
Iran	3,387	3,113	3,239	3,293	4,151	4,469	4,255	2972.00	2666.00
USA	6,521	7,494	8,789	9,446	8,852	9,371	10,964	12248.00	11308.00
Algeria	1,532	1,462	1,420	1,429	1,348	1,306	1,259	1259.00	1122.00
Venezuela	2,500	2,500	2,500	2,489	2,254	1,995	1,486	877.00	527.00
Nigeria	2,457	2,307	2,347	2,171	1871	1,946	1,909	1946.00	1776.00
Mexico	2,593	2,562	2,469	2,302	2,187	1,981	1,852	1704.00	1710.00
China	4,074	4,164	4,208	4,278	3,983	3,821	3,787	3825.00	3889.00
Oman	919	940	943	981	1,004	970	979	972.00	949.00

Source: World Bank's Global Gas Flaring Tracker Data (2020).

energy production continued to fluctuate from 2012 (2,457 kb/d) to 2020 (1776
kb/d).

However, the gas flaring intensities among the top ten (10) flaring countries
are shown in Table 2. Ajugwo (2013) noted that oil companies in Nigeria flare
17.2 billion m^3 of natural gas annually during crude oil exploration in oil wells.
He further explained that gas flaring is a manifestation of energy inefficiency
because of the associated economic loss, social problems and environmental
degradation stemming from oil fields in local communities in Nigeria. From the
listed top gas flaring countries, Nigeria occupied the fifth position, and the volume of gas flaring continued to increase from 2012 to 2020. To mitigate huge
revenue and foreign exchange losses from gas flaring, Ibitoye (2014) explained
that several measures have been made at the policy circle to curtail gas flaring in

Table 2. Flaring Intensity – Top 10 Flaring Countries.

Category	2012	2013	2014	2015	2016	2017	2018	2019	2020
Russia	6.19	5.43	4.97	5.24	5.81	5.16	5.42	5.86	6.91
Iraq	11.62	11.91	11.40	10.98	10.93	10.98	10.58	10.38	11.61
Iran	8.96	9.76	10.33	10.06	10.83	10.83	11.13	12.59	13.63
USA	4.00	3.36	3.53	3.44	2.75	2.78	3.51	3.87	2.84
Algeria	13.59	15.35	16.78	17.50	18.49	18.47	19.61	20.33	22.73
Venezuela	8.93	10.14	10.91	10.23	11.25	9.55	15.17	29.81	44.50
Nigeria	7.24	13.09	12.46	10.30	9.98	9.77	10.12	10.32	11.05
Mexico	4.55	4.61	5.39	5.95	5.98	5.24	5.76	7.21	9.24
China	1.31	1.26	1.37	1.33	1.35	1.12	1.32	1.45	1.92
Oman	6.30	6.87	7.53	6.79	7.68	7.34	7.10	7.42	7.27

Source: World Bank's Global Gas Flaring Tracker Data (2020).

the country through the establishment of a liquified natural gas plant, the constriction of pipelines to transport gas to neighbouring countries and the promulgation of laws to regulate excesses of the oil and gas companies. Other measures directed at curtailing the unethical practice of gas flaring include enforcement of international protocols on carbon emissions, sanctioning of culpable multinational oil companies and optimal gas utilisation through energy liberalisation and public–private partnership (PPP) involvements (Raimi, Towobola, & Madueke, 2013).

Empirical Review

The new industrialisation agenda advocates that all countries strive to integrate energy efficiency, economic development SOS, and EVS (Ibrahim & Alola, 2020). To what extent has this new thinking impacted SD across the globe? A number of empirical studies have found that there is a positive relationship between energy consumption/production and economic growth in several contexts (Ibrahim & Alola, 2020; Kahia, Aïssa, & Charfeddine, 2016; Ozturk, 2010; Rashid & Kandemir, 2016). In the United States, Ayres et al. (2007) found that economic growth/GDP from 1900 through 1998 suggests that energy efficiency is economically beneficial because the net social benefit is higher than the costs. In Scotland, it was found that energy efficiency resulted in economic gain (as the ratio of GDP to CO_2 emissions falls) because it reduces energy prices, produces high output, stimulates energy demands and boosts incomes. However, the positive economic effects are insufficient to generate environmental improvements (Hanley et al., 2009).

Furthermore, a firm-level study found that there is a nexus between energy efficiency and ECS (financial investment decisions) in Romania. In particular, the payback period of investments in energy efficiency measures depends largely on two economic factors, namely, potential energy savings and the added value of buildings (Popescu, Bienert, Schützenhofer, & Boazu, 2012). Another firm-level study in the building environment found that using the right energy-saving technologies within a given budget helps achieve energy efficiency, which translates to optimisation of economic (financial) and environmental benefits (Tan, Yavuz, Otay, & Çamlıbel, 2016).

In Middle East and North African (MENA) countries, Ibrahim and Alola (2020) found that conventional energy and renewable energy produced different results. A conventional energy efficiency of 98% has a positive impact on ECS but has a negative impact on EVS because of externalities on environmental quality. Conventional energy and renewable energy produced different results. However, a renewable energy inefficiency of 69.5% was found to be caused by scale size inadequacy rather than operational deficiency. Overall, economic growth arising from energy prosperity was found to be detrimental to the region's EVS because the MENA region is one of the largest consumers of energy resources alongside Asia (El-Katiri, 2014).

Regarding energy efficiency and social and EVS, Goodacre et al. (2002) found that the net social benefit of attaining energy efficiency exceeds costs for discount rates by 14% when the relationships among fuel expenditure, energy and CO_2 emissions savings are correlated. Another study found that inefficient utilisation of energy resources has negatively impacted the environment. By 2030, to return the global environment to what it was in 1977, there is a need to have 100% energy efficiency and annual reductions (2 and 3%) in energy demand (Vance, Eason, & Cabezas, 2015). Moreover, the effect of energy efficiency on economic growth (GDP) and EVS (carbon emissions) in 15 developing countries indicated that high energy consumption leads to a high economic upswing and high ecological disorder. An indication of economic upswing through GDP growth leads to pollution of the environment due to high energy intensity and low energy efficiency (Zhang et al., 2020).

Summarising the multiple results, it is evident that energy efficiency has impacted ECS due to the positive impact on economic growth worldwide. However, the positive impact of energy efficiency is detrimental to social and EVS because externalities such as the emission of GHGs, nitrous oxide (N_2O), carbon dioxide (CO_2), methane (CH_4) and chlorofluorocarbons (CFCs) have inflicted serious harm on people and their socioeconomic wellness (Zhang et al., 2020).

METHODOLOGY

This study adopts a quantitative research method, which is a positivist research paradigm. The data used were extracted from World Development Indicators of the World Bank for a period of 30 years (1991–2020). Before the analysis, data cleaning procedures were carried out. First, data for missing years were computed by taking an average of the previous three years, assuming that there was no significant change for the computed year. Due to the large digits, logarithmic data transformation was carried out. The transformation is necessary to normalise datasets, mitigate the chances of producing errors, aid better prediction/generalisation of the dataset and improve the fit of the model (DEV Community, 2021; Soczewica, 2021). After the data cleaning procedures, the data were analysed using correlation analysis, linear regression and path analysis. We used correlation analysis prior to regression analysis to establish the extent of dependability among the macroeconomic data used in a quantitative study with big data (Pandey, Dhoundiyal, & Kumar, 2015). Furthermore, we used regression analysis to test the causality or functional relationship in our specified model among dependent variables and predictors (Fumo & Biswas, 2015). Linear regression analysis is necessary because a correlation test is only useful for determining the strength and direction of the linear relationship between two or more continuous variables (Frost, 2021). To determine the effects of EFF on the triple dimensions of SD (ECS, SOS, EVS), the following models were used:

Model specifications:

$$\text{Model 1: } ECS_t = \sigma_1 + \sigma_2 EFF + \sigma_3 COG + \xi_t$$

$$\text{Model 2: } SOC_t = \sigma_1 + \sigma_2 EFF + \sigma_3 COG + \xi_t$$

$$\text{Model 3: } EVS_t = \sigma_1 + \sigma_2 EFF + \sigma_3 COG + \xi_t$$

where

EFF = Energy resource efficiency,
ECS = Economic sustainability,
SOS = Social sustainability,
Environmental sustainability,
Claim on Central Government (COG) and
ξ = Error term.

The subscript t denotes the time period covered by the analyses in this study (1991–2020). Furthermore, $\sigma_1, \sigma_2, \sigma_3$ are the parameters being estimated. Given the above exposited empirical model, the various a priori expectations are stated. First, empirical evidence advancing the nexus between EEF and ECS has revealed the existence of positive impacts of the former on the latter. Following these arguments, we expect EEF to exert a positive sign on ECS $\sigma_1 = \frac{\delta ECS}{\delta EEF} > 0$. Second, since EEF implies the utilisation of fewer energy resources for the optimisation of similar or better outcomes, it is expected that social benefits should outweigh the costs. In this way, EEF enhances SOS. Hence, EEF is hypothesised to exert a positive effect on SCO.

A-priori expectation: $0 < \beta 1-3 < 1 \ \sigma_1 = \frac{\delta SOC}{\delta EEF} > 0$. Lower energy consumption that does not reduce the number of outputs is analogously expected to lessen the level of carbon emitted into the atmosphere. By implication, EEF serves as a positive predictor of EVS such that $\sigma_1 = \frac{\delta EVS}{\delta EEF} > 0$. All things being equal, we expect a positive nexus between claims on the central government (COG) and the three dimensions of sustainability since the government is responsible for pursuing green agenda major planners and executors of economic agendas. Hence, $\sigma_2 = \frac{\delta ECS}{\delta CPG} > 0, \frac{\delta SOC}{\delta COG} > 0, \frac{\delta EVS}{\delta COG} > 0$

From the above model supported by the insights from the reviewed literature, it could be hypothesised as follows:

H1. Energy resource efficiency has a significant positive effect on economic sustainability in Nigeria.

H2. Energy resource efficiency has a significant positive effect on social sustainability in Nigeria.

H3. Energy resource efficiency has a significant positive effect on environmental sustainability in Nigeria.

RESULTS AND DISCUSSIONS

Descriptive Statistics

The descriptive statistics of the indicators employed in this study are presented in Table 3. Among the components of sustainability indicated in the table, EVS is the only one with a negative sign, which denotes the deteriorating state of the environment due to the effects of global warming. The positive sign of energy efficiency suggests that the indicator has the potential to drive sustainability across the three indicators of sustainability.

Inferential Analysis/Test of Hypotheses

This section examines the plausibility of a nexus between EEF and SD in Nigeria. Three hypotheses were formulated and empirically tested using (1) Pearson's partial correlation at a significance level of 0.05, (2) linear regression at a significance level of 0.05 and (3) path analysis. The estimates from the correlation analysis with explanations are presented in Table 4.

Correlation Analysis

From Table 4, there are three correlation estimates. The first correlation estimate shows that there is a significant positive relationship between EFF and ECS,

Table 3. Description of the Variables.

	N	Mean	Median	SD	Minimum	Maximum	Shapiro–Wilk	
							W	p
LOG (EEF)	31	0.893	0.881	0.1129	0.750	1.020	0.792	<0.001
LOG (ECS)	31	1.161	1.219	0.1905	0.682	1.502	0.945	0.113
LOG (SOS)	31	1.665	1.679	0.0780	1.436	1.773	0.929	0.042
LOG (EVS)	31	−1.170	−1.036	0.3698	−2.065	−0.598	0.903	0.008
LOG (COG)	31	0.347	0.432	0.5453	−1.595	1.212	0.884	0.003

Source: Author's computation (2021).

Table 4. Partial Correlation.

		EEF	ECS	SOS	EVS
EEF	Pearson's *r*	—			
	p Value	—			
	N	—			
ECS	Pearson's *r*	0.58	—		
	p Value	*< 0.001*	—		
	N	31	—		
SOS	Pearson's *r*	−0.799	−0.663	—	
	p Value	<0.001	<0.001	—	
	N	31	31	—	
EVS	Pearson's *r*	−0.516	−0.398	0.244	—
	p Value	0.003	0.029	0.195	—
	N	31	31	31	—

Source: Author's computation (2021).
Note: controlling for COG, $*p < 0.05$, $**p < 0.01$, $***p < 0.001$.

based on $r = 0.58$ and $p < 0.05$. The second correlation estimate shows that there is a significant negative relationship between EFF and SOS, with a strength of $r = −0.799$ and $p < 0.05$. The third correlation estimate shows that there is a significant negative relationship between EFF and EVS, $r = −0.516$, $p < 0.05$. All estimates were controlled by COG. After the partial correlation analysis, the next step is to carry out a linear regression to determine the effects of EFF on the triple dimensions of SD (ECS, SOS and EVS).

Linear Regression Analysis
Three models were analysed and reported in this section.
    Model 1:

$$ECS_t = \sigma_1 + \sigma_2 EFF + \sigma_3 COG + \xi_t$$

In Table 5, the linear regression estimations in Model 1 ($R^2 = 0.58$, *Adj. R^2* = 0.337, $F_{(2,28)} = 7.1$, $p < 0.05$; ECS: $\beta_1 = 0.9884$, and COG: $\beta_2 = −0.0331$)

Table 5. Model Fit Measures and Model Coefficient – LOG ECS.

Model	*R*	*R²*	Adjusted *R²*	*F*	df1	df2
1	**0.58**	**0.337**	**0.289**	**7.1**	**2**	28
Predictor	Estimate	SE	*t*	*p*	Stand. Estimate	
Intercept	0.2899	0.2342	1.238	0.226		
LOG (EEF)	0.9884	0.2624	3.767	<0.001	0.5857	
LOG (COG)	−0.0331	0.0543	−0.610	0.547	−0.0948	

Source: Author's computation (2021).

suggest that EFF exerted a significant positive effect on ECS. The economic intuition derived from this nexus is that a percentage increase in EEF leads to a significant increase in ECS. In addition, the result suggests that the roadmap to ECS is achieved by adopting a pattern of energy consumption that is efficient. In contrast, claims on government (COG) exerted an insignificant negative effect on ECS. The growing COG by all levels of government have made EEF in Nigeria economically unsustainable. This finding is consistent with several studies, such as Ayres et al. (2007), Hanley et al. (2009), Ibrahim and Alola (2020) and Zhang et al. (2020), that suggest that energy efficiency is economically beneficial because it impacts the economic growth of oil-rich countries when measured in terms of GDP growth.

Model 2:

$$SOC_t = \sigma_1 + \sigma_2 EFF + \sigma_3 COG + \xi_t$$

In Table 6, the linear regression estimations in Model 2 ($R^2 = 0.662$, *Adj.* $R^2 = 0.638$, $F(2,28) = 27.5$, $p < 0.05$; SOS: $\beta_1 = -0.5387$; COG: $\beta_2 = -0.0211$) suggest that EFF exerted a significant negative effect on SOS. Additionally, COG exerted an insignificant negative effect on SOS. The growing COG by all levels of government partially impact SOS because a large portion of the claims are being used to redress growing social problems in Nigeria. The finding is not consistent with the empirical analysis of Goodacre et al. (2002), which found that the net social benefit of attaining energy efficiency exceeds costs when the relationships among fuel expenditure, energy and CO_2 emissions savings are correlated.

Model 3:

$$EVS = \alpha + \beta_1 EFF + \beta_2 COG + \varepsilon$$

In Table 7, the linear regression estimations in Model 3 ($R^2 = 0.442$, *Adj.* $R^2 = 0.402$, $F(2,28) = 11.1$, $p < 0.05$; EVS: $\beta_1 = -1.4909$, and COG: $\beta_2 = 0.3743$) suggest that EFF exerted a significant negative effect on EVS. However, COG exerted a significant positive effect on environmental social sustainability (EVS). The growing COG by all levels of government impact EVS because a large portion of the claims are being used to redress environmental problems. The above finding aligns with previous empirical studies, such as Hanley et al. (2009),

Table 6. Model Fit Measures and Model Coefficient – LOG SOC.

Model 2	R	R^2	Adjusted R^2	F	df1	df2
1	0.814	0.662	0.638	**27.5**	**2**	28
Predictor	Estimate	SE	t	p	Stand. Estimate	
Intercept	2.1532	0.0684	31.48	0.226		
LOG (EEF)	−0.5387	0.0766	−7.03	<0.001	0.5857	
LOG (COG)	−0.0211	0.0159	−1.33	<0.001	0.194	

Source: Authors' computation (2021).

Table 7. Model Fit Measures and Model Coefficient – LOG EVS.

Model 3	R	R^2	Adjusted R^2	F	df1	df2
1	0.664	0.442	0.402	11.1	2	28
Predictor	Estimate	SE	t	p	Stand. Estimate	
Intercept	0.0317	0.4172	10.0759	0.940		
LOG (EEF)	−1.4909	0.4673	−3.1904	0.003	−0.455	
LOG (COG)	0.3743	0.0967	3.8703	<0.001	0.552	

Source: Authors' computation (2021).

Vance et al. (2015) and Zhang et al. (2020), who found that the positive economic effects of enemy efficiency negatively impacted the environment.

Path Analysis
The path analysis was analysed to provide more explanation on the direct and indirect effects of EFF and COG (predictors) on ECS, SOS and EVS (dependent variables) in the test models. The path analysis diagram depicts the parameter estimates, covariance and path coefficients. Table 8 estimates suggest five results:

   i. Energy resource efficiency (EFF) exerted a significant positive effect on economic sustainability (ECS);
  ii. Claims on government (COG) exerted an insignificant negative effect on ECS;
 iii. EFF exerted a significant negative effect on social sustainability (SOS);
  iv. COG exerted an insignificant negative effect on SOS;
   v. EFF exerted a significant negative effect on EVS and
  vi. COG exerted a significant positive effect on EVS.

Table 8. Parameter Estimates of the Path Analysis.

Dependent	Predictor	Estimate	SE	β	p
LOG (ECS)	LOG (EEF)	0.9884	0.2493	0.5857	<0.001
LOG (ECS)	LOG (COG)	−0.0331	0.0516	−0.0948	0.521
LOG (SOS)	LOG (EEF)	−0.5387	0.0728	−0.7799	<0.001
LOG (SOS)	LOG (COG)	−0.0211	0.0151	−0.1476	0.161
LOG (EVS)	LOG (EEF)	−1.4909	0.4441	−0.455	<0.001
LOG (EVS)	LOG (COG)	0.3743	0.0919	0.552	<0.001

Source: Authors' computation (2021).

CONCLUSION AND OUTLOOK

The study set out to determine the effects of EFF on the triple dimensions of SD (ECS, SOS, EVS) with COG as a control variable. Ultimately, it was found that EFF exerted a significant positive effect on ECS, a significant negative effect on SOS, and a significant negative effect on EVS. In addition, COG exerted an insignificant negative effect on ECS, an insignificant negative effect on SOS and a significant positive effect on environmental social sustainability (EVS).

Policy, Managerial and Theoretical Implications

The policy/managerial implications of the present research are that policymakers and managers of Nigeria's energy sector need to explore optimal and efficient energy resource utilisation in a manner that is environmentally, economically and socially sustainable. In particular, a nation can be described as energy efficient when it is able to meet future energy demand and supply in a way that reduces associated GHG emissions and promotes sustainable climate change lifestyles. From a theoretical standpoint, the research validates XET and RCT, which provide a further logical explanation for why resource-rich countries failed to effectively, productively and efficiently utilise their natural resource wealth to respond to public welfare needs, develop infrastructural facilities and achieve SD. Inefficient utilisation of economic resources is associated with eight (8) elements, namely, (1) inefficiency in labour utilisation, (2) inefficiency capital utilisation, (3) inefficiency time sequence, (4) inefficiency in the extent of employee cooperation, (5) inefficiency in information flow, (6) inefficiency in bargaining effectiveness, (7) inefficiency in credit availability utilisation and (8) inefficiency in heuristic procedures. Logically, a high level of X-efficiency without the resource curse phenomenon in the economy would significantly and positively impact the three dimensions of SD.

Implications for Enterprise Development

The first policy implication is that if energy resources are effectively and efficiently exploited and managed in Nigeria's energy sector, there would be sustainable stability, reliability, safety and security in the supply of diversified energy products to all sectors of the economy. This exploitation would increase the gross domestic product (GDP) and boost citizens' welfare and livelihood.

Second, EEF that aligns with the three themes of SD (economic, social and environmental) would attract foreign direct investments (FDIs) into the energy sector industries with substantial participation by local, regional and foreign investors. The multiplier effect of FDI injections would lead to increased employment opportunities for citizens, poverty reduction, better international trade, economic cooperation on energy resources and, more importantly, the acquisition and diffusion of new energy technologies and managerial expertise for improved productivity in the energy sector.

Third, EEF, which stimulates economic growth and SD, has the propensity to reduce the endemic rent-seeking mentality, poverty and excessive claims from the government.

Another implication of EEF in relation to SD is the propensity to create a reliable, secure, safe eco-friendly energy sector that would directly lead to good health and wellbeing for citizens (SDG 3), encourage responsible production and consumption of energy resources (SDG 12), careful management of energy resources to safeguard life below water and life on land (SDG 14 and 15), embed peace, justice and strong institutions through transparency and corrupt-free management of energy resources (SDG 16) and indirectly support SDG 1 (no poverty), SDG 2 (Zero Hunger), SDG 3 (Good Health and Wellbeing), SDG 4 (Quality Education), SDG 5 (Gender Equality) and SDG 17 (Partnerships for the Goals).

Long-Term Implications and Prognoses for the Future

In view of the fact that the nexus of energy efficiency and SD has far-reaching effects beyond Nigeria, the following implications need to be considered as prognoses in the shift towards a sustainable energy future at regional and global levels.

First, to achieve a nexus of energy efficiency and SD in Nigeria, there is a need for commitment to the Net Zero target. At present, Nigeria has made a policy commitment to end flaring and CO_2 emissions by limiting warming to 1.5°C, as recommended by the international community. This is an indication that the country is progressing towards 1.5°C, but massive support is needed from international energy agencies to forestall failure to meet set targets on domestic full decarbonisation (Climate Action Tracker, 2022).

Second, commitment to sustainable energy for the SE4ALL initiative is equally key in achieving the anticipated nexus. Nigeria is a signatory sustainable development goal (SDG) as well as SE4ALL. Both agendas promote universal access to clean, reliable, sustainable and affordable energy by 2030, including the overarching climate goal of limiting the global temperature increase to below 2°C (Dioha & Emodi, 2018; Rogelj, McCollum, & Riahi, 2013). Particularly, Nigeria must enforce SDG 12 (responsible production and consumption), which suggests that the utilisation of Earth's resources for production and consumption should be carried out in a manner that would not aggravate climate change impacts. SDG 13 (climate action) underscores the need for nations to vigorously pursue all climate protocols, including limiting warming to 1.5°C (Raimi, Che, & Mutiu, 2021).

Third, strong regulatory agencies and institutions are required to achieve a nexus of energy efficiency and SD. At present, Nigeria has several energy regulatory agencies with complementary roles and functions, namely, the National Council on Climate Change ('the Council'), Federal Ministry of Environment (FME), Department of Climate Change, Inter-Ministerial Committee on Climate Change (ICCC) and National Council on Environment. Unfortunately, the government ministries and regulatory agencies in charge of climate change action are poorly coordinated; they have weak institutional capacities, as they depend on external consultants for most tasks, and worse, they still face capital and resource constraints (Climate Action Tracker, 2022). The weaknesses of regulatory agencies and institutions need to be redressed.

Fourth, an effective legal and regulatory regime can better drive the agenda of a nexus of energy efficiency and SD. Currently, Nigeria has an adequate legal regime, as evident from the following laws and national legislations.

- Petroleum Drilling and Production Act (PDPA), 1969: This law obligates oil and gas companies to submit 5-year plans for the utilisation of natural oil after the commencement of oil exploration and operations.
- Associated Gas Re-Injection Act (AGRA), 1979: The ineffectiveness and poor compliance with the PDPA led to the promulgation of AGRA. The new legal instrument in support of climate change compels oil and gas companies in Nigeria to submit a plan of action for gas reinjection and viable use of gas resources being flared in oil fields.
- Associated Gas Re-Injection (Amendment) Act 2004: In 2004, it was amended as AGRA 1979. It was an enriched version of the previous legislation.
- Flare Gas (Prevention of Waste and Pollution) Regulation, 2018: The legislation is enacted to consciously reduce the environmental and social impacts of flaring of methane and natural gas in Nigeria.
- Petroleum Industry Bill (PIB), 2021: The new legislation seeks to reform the oil and gas sector, attract investment in the sector, ensure better transparency, develop infrastructure and comply with the Paris Agreement temperature limit and promote net zero emissions in 2050.
- Flare Gas (Prevention of Waste and Pollution) Regulations, 2018: This important law provides the legal foundation the Nigerian Gas Flare Commercialisation Programme. It also imposed a new payment regime for gas flaring on gas companies based on the polluter pays principle and mandated data reporting on producers.
- National Building Energy Efficiency Code or BEEC, 2017: The BEEC sets minimum national energy efficiency standards for new buildings in the country.
- Nigeria's Climate Change Act (2021): The Act provides a detailed and sound framework for achieving low GHG emissions and mainstreams climate change actions into consistent national plans and programmes. To make the Act actionable, the National Council on Climate Change (NCCC) was established and empowered to make policies and decisions on all matters relating to climate change in Nigeria in collaboration with the Federal Inland Revenue Service (FIRS) to develop a mechanism for carbon tax and emissions trading to serve as a sustainable funding source fund for climate change, including developing a proposal for the enactment of the Climate Change Fund (the Fund) Act in Nigeria.
- International protocols and agreement: Nigeria is a signatory to the United Nations Framework Convention on Climate Change (UNFCCC), the Kyoto

Protocol and Paris Agreement) and the UN Climate Change Conference (COP26), among others (Mohammed, 2020).

Fifth, policymakers require solid plans and strategies to achieve a nexus of energy efficiency and SD. Some of the strategic vision of Nigeria include: the 2021 Energy Transition Plan that provides a clear roadmap to achieve net zero target; 2050 Long-Term Vision (LTV) for Nigeria (2021) aims to reduce the current level of emissions by 50% by 2050 and ensure all sectors of the economy adopt net-zero emissions; Revised 2021 National Climate Change Policy (NCCP) and the National Climate Change Programmes for Nigeria; the Medium Term National Development Plan (2021–2025) that prioritises the implementation of the Climate Change Act for developing decarbonisation pathways in the country; the National Action Plan on Gender and Climate Change for Nigeria (2020) that mainstreams gender inclusion and recognition in national climate change initiatives, programmes and policies; the 2020 Economic Sustainability Plan (ESP); the Economic Recovery and Growth Plan (2017–2020) promotes sustainable economic development through multiple climate-related projects; the 2015 National Integrated Infrastructure Master Plan (NIIMP) serves as a blueprint for infrastructure development and investment in climate-friendly projects for the period 2014–2043; and the 2012 National Climate Change Policy Response and Strategy provides guidance and policy direction on climate change mitigation and adaptation measures on climate-related R&D, institutional capacity development, sensitisation and public awareness among others (Climate Action Tracker, 2022; Department of Climate Change, 2021a).

Finally, innovation adoption and diffusion are key imperatives for the nexus of energy efficiency and SD. Nigeria's Department of Climate Change (2021b) noted that the country's vision by 2050 is to become a low-carbon, climate-resilient, high-growth circular economy through the deliberate reduction of the current level of emissions by 50% by using four types of innovation: social innovation, economic innovation, technological innovation and environmental innovation (Department of Climate Change, 2021b). Social innovation entails the pursuance of social change by reinventing institutional factors that inhibit progression towards a low-carbon economy. Economic innovation entails diversifying the economy and adopting a new paradigm that balances economic growth and EVS by rejecting a trade-off of both goals. Technological innovation focuses on the adoption and utilisation of green devices and eco-friendly technologies such as the internet of things (IoT), smart home devices, climate smart agriculture, energy smart and water-smart technologies to mitigate climate change and control carbon emissions. Environmental innovation seeks to change the way of doing things in a manner that promotes environmental integrity. It extends to the use of novelty in science, technology, manufacturing processes and agriculture in a way that enhances positive social and environmental outcomes while avoiding environmental risks and externalities (Department of Climate Change, 2021b).

Limitations and Further Research Direction

The current study is unique because it empirically determines the nexus between EFF and SD in an oil-dependent economy in Nigeria. We used a combination of correlation analysis, linear regression analysis, and path analysis in time-series data for a single country. However, future research should consider using panel data to determine the nexus between EEF among African countries.

REFERENCES

Adebakin, M. A., & Raimi, L. (2012). National security challenges and sustainable economic development: Evidence from Nigeria. *Journal of Studies in Social Sciences, 1*(1), 1–30.

Adedoyin, F. (2019). *Government bailout of distressed states in Nigeria: An analysis of the 2015 fiscal crisis.* Working Paper, 1–33. Retrieved from https://papers.ssrn.com/sol3/papers.cfm?abstract_id=3342552

Agu, C. (2011). Fragile states! Why subnational governments in Nigeria cannot subsist on internally generated revenue? *IUP Journal of Public Finance, 9*(1), 25–53.

Ajugwo, A. O. (2013). Negative effects of gas flaring: The Nigerian experience. *Journal of Environment Pollution and Human Health, 1*(1), 6–8.

Akuru, U. B., & Okoro, O. I. (2014). Renewable energy investment in Nigeria: A review of the Renewable Energy Master Plan. *Journal of Energy in Southern Africa, 25*(3), 62–67.

Andersson, T., & Djeflat, A. (Eds.). (2012). *The real issues of the Middle East and the Arab Spring: Addressing research, innovation and entrepreneurship.* Springer Science & Business Media.

Ang, B. W., & Choi, K. (2002). Boundary problem in carbon emission decomposition. *Energy Policy, 30*, 1201–1205.

Ayres, R. U., Turton, H., & Casten, T. (2007). Energy efficiency, sustainability and economic growth. *Energy, 32*(5), 634–648.

Bizikova, L., & Denton, P. (2016). How should we measure sustainable development? *Huffpost.* Retrieved from https://www.huffingtonpost.ca/development-unplugged/sustainable-development-goals_b_9829340.html

Blomqvist, H. C. (2010). Brunei Darussalam: Resource curse and economic development. In *Globalisation and development: Country experiences.* New York, NY: Nova Science Publisher.

Button, K. J., & Weyman-Jones, T. G. (1994). X-efficiency and technical efficiency. *Public Choice, 80*(1–2), 83–104.

Byrne, J., & Taminiau, J. (2016). A review of sustainable energy utility and energy service utility concepts and applications: Realising ecological and social sustainability with a community utility. *Wiley Interdisciplinary Reviews: Energy & Environment, 5*(2), 136–154.

Centobelli, P., Cerchione, R., & Esposito, E. (2018). Environmental sustainability and energy-efficient supply chain management: A review of research trends and proposed guidelines. *Energies, 11*(2), 275.

Climate Action Tracker. (2022). *Climate Governance Assessment of the government's ability and readiness to transform Nigeria into a zero emissions society.* Retrieved from https://climateactiontracker.org/documents/1014/2022_02_CAT_Governance_Report_Nigeria.pdf

Climate Change Act. (2021). Law of Federal Republic of Nigeria, Abuja. Retrieved from http://extwprlegs1.fao.org/docs/pdf/NIG208055.pdf

Demirel, Y. (2016). Energy sources, *Energy. Green energy and technology.* Cham: Springer. doi:10.1007/978-3-319-29650-0_2

Department of Climate Change. (2021a). 2050 Long-Term Vision for Nigeria (LTV-2050), Federal Ministry of Environment, Nigeria. Retrieved from https://unfccc.int/sites/default/files/resource/Nigeria_LTS1.pdf

Department of Climate Change. (2021b). National climate change policy for Nigeria (2021–2030). Retrieved from https://climatechange.gov.ng/wpcontent/uploads/2021/08/NCCP_NIGERIA_REVISED_2-JUNE-2021.pd

DEV Community. (2021). Logarithmic transformation in linear regression models: Why & when. Retrieved from https://dev.to/rokaandy/logarithmic-transformation-in-linear-regression-models-why-when-3a7c

Dioha, M. O., & Emodi, N. V. (2018). *Energy-climate dilemma in Nigeria: Options for the future* (Vol. 2, pp. 29–32). Abuja: IAEE Energy Forum.

El-Katiri, L. (2014). *A roadmap for renewable energy in the Middle East and North Africa*. Oxford institute for energy studies. OIES Working Paper No. MEP 6. Retrieved from https://www.arabdevelopmentportal.com/sites/default/files/publication/286.a_roadmap_for_renewable_energy_in_the_middle_east_and_north_africa.pdf

Eleri, E. O., & Onuvae, P. (2011). *Low-carbon Africa: Leapfrogging to green future: Low carbon Nigeria*. Retrieved from www.christainaid.org.uk/resources/policy/climate/low-carbon-africa.aspx

Eleri, E. O., Ugwu, O., & Onuvae, P. (2012). *Expanding access to pro-poor energy services in Nigeria*. Retrieved from https://www.osti.gov/etdeweb/servlets/purl/1057727

Emodi, N. V., & Boo, K. J. (2015). Sustainable energy development in Nigeria: Overcoming energy poverty. *International Journal of Energy Economics and Policy, 5*(2), 580–597.

Emodi, N. V., Emodi, C. C., Murthy, G. P., & Emodi, A. S. A. (2017). Energy policy for low carbon development in Nigeria: A LEAP model application. *Renewable and Sustainable Energy Reviews, 68*, 247–261.

Emodi, N. V., & Yusuf, S. D. (2015). Improving electricity access in Nigeria: Obstacles and the way forward. *International Journal of Energy Economics and Policy, 5*(1), 335–351.

Energy Commission of Nigeria. (2003). *National Energy Policy*. Abuja: LFN.

Energy Commission of Nigeria. (2005). *Renewable Energy Master Plan (Final Draft)*. ECN-UNDP. Retrieved from http://www.ecowrex.org/system/files/repository/2005_re_master_plan_-_min_power.pdf

FAO. (2021). Nigeria. Retrieved from http://www.fao.org/countryprofiles/index/en/?iso3=NGA

Forsberg, A., & Von Malmborg, F. (2004). Tools for environmental assessment of the built environment. *Building and Environment, 39*(2), 223–228.

Frost, J. (2021). Interpreting correlation coefficients. *Making Statistics Intuitive*. Retrieved from https://statisticsbyjim.com/basics/correlations/

Fumo, N., & Biswas, M. R. (2015). Regression analysis for prediction of residential energy consumption. *Renewable and Sustainable Energy Reviews, 47*, 332–343.

Ganda, F., & Ngwakwe, C. C. (2014). Role of energy efficiency on sustainable development. *Environmental Economics, 5*(1), 86–99.

Glasson, J., & Wood, G. (2009). Urban regeneration and impact assessment for social sustainability. *Impact Assessment and Project Appraisal, 27*(4), 283–290.

Goodacre, C., Sharples, S., & Smith, P. (2002). Integrating energy efficiency with the social agenda in sustainability. *Energy and Buildings, 34*(1), 53–61.

Hanley, N., McGregor, P. G., Swales, J. K., & Turner, K. (2009). Do increases in energy efficiency improve environmental quality and sustainability? *Ecological Economics, 68*(3), 692–709.

Ibitoye, F. I. (2014). Ending natural gas flaring in Nigeria's oil fields. *Journal of Sustainable Development, 7*(3), 13–22.

Ibrahim, M. D., & Alola, A. A. (2020). Integrated analysis of energy-economic development-environmental sustainability nexus: Case study of MENA countries. *Science of the Total Environment, 737*, 139768.

Ibrahim, O. R., & Olasinde, Y. T. (2020). Coronavirus disease (COVID-19) in Nigeria: Mitigating the global pandemic. *Journal of Clinical Medicine of Kazakhstan, 1*(55), 36–38.

Ingrao, C., Messineo, A., Beltramo, R., Yigitcanlar, T., & Ioppolo, G. (2018). How can life cycle thinking support sustainability of buildings? Investigating life cycle assessment applications for energy efficiency and environmental performance. *Journal of Cleaner Production, 201*, 556–569.

Ioppolo, G., Cucurachi, S., Salomone, R., Shi, L., & Yigitcanlar, T. (2019). Integrating strategic environmental assessment and material flow accounting: A novel approach for moving towards sustainable urban futures. *International Journal of Life Cycle Assessment, 24*(7), 1269–1284.

Kahia, M., Aïssa, M. S. B., & Charfeddine, L. (2016). Impact of renewable and nonrenewable energy consumption on economic growth: New evidence from the MENA Net Oil Exporting Countries (NOECs). *Energy*, *116*, 102–115.

Kalu, B. (2020). COVID-19 in Nigeria: A disease of hunger. *The Lancet Respiratory Medicine*, *8*(6), 556–557.

Karl, T. L. (2007). Oil-led development: Social, political, and economic consequences. *Encyclopedia of Energy*, *4*(8), 661–672.

Kaygusuz, K. (2012). Energy for sustainable development: A case of developing countries. *Renewable and Sustainable Energy Reviews*, *16*(2), 1116–1126.

Kerimray, A., De Miglio, R., Rojas-Solórzano, L., & Ó Gallachóir, B. P. (2018). Causes of energy poverty in a cold and resource-rich country: Evidence from Kazakhstan. *Local Environment*, *23*(2), 178–197.

Kluczek, A. (2019). An energy-led sustainability assessment of production systems–an approach for improving energy efficiency performance. *International Journal of Production Economics*, *216*, 190–203.

Kok, B., & Benli, H. (2017). Energy diversity and nuclear energy for sustainable development in Turkey. *Renewable Energy*, *111*, 870–877.

Lashitew, A., & Werker, E. (2020). Are natural resources a curse, a blessing, or a double-edged sword? *Brookings' Future Development Publication*. Retrieved from https://www.brookings.edu/blog/future-development/2020/07/16/are-natural-resources-a-curse-a-blessing-or-a-double-edged-sword/

Leibenstein, H. (1979). X-efficiency: From concept to theory. *Challenge*, *22*(4), 13–22.

McKenzie, S. (2004). *Social sustainability: Towards some definitions*. Hawke Research Institute: Working Paper Series. Hawke Research Institute, Magill.

Michael, Y. M. A. K., & Peacock, C. J. (2011, January). Social sustainability: A comparison of case studies in UK, USA and Australia. In *17th Pacific Rim Real Estate Society Conference*, Gold Coast (pp. 16–19).

Mohammad, M. T. S. H. (2010). Principles of sustainable development in Ibn Khaldun's economic thought. *Malaysian Journal of Real Estate*, *5*(1), 1–18.

Mohammed, S. D. (2020). Clean development mechanism and carbon emissions in Nigeria. *Sustainability Accounting, Management and Policy Journal*, *11*(3), 523–551. doi:10.1108/SAMPJ-05-2017-0041

Mukund, K. (2016). The resource curse: The political and economic challenges of natural resource wealth. Retrieved from https://www.linkedin.com/pulse/resource-cursethe-political-economic-challenges-natural-kumar-mukund/

Nagesha, N., & Subramanian, M. B. (2006). Energy efficiency for sustainable development of small industry clusters: What factors influence it? *International Journal of Economic Policy Studies*, *1*(1), 133–153.

Oparaocha, S., & Dutta, S. (2011). Gender and energy for sustainable development. *Current Opinion in Environmental Sustainability*, *3*(4), 265–271.

Oyedepo, S. O. (2012). Energy efficiency and conservation measures: Tools for sustainable energy development in Nigeria. *International Journal of Energy Engineering*, *2*(3), 86–98.

Oyedepo, S. O. (2014). Towards achieving energy for sustainable development in Nigeria. *Renewable and Sustainable Energy Reviews*, *34*, 255–272.

Ozturk, I. (2010). A literature survey on energy–growth nexus. *Energy Policy*, *38*(1), 340–349.

Pandey, R., Dhoundiyal, M., & Kumar, A. (2015, April). Correlation analysis of big data to support machine learning. In *2015 Fifth International Conference on Communication Systems and Network Technologies* (pp. 996–999). IEEE.

Perelman, M. (2011). Retrospectives: X-efficiency. *The Journal of Economic Perspectives*, *25*(4), 211–222.

Popescu, D., Bienert, S., Schützenhofer, C., & Boazu, R. (2012). Impact of energy efficiency measures on the economic value of buildings. *Applied Energy*, *89*(1), 454–463.

Raimi, L. (2010). Need for strategic planning for sustainable power and energy development in Nigeria. In *Award Winning Essay, National Young Managers' Essay Competition*, Nigeria. Nigerian Institute of Management (NIM) at the grand finale. IGI Global.

Raimi, L., & Aljadani, A. (2020). Sustainability of public finance of rentier states. In A. Gurtu (Ed.), *Recent advancements in sustainable entrepreneurship and corporate social responsibility*. Hershey, PA: IGI Global.

Raimi, L., Che, F. N., & Mutiu, R. M. (2021). Agricultural information systems (AGRIS) as a catalyst for sustainable development goals (SDGs) in Africa: A critical literature review. In F. Che, K. Strang, & N. Vajjhala (Eds.), Opportunities and strategic use of agribusiness information systems (pp. 109–133). IGI Global, US. doi:10.4018/978-1-7998-4849-3.ch007

Raimi, L., & Olowo, R. (2021). Perceptions of energy resources efficiency for sustainable development in the developing context of Nigeria: Implications for enterprise development in the energy sector. Presentation at the *1st ASEAN International Conference on Energy and Environment (1st AICEE)*, Brunei Darussalam, Virtual Platform, 15–16 September 2021.

Raimi, L., Towobola, W. L., & Madueke, L. I. (2013). Redressing the energy challenge of gas flaring in Nigeria: The MEEs approach. *Journal of Sustainable Development Studies, 2*(2), 242–257.

Rashid, A., & Kandemir, Ö. (2016). Variations in energy use and output growth dynamics: An assessment for intertemporal and contemporaneous relationship. *Energy, 102*, 388–396.

Riti, J. S., & Shu, Y. (2016). Renewable energy, energy efficiency, and eco-friendly environment (R-E5) in Nigeria. *Energy, Sustainability and Society, 6*(1), 1–16.

Rogelj, J., McCollum, D. L., & Riahi, K. (2013). The UN's' Sustainable Energy for All'initiative is compatible with a warming limit of 2 C. *Nature Climate Change, 3*(6), 545–551.

Salvia, A. L., & Schneider, L. L. (2019). Overall energy efficiency and sustainable development. In W. Leal Filho (Ed.), *Encyclopedia of sustainability in higher education*. Cham: Springer. doi:10.1007/978-3-319-63951-2_463-1

Smart Energy Education. (2016). Primary resources and secondary energy. *Publication of Disco Learning Media*. Retrieved from https://stem.guide/topic/primary-resources-and-secondary-energy/

Soczewica, R. (2021). Quantitative Analyst hunting for alpha. Passionate about market research, automatization, and nonobvious solutions utilising alternative data. *Towards Data Science Publication*. Retrieved from https://towardsdatascience.com/when-should-we-use-the-log-linear-model-db76c405b97e

Sorrell, S. (2010). Energy, economic growth and environmental sustainability: Five propositions. *Sustainability, 2*(6), 1784–1809.

Tadjoeddin, M. Z. (2007). *A future resource curse in Indonesia: The political economy of natural resources, conflict and development*. Department of International Development, University of Oxford.

Tan, B., Yavuz, Y., Otay, E. N., & Çamlıbel, E. (2016). Optimal selection of energy efficiency measures for energy sustainability of existing buildings. *Computers & Operations Research, 66*, 258–271.

University of Gävle. (2018a). *Ecological sustainability*. Stockholm, Stockholm County, Sweden. Retrieved from https://www.hig.se/Ext/En/University-of-Gavle/About-the-University/Environmental-Work/What-is-sustainable-development-at-HiG/Ecological-sustainability.html

University of Gävle. (2018b). *Economic sustainability*. Stockholm, Stockholm County, Sweden. Retrieved from https://www.hig.se/Ext/En/University-of-Gavle/About-the-University/Environmental-Work/What-is-sustainable-development-at-HiG/Economic-sustainability.html

Vance, L., Eason, T., & Cabezas, H. (2015). Energy sustainability: Consumption, efficiency, and environmental impact. *Clean Technologies and Environmental Policy, 17*(7), 1781–1792.

World Bank's Global Gas Flaring Tracker Data. (2020a). Flaring intensity – Top 10 flaring countries. Retrieved from https://www.ggfrdata.org/

World Bank's Global Gas Flaring Tracker Data. (2020b). Oil production – Top 10 flaring countries. Retrieved from https://www.ggfrdata.org/

World Development Indicators database. (2021). Nigeria country profile. Retrieved from https://
    databank.worldbank.org/reports.aspx?source=2&country=NGA
Zhang, J., Alharthi, M., Abbas, Q., Li, W., Mohsin, M., Jamal, K., & Taghizadeh-Hesary, F. (2020).
    Reassessing the environmental kuznets curve in relation to energy efficiency and economic
    growth. *Sustainability*, *12*(20), 8346.
Zhang, N., & Kim, J. D. (2014). Measuring sustainability by energy efficiency analysis for Korean
    power companies: A sequential slacks-based efficiency measure. *Sustainability*, *6*(3),
    1414–1426.

JUST TRANSITIONS FROM FOSSIL FUELS TO A REGENERATIVE AND RENEWABLE FUTURE: CHALLENGES AND OPPORTUNITIES

Georgia Beardman, Naomi Godden, Mehran Nejati, Jaime Yallup Farrant, Leonie Scoffern, James Khan, Joe Northover and Angus Morrison-Saunders

ABSTRACT

Climate change is a global issue with far-reaching environmental, social and economic consequences. As more people become aware of these consequences, pressure is mounting on governments and businesses to implement ambitious and required climate mitigation and adaptation plans to reduce and finally stop making the climate crisis worse. One of these strategies is just transition, which is defined as the call for climate transformation that prioritises the social and environmental needs of workers and vulnerable groups, especially in the context of transitioning away from fossil fuels, while leaving no one behind. This chapter first provides an overview of just transition through a review of the literature and bibliometric analysis. Then, it discusses just transition in policymaking, comprising reactive, proactive and transformational just transition approaches. This is followed by a discussion on barriers to just transition. Finally, the chapter offers a practical example of transformational just transition approach by reporting some preliminary findings from a case study in the coal mining town of Collie on Wilman Boodja, Western Australia.

Keywords: Climate change; just transition; climate justice; social justice; coal; bibliometric analysis

Achieving Net Zero
Developments in Corporate Governance and Responsibility, Volume 20, 177–201
Copyright © 2023 by Emerald Publishing Limited
All rights of reproduction in any form reserved
ISSN: 2043-0523/doi:10.1108/S2043-052320230000020008

INTRODUCTION

The latest report of the Intergovernmental Panel on Climate Change (IPCC) explicitly linked the impacts of ecological degradation and climate change with broader global and social trends, recognising that the climate, biodiversity and human systems are all interdependent (IPCC, 2022). This is a marked shift in language away from climate change being phenomena happening to the planet out there, towards climate change being a pervasive crisis that will have wide-reaching social, economic and health impacts. As the knowledge and direct experience of these impacts grow, so too does the global pressure on governments and industries to enact ambitious and necessary climate mitigation and adaptation strategies to slow and eventually stop the climate crisis from worsening. One such globally recognised strategy is known as the 'just transition' from fossil fuels to renewables (United Nations, 2015).

The term 'just transition' first emerged as a policy framework, devised by the labour union movement in the United States as a means for protecting workers in high emission industries, while also acknowledging the need to address the emerging climate crisis (Heffron & McCauley, 2018; Pai, Harrison, & Zerriffi, 2020). Advocates of the early iterations of just transition policy focussed on the importance of finding like-for-like jobs for affected workers, measuring success by predominantly economic markers (Krawchenko & Gordon, 2021; McCauley et al., 2019). Towards the turn of the century, with the emergence of climate change mainstreaming, the focus and language of just transition shifted to be more environment-centred and effectiveness was evaluated predominantly on the ability to enable a transition to carbon neutrality (Krawchenko & Gordon, 2021). However, in the last decade, as the social implications of just transitions and climate change have become more widely understood, the implementations of just transition, together with just transition scholarship has expanded to have a whole of society focus (Johnstone & Hielscher, 2017; Olson-Hazboun, 2018; Vona, 2019; Weller, 2019). In contemporary applications of just transition concepts, success is measured by the transition's effectiveness in reducing carbon emissions, while also uplifting and supporting the social and economic wellbeing of whole communities, and in its function as a vehicle for structural change and system transformation (Heffron & McCauley, 2018; Krawchenko & Gordon, 2021).

A simple search of the term 'just transition' on Google Scholar returns more than 14,000 results spanning the last three decades. Of those, more than 11,000 have emerged since 2015, an almost 400% increase in the number of search results. This could be due to the mainstreaming of the just transition concept as a means for tackling climate change, following its inclusion in the preamble of the 2015 Paris Agreement (United Nations, 2015). Analysis of a wide range of this literature shows that frameworks for understanding just transitions can be narrowed to three main streams, being jobs-focussed, environment-focussed and society-focussed (Heffron & McCauley, 2018; Krawchenko & Gordon, 2020; Pai et al., 2020). Further analysis identifies emerging areas of just transition scholarship studying the importance of intersectional approaches to just transition policymaking to ensure that transition processes do not exacerbate existing structural inequalities (Kaijser & Kronsell, 2014). Lastly, some key trends develop across the literature, showing three main policy platforms exist in just transition research, being reactive, proactive and transformational (Bennett, Blythe, Cisneros-Montemayor, Singh, & Sumaila, 2019).

The research we report on here seeks to understand the challenges and opportunities just transitions present for addressing climate change and facilitating an end to fossil fuels, with a particular focus on coal mining and associated power generation. Given the global nature of climate change and fossil fuel usage, just transition could be investigated at any scale from the local to the international. In this research, our approach is 'placed-based', focussing solely on a local region (i.e. subnational scale and within Australia) historically reliant on local coal mining and associated power generation projects. We first provide an overview of just transition, exploring different framings or typologies, through a review of the literature and bibliometric analysis. Then, we discuss the just transition in policymaking, comprising reactive, proactive and transformational just transition approaches, followed by a discussion on barriers to just transition identified in the literature. Finally, we provide a practical example of transformational just transition approach by reporting some preliminary findings from a case study in the coal mining town of Collie, situated on Wilman Boodja in the South West of Western Australia. We conclude the chapter with some reflections on how policymakers, communities and researchers alike might usefully frame, plan for and implement just transitions for climate change and the end of fossil fuels.

FRAMING JUST TRANSITION

Three broad framings of just transition are evident in the literature, based upon the target subject; being worker or job focussed, environmental outcome related and taking a whole of society approach. These are addressed in turn.

Job-Focussed Just Transition

Emerging out of the US trade union movement, the concept of the 'just transition' was introduced by unionists as a means for reconciling environmental goals with economic security for workers in polluting industries (Meadowcroft, 2009; Pai et al., 2020; Vachon, 2021). Early pioneers of the just transition saw it as an opportunity to collaborate with environmentalists to bridge the divide between worker justice and environmental goals, as fossil fuel industries were phased out (MacNeil & Beauman, 2022; Vachon, 2021). For the first time in history, unions were advocating action that not only protected workers but also acknowledged the impacts of polluting industries on the environment (Evans & Phelan, 2016; Pai et al., 2020; Rosemberg, 2010). Over time, the increasing politicisation of the climate movement led to just transitions being framed via the false dichotomy of 'jobs vs the environment', a narrative driven by fossil fuel companies and their political allies to mobilise the support of blue-collar workers in fossil fuel dependent communities (Evans & Phelan, 2016; Hackett & Adams, 2018; Kalt, 2021; Vona, 2019). Scholars in North America and Australia observe that this has contributed to an unwillingness by governments to be seen as preferencing the environment over workers, for fear of losing votes. This translates in practice, to a strong worker and jobs-focussed policy approach to transition and minimal focus being drawn to climate change (Goddard & Farrelly, 2018; Lewin, 2017; Lobao, Zhou, Partridge, & Betz, 2016; MacNeil & Beauman, 2022).

Environment-Focussed Just Transition

By comparison, the concept of an environment-focussed just transition approach emerged in the early 2000s, when climate change issues began to mainstream, and the concept of carbon neutrality dominated climate action discourse globally (Pai et al., 2020). Advocates of this approach propose that measures of success shift so that just transitions are evaluated primarily on their ability to deliver carbon neutrality (Krawchenko & Gordon, 2020; Pai et al., 2020), although other environmental outcome changes could also be envisaged. Under this model, just transitions are used predominantly as tools for climate action. In turn, the focus narrows to environmental outcomes, examining production and consumption patterns as markers of success (Krawchenko & Gordon, 2020). Olson-Hazboun (2018) notes that this shift in focus could lead to intensified sentiment amongst workers that city-based policy writers are being too heavily influenced by environmentalists, putting the needs of the environment before workers' needs to support themselves and their families. This approach is attributed to an ever-widening gap between blue-collar workers and policymakers, purporting that it has further entrenched the 'jobs vs environment' discourse in affected communities (Olson-Hazboun, 2018). A similar sentiment in this regard is also reflected in studies conducted in coal-dependent towns in Australia and the United States (Hackett & Adams, 2018; Vona, 2019).

Society-Focussed Just Transition

The previous two approaches have both drawn criticism from contemporary scholars for their narrow focus and inability to acknowledge the broader impacts of transition policy (Emden, Ahmad, Murphy, & Cameron, 2020; MacNeil & Beauman, 2022; McCauley et al., 2019; Pai et al., 2020; Stevis, 2020). Heffron and McCauley (2018) saw an opportunity to develop a new theoretical lens that focussed on the justice element of a just transition that applies a more critical and inclusive approach. In doing so, their approach attempts to balance the needs of workers, the environment and the community, in concert with the needs of society more broadly. This contemporary just transition framework is one underpinned by socio-ecological justice, urging decision-makers to have a developed understanding of the broader issues of energy, climate and environmental justice (McCauley & Heffron, 2018). Their work considers how structures of power, ethics, equity and participation might factor into a transition and what opportunities might exist to use just transitions as a tool for achieving structural change. In its application, a society-focussed transition requires communities, researchers and policy developers to be attentive to social issues, such as who holds power in a transition process and how this power and the benefits that come with it might be more equitably distributed (McCauley & Heffron, 2018; McCauley et al., 2019). While McCauley and Heffron (2018) were two of the first to conceptualise just transitions in this way, their work has since been supported by the work of other scholars globally in the last five years (Bennett et al., 2019; Braunger & Paula, 2022; Goldtooth, 2020; Hurlbert & Rayner, 2018; Jafry, Watson, Mattar, & Mikulewicz, 2022; McCauley & Heffron, 2018).

BIBLIOMETRIC ANALYSIS

The previous account of our literature review was brief and restricted in scope. To further characterise framing and understanding of just transitions in the literature, we carried out a more comprehensive bibliometric analysis. Our methods and key findings are addressed in turn.

Method

Following the guideline provided by Higgins et al. (2019) for a systematic review process, we first determined the aim of this bibliographic analysis to be discovering emerging trends in the just transition literature. For the protocol of systematic review, our selection criteria included peer-reviewed research papers published in journals, books or conference proceedings which have been indexed in Web of Science (WOS). We used 'just transition' as our key search term which returned 359 articles published in the 2000–2022 timespan, including 309 journal articles. The following sections include our analysis of the literature and a summary of key findings.

Findings

While the first papers on just transition appear in 2000, the number of articles on the topic has grown exponentially since 2018 (Fig. 1) indicating an annual percentage growth rate of 20.5. There have been 858 authors publishing in the field. The top 10 countries with highest number of publications on just transition include the United States (77), United Kingdom (58), Germany (28), Australia (18), South Africa (18), Netherlands (15), Ireland (14), Canada (13), Finland (12) and Poland (10).

Most productive authors in the field include Heffron, McCauley, Oei and Sovacoo. As highlighted in Fig. 2, authors publishing on just transition have particularly been more active in the past 5 years, i.e. from 2018 to 2022.

Descriptive analysis of the documents revealed that the top 10 author keywords used in publications include just transition (155), climate change (42), energy justice (32), energy transition (31), transition (31), just (24), energy (22),

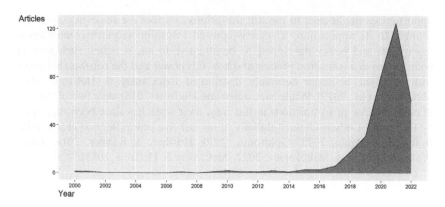

Fig. 1. Annual Scientific Production.

climate justice (21), justice (21) and coal (19). Fig. 3 shows the keyword co-occurrences for the analysed articles.

Lastly, to identify the key themes emerging from previous studies, we used Bibliometrix's machine learning based visualisation of the author keywords in R following the guidelines by Aria and Cuccurullo (2017). Using the Multiple Correspondence Analysis (MCA) method, keywords were grouped to generate a conceptual structure map as depicted in Fig. 4. The algorithm generated only one main cluster (red cluster) which is more focussed on climate justice, policies, unions and future. Other topical areas are not significant enough to form a unique cluster yet. This shows a concentrated approach on climate justice from the angle of policy, law and unions in the current publications and reveals an opportunity for future studies to investigate other angles including perspectives of stakeholders and their potential resistance to the transition (i.e. purple focus area on the map).

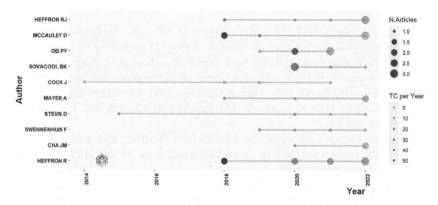

Fig. 2. Top Authors' Production Over Time.

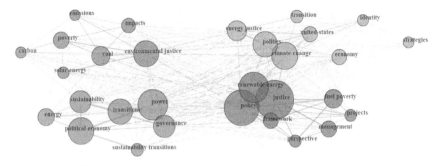

Fig. 3. Keyword Co-occurrences.

Overall, our bibliometric analysis serves to demonstrate the rapidly expanding and evolving nature of just transition research. In the next section, we discuss trends in just transition policy evolution in this regard, specifically targeting literature on energy transition for the end of fossil fuels extraction and burning.

JUST TRANSITION IN POLICYMAKING

The blueprint for a successful transition to a greenhouse gas emissions-neutral world is notably absent from the literature. Pellegrini-Masini, Pirni, and Maran (2020) posit that this is due to the lack of empirical research available, noting that just transition literature remains largely theoretical and methods for accurately measuring the effectiveness of transitions, elusive. While there is broad agreement globally of what a just transition is, the goals and aspirations of each transition vary greatly. For some, success is measured by alternative job creation, for others it's in neutralising carbon emissions (Krawchenko & Gordon, 2020). Only

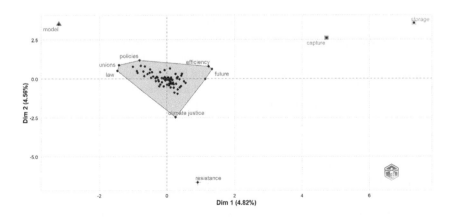

Fig. 4. Conceptual Structural Map.

recently have some regions, such as Germany, begun to consider if success markers could lie in the social wellbeing and quality of life in communities undergoing transition (Furnaro et al., 2021; Herpich, Brauers, & Oei, 2018).

Despite the continuing evolutions of how just transitions are conceptualised and framed, three main schools of thought have emerged pertaining to policy development, being reactive, proactive and transformational policy approaches (Bennett et al., 2019; Mertins-Kirkwood, 2018).

Reactive Policies

Reactive, or defensive just transition policies have a narrow focus, usually not extending past workers and communities who are directly impacted (Mertins-Kirkwood, 2018). Policy initiatives tend to be individually focussed and success is measured primarily using economic markers, such as employment rates (Krawchenko & Gordon, 2020). Typical elements of a reactive just transition policy include (Krawchenko & Gordon, 2020; Mertins-Kirkwood, 2018):

- Income support for displaced workers, usually via social security payments
- Funded retraining and career support for affected workers
- Job transfers
- Pension bridging or redundancy incentives
- Workforce transition plans

Critics of reactive just transition policy approaches argue that the focus is too narrow and risks exacerbating existent structural inequalities (MacNeil & Beauman, 2022; McCauley et al., 2019; Pai et al., 2020; Stevis, 2020). Examples of reactive just transition policymaking include UK transition policies from the 1980s, early German transition policies and the current Canadian policy platform (Emden et al., 2020; Furnaro et al., 2021; Herpich et al., 2018; Rising et al., 2021).

Proactive Policies

By comparison, proactive policymaking is intended to maximise the long-term benefits of the transition to a carbon-neutral economy (Mertins-Kirkwood, 2018). Proactive policies are characterised by a slightly broader focus, beyond individual workers and also makes some attempts to address inequities, although usually only those in the workforce, compared with society more broadly (Krawchenko & Gordon, 2020). Common platforms for proactive transition policy initiatives include:

- Future labour market modelling
- Targeted skills training – based on labour market modelling
- Industrial transition support
- Geographically targeted spending to support the economic viability of vulnerable regions

Critics of proactive just transition policy approaches argue that they fail to redress wider social inequities, such as climate, energy and environmental injustice (Bennett et al., 2019; Johnson et al., 2020; Krawchenko & Gordon, 2020).

Transformational Policies

Bennett et al. (2019) argue that policies pertaining to energy transitions need to be transformational if they are to address the profound environmental and social challenges that climate change presents. They propose deliberate governance processes to facilitate the radical transformation of fossil fuel dependent societies from an unsustainable, unjust system to a sustainable one that balances both the social justice and environmental needs of the planet (Bennett et al., 2019). This approach aligns with the intersectional transition approaches and is supported by comprehensive comparative policy analyses conducted by Jafry et al. (2022) and Krawchenko and Gordon (2021). Eight key considerations for achieving a transformational energy transition can be identified, which we address in turn.

Planning

Studies show that long-term, proactive, multi-level planning that is sufficiently funded at all levels is essential for transformational energy transitions (Campbell & Coenen, 2017; Furnaro et al., 2021). Planning must allow for long-term, community-based, meaningful engagement that fosters whole of community participation (Jafry et al., 2022). Scholars argue that effective, collaborative planning can create a shared sense of ownership and involvement across the community, which can mitigate the risk of excluding marginalised members of the community (Goddard & Farrelly, 2018; Sartor, 2018).

Engagement Versus Consultation

Community-based, participatory engagement that seeks the input and voices of a representative cross section of all members of affected communities is a proven way of effectively engaging communities in place-based problem-solving (Blomkamp, 2018; Kronsell, 2013). Co-design of policies with community members increases a sense of ownership over the process and strengthens community participation (Sartor, 2018; Wooltorton, Collard, Horwitz, Poelina, & Palmer, 2020). By comparison, government-initiated, tokenistic community consultation that is narrow and excludes community members not deemed to be directly impacted is shown to result in disenfranchisement, reduced trust and decreased participation (Carley & Konisky, 2020; MacNeil & Beauman, 2022; Snyder, 2018).

Inclusion of Indigenous Knowledges

A transformational approach to transition policy will actively seek to mitigate the prejudicial impacts of colonisation by acknowledging how the history and legacy of colonisation has contributed to climate change and how that has impacted local Indigenous communities (Abimbola, Aikins, Makhesi-Wilkinson, & Roberts, 2021). Furthermore, in regions that are colonised, localised Indigenous knowledge and voices should be sought throughout, and used to inform transition policy at every stage of the process, from planning to development to implementation (Cha, Price, Stevis, Vachon, & Brescia-Weiler, 2021; Goldtooth, 2020; Weeramanthri, Joyce, Bowman, Bangor-Jones, & Law, 2020). This has been shown to be essential to ensuring transition processes address existing social inequities (Abimbola et al., 2021; Bainton, Kemp, Lèbre, Owen, & Marston, 2021; Leonard, Parsons, Olawsky, & Kofod, 2013; Petzold, Andrews, Ford, Hedemann, & Postigo, 2020; Shaffril, Ahmad, Samsuddin, Samah, & Hamdan, 2020).

Justice-Oriented
Complementary to the inclusion of Indigenous knowledges, the literature states that recognitional, procedural and distributional justice should inform and underpin all transformational policymaking to ensure that structural inequalities are addressed and redressed (Braunger & Paula, 2022; Evans & Phelan, 2016; Goddard & Farrelly, 2018; McCauley & Heffron, 2018; McCauley et al., 2019).

Climate Informed
Climate science is dynamic and fast evolving. In a comparative review, Krawchenko and Gordon (2021) found that policymaking informed by a strong scientific evidence base that reflects the most current available research and modelling were more effective than those that were silent on climate. In addition, Snyder (2018) argues that climate data should be specific to local geographical contexts and included in a way that links the climate change vulnerabilities of a region to decarbonisation.

Economics and Governance
The more recent policy position of Germany's energy transition shows the important role that strong governance structures can play in facilitating a coordinated, multi-level approach (Herpich et al., 2018). Researchers found that when financial autonomy is granted to local governments, communities are empowered and resourced to implement local transition processes that are relevant to them (Furnaro et al., 2021). In addition, they found that local infrastructure development, such as public transport initiatives, together with investment in the area, can prevent outwards skills migration and provide wide-reaching social benefits, such as reduced poverty and increased local mobility (Furnaro et al., 2021). Complementing these localised levels of governance and funding, needs to be state and national level policy cohesion (Mertins-Kirkwood, 2018).

Fostering Trust and Positive Public Perception

Public perception and attitudes towards transition processes can have a marked impact on their success (Wang & Lo, 2021). A transformational transition process requires leading agencies to have clear messaging, derived from a locally co-designed, community-based process that fosters positive public perception of the energy transition (Cherry et al., 2022). Misinformation, distrust and unclear messaging can create polarisation and be counterproductive to transition efforts (Carvalho, Riquito, & Ferreira, 2022; Hackett & Adams, 2018; MacNeil & Beauman, 2022; Vona, 2019).

Localised, Spatially Targeted Approach

There can be no 'one size fits all' approach to transition policy (Campbell & Coenen, 2017). In a study in the Appalachian region of the United States, researchers found that socioeconomic impacts of energy transition could be mitigated if policymakers took a locally informed, spatially targeted approach (Snyder, 2018). Spatially targeted policy approaches are derived from specific local needs, as identified through community-led, place-based engagement (Blomkamp, 2018; Sartor, 2018). They enable targeted investment to support the increase in community functioning and social outcomes, as well as fostering social and economic resilience through the process of transition (Campbell & Coenen, 2017; Cherry et al., 2022; Evans & Phelan, 2016; Jafry et al., 2022; Kais & Islam, 2016).

Despite a clear understanding and articulation of what is necessary for achieving just transition, there are currently no concrete examples of transformational just transition policymaking that have been fully implemented to date, especially in the context of climate change and the end of fossil fuels extraction and burning. Later in this chapter, we introduce a case study of just transition in the coal mining town of Collie, on Wilman Boodja in Western Australia, which is among the first attempts towards transformational just transition policymaking in Australia. However, realising transformational just transition policymaking requires overcoming some significant barriers which will be discussed in the next section.

BARRIERS TO JUST TRANSITION

Climate change is a 'wicked problem' with no single solution. Different approaches to solving the problem of climate change come with complex barriers. Just transitions are no exception. The literature identifies several key barriers to achieving a just and transformational energy transition, all of which intersect as they attempt to balance competing tensions and needs. The barriers of just transition are varied and complex, encompassing a full spectrum of socio-political and cultural issues. They deal with systems of power (Abimbola et al., 2021), the harmful dichotomy of 'jobs vs environment' (Hackett & Adams, 2018), short political cycles (Emden et al., 2020), 'lock-in' (Campbell & Coenen, 2017) and perceived loss of identity in coal communities (Della Bosca & Gillespie, 2018; Lewin, 2017; Mayer, 2018). We address each briefly in turn.

Systems of Power

Perhaps the most pervasive barrier to a just transition that achieves lasting, structural change, as well as addressing the climate crisis, are the systems of power that currently inform and influence all aspects of life in the Western world. The literature highlights how patriarchy, colonialism, imperialism, capitalism and neoliberalism all contribute to the complex and layered barriers arising out of transition processes around the world (Abimbola et al., 2021; Braunger & Paula, 2022; Johnson et al., 2020; Kaijser & Kronsell, 2014; Tuana, 2019; Velicu & Barca, 2020). An example of this is the work of Abimbola et al. (2021) who argue that while colonialism and racism are embedded in the structures, institutions and organisations confronting the climate crisis, climate policy at all levels will fail to address structural inequalities. Similarly, Braunger and Paula (2022) points to the gendered power asymmetries of past coal transitions to show that while women often bear the brunt of the transition process, their contributions remain largely invisible. A transformational just transition must address these structural power inequalities to overcome this barrier.

Politicisation of Climate and Just Transition Policy

The increasing politicisation of the climate crisis has led to just transitions being framed via the false dichotomy of 'jobs vs the environment', a narrative adopted by fossil fuel companies and their political allies to mobilise the support of blue-collar workers in fossil fuel dependent communities (Evans & Phelan, 2016; Hackett & Adams, 2018; Kalt, 2021; Lewin, 2017; Olson-Hazboun, 2018; Vachon, 2021). A recent example of this in Australia is the 2019 election, when the discourse in Queensland about a proposed coal mine positioned the mining company responsible as totemic of regional economic development more broadly (Tranter & Foxwell-Norton, 2021; Williams, 2021). Australia's Labour Party chose not to vocally support the mine, which some critics say was the reason they lost the election, with swings towards their opponents in Queensland 3% higher than the national average (Williams, 2021). By comparison, in the 2022 election campaign, both major parties showed a reluctance to speak explicitly about any issues relating to coal or climate, which some predicted would see a swing away from Labour in previously safe electorates, such as the coal-dependent seat of Hunter, New South Wales (Butler, 2022). However, this swing did not eventuate.

In a recent study, MacNeil and Beauman (2022) found that coal miners in the Eastern states of Australia felt abandoned by politicians, expressing that transition processes were failing to understand and address local needs and aspirations, a feeling echoed in coal communities abroad as well (Lewin, 2017). The 'jobs vs environment' discourse has become so polarising to the just transition movement, that there are anecdotal examples of people and organisations no longer using the term 'just transition' for fear that it will provoke a negative response from workers and communities in the industry. These examples show that the continued use of the 'jobs vs environment' narrative poses a significant barrier to achieving a just transition (Evans & Phelan, 2016; Goddard & Farrelly, 2018; Hackett & Adams, 2018; Kalt, 2021; MacNeil & Beauman, 2022; Olson-Hazboun, 2018; Vona, 2019; Weller, 2019).

Short Political Cycles

Addressing climate change via transformational just transition policymaking and implementation requires multi-partisan, long-term political leadership and vision (Cha et al., 2021; Meadowcroft, 2009; Mertins-Kirkwood, 2018; Weller, 2019). Analysis of policy interventions in Victoria's Latrobe Valley during the Gillard time in office found that Australia's short political cycles created a significant barrier to effective local transition policymaking (Weller, 2019). Further exacerbating this barrier is the absence of a national approach to the transition away from coal-fired power (Edwards et al., 2022), as evidenced by Australia refusing to sign up as a member of the Powering Past Coal Alliance, despite several states signing up independent of their federal counterparts (Jewell, Vinichenko, Nacke, & Cherp, 2019). This fragmented approach, coupled with short political cycles, creates a barrier to cohesive, effective just transition policymaking (Campbell & Coenen, 2017; Edwards et al., 2022; Mertins-Kirkwood, 2018; Weller, 2019).

'Lock-in'

In a critical analysis of coal transitions across Europe's old industrial regions, Campbell and Coenen (2017) identified that over-specialisation and industrial mono-structuring can lead to 'lock-in'. They observed that the same elements that enable a region's economic success – extensive and specialised knowledge infrastructure, strong organisational networks, industrial atmosphere and local political support for a given industry – can ultimately become obstacles to the innovation required to diversify the industry and economy of that region (Campbell & Coenen, 2017). Scholars argue that if a region's economic development becomes rigidly specified, it can become 'locked in' by the same conditions that once made them stand out, creating a barrier to change (Campbell & Coenen, 2017; Carley & Konisky, 2020; Mayer, 2018; Olson-Hazboun, 2018).

Perceived Loss of Identity

For many people living and working in coal mining regions, coal forms a central part of their identity (Lewin, 2017; Mayer, 2018). For many of the workers, there are generational links to the industry, and it carries with it a sense of belonging and community (Cha et al., 2021; Cherry et al., 2022; Mayer, 2018). This creates a barrier to transition because it presents a challenge to communities to reimagine their identity and sense of being beyond coal, which, in the context of 'lock-in', a future without coal can be seemingly unimaginable (Campbell & Coenen, 2017; Lewin, 2017; Vona, 2019).

CASE STUDY OF COLLIE

In this section, we discuss a case study of the rural community of Collie, situated on Wilman Boodja in Western Australia. Collie is a town undergoing a significant economic and social transition from its main economic industry of coal mining and coal-fired power generation. The case study highlights the importance of a social justice lens in transition planning and in the context of a changing climate.

Context

The Shire of Collie is situated in Western Australia, 200km southeast of Perth. It is part of the Bibbulmun Nation, and home to the Wilman tribe, or Freshwater Peoples (Australian Bureau of Statistics, 2020; South West Aboriginal Land and Sea Council, n.d.). The Wilman people have preserved and protected their boodja (land) and moort (family) since time immemorial, sustaining cultural practices for thousands of generations. Despite two centuries of colonisation, they have maintained traditions which care for the land and waters of Collie and surrounds (J. Khan, personal communication, n.d.; Northover, n.d.).

Totalling 171,000 hectares, Collie is 57 kilometres inland from the southwest city of Bunbury and is surrounded by state forest. The Shire of Collie is home to two coal mines, Premier and Griffin, and three power stations, Bluewaters, Collie and Muja.

Knowledge shared by traditional custodians for the Wilman People of the Bibbulmun Nation, Joe Northover and James Khan demonstrates that the Wilman people have coexisted as part of the ecosystem of this *boodja* for tens of thousands of years, and their connection to this Country is a significant part of Collie's history, present day, and its future (J. Khan, personal communication, n.d.; Northover, n.d.). Since time immemorial, the Wilman people have cared for this *boodja* and sustained life in the region in a way that is regenerative, sustainable and respectful of the interconnectedness of the entire ecosystem. A recent Aboriginal Heritage Assessment prepared for the Shire of Collie showed that the region is home to several sites of Cultural and spiritual importance, in particular its waterways, including the Collie River, Minninup Pool, Collie Spring and the Brunswick and Preston Rivers. The Wilman people know the *Ngarngungudditj Waugal* (hairy-faced snake) to be the creation spirit of the Collie River and the fresh waters of this region are the spiritual heart of the custodians here (Michell & Halsmith, 2019). The following quotation illustrates this:

> The Ngarngungudditj Waugal came from the north of Collie, passed through the Collie area and moved towards Eaton, forming all local waterways, including the Collie, Preston and Brunswick Rivers. When the snake reached Eaton, it turned its body creating the Leschenault Estuary and then travelled back up the river to rest at Minninup Pool, known also as Koolingup, or swimming place. (Beckwith Environmental Planning, 2009)

The Collie region was first colonised in the 1880s, following the accidental discovery by settlers of coal in the Collie basin. Within two decades, Collie was transformed into a coal town, and soon became the energy-generating epicentre of Western Australia (Government of Western Australia, 2020). Unlike other coal producing regions in Australia, the Collie coal has not become an export commodity, being used primarily or solely to meet local energy needs. The 1900s saw a century of boom and bust for the region, with its economic health almost entirely dependent on the coal market (Beyond Zero Emissions, 2019). The second half of the twentieth century saw record population growth in Collie as the power demands across the post-war world grew (Department of Primary Industries and Regional Development, 2021). To date, the coal community in Collie has seen the closure of the amalgamated collieries, the closure of all underground coal mines and the retirement of two regionally significant power stations – known as Muja A and B (Beyond Zero Emissions, 2019).

As the market for coal declines globally, and the pressure for decarbonisation grows, Collie is facing an imminent shift away from coal for the first time in its colonial history (Government of Western Australia, 2020). Collie is also highly vulnerable to a number of climate change-related threats. The IPCC has predicted, with high confidence, that the region Collie sits within, South-Western Australia, will be severely impacted by the changing climate (Lawrence et al., 2022). The IPCC warns that extreme events, such as heatwaves, droughts, floods, fires, the collapse of the northern jarrah forests and severe storms/cyclones will have rippling effects to households, communities, businesses, critical infrastructure, essential services, food production, the economy and employment (Lawrence et al., 2022). Declining rainfall is predicted to have a significant impact on agriculture, increasing stress in rural communities (Lawrence et al., 2022). Places that are surrounded by forest, like Collie, are at increasing risk of extreme fire events, as well as disruption and decline in local production (Lawrence et al., 2022). Furthermore, environment groups identify that 'the coal measures in Collie are below the water table and constant dewatering is required to safely mine that coal' (Commonwealth of Australia, 2017, p. 11), and this will have a significant regional impact on the drying of rivers, streams and water courses, with regular health warnings about eating fish from the Collie River as they contain elevated levels of mercury and other toxic by-products of coal burning.

The 2016 Australian Census data (Australian Bureau of Statistics, 2020) show that statistically, Collie is a largely blue-collar, working-class town with high rates of disadvantage. The population of Collie is 8,601 people (a decline from 9,132 in 2015), and 42% of the population are aged 50 or older. Just 11.2% of its residents were born overseas, and 4% of the community are Aboriginal and Torres Strait Islander, and 21.4% of the Collie population is living with a disability. The education rates in Collie show lower than average rates of engagement in tertiary studies, with just 4.3% of persons aged 15 years and over going on to study a bachelor's degree, compared with 20.5% of Western Australians more broadly. Collie has a labour force participation rate of 51.8%, and the unemployment rate of 11% is higher than the state and national average, with Aboriginal and Torres Strait Islander residents experiencing a substantially higher unemployment rate, at 35.2%. There is a large cohort of low-income households in Collie, with 34% of the population aged 15 and over in Collie earning less than AU$500 per week.

More than half of the population of Collie receive Government financial assistance (54.6%), including 778 persons receiving unemployment benefits.

The most common occupations of employed persons in Collie include technicians and trade workers (23.5%), machinery operators and drivers (17%), labourers (14.5%) and community and personal service workers (10.4%). Managers and professionals make up just 15.4% of total occupations in Collie. According to 2016 census data, the primary industry of employment in Collie is mining (18.2%), with health care and social assistance (10%) and retail trade (9.8%) the next biggest employers. Education and training (8.7%), accommodation and food services (7.9%) and electricity, gas, water and waste services (7.3%) also feature strongly. Notably, manufacturing and construction experienced significant decreases in employees between 2011 and 2016, down 4.6% and 9.2%, respectively.

In recent times, it has become clear that there is reduced competitiveness of coal in the future energy market, and improved affordability and availability of renewable alternatives. Collie's economic dependence on coal is a risk factor for future economic security. In August 2019, the government of Western Australia announced that it would retire two of four coal-fired operating units at the state-owned Muja Power Station in Collie in October 2022 (Government of Western Australia, 2020). Then in June 2022, the WA government announced that it would begin the process of phasing out the remaining state-owned coal-fired power stations in Collie by 2029. This forthcoming phase-out of coal-fired power generation in Collie will have major ramifications for the people of the town and region; in addition to the impacts of climate change that are already being experienced.

In response to calls from unions and other civil society organisations (Beyond Zero Emissions, 2019), in December 2020, the state government released its Collie Just Transition Plan to fund and implement a just transition for Collie's coal workers and wider community away from its economic dependence on coal (Government of Western Australia, 2020). This process involves the Department of Premier and Cabinet's Collie Just Transition Working Group, together with industry, unions, business groups and the Shire of Collie, but it has limited community sector engagement or input specifically built into it, rather focussing on maximising opportunities for affected workers.

The Collie Just Transition Plan (Government of Western Australia, 2020) focusses on diversifying the local economy, maximising opportunities for affected workers, celebrating Collie's history and promoting its future. However, it could be seen as short term and focussed almost exclusively on the economic transition for Collie. Notably, the term 'climate change' is mentioned just once throughout the whole document and while 'justice' is mentioned in relation to the Working Group's guiding principles, it is not clear how the Plan incorporates justice into its implementation process.

The Climate Justice Union WA (CJU) is a community union that aims for Western Australia to rapidly transition to net-zero emissions, including exports, while taking care of people and place (Climate Justice Union, n.d.). In 2019, the CJU supported not-for-profit organisation Beyond Zero Emissions to produce a report, *Collie at the Crossroads: Planning a Future Beyond Coal* (Beyond Zero Emissions, 2019), which identified industry opportunities for the Collie community to transition from coal extraction and energy generation to alternatives, such as land regeneration, social care, renewable manufacturing and low emission industries. Through this process, the CJU identified that the state government's transition process in Collie did not yet reach a whole-of-community approach; did not yet apply a social justice lens to ensure that no one in the community is left behind; and was limited in accounting for the diverse range of expected social and environmental impacts of climate change in the region. In its limited scope (which was hard won over years of collaboration) it is insufficient to ensure no one is left behind.

A Just Transition for Collie that Leaves No One Behind: Research Methodology

In 2021, the CJU and Edith Cowan University's Centre for People, Place and Planet commenced a pilot participatory action research (PAR) study to directly collaborate with Collie community members, including people experiencing systemic disadvantage, to explore a just transition for Collie that leaves no one behind. This is the research we report on here. It involves supporting the Collie community to achieve the type of transition they need and deserve; one which reduces inequity and provides a positive future for the whole community for generations to come. In collaboration with Collie community members and stakeholders, the project builds on the decades of community-based work that has come before it, to produce a local baseline social justice profile which highlights the key ways in which diverse community members are likely to be impacted by the energy transition, and/or by the increasing and expected local impacts of climate change. It aims to accelerate the achievement of key just transition priorities in the transition away from coal. ECU, CJU and Collie community members will then work together to identify key priorities for reducing these vulnerabilities that can be included in the ongoing transition planning and implementation processes. This work aims to elevate and build on the work of many in the community over decades, which has long sought to address the complex environmental, social and justice issues that coexist with climate change, coal mining and coal-fired power generation. Ultimately, the team envisages this project becoming a multi-year undertaking for on-going collaboration with the Collie community to support a just and inclusive transition process that works for all in the community and enables a sustainable and bright future for generations to come.

The pilot study methodology is informed by an intersectional feminist analysis of justice and equity in the context of climate change (Kaijser & Kronsell, 2014; Tuana, 2019); and the participatory methodological paradigm that prioritises community-led enquiry and activism that is grounded in place (Godden, Macnish, Chakma, & Naidu, 2020; Wooltorton et al., 2020). The project design and implementation are strongly influenced by Indigenous knowledge holders, through relationship-building with Wilman Elders and community members, and inclusion of their priorities and needs in transition planning and responding to economic disruption and localised climate impacts. Thus, our approach is consistent with transformative policymaking discussed previously and our design is intended to avoid the barriers to just transition we identified earlier.

Specifically, in this iterative project we use a range of participatory methods to engage community members in identifying issues and possibilities for action:

- *Community Relationship-Building:* Meetings (yarns) with key stakeholders, including Elders and Noongar community members, residents of Collie, Department of Premier and Cabinet, local government, Unions and workers within local social and community services.
- *Desktop Review:* Collect and analyse demographic data and grey literature about the Collie community, and the Collie transition process.
- *Social Mapping:* A series of workshops with a cross section of community members to map the social justice impacts of economic transition and climate change, and opportunities for action to address these issues.
- *Baseline Survey:* A baseline survey with up to 350 people (5% of the Collie population) to capture perceptions of the transition process, the impacts of climate change and opportunities for action.
- *Personas:* Data from stages 1 to 4 are used to compile up to 10 diverse personas (case studies) that reflect the range of community experiences of the transition process and climate change.
- *Action Planning:* Workshops with community members and stakeholders to collectively analyse the data and personas, and identify possible actions to support the Just Transition process. It is intended that the data can inform just transition planning and a fairer distribution of resources in the Collie community.

Initial Research Findings

Although the study is not yet completed, we can report some initial findings based on the desktop review, community relationship-building and a series of social mapping workshops that were held in Collie in early 2022 with Wilman Traditional Owners and community members, parents of young children with disabilities, people on low income, local business owners, workers in coal-related industries, union representatives, young people and local government Councillors. While by no means capturing the views of all stakeholder groups within the Collie community, our approach aims to extend further than that adopted by the Government of Western Australia (2020) which focusses on those employed directly in coal mining and associated power generation industries.

Strongly evident in all encounters we have had in our research so far is that Collie community members express a deep connection to place and pride in the community. They feel that Collie people are strong and resilient, and they look after each other, as the quotation from a workshop participant in Box 1 demonstrates. Nevertheless, they articulate fears about the economic transition from coal, including uncertainty about future jobs opportunities and the risk of economic decline. They also identify a range of current and predicted climate change impacts for Collie, particularly extreme risk of bushfire and reduced rainfall. Community members explain that people who are already experiencing disadvantage in Collie will be worse off with these economic and climatic changes.

BOX 1. Transcripts From a Male Participant in the Workshops.

If you're a part of the community and you're in a bit of strife, say with a health issue or something like that and the community finds out about it, then the community will get in and help you. They'll drop you a load of wood off or the wife will cook a cake or a feed and or you know, they might whip the hat around and we've always, in the mines anyway I think the guys out at the power station ... and that we're pretty well the same, every, any time there's a problem with someone your hand would always go in your pocket, you know.

The workshop participants greatly appreciated being included in the just transition process embodied in the research, with many explicitly thanking us for including them in the workshops and research processes thus far. While it is evident that the WA government's transition process is concentrated on industries and workers that are directly affected by the forthcoming closure of the coal-fired power station, including significant transition planning underway for each individual worker, participants in our process greatly value the opportunity to engage with and direct this transition. The WA Government is investing funds into alternative economic industries in the community, such as the development of a magnesium refinery, mountain bike trails and tourism (Government of Western Australia, 2020). However, our data suggest that the government's economic development agenda for Collie fails to currently address all of the rights and needs of community members who experience systemic disadvantage. Participants have informed us that there is a significant lack of social services in Collie, such as mental health services and childcare, limited local post-secondary education opportunities, and housing is increasingly unaffordable due to the impacts of the COVID pandemic. The conceptualisation and resourcing of 'just transition' by the Western Australian government has not yet extended to the provision of necessary social protections to address the drivers of disadvantage and marginalisation for different groups of people in the community.

We also observe the importance and value of Aboriginal peoples' perspectives on economic transition and climate change in Collie. One Elder explained that our workshop was the first time he had been asked for his opinion and input about Collie's future despite holding a significant cultural position in the community. Wilman Noongar workshop attendees highlight the cultural and spiritual significance of the Collie River and recognise the impacts of the drying climate on the river. They promote opportunities for alternative industries through cultural ranger programmes, environmental rehabilitation and restoration and cultural tourism.

Numerous community members also discuss prevailing economic and social disparities in the community, with a growing divide between the 'haves' and the 'have nots'. This is exacerbated by increased cost of living due to rising prices for fuel, food and housing. In a patriarchal context with male-dominant economic industries, some women are disadvantaged by the lack of governmental focus on gender equity in new economic opportunities, lack of affordable childcare and lack of local family and domestic violence services. Furthermore, community members express concern about limited education and work opportunities for young people.

Although we have not yet completed the data collection for this research, already participants are providing initial suggestions to enhance equity and inclusion in the just transition and the climate change context. Some identify the need for safe and inclusive public spaces for queer young people and children with a disability. Others suggest the creation of regenerative and low emissions jobs in culturally responsive environmental conservation, social services and education. It has also been suggested that decision-making spaces must be inclusive of diverse worldviews and lived experiences to enable a transformative just transition that leaves no one behind.

CONCLUSION

The urgent need to decarbonise through cessation of fossil fuel use and energy transition to renewables as well as to respond to the consequences of climate change is a challenge facing all of humankind. In this chapter we have briefly explained the localised evolving nature of just transition thinking and framing in this context based on a literature review. It will not be sufficient to focus only on those employed in fossil fuel based industries or other economic-only based solutions, nor on simply attaining the kinds of environmental targets and outcomes needed for a sustainable future. Instead, a whole of society approach is needed, and we have argued that a truly 'just' transition must include all community members, be transformative and ensure that no one is left behind. Using a case study of the Collie region on Wilman Boodja in Western Australia, we have explained how such a process can be instigated through a participatory action research approach. However, it is worth reiterating that an energy transition away from fossil fuels to a regenerative economy is a complex challenge impacting multiple stakeholders, and is influenced by institutions, technologies and finances operating at all scales from the local to the global. While we do not profess to have all the answers, it is clear to us that such an approach can and will generate the kinds of visions and solutions needed for a successful transition. Most importantly, by being collaborative and inclusive, a strong sense of community empowerment and ownership emerges. We believe that the kind of transformative just transition approach we advocate for in this chapter can usefully serve community members, policymakers and researchers alike in framing and attaining just transitions for addressing the climate crisis and ending the extraction and burning of fossil fuels. Nonetheless, as the S-Curve model suggests, it can be expected that for the transformation to a decarbonised and regenerative economy to occur, things will get worse before they get better and a just transition process will need to accommodate this ultimately ensuring that no one gets left behind.

REFERENCES

Abimbola, O., Aikins, J. K., Makhesi-Wilkinson, T., & Roberts, E. (2021). Racism and climate (in) justice: How racism and colonialism shape the climate crisis and climate action. Retrieved from https://www.researchgate.net/profile/Erin-Roberts-2/publication/357605723_Racism_and_Climate_InJustice_How_Racism_and_Colonialism_shape_the_Climate_Crisis_and_Climate_Action/links/61d600afb8305f7c4b258221/Racism-and-Climate-InJustice-How-Racism-and-Colonialism-shape-the-Climate-Crisis-and-Climate-Action.pdf

Aria, M., & Cuccurullo, C. (2017). Bibliometrix: An R-tool for comprehensive science mapping analysis. *Journal of Informetrics, 11*(4), 959–975.

Australian Bureau of Statistics. (2020). *Region summary: Collie (S)*. Region code: 51890. Retrieved from https://dbr.abs.gov.au/region.html?lyr=lga&rgn=51890

Bainton, N., Kemp, D., Lèbre, E., Owen, J. R., & Marston, G. (2021). The energy-extractives nexus and the just transition. *Sustainable Development, 29*(4), 624–634.

Beckwith Environmental Planning. (2009). *Nyungar values of the Collie River*. Department of Water. Retrieved from https://www.water.wa.gov.au/__data/assets/pdf_file/0016/5443/91172.pdf

Bennett, N. J., Blythe, J., Cisneros-Montemayor, A. M., Singh, G. G., & Sumaila, U. R. (2019). Just transformations to sustainability. *Sustainability, 11*(14), 3881. Retrieved from https://www.mdpi.com/2071-1050/11/14/3881

Beyond Zero Emmissions. (2019). *Collie at the Crossroads: Planning a future beyond coal*. Beyond Zero Emmissions Inc. Retrieved from https://bze.org.au/wp-content/uploads/2020/12/Collie-at-the-Crossroads-FINAL-2.pdf

Blomkamp, E. (2018). The promise of co-design for public policy. *Australian Journal of Public Administration, 77*(4), 729–743. doi:10.1111/1467-8500.12310

Braunger, I., & Paula, W. (2022). Power in transitions: Gendered power asymmetries in the United Kingdom and the United States coal transitions. *Energy Research & Social Science, 87*. doi:10.1016/j.erss.2021.102474

Butler, J. (2022, May 4). In Hunter, where coal is king, a Labor heartland seat faces a strong Coalition challenge. *The Guardian*. Retrieved from https://www.theguardian.com/australia-news/2022/may/04/in-hunter-where-coal-is-king-a-labor-heartland-seat-faces-a-strong-coalition-challenge?CMP=Share_iOSApp_Other

Campbell, S., & Coenen, L. (2017). *Transitioning beyond coal: Lessons from the structural renewal of Europe's old industrial regions*. Melbourne: Australian National University.

Carley, S., & Konisky, D. M. (2020). The justice and equity implications of the clean energy transition. *Nature Energy, 5*(8), 569–577. Retrieved from https://www.nature.com/articles/s41560-020-0641-6

Carvalho, A., Riquito, M., & Ferreira, V. (2022). Sociotechnical imaginaries of energy transition: The case of the Portuguese roadmap for carbon neutrality 2050. *Energy Reports, 8*, 2413–2423. doi:10.1016/j.egyr.2022.01.138

Cha, J. M., Price, V., Stevis, D., Vachon, T. E., & Brescia-Weiler, M. (2021). *Workers and communities in transition: Report of the just transition listening project*. Labor for Sustainability Network. Retrieved from https://www.researchgate.net/profile/Dimitris-Stevis/publication/350327955_JTLP_report2021/links/605a58d1458515e83467e9d0/JTLP-report2021.pdf

Cherry, C., Gareth, T., Groves, C., Roberts, E., Shirani, F., Henwood, K., & Pidgeon, N. (2022). A personas-based approach to deliberating local decarbonisation scenarios: Findings and methodological insights (Original Research). *Energy Research & Social Science, 87*. doi:10.1016/j. erss.2021.102455

Climate Justice Union. (n.d.). About us. Retrieved form https://www.climatejusticeunion.org/About-Us

Commonwealth of Australia. (2017). *Retirement of coal fired power stations: Final report.* Canberra: Senate Printing Unit. Retrieved from https://www.aph.gov.au/Parliamentary_Business/ Committees/Senate/Environment_and_Communications/Coal_fired_power_stations/Final_ Report

Della Bosca, H., & Gillespie, J. (2018). The coal story: Generational coal mining communities and strategies of energy transition in Australia. *Energy Policy, 120*, 734–740. doi:10.1016/j.enpol. 2018.04.032

Department of Primary Industries and Regional Development. (2021). *Climate projections for Western Australia.* Retrieved from https://www.agric.wa.gov.au/climate-change/climate-projections-western-australia

Edwards, G. A., Hanmer, C., Park, S., MacNeil, R., Bojovic, M., Kucic-Riker, J., ... Viney, G. (2022). Towards a just transition from coal in Australia? *The British Academy.* Retrieved from https://research-management.mq.edu.au/ws/portalfiles/portal/200633363/Publisher_version.pdf

Emden, J., Ahmad, H., Murphy, L., & Cameron, C. (2020). Lessons learned: Just transitions from around the world. *Institute for Public Policy Research.* Retrieved from https://www.ippr.org/ files/2020-12/lessons-learned-dec2020.pdf

Evans, G., & Phelan, L. (2016). Transition to a post-carbon society: Linking environmental justice and just transition discourses. *Energy Policy, 99*, 329–339. doi:10.1016/j.enpol.2016.05.003

Furnaro, A., Herpich, P., Brauers, H., Oei, P.-Y., Kemfert, C., & Look, W. (2021). *German just transition: A review of public policies to assist German coal communities in transition.* Resources for Future. Retrieved from https://media.rff.org/documents/21-13-Nov-22.pdf

Goddard, G., & Farrelly, M. (2018). Just transition management: Balancing just outcome with just processes in Australian renewable energy transitions. Special Issue: Low Carbon Energy Systems and Energy Justice. *Applied Energy, 225*, 110–123. doi:10.1016/j.apenergy.2018.05.025

Godden, N. J., Macnish, P., Chakma, T., & Naidu, K. (2020). Feminist participatory action research as a tool for climate justice. *Gender and Development, 28*(3), 593–615. doi:10.1080/13552074. 2020.1842040

Goldtooth, T. (2020). Indigenous just transition: Reflections from the field. In B. G. Tokar & T. Gilbertson (Eds.), *Climate justice and community renewal: Resistance and grassroots solutions* (1st ed., p. 15). Routledge. doi:10.4324/9780429277146

Government of Western Australia. (2020). *Collie's just transition plan.* Perth: Department of Premier and Cabinet. Retrieved from https://www.wa.gov.au/government/publications/collies-just-transition-plan

Hackett, R. A., & Adams, P. R. (2018). *Jobs vs the environment?* Canadian Centre for Policy Alternatives. Retrieved from https://policyalternatives.ca/sites/default/files/uploads/publications/BC %20Office/2018/12/CCPA-BC_JobsvsEnvt_web.pdf

Heffron, R. J., & McCauley, D. (2018). What is the 'just transition'? *Geoforum, 88*, 74–77. doi:10.1016/ j.geoforum.2017.11.016

Herpich, P., Brauers, H., & Oei, P.-Y. (2018). *An historical case study on previous coal transitions in Germany.* Berlin: IDDRI and Climate Strategies. Retrieved from https://coaltransitions.files. wordpress.com/2018/07/2018-historical-coal-transitions-in-germany-report1.pdf

Higgins, J. P., Thomas, J., Chandler, J., Cumpston, M., Li, T., Page, M. J., & Welch, V. A. (Eds.). (2019). *Cochrane handbook for systematic reviews of interventions.* Hoboken, NJ: John Wiley & Sons.

Hurlbert, M., & Rayner, J. (2018). Reconciling power, relations, and processes: The role of recognition in the achievement of energy justice for Aboriginal people. *Applied Energy, 228*, 1320–1327. doi:10.1016/j.apenergy.2018.06.054

IPCC. (2022). *Climate change 2022: Impacts, adaptation, and vulnerability summary for policy makers.* Working Group II Contribution to the Sixth Assesment Report of the IPCC, WMO and

UNEP. Retrieved from https://report.ipcc.ch/ar6wg2/pdf/IPCC_AR6_WGII_FinalDraft_ FullReport.pdf

Jafry, T., Watson, E., Mattar, S. D., & Mikulewicz, M. (2022). Just transitions and structural change in coal regions: Central and Eastern Europe. In *Civil engineering and environmental management*. Glasgow: Glasgow Caledonian University.

Jewell, J., Vinichenko, V., Nacke, L., & Cherp, A. (2019). Prospects for powering past coal. *Nature Climate Change, 9*(8), 592–597. doi:10.1038/s41558-019-0509-6

Johnson, O. W., Han, J. Y.-C., Knight, A.-L., Mortensen, S., Aung, M. T., Boyland, M., & Resurrección, B. P. (2020). Intersectionality and energy transitions: A review of gender, social equity and low-carbon energy. *Energy Research & Social Science, 70*, 101774. doi:10.1016/j. erss.2020.101774

Johnstone, P., & Hielscher, S. (2017). Phasing out coal, sustaining coal communities? Living with technological decline in sustainability pathways. *The Extractive Industries and Society, 4*(3), 457–461. doi:10.1016/j.exis.2017.06.002

Kaijser, A., & Kronsell, A. (2014). Climate change through the lens of intersectionality. *Environmental Politics, 23*(3), 417–433. doi:10.1080/09644016.2013.835203

Kais, S. M., & Islam, M. S. (2016). Community capitals as community resilience to climate change: Conceptual connections. *International Journal of Environmental Research and Public Health, 13*(12), 1211. Retrieved from https://www.mdpi.com/1660-4601/13/12/1211

Kalt, T. (2021). Jobs vs. climate justice? Contentious narratives of labor and climate movements in the coal transition in Germany. *Environmental Politics, 30*(7), 1135–1154. doi:10.1080/09644016. 2021.1892979

Krawchenko, T., & Gordon, M. (2020). Policies for a just transition. In *The Palgrave encyclopedia of urban and regional futures*. London: Palgrave Macmillan. doi:10.1007/978-3-030-51812-7_95-1

Krawchenko, T. A., & Gordon, M. (2021). How do we manage a just transition? A comparative review of national and regional just transition initiatives. *Sustainability, 13*(11), 6070. doi:10.3390/ su13116070

Kronsell, A. (2013). Gender and transition in climate governance. *Environmental Innovation and Societal Transitions, 7*, 1–15. doi:10.1016/j.eist.2012.12.003

Lawrence, J., Mackey, B., Chiew, F., Costello, M. J., Hennessy, K., Lansbury, N., ... Wreford, A. (2022). Australasia. In H.-O. Pörtner, D. C. Roberts, M. Tignor, E. S. Poloczanska, K. Mintenbeck, A. Alegría, ... B. Rama (Eds.), *Climate change 2022: Impacts, adaptation, and vulnerability. Contribution of Working Group II to the Sixth Assessment Report of the Intergovernmental Panel on Climate Change*. Cambridge University Press.

Leonard, S., Parsons, M., Olawsky, K., & Kofod, F. (2013). The role of culture and traditional knowledge in climate change adaptation: Insights from East Kimberley, Australia. *Global Environmental Change, 23*(3), 623–632. doi:10.1016/j.gloenvcha.2013.02.012

Lewin, P. G. (2017). "Coal is not just a job, it's a way of life": The cultural politics of coal production in Central Appalachia. *Social Problems, 66*(1), 51–68. doi:10.1093/socpro/spx030

Lobao, L., Zhou, M., Partridge, M., & Betz, M. (2016). Poverty, place, and coal employment across Appalachia and the United States in a new economic era. *Rural Sociology, 81*(3), 343–386. doi: 10.1111/ruso.12098

MacNeil, R., & Beauman, M. (2022). Understanding resistance to just transition ideas in Australian coal communities. *Environmental Innovation and Societal Transitions, 43*, 118–126. doi:10.1016/ j.eist.2022.03.007

Mayer, A. (2018). A just transition for coal miners? Community identity and support from local policy actors. *Environmental Innovation and Societal Transitions, 28*, 1–13. doi:10.1016/j.eist.2018.03. 006

McCauley, D., & Heffron, R. (2018). Just transition: Integrating climate, energy and environmental justice. *Energy Policy, 119*, 1–7. doi:10.1016/j.enpol.2018.04.014

McCauley, D., Ramasar, V., Heffron, R. J., Sovacool, B. K., Mebratu, D., & Mundaca, L. (2019). Energy justice in the transition to low carbon energy systems: Exploring key themes in interdisciplinary research. *Applied Energy, 233–234*, 916–921. doi:10.1016/j.apenergy.2018.10.005

Meadowcroft, J. (2009). What about the politics? Sustainable development, transition management, and long term energy transitions. *Policy Sciences, 42*(4), 323. doi:10.1007/s11077-009-9097-z

Mertins-Kirkwood, H. (2018). *Making decarbonization work for workers: Policies for a just transition to a zero-carbon economy in Canada*. Canadian Centre for Policy Alternatives. Retrieved from https://www.policyalternatives.ca/sites/default/files/uploads/publications/National%20Office/2018/01/Making%20Decarbonization%20Work.pdf

Michell, M., & Halsmith, R. (2019). *Minninup Pool Precinct Project: Aboriginal Heritage Assessment*. S. o. Collie. Retrieved from https://www.collie.wa.gov.au/wp-content/uploads/2020/11/Noongar-Heritage-Report.pdf

Northover, J. (n.d.). Joe Northover talks about Minningup Pool on the Collie River. South West Aboriginal Land & Sea Council. Retrieved from https://www.noongarculture.org.au/joe-northover-minningup-pool/

Olson-Hazboun, S. K. (2018). "Why are we being punished and they are being rewarded?" Views on renewable energy in fossil fuels-based communities of the US west. *The Extractive Industries and Society, 5*(3), 366–374. doi:10.1016/j.exis.2018.05.001

Pai, S., Harrison, K., & Zerriffi, H. (2020). *A systematic review of the key elements of a just transition for fossil fuel workers*. Ottawa, ON: Smart Prosperity Institute.

Pellegrini-Masini, G., Pirni, A., & Maran, S. (2020). Energy justice revisited: A critical review on the philosophical and political origins of equality. *Energy Research & Social Science, 59*, 101310. doi:10.1016/j.erss.2019.101310

Petzold, J., Andrews, N., Ford, J. D., Hedemann, C., & Postigo, J. C. (2020). Indigenous knowledge on climate change adaptation: A global evidence map of academic literature. *Environmental Research Letters, 15*(11), 113007. doi:10.1088/1748-9326/abb330

Rising, J., Dumas, M., Dicker, S., Propp, D., Robertson, M., & Look, W. (2021). *Regional just transitions in the UK: Insights from 40 years of policy experience*. Resources for the Future. Retrieved from https://media.rff.org/documents/UK_Report_-_with_Appendix.pdf

Rosemberg, A. (2010). Building a just transition: The linkages between climate change and employment. *International Journal of Labour Research, 2*(2), 125–161. Retrieved from https://www.proquest.com/docview/884976739?pq-origsite=gscholar&fromopenview=true

Sartor, O. (2018). Implementing coal transitions. Insights from case studies of major coal-consuming economies. A summary report of the coal transitions project based on inputs developed under the coal transitions research project - September 2018. *Institute for Sustainable Development and International Relations, 52*(48), 45–76.

Shaffril, H. A. M., Ahmad, N., Samsuddin, S. F., Samah, A. A., & Hamdan, M. E. (2020). Systematic literature review on adaptation towards climate change impacts among indigenous people in the Asia Pacific regions. *Journal of Cleaner Production, 258*, 120595. doi:10.1016/j.jclepro.2020.120595

Snyder, B. F. (2018). Vulnerability to decarbonization in hydrocarbon-intensive counties in the United States: A just transition to avoid post-industrial decay. *Energy Research & Social Science, 42*, 34–43. doi:10.1016/j.erss.2018.03.004

South West Aboriginal Land and Sea Council. (n.d.). Connection to country. Retrieved from https://www.noongarculture.org.au/connection-to-country/

Stevis, D. (2020). Planetary just transition? How inclusive and how just? Discussion Paper. *Earth System Governance, 6*. doi:10.1016/j.esg.2020.100065

Tranter, B., & Foxwell-Norton, K. (2021). Only in Queensland? Coal mines and voting in the 2019 Australian federal election. *Environmental Sociology, 7*(1), 90–101. doi:10.1080/23251042.2020.1810376

Tuana, N. (2019). Climate apartheid: The forgetting of race in the Anthropocene. *Critical Philosophy of Race, 7*(1), 1–31. doi:10.5325/critphilrace.7.1.0001

United Nations. (2015). United Nations Paris Agreement. Retrieved from https://unfccc.int/sites/default/files/english_paris_agreement.pdf

Vachon, T. (2021). The greens new deal and just transition frames within the American labour movement. In N. Räthzel, D. Stevis, & D. Uzzell (Eds.), *The Palgrave handbook of environmental labour studies*. London: Palgrave Macmillan. doi:10.1007/978-3-030-71909-8_5

Velicu, I., & Barca, S. (2020). The just transition and its work of inequality. *Sustainability: Science, Practice and Policy, 16*(1), 263–273. doi:10.1080/15487733.2020.1814585

Vona, F. (2019). Job losses and political acceptability of climate policies: Why the 'job-killing' argument is so persistent and how to overturn it. *Climate Policy, 19*(4), 524–532. doi:10.1080/14693062.2018.1532871

Wang, X., & Lo, K. (2021). Just transition: A conceptual review. *Energy Research & Social Science, 82*, 102291. doi:10.1016/j.erss.2021.102291

Weeramanthri, T., Joyce, S., Bowman, F., Bangor-Jones, R., & Law, C. (2020). *Climate Health WA Inquiry: Final report.* Department of Health.

Weller, S. A. (2019). Just transition? Strategic framing and the challenges facing coal dependent communities. *Environment and Planning C: Politics and Space, 37*(2), 298–316. doi:10.1177/2399654418784304

Williams, P. D. (2021). Queensland's role in the 2019 Australian Federal Election: A case study of regional difference. *Australian Journal of Politics & History, 67*(1), 150–168. doi:10.1111/ajph.12760

Wooltorton, S., Collard, L., Horwitz, P., Poelina, A., & Palmer, D. (2020). Sharing a place-based indigenous methodology and learnings. *Environmental Education Research, 26*(7), 917–934. doi:10.1080/13504622.2020.1773407

ENERGY CONSUMPTION FOR TRANSPORTATION IN SUB-SAHARAN AFRICA

Adetayo Olaniyi Adeniran, Mosunmola Joseph Muraina and Josiah Chukwuma Ngonadi

ABSTRACT

Energy consumption in transportation accounted for over 29% of total final consumption (TFC) of energy and 65% of global oil usage, and it is highly connected to mobility. Mobility is essential for access to day-to-day activities such as education, leisure, healthcare, business activities, and commercial and industrial operations. This study examines the energy consumption for the transport industry, and the level of renewable energy development in some selected Sub-Saharan African (SSA) nations. This study relied on previous publications of government, reports and articles related to the subject matter. Vehicle ownership is fast increasing, particularly in cities. Still, it begins at a relatively low level because the area is home to countries with the lowest ownership rates worldwide. In its current state, the energy sector faces significant challenges such as inadequate and poorly maintained infrastructure, dealing with increasing traffic congestion in cities, large-scale imports of used vehicles with poor emission standards that affect air quality in cities, a lack of safe and formally operated public transportation systems, and inadequate consideration for women and disabled mobility needs. Motorcycle and tricycle are dominating the rural areas, accounting for a substantial amount of this growth. Aviation is the largest non-road user of energy, and this trend is predicted to continue through 2040 as Gross Domestic Product (GDP) grows and urbanisation expands. This study revealed the energy consumption for the transport industry, and the level of renewable energy development in some selected SSA. Rail and navigation lag behind current global levels. The usage of biofuel and rail transport was recommended.

Achieving Net Zero
Developments in Corporate Governance and Responsibility, Volume 20, 203–231
Copyright © 2023 by Emerald Publishing Limited
All rights of reproduction in any form reserved
ISSN: 2043-0523/doi:10.1108/S2043-052320230000020009

Keywords: Energy sources; energy consumption; transportation; infrastructure; emission; Sub-Saharan Africa

INTRODUCTION

Economic activities can impact energy demand, hence it is likely that energy consumption has influenced economic activity. Because it is an essential input in the manufacture and transportation of commodities for both foreign and domestic enterprises, energy demand governs economic activity. The equipment and machinery in factories and industries need a lot of energy to make and deliver items for businesses. As a result, as the need for energy grows, so does the volume of transported goods for trade and the volume of goods produced.

Energy consumption estimates are critical tools for planners, policymakers, scientists, engineers, stakeholders, and the general public including investors that are users of energy data to analyse the future data of energy consumption in the country and comprehend the social, economic, technical, and environmental implications of achieving that demand. Such technologies are much more important in emerging nations since previous consumption trends alone cannot predict the trajectory of future energy consumption.

Transportation energy usage comprises the energy used to move people and products by road, rail, air, water, and pipeline. Energy consumption in the transportation sector is determined by growth rates in both economic activity and the driving-age population (Georgia, 2019). Economic expansion stimulates increases in industrial production, which necessitates the transportation of raw materials to manufacturing locations as well as the transportation of completed commodities to end customers. Vehicles that are land-based, air-based, or water-based consume energy (Chukwu, Isa, Ojosu, & Olayande, 2015). The compilation of trustworthy data that identifies and quantifies the energy provided and consumed in an economy is important to any energy research. Since mobility is germane to the existence of human beings, so also is energy because it drives the mobility power.

Both mobility and energy are indispensable for achieving quality living (Chioma, 2019). Energy is utilised by practically all of the economy's activities across the continent, and homes consume it every day for enhancing comfort and facilitate travel. Energy is utilised in a variety of ways (Felix, 2019). As a result, growth rates for both the driving-age population and economic activity influence transportation sector energy consumption. Economic expansion stimulates increases in industrial production, which necessitates the transportation of raw materials to manufacturing locations as well as the transportation of completed commodities to end customers (Ogunbodede, Ilesanmi, & Olurankinse, 2019). The most common energy available in Africa is gasoline, natural gas, and electricity. Other forms such as biomass and solar energy are not common in all African countries. Today, road transport dominates the region's energy consumption for transportation, and this trend is expected to continue through 2040.

Among all end-use sectors, transportation consumes the most energy. In 2018, it accounted for over 29% of total final consumption (TFC) of energy and 65% of global oil usage. Mobility is essential for access to day-to-day activities, education, leisure, health care, business activities, and commercial and industrial operations. The energy consumption in the transport industry in 11 Sub-Saharan African nations was studied: Angola, Côte d'Ivoire, the Democratic Republic of the Congo, Ethiopia, Ghana, Kenya, Mozambique, Nigeria, South Africa, Senegal, and Tanzania. The nations were picked based on economic power, population dominance, and data availability. Large amounts of mineral deposits required for modern energy transitions are also found in Africa, including one-fifth of the world's uranium resources and large amounts of strategic metals and minerals, such as 90% of world cobalt reserves in the Democratic Republic of the Congo, which serves as important components of batteries required for the electric vehicle revolution.

The Sustainable Development Goals (SDGs), investigate what it would take to meet the key energy-related components of the '2030 Agenda for Sustainable Development', which was endorsed in 2015 by United Nations member states. Among the SDGs, the three relevant targets for energy consumption are:

i. To achieve universal energy access to modern energy by 2030;
ii. To embark on pressing action to address climate change; and
iii. To minimise pollutant emissions that lead to poor air quality.

It is vital to emphasise that access to modern energy has become a trademark problem, with systematic monitoring of the worldwide population's lack of basic energy services, as well as the study of the policies, technology, and investment needed to bridge this gap. While Agenda 2063 lays out a comprehensive and ambitious plan for Africa, its success is dependent on overcoming several obstacles.

The paucity of resources for its execution, as well as the need to build government capacity, transparency, and intra-African cooperation institutional change, are among the most significant. The Africa Case gross domestic product (GDP) estimates are based on Agenda 2063 and take into consideration each country's own goal for economic growth, which is based on regional economic blueprints and energy master plans. It lays forth a realistic route to inclusive and long-term economic growth and development. In the case of Africa, the GDP rises at an average annual pace of 6.1% from now to 2040, while Sub-Saharan Africa grows at an average rate of 7.3% annually. The essence of monitoring energy consumption in transportation is to achieve sustainable environmental development through the encouragement of renewable energy.

The term 'renewable energy' was first used in the specialist literature over two decades ago, and it was defined as 'new goods and processes that give the customer and corporate value while dramatically reducing environmental consequences' (Hellstrom, 2016). The term 'renewable energy' is frequently used in combination with other terms in comparable settings, such as 'environmental innovation', and 'sustainable innovation'. Renewable energy, as a critical component of innovation, is a driver of social and economic advancement, with a particular focus on providing chances for long-term economic growth (Fussler & James, 1996; James, 1997). This phenomenon, which offers a wide range of applications, is thought to be capable of ensuring societal economic development, company competitiveness, increased productivity, and profitability through resource management and access to environmentally friendly products, technologies, and markets (International Energy Agency, 2017a; Rennings, 2018).

Concerning the economy, renewable energy strives to minimise energy and material costs while also boosting goods, services, markets, customers, and new business models. Renewable energy attempts to improve people's quality of life and generate new, long-term jobs on a social level. In terms of the environment, renewable energy attempts to protect biodiversity and maintain ecological balance through fostering environmental effect reduction, sustainable and innovative views on climate change, and responsible natural resource management (Dogaru, 2017).

In recent years, research into the origins of carbon-dioxide emissions has exploded (Chaabouni & Saidi, 2017; Iwata, Okada, & Samreth, 2020; Mui-Yin, Chin-Hong, Teo, & Joseph, 2018; Sadikov, Kasimova, Isaeva, Khachaturov, & Salahodjaev, 2020; Solarin, 2021). The existence of a nonlinear (inverted U-shaped) link between GDP per capita and carbon-dioxide emissions across nations, known as the environmental Kuznets curve (EKC) phenomenon, was one of the most significant frameworks investigated in this area. Malaysia (Saboori, Sulaiman, & Mohd, 2020), China (Jalil & Mahmud, 2015), Croatia (Ahmad et al., 2017), Turkey (Pata, 2018), Algeria (Lacheheb, Rahim, & Sirag, 2015), and Sub-Saharan Africa (Lacheheb et al., 2015) have all used the EKC framework (Bah, Abdulwakil, & Azam, 2019).

Also, research suggests that economic development, urbanisation, commerce, and the usage of renewable energy are all key predictors of carbon-dioxide emissions among nations (Hossain, 2019; Mirzaei & Bekri, 2017; Shahbaz, Hye, Tiwari, & Leitão, 2021). Due to the need for examining the energy consumption for the transport industry, this study examines energy consumption for transportation in some selected Sub-Saharan African (SSA) nations: Angola, Côte d'Ivoire, the Democratic Republic of the Congo, Ethiopia, Ghana, Kenya, Mozambique, Nigeria, Senegal, South Africa, and Tanzania, and the level of renewable energy development in some selected SSA countries such as Morocco, Tunisia, Egypt, Benin, Ghana, Guinea, Mali, Senegal, Sierra Leone, Togo, Mauritius, Burundi, Kenya, Malawi, Uganda, Rwanda, Tanzania, Cameroon, Swaziland, Botswana, and South Africa based on the availability of information.

EMPIRICAL REVIEW
The Replacement of Fossil Fuels, Why?

The curiosity of human and the need for survival led to a slew of energy-related discoveries. Gaining energy from food (nutrients) prompted man to devise methods to turn some inedible raw materials edible and to gain simple access to food. As a result, man sought energy (through wood burning) to cook and manufacture food. Humanity desired more after obtaining energy for the body in order to raise their level of existence. As a result, new and 'simple' energy-producing sources were discovered. Fossil fuels are naturally occurring hydrocarbons that build up in the environment over millions of years when living species die.

The first fossil energy discovered was 'black stone' (coal) in the thirteenth century, followed by natural gas, petroleum, and oil shale later (commercially in the nineteenth century) (Keeling, 1973; UNDP, 2016). The primary uses of fossil fuels are transportation, industry, and power generation (Bertine & Goldberg, 1971; Hubbert, 1949; Keeling, 1973). Continuous usage of fossil energy (which cancels out its creation and use) will cause less environmental damage than increasing rates of use. As of the end of 1947, total coal output was 81 billion metric tons. The fact that half of this was consumed during a 27-year period sparked concerns about environmental effect (Hubbert, 1949).

An exponential growth in population, according to Thomas Malthus' concept, leads to poverty. Adam Smith, on the other hand, contends that individuals or societies behave cooperatively to increase prosperity (Thomson, 1998). These concepts support the previous premise that human nature harms the environment. Concerns about global warming and climate change arose as a result of population growth and the exponential expansion in the usage of fossil fuels (Wuebbles & Jain, 2018). This is mostly due to anthropogenic activity such as fossil fuel combustion, which emits greenhouse gases into the atmosphere. Furthermore, because fossil fuels are generated over time (centuries), their annihilation without a substitute will be damaging to human life.

The effect of rising atmospheric temperatures and climate change on the ecosystem may be observed in the loss of biodiversity owing to excessive flooding, storms, certain volcanic eruptions, landslides, and so on. Some valuable creatures and plant species have become extinct as a result of this. Even though fossil energy has and continues to improve humanity's level of life, the necessity for additional alternative energy sources is critical in light of the aforementioned problems.

Sustainable Substitutes of Energy Sources

The major difference between renewable energy sources (RES) and traditional energy sources is that RES regenerates continually during human existence while it takes several years for traditional energy sources to create (Kaygusuz, 2020). The endeavour to ensure energy supply and reduce energy's role to climate change are often regarded as the two 'overarching problems' of the energy industry in pursuit of a sustainable future (Abbasi & Abbasi, 2020; Edenhofer et al., 2019; Kaygusuz, 2020). Energy security is critical, and we must not forget that its form and use are both sustainable. This prompted a number of studies that resulted in a return to RES, which are long-term energy sources. 'Return' because before the discovery of fossil energy, humans used bio-energy (for cooking and heating).

One of the earliest reasons in favour of transitioning from fossil fuels to renewables occurred in the early 1970s, when the Organization of Petroleum Exporting Countries (OPEC) dramatically and unilaterally raised the price of crude petroleum, just as the world was becoming more aware of environmental degradation (Abbasi, Premalatha, & Abbasi, 2019). In the last decade, renewable energy has emerged as a fascinating and quickly expanding business. The most significant renewable energy sources include hydropower, geothermal energy, solar energy, ocean (tide and wave) energy, wind energy, and bioenergy since they can replace themselves spontaneously and without depletion.

The principal sources, usage and conversions of the RES can be summarised as hydropower energy source that can be used for power generation; modern biomass energy source that can be used for heat and power generation, pyrolysis, gasification, digestion; geothermal energy source that can be used for urban heating, power generation, hydrothermal, hot dry rock; solar energy source that can be used for solar home systems, solar dryers, solar cookers; direct solar energy source that can be used for photovoltaic, thermal power generation, water heaters; wind energy source that can be used for power generation, wind generators, windmills, water pump; and wave and tide energy source that can be used for numerous designs, barrage, tidal stream (Panwar, Kaushik, & Kothari, 2019).

Literature Gap

Scientifically, energy is the proclivity and tendency to do work concerning force and distance covering. It is a multiplier of force that improves man's ability to turn raw resources into useable goods (Acar & Dincer, 2019), allowing him to provide a variety of valued services (Edward, 2021). As a result, it is an essential element of progress and has always been a critical and indispensable contribution to the current civilization's economic demands (Sambo, 2015). Energy comes in many forms, including electrical, chemical, mechanical, heat, light, and so on, and may be divided into renewable and non-renewable sources (Edward, 2021).

It is undeniably crucial in the growth process. It has been suggested that without energy, achieving sustainable development is nearly impossible (Edifon, Edwin, & Ben, 2016). Because access to contemporary energy is at the centre of human progress, it is clear that to accomplish the SDGs (Sustainable Development Goals), significant improvements in the kind of energy services to which the poor have access to fundamental requirements of life are required (Twidell & Weir, 2015). According to the World Health Organization (WHO), the Millennium Development Goals (MDGs) may be met if the energy issue is handled in terms of quantity and quality (GNESD, 2016).

It asserts that, while there is no SDG for energy, the global ambitions contained in the targets will not be met unless the quantity and quality of energy services are significantly expanded (Edifon et al., 2016). Energy is certainly an essential element of socioeconomic growth, affecting virtually every aspect of human existence and serving as a vital requirement for human advancement (Bhusare, 2015). Improved household energy technology for the poor can prevent around 2 million deaths per year from indoor air pollution caused by solid fuel use (Word Bank, 2015). The common merits of RES are their inexhaustibility and low environmental effect, and the demerits are their low energy density and the fact that the technology is still in its early stages (Iwata et al., 2020). In reality, RES technology has only just become commercially available Saboori et al. (2020).

Ajayi and Ajanaku (2016) contend that energy is essential for human development and livelihood transformation, considering energy as a catalyst that may stimulate livelihood transformation by increasing numerous socioeconomic activities at the household level such as agriculture, health care, and education (Kalogirou, 2021). Energy, according to Chambers and Conway (1991), is a necessary component of greater economic growth. The fact that greater availability and use of energy services are strongly linked to economic growth indicates the pertinence of energy in socio-economic development (Ellabban, Abu-Rub, & Blaabjerg, 2019).

Carbon emission is known to be the end product of fossil fuel which is widely consumed in African countries. In recent years, studies on carbon emissions were conducted by Chaabouni and Saidi (2017), Iwata et al. (2020), Mui-Yin et al. (2018), Sadikov et al. (2020), and Solarin (2021). Some studies found a nonlinear relationship between carbon emissions and GDP per capita across different countries of the world. For instance, Saboori et al. (2020) found the relationship in Malaysia, Jalil and Mahmud (2015) found the relationship in China, Ahmad et al. (2017) in Croatia, Pata (2018) in Turkey, Lacheheb et al. (2015) in Algeria, and Lacheheb et al. (2015) in Sub-Saharan Africa. Those studies further revealed that transportation, urbanization, economic development, and commerce are drivers of renewable energy usage, and are all significant factors influencing carbon emissions.

Nonetheless, those studies may not have considered the energy consumption in transportation and the level of renewable energy development in SSAs, as they are crucial in sustainable development. On this note, this study examines the energy consumption for the transport industry in some selected SSA nations: Angola, Côte d'Ivoire, the Democratic Republic of the Congo, Ethiopia, Ghana, Kenya, Mozambique, Nigeria, Senegal, South Africa, and Tanzania, and the level of renewable energy development in some selected SSA countries: Morocco, Tunisia, Egypt, Benin, Ghana, Guinea, Mali, Senegal, Sierra Leone, Togo, Mauritius, Burundi, Kenya, Malawi, Uganda, Rwanda, Tanzania, Cameroon, Swaziland, Botswana, and South Africa based on the availability of information.

RESULTS AND DISCUSSION

Transport is a consumer of energy through the burning of fuel. It accounts for more than 20% of current global CO_2 emissions. Regarding the global share of transport energy usage in the world, automobiles account for more than 40% of energy usage, trucks account for more than 34% of energy usage, aviation and maritime account for more than 11% of energy usage each, and railways account for more than 4% energy usage. It was revealed that there is more passenger mobility than freight. Hence, there is a need for a modal shift such that there will be more efficient usage within the same mode (for example, more freight per ride).

Renewable Energy Development in Some Selected African Countries

There are five regions in Africa: north, west, east, central, and south. It consists of 54 self-governing countries. Each region has distinct cultures and magnificent geographical features (language, visual arts and indigenous traditions). Africa is the world's second-largest continent, bordered to the north by the Mediterranean and Red Seas, to the east and south by the Indian Ocean, and to the west and south by the South Atlantic Ocean. African countries affected by slavery and colonialism, with the exception of Ethiopia, had to battle for their liberty. The Country of South Africa (Union of South Africa) gained independence as the first African republic in 1931. With Africa's longest river, the Nile in Egypt, capable of producing hydropower, and the world's biggest desert, the Sahara, capable of producing solar energy, there is no doubt that its climatic conditions would differ across the continent.

Africa has a diverse range of climatic conditions, including tropical rainforest in the Western, Central, and Eastern areas, humid subtropical in the South-west, Mediterranean in the South-east and North-west, and desert and semi-desert climate in the Sahara and Sub-Sahara regions in the north. The continent is still evolving, with some nations thriving and others remaining impoverished. Climate conditions in the 1700s were different. Climate change has previously been documented in Africa, according to research publications (Barrios, Bertinelli, & Strobl, 2016; Besada et al., 2015; Challinor, Wheeler, Garforth, Craufurd, & Kassam, 2016; Collier, Conway, & Venables, 2015). This may be seen in extreme weather patterns such as protracted drought and increased rainfall intensity creating floods, as well as certain places becoming hotter, harming agricultural production and livelihood. These changes can be attributed to increased pollution, the use of fossil fuels to provide electricity to most regions of the world, and deforestation for development.

While seeking to improve countries, the methods used to do so are simultaneously damaging the environment, which inhibits economic growth and development. As a result of the availability of renewable energy resources, most African governments are attempting to build laws and strategies to develop them in a sustainable manner (Bugaje, 2016). The subsections that follow will examine the growth of renewable energy consumption in the 21 nations included in this article. Benin, Burundi, Botswana, Cameroon, Egypt, Ghana, Guinea, Kenya, Malawi, Mali, Mauritius, Morocco, Rwanda, Senegal, Sierra Leone, South Africa, Swaziland, Tanzania, Togo, Tunisia, and Uganda are among the nations involved.

Morocco

Morocco's location in the Southern Mediterranean area provides tremendous solar and wind energy potential (1300 MW estimated power capacity, 2020). The nation also has hydropower potential. Morocco's government adopted a National Renewable Energy and Efficiency Plan in 2015. The goal of this strategy is to expand renewable energy percentages in the fossil-dominated energy mix to 42% by the end of 2020 (solar – 14%, wind – 14%, and hydro – 14% installed capacity) and 52% by 2030. It also intends to cut its energy use by 12% by 2020 in order to increase energy efficiency (De Arce, Mahía, Medina, & Escribano, 2020; Hochberg, 2017; International Energy Agency, 2017b; Mentis, Hermann, Howells, Welsch, & Siyal, 2015). Morocco is far and away the leader in the implementation and adoption of renewable energy programs for sustainable development in North Africa and Africa as a whole.

Tunisia

Despite the fact that RES have been used in Tunisia for decades, there was no dedicated regulatory authority (Ministry of Industry, Energy, and Mines) that focussed entirely on renewable energy until January 2016. The new Mining, Energy, and Renewables industry will aid in the emphasis on decrease of fossil energy imports (over 90%) that began in 2018 (Jebli & Youssef, 2015; Oxford Business Group, 2016). In Tunisia, there are several renewable energy potentials, the most notable of which is solar energy, with yearly radiation rates ranging from 1,800 to 2,600 kWh/m^2.

Tunisia's connected-grid generation capacity increased by 3% in 2015 due to the addition of renewable energy from the country's two wind farms. The TuNur project, which is under ongoing, seeks to build Tunisia's first large-scale solar farm and a 10 MW Concentrated Solar Power Plant. Despite these incremental gains, numerous regulatory obstacles must to be resolved before the new ministry can fulfil its objectives (Oxford Business Group, 2017).

Egypt

Egypt generates a substantial amount of oil and natural gas because it bridges the gap between North Africa and the Middle East (second largest after Algeria). More than 80% of Egypt's primary energy consumption is derived from fossil fuels (oil, natural gas, and coal), with the remaining derived from hydroelectricity and other renewables (British Petroleum PLC, 2017; EIA, 2015). According to the BP Statistical Review of World Energy (2017), Egypt's primary energy consumption by fuel source in 2016 were through oil, natural gas, hydro-eletricity, annd renewables. From all these, natural gas is the major source of energy consumption.

Because of Egypt's geographic position, the most important RES are the'sun' (solar energy) and wind energy. The New and Renewable Energy Authority (NREA) was founded in 1986 to monitor and encourage the use of renewable energy in the country in order to minimise the country's usage of fossil energy and thereby safeguard the environment.

NREA has continued to improve its research and development in the solar and wind potential energy industries throughout the years, with several future projects planned. Egypt's direct solar radiation potential ranges between 1970 to 2,600 kWh/m^2 per year, with an average of 9–11 hours of sunshine every day (New and Renewable Energy Authority, 2017). According to Shata and Hanitsch (Shata & Hanitsch, 2016), the finest three places for wind farms in Egypt are Sidi Barrani, Mersa Matruh, and EI Dabaa. These stations are predicted to provide an annual mean wind speed of more than 5.0 m/s along Egypt's Mediterranean coast. Since the adoption of the NREA, it has experienced its fair share of problems and possibilities, and it currently plays an important part in the country's economy and energy security.

Benin
The Republic of Benin is bordered by Togo to the west and Nigeria to the east, as well as Burkina Faso and Niger. The country has a variety of renewable energy potentials, the most important of which are hydropower and bio-energy, followed by sun and wind. The geothermal potential has not been scientifically tested. As evidenced in the REEP policy database, the main renewable energy sources (RES) in Benin were solar wind, bio-energy, geothermal, and hydro. In 2015, the gross generation of power from solar photovoltaic and hydro was 5 GWh and 14 GWh, respectively. In addition, primary solid biofuels consumed 60,584 TJ in total (International Energy Agency, 2015a).

Ghana
Togo, Burkina Faso, and Ivory Coast are Ghana's neighbours. Ghana's fuel energy mix consists mostly of traditional biomass (approximately 18% charcoal and firewood), fossil fuel, and hydropower (over 20%). Due to decreasing hydropower station energy output, the country has experienced an increase in power outages and load shedding during the last decade (hydrologic shocks in Akosombo and Kpong). Other RES have the ability to alleviate the current electricity problem. In Ghana, the renewable energy potential comprises sun, wind, hydropower, and bio-energy (modern biomass) (Arthur, Baidoo, & Antwi, 2019; Gyamfi, Modjinou, & Djordjevic, 2015).

Since the late 1990s, Ghana has worked to incorporate legislation that promote renewable energy use into the energy mix, and the Renewable Energy Act was approved in 2019. This Act includes provisions such as feed-in tariffs, renewable energy purchase mandates, the establishment of a renewable energy fund, and tax benefits. The daily sun irradiation potential of the nation is between 4 and 6 kWh/m^2, and select areas have an estimated wind speed potential of 6 m/s at 50 m (Gyamfi et al., 2015).

Guinea

Guinea is a West African country surrounded by Mali, Senegal, and Guinea-Bissau to the north and Liberia, Cote d'Ivoire, and Sierra Leone to the south. In 2021, just 26% of the population had access to power. Given the circumstances and the country's abundance of 12 major rivers and other renewable energy sources, the Ministry of Energy and government are attempting to improve matters. Hydropower and biomass are significant RES in the country. In order to diversify the country's energy mix, the government built a 240 MW hydropower plant (Kaleta Hydropower Plant) in 2015 (USAID, 2017).

Mali

Mali shares borders with Algeria to the north, Mauritania to the west, Niger to the east, Senegal, Guinea-Bissau, Guinea, and Cote d'Ivoire to the north, and Burkina Faso to the east. In 2016, 27% of the population had access to electricity produced by hydropower and imported fossil fuels. Other RES can help to solve the situation (The World Bank, 2017). Renewable energy sources such as hydropower, solar energy, wind energy, and bio-energy can assist Malians improve their energy balance. According to Nygaard et al. (2019).'s research, the modelled annual mean wind speed at a height of 50 m is 4.46 m/s, with an observed value of 5.3 m/s at a height of 41 m.

Wind speed is more intense in the north than in the south. Solar radiation in the north varies between 4,000 and 7,000 kWh/m^2/day all year. From May to September, it swings between 5,000 and 6,000 kWh/m^2/day, with daily fluctuations in the south being larger and more regular than in the north.

Senegal

The energy mix of the country is dominated by fossil fuels, and not everyone has access to electricity. With the instability of fossil energy costs, as well as pollution and deterioration of the environment, RES has the potential to improve the situation. Wind energy in Senegal has advanced differently from other RES in the country during the previous two decades. Sabaly, Basse, Diba, Sarr, and Camara (2021) observed that wind speed averages 3–5 m/s in three places, Kaolack, Fatick, and Thies, with most years above 4 m/s. Even though wind speed is not particularly high in the researched regions, it is higher near bodies of water (river or sea) and in mountainous areas of the country.

Senegal's geographical location provides it with a maximum potential of 5.8 kWh/m^2/day. Irradiation levels are normally high throughout the year, with the exception of January and December (minimal irradiations). According to the findings of this study, bio-energy (especially biogas from cow dung) holds promise in the country but is not feasible for power generation in these areas.

Sierra Leone

In May 2016, the government of the Republic of Sierra Leone established a renewable energy strategy. It attempts to minimise the country's dependency on fossil fuels while improving access to and production of energy (Jalloh, 2018). Renewable energy accounts for 4,703 ktoe/annum of the final energy mix consumption objectives for 2020 and 2030, respectively. Wind, hydro, solar, and bio energy are all renewable energy sources in the nation. In 2019, RES supplied 1,276 ktoe/year of energy to final consumption (Hydro and wood fuel) (Thomas, 2016). The estimated potential for hydro source is 5000 MW from 300 sites countrywide in 2021, while the installed hydro capacity as at 1982 in Dodo is 6 MW and 50 MW in Bumbuna as at 2015.

The estimated potential for Bioenergy source is 2706 GWh, while the installed Bioenergy capacity at Addax ethanl project from sugarcane in Makani was 5 MW power. The estimated potential for Solar is between 1,460 and 1,800 kWh/m^2, while the installed capacity is 2.5 MW Solar photovolatic as at 2019. The estimated potential for wind energy is between 3 m/s and 5 m/s wind speed country wide, while 8 m/s in hilly areas (Conteh et al., 2021; Thomas, 2016).

Togo
The country's energy mix includes thermal plants, imported power from Ghana and Nigeria, and hydro-energy. Solar, biofuel, wind, and hydropower are examples of renewable energy possibilities in the nation. Annual solar radiation is projected to range between 1,700 and 2,100 kWh/m^2, with average wind speed potential in coastal places approaching 5 m/s. In 2015, hydro generated 56 GWh of gross electricity, while primary solid biofuel generated 5 GWh (International Energy Agency, 2015b; USAID, 2017).

Mauritius
Mauritius, an island in the southwest Indian Ocean, is endowed with stunning natural beauty, animals, and breathtaking mountains. Despite the fact that the Mauritius government emphasises energy project building, some of its inhabitants lack access to electricity. The energy mix of Mauritius consists of fossil fuels (petroleum and coal), bioenergy (bagasse and wood fuel), and hydropower. Because renewable energy sources (RES) have the potential to help close the electricity gap, the government (Ministry of Public Utilities) has established policies aimed at expanding RES use from 22% to 35% (International Trade Administration, 2017; Mohee, Surroop, & Jeeta, 2020; Palanichamy, Babu, & Nadarajan, 2017) The renewable energy potential of the country includes hydro, solar, wind, and biofuel. The yearly mean wind speed potential at 30 metres and above is between 3 and 7 metres per second (Mohee et al., 2020).

Burundi
Burundi is a landlocked nation in East Africa. Traditional biomass (almost 90%), hydropower, and fossil fuels dominate their energy mix. The great majority of electricity is generated by hydropower, with bagasse accounting for around 10%. Power is held by less than 10% of the people, which does not foster economic advancement (Energypedia, 2016). Only hydro (32 MW of the 1,700 MW

anticipated potential capacity) and bioenergy (bagasse and wood fuel) are being used from the country's RES potential. The country's solar energy potential is between 4 and 5 kWh/m² per day, with wind speed potential ranging between 4 and 6 m/s (Multi News, 2019).

Kenya

Kenya is bounded on the west by Uganda, on the northwest by Sudan, on the north by Ethiopia, on the east by Somalia, and on the south by Tanzania. It was the first country on the continent's east coast to access and use geothermal resources, and its renewable energy sector is rapidly expanding. The great bulk of the country's primary energy usage is accounted for by traditional biomass, petroleum, electricity, and coal. Kenya's installed power production capacity includes hydro, fossil fuel, geothermal, bioenergy (bagasse), and wind. Kenya Renewable Energy Association (KREA), created in 2017, promotes the growth and development of renewable energy in Kenya. Solar, wind, geothermal, bio-fuel, and hydropower are all examples of renewable energy sources.

Wind energy potential in the nation ranges from 5 to 7 m/s at 50 m along the coast to 9 m/s in the northern and hilly (Rift Valley) areas. The nation's entire hydro potential (small, mini, and micro) is estimated to reach 3,000 MW. Menegei has a 1,600 MW potential, Baringo-Silali has a 3,000 MW potential, Suswa has a 750 MW potential, and Olkaria has a 412 MW potential, among others (GDC, 2017; Kenya Renewable Energy Association, 2016).

Malawi

Malawi, located in the region's south, has borders with Tanzania to the north, Mozambique to the south and east, and Zambia to the west (west). Traditional biomass (89% as of 2019), hydropower (Shire River), fossil fuel, and bioenergy are the key sources of primary energy usage (ethanol). Solar, wind, hydro, geothermal, and bioenergy resources abound in the United States (Zalengera et al., 2019). The daily solar energy potential is calculated to be 5.8 kWh/m². An 850 kW grid-connected photovoltaic system was installed at Lilongwe's Kamuzu International Airport in September 2021.

The average monthly wind speed at a height of 2 m was more than 2 m per second in 2015. There is an untapped hydropower potential of 1.478 GW in rivers around the country. Over 50 recognized hot springs across the country have geothermal energy potential (18 with average surface temperatures above 50°C and as high as 82°C in Mphizi – Rumphi) (Zalengera et al., 2019).

Uganda

Uganda has a diversified terrain (mountains and Lake Victoria) and animals. It is also famous for its 43-metre-high waterfall (Murchison Falls National Park). Sudan borders the nation to the north, Kenya to the east, Congo to the west, and Tanzania to the south. The country's electrification rate is low, with 20.4% of the population having access as of 2019, and power is generated by hydro (80%), fossil oil (diesel), and bioenergy (bagasse) (Mathias-Gustavsson, Mark, & Karin, 2015; The World Bank, 2017). As Uganda's energy consumption rises at a 10–12% yearly pace, RES with a potential capacity of 5,300 MW can help to reduce the problem.

The Ministry of Energy, Minerals, and Development's (MEMD) renewable energy programme, launched in 2016, demonstrates the government's resolve to efficiently exploit their RES. With about 2018 MW of hydropower potential, less than half (783 MW big scale project to be finished in 2018) is being used. The average of 8 hours of sunshine is expected to emit between 1,825 and 2,500 kWh/m^2 of radiation each year. The country's sustainable bioenergy potential is projected to be 45 million tons. An empirical research of geo-energy is now underway, with 43 plausible estimations totaling 450 MW. Large-scale power generation is not economically viable due to the low wind speed (mean observations of 3.7 m/s at 20 m in Mukono and Kabale) (Mathias-Gustavsson et al., 2015).

Rwanda

Rwanda is a non-coastal nation bordered to the north by Uganda, to the north-east and east by Tanzania, to the north-west and west by the Democratic Republic of the Congo, and to the south by Burundi. Following the mid-1990s genocide, the country made considerable strides towards development. Energy access will boost socioeconomic growth. Rwanda has less than 50% of the country's power. The majority of the country's energy is generated by fossil fuels (petroleum products), conventional biomass (wood fuel and charcoal), agricultural wastes, and peat bogs (de-Dieu Uwisengeyimana, Teke, & Ibrikci, 2017). Rwanda benefits from solar energy, which has an estimated daily irradiation of 5.2 kWh/m^2.

Agahozo-Shalom Youth Village features an 8.5 MW photovoltaic facility with this potential (Rwamagana District). Geo-energy with temperatures as high as 150°C and power generation capacity ranging from 170 to 320 MW is a possibility. The country's wind potential is modest, with only the eastern counties showing some promise. Hydropower is used to generate energy in the nation (28 MW installed capacity). Rwanda's government has set a goal of providing its population with 100% access to electricity by 2020, and renewable energy has the ability to make that a reality (de-Dieu Uwisengeyimana et al., 2017; USAID, 2017).

Tanzania

The country is well-known for its huge forests and attempts to safeguard animals. The country is bounded to the north-west by Uganda, Rwanda, and Burundi, to the north by Kenya, to the west by the Democratic Republic of the Congo, to the south by Zambia, Malawi, and Mozambique, and to the east by the Indian Ocean. Their primary energy sources are water, traditional biomass, and imported fossil fuel. Despite the fact that the country's energy consumption is increasing as a result of population increase and industrial expansion, access remains restricted (15.5% of the population in 2019). According to African Development Bank Group (2015), despite the fact that hydro is Tanzania's largest source of electricity generation, the country's renewable energy potential is untapped.

Large hydro installed capacity was 562 MW in 2015, with a potential of 4,000 MW, while small hydro, largely created by private enterprises, was predicted to be 480 MW. The geothermal potential in the Mbeya region has not been properly examined, although it is predicted (through analog methods) to be greater than 650 MW from hot springs with temperatures reaching 200°C. The vast bulk of the country's wind potential can be harnessed to create electricity. At 30 m, the mean speed of Kititimo-Singida and Makambako-Iringa is 9.9 m/s and 8.9 m/s, respectively. Solar irradiation varies between 4 and 6 kWh/m^2/day for photovoltaic and thermal potentials, with 2,800–3,500 sunlight hours per year. Tanzania's government is taking steps to boost the contribution of modern RES, notably bioenergy, to the country's energy mix (African Development Bank Group, 2015).

Cameroon

Cameroon features a diverse range of animal and forest habitats. Nigeria borders the country on the north, west, and west, Chad on the north, east, and east, and Gabon and Congo on the south. To the south-west, the country is bounded by the Atlantic Ocean (Abanda, 2020). Despite the energy ministry's intention to increase electrification from 55% to 75% by 2020, power outages are on the rise. Hydro (60%), fossil fuel (oil and gas), and biomass produce the bulk of power (Abanda, 2020). According to the World Bank (2020), Cameroon's renewable energy potential are Hydro (23 GW in Sanaga basin); Solar (irradiation) (5.8 kW/m^2/day in the nothern Camerooon; 4.5 kW/m^2/day in the southern Cameroon); Wind (5–7 m/s in the north and coastal areas of Cameroon; 2–4 m/s at 100 m in most areas of Cameroon); Bioenergy (biomas residue) with approximately 1 GWh. Although geothermal energy has yet to be empirically quantified, it exists as a result of volcanic activity in numerous parts of the planet.

Swaziland

The northern region of the country has the most potential solar energy. This RES is generally developed by private entities or in collaboration with the government. The largest wind speed potential is situated around South Africa's coastline, with modest wind speed in certain interior places. The average wind speed at 100 m is between 4 and 8 m per second. South Africa has a hydro energy capacity of 38 MW installed. Some places have some recent estimates (247 MW) of small-scale hydro (Free State, KwaZulu-Natal, Mpumalanga and Eastern Cape). Bioenergy potential research and development is currently underway, with complete implementation predicted by 2022 (Africa-EU Renewable Energy Cooperation Programme, 2017).

Botswana

Botswana is a non-coastal country bordered by South Africa to the south, Namibia to the west, Zimbabwe to the east, and Angola and Zambia to the north. The country is endowed with vast green forests (Kalahari Game Reserve) and rare fauna. Electricity and traditional biomass are the country's primary energy sources. Because coal is abundant in the nation, it is the major source of electrical generation (Fagbenle, 2018). In Botswana, solar and bioenergy (biogas from bovine dung) have significant potential, although wind has minimal promise.

With around 3,200 hours of sunlight each year, the solar radiation potential is estimated to be 21 MJ/m²/day. Wind speed is normally modest in the nation at a height of 10 m, with a mean of 3 m/s (Africa-EU Renewable Energy Coorperation Programme, 2017). Because of the country's geography and lack of rainfall, hydropower for electricity generation is not feasible. Botswana's government is determined to increase its contemporary utilization of RES (particularly bioenergy) in its energy mix (Fagbenle, 2018).

South Africa

The country is located at the southern tip of Africa, with coasts on the South Atlantic and Indian Oceans. The landscape and wildlife of the country attract visitors all year. With an electrification rate of about 90%, South Africa is one of the few countries on the continent with adequate energy access. The country's electricity is generated by fossil fuels (coal and gas), hydro, nuclear, and wind energy (Africa-EU Renewable Energy Cooperation Programme, 2017). Solar and wind energy are the country's most established renewable energy sources. Solar irradiation ranges between 4.5 and 6.5 kWh/m²/day, with an annual average of roughly 2,500 hours of sunlight.

The northern region of the country has the most potential solar energy. This RES is generally developed by private entities or in collaboration with the government. The largest wind speed potential is situated 45 around South Africa's coastline, with modest wind speed in certain interior places. The average wind speed at 100 m is between 4 and 8 m per second. South Africa has a hydro energy capacity of 38 MW installed. Some places have some recent estimates (247 MW) of small-scale hydro (Free State, KwaZulu-Natal, Mpumalanga and Eastern Cape). Bioenergy potential research and development is currently underway, with complete implementation predicted by 2022 (Africa-EU Renewable Energy Cooperation Programme, 2017).

In summary, the circumstances around better living has spured living standards through numerous technical phases of progress. Despite the fact that these advances were necessary and helpful, it has come to our attention that natural resources must be protected via a collaborative effort. As a result, we must strive for long-term growth. Africa continues to have poor rates of energy access and security. Renewable energy can help address these issues while also safeguarding the environment.

Energy Consumption in Africa

African energy consumption has been pushed in recent decades by the expanding demands of North Africa, Nigeria, and South Africa. In 2017, Africa's main energy consumption was 815 million tonnes of oil equivalent (MTOE), with North Africa (24%), Nigeria (18%), and South Africa (16%) accounting for more than half of the total but accounting for just 35% of the population. Nonetheless, most African nations' average energy consumption per capita is significantly below the global average of roughly 2 tonnes of oil equivalent per capita. South Africa and Nigeria have the largest per capita consumption at 2.32 and 0.8 toe/capita, respectively, whereas most other nations have a consumption of approximately 0.5 and Senegal has the lowest at 0.3.

In most nations, a considerable portion of per capita energy consumption is accounted for by the comparatively inefficient utilisation of solid biomass. Energy consumption growth has slowed dramatically in recent years and is now lower than GDP growth. Energy consumption climbed at an annual average rate of 3.4% between 2018 and 2019, but this dropped to 2.7% from 2019 to 2018. There are also significant geographical differences. Countries such as the Democratic Republic of the Congo (Africa's fourth most populated nation) had their main energy consumption nearly quadruple between 2019 and 2018, whilst others such as Côte d'Ivoire, Ghana, and Mozambique saw just a moderate growth if any at all.

The decrease in demand does not imply a decrease in energy services. In reality, in both Mozambique and Côte d'Ivoire, the drive towards LPG for cooking has resulted in a decrease in solid biomass consumption, a substitution that also accounts for a significant increase in efficiency. Fossil fuels now account for about 40% of the total energy mix in Sub-Saharan Africa and more than half of the whole African energy mix. The usage of oil is around four million barrels per day (mb/d). The transportation sector accounts for the majority of oil use (about 60%), although it is also used as diesel for backup generators, in households as kerosene or LPG for lighting and cooking, and industry.

Transport Situation in Africa

Mobility for access to day-to-day activities, education, leisure, health care, business activities, and commercial and industrial operations is an essential constituent of economic growth. Mobility of raw materials and commodities is also critical for seamless industry operations, agricultural produce transit, and trade between various locations. Transportation services have the potential to propel growth. As the globe gets more urbanised, it becomes increasingly critical to have appropriate access to efficient, safe, and sustainable transportation alternatives. Certain transport studies in Africa give some important insights on the subject. GIZ research examines mitigation options for GHG emissions from the transport sector in Kenya (Notter, Weber, & Fuessler, 2018) and concludes that in the absence of fuel economy improvements in imported used vehicles and a shift from road to rail, emissions from road transport are set to rise dramatically by 2050.

Another GIZ research in Kenya focuses on the features of in-service road vehicle fleets in the country's major cities (GIZ, 2017). According to their figures, the average age of automobiles in Kenya is more than 12 years, with 9% of the fleet being more than 20 years old. According to research conducted by the Addis Ababa Institute of Technology, UNEP, and GFEI on Ethiopia's transportation industry, GHG emissions from passenger automobiles would rise from 2.5 million tonnes in 2019 to 13.1 million tonnes of CO_2 equivalent in 2030, emphasising the need for fuel economy (UNEP, 2021). Further research on the relevance of vehicle fuel economy and fleet age in Côte d'Ivoire and Senegal is available.

Nonetheless, there remains a significant research gap in modelling the region's entire transport energy use. South Africa is the only country in Sub-Saharan Africa that has research released in 2020 by the University of Cape Town that quantifies the energy consumption of the transport industry (Merven, Stone, Hughes, & Cohen, 2020). Under a 'business as usual' scenario, South Africa's transport energy consumption will quadruple by 2050, but this rise can be limited to less than 30% under an alternative case that assumes an annualised 2% improvement in fuel efficiency across all vehicle categories (Merven et al., 2020).

Furthermore, all studies identified on the issue emphasise the critical need for improved data collecting in the region as well as the industry, which is currently the biggest restriction for more elegant modelling and study in the field. Transport is a sector with immense potential for improving Africa's social and economic status, and an evaluation of its future energy demands is critical. Approximately 60% of the continent's population lacks access to modern transportation infrastructure (UN, 2015), and high transportation costs are believed to increase the cost of commodities exchanged between African nations by 30–40% (EXIM Bank of India, 2018).

The continent's transportation sector is now facing significant challenges in terms of infrastructure and legislation. These obstacles may be overcome with a comprehensive approach that combines strong policy and increased investment. Car ownership remains a luxury in many regions of Africa, although motorcycle and tricycle ownership is comparably greater. Many nations are expanding the number of light-duty cars as wages grow, but the efficiency of the vehicle fleet is poor since many of these are imported second-hand from Europe and Asia. Public transportation is similarly underdeveloped in many areas, but it has the potential to be critical in boosting economic and social wellbeing in the world's most quickly urbanising region.

Rail networks are limited, and many were traditionally developed to serve the requirements of extractive industries rather than to offer passenger services. Households instead rely on unofficially running, dangerous buses and minibuses to move within or between cities in various regions of the continent. Among the many advantages of investing in these forms of mass, transportation would include providing safer and faster alternatives for carrying huge numbers of people at the same time, as well as connecting rural/agricultural producing regions to large commercial centres.

Aviation in Africa

Africa's need for air passenger travel has been constantly increasing. African airlines carried 79.5 million passengers in 2015, accounting for 2.2% of global air passenger transport, a 1.8% increase over 2019. In 2015, foreign lines handled 48.3 million passengers, while domestic routes carried 31.2 million. African airlines handled 817,000 tonnes of freight, up from 777,000 tonnes the previous year. In 2015, African airlines carried 1.6% of total worldwide freight transported (EXIM Bank of India, 2018). Although air travel in Africa is expanding rapidly, it is still at a relatively low level. It lags significantly behind other emerging regions, is costly, and has spotty connectivity.

Despite Africa's approximately 4,000 airports and airfields (UNECA, 2015), many of them fail to meet International Civil Aviation Organization (ICAO) standards and recommended procedures. Only around a quarter of these airports have paved runways. The spread of intra-African air transport has been hindered in part due to inadequate infrastructure and in part due to African governments' lack of a clear liberalisation policy. Despite Africa's small share of the global aviation business, the International Air Transport Association (IATA) estimates that it employs 6.9 million people and provides $80 billion to the African economy (World Economic Forum, 2019).

Road Transport in Africa

Most African countries' transportation sectors are dominated by roads, which account for 80–90% of total passenger and freight traffic (AfDB, 2019). Although road transport is projected to be responsible for $200 billion in trade in Africa, the density of the road network, both per person and a square kilometre of land area, is significantly lower than in other parts of the world. Furthermore, a lack of effective and consistent maintenance and improvements results in the deterioration of road surfaces. Only 0.8 million kilometres of Sub-Saharan Africa's total 2.8 million kilometres of road networks are paved (EXIM Bank of India, 2018).

Only about half of all paved roads are in good condition. In Sub-Saharan Africa, the road to population ratio is barely 27 km per 10,000 people, compared to 101 km per 10,000 in the European Union (EXIM Bank of India, 2018). Africa has an average of 204 km of roads per 1,000 km², with just one-quarter of them paved (World Bank, 2019). Thus, Africa's national road density lags well behind the global average of 944 km per 1,000 km², of which more than half is paved. Regionally, North Africa and South Africa fare significantly better than the rest of the continent. The lack of transportation to connect rural areas to cities also results in a loss of agricultural earnings, which employs a sizeable portion of the African population (Bloemen, 2019).

According to studies, more than half of Sub-Saharan Africa's untapped agricultural potential is located more than six hours from a major market, and less than 40% of rural Africans live within 2 km of an all-season road, by far the lowest level of rural accessibility in the developing world (Bloemen, 2019). Road mobility is also a significant source of outdoor air pollution in Africa. A primarily used, ageing, and expanding car fleet imported from Japan and Europe, low fuel quality, the absence of rigorous and universal pollution rules, and fast, poorly planned urban expansion all contribute to increasingly congested cities (UNECA, 2015).

Commercial road vehicles (buses and lorries) have an average age of 20 years in Africa, compared to 8–12 years in other rising economies and fewer than 10 years in wealthy nations (UNECA, 2015). Improving public transportation networks via solid legislation, effective urban planning, and capacity building has the potential to reduce the number of smaller, less efficient automobiles on the road. Nonetheless, increasing fuel quality, particularly in terms of reducing sulphur content, is a vital step towards the usage of better vehicle technology that minimises exhaust emissions.

Maritime Transport or Navigation in Africa

Maritime transport is critical to international trade, accounting for more than 90% of all international trade transiting through ports worldwide. It is much more prevalent in Africa, where ports account for 92–97% of foreign commerce (UNECA, 2015). Poor maintenance and inefficient operations, on the other hand, hamper this means of transit on the continent. Only 6% of world marine traffic is handled by Africa's 90 largest ports. Only six of these ports, three in Egypt and three in South Africa, account for 50% of all African maritime volume. Africa's port productivity is poor in comparison to the worldwide average, with an estimated 30% of the global level.

Stay time for boats at a port is an essential metric of port efficiency, and the average dwell time documented at several major African ports is roughly 11 days, which is three times longer than the average dwell periods at ports in other developing areas. Dar-es-Salam, one of East Africa's largest ports, had a documented dwell duration of 15 days (UNECA, 2015). Efficient management and better equipment maintenance might greatly minimise dwell time and increase profits from foreign trade.

Railways in Africa

The bulk of railway lines in Africa was built by colonial powers to connect mines and other natural resources to ports for extraction and transfer of resources. While much of Sub-Saharan Africa has remained largely unchanged, South Africa is an exception. According to the United States Department of Commerce (United States Department of Commerce, 2019), South Africa now has the best rail infrastructure on the continent, including the upgraded famous luxury Blue Train for tourists and new projects in the works such as the Tambo Springs Intermodal Terminal (Tambo Springs, 2019) for freight transport, which is set to be fully operational by 2022.

However, the sector has not seen the same amount of growth as the rest of the region, and it is still plagued by outmoded railroad infrastructure. The total length of Africa's rail network is 82,000 km (World Bank, 2015), with 84% of it operational and the remainder closed due to war damage, natural disasters, or a lack of maintenance and funds. Passenger services account for around 20% of train traffic. According to financial analyses, railways that transport fewer than one million net tonnes of freight per year do not generate enough revenue to cover infrastructure capital expenditures (World Bank, 2021). Except for South Africa and North African countries, few African countries presently have enough freight traffic.

Africa's contribution to total world tonne-kilometres of freight hauled was under 2% in 2016. With the continent's demographics rapidly changing and GDP expanding, this position might fast alter. Rising urbanisation and industry in the region will create new transportation difficulties that will be best met by railroads. Africa, which is rich in natural resources and minerals, has the potential to use railways to move vast amounts of products.

About 2.8 billion people (roughly 40% of the world's population) use unsustainable solid fuels (such as wood, agricultural waste, and animal waste) for cooking and heating. Electricity is unavailable to 1.2 billion people. Table 1 below shows the consumption pattern of electricity, natural gas, fossil fuel, nuclear power, and renewable energy based on per capita in some selected Sub-Saharan African countries as of 2019. From the Table, it was revealed that the rate of electricity consumed in South Africa (3,449.25 kWh) is far more than in other selected SSA countries. This is because the level of electricity generated in that country is higher. The implication of high electricity production in transportation is that more vehicles will be powered by electricity without delay.

Furthermore, there was a record of natural gas consumption in all the selected countries except DR Congo, Ethiopia and Kenya. This implies that natural gas is not produced in those three countries, and not imported from other neighbouring countries that have natural gas in abundance. It is recommended that the

Table 1. Energy Consumption Levels.

Consumption Per Capita	Electricity (kWh)	Natural Gas (m³)	Fossil Fuel (kWh)	Nuclear Power (kWh)	Renewable Energy (kWh)
Angola	266.26	24.20	229.35	0.00	13.49
Côte d'Ivoire	230.84	85.83	371.85	0.00	0.00
DR Congo	80.43	0.00	4.91	0.00	0.00
Ethiopia	76.88	0.00	6.21	0.00	22.76
Ghana	295.06	38.83	608.60	0.00	10.49
Kenya	143.00	0.00	126.23	0.00	126.23
Mozambique	359.73	57.24	114.44	0.00	7.15
Nigeria	116.93	81.55	348.74	0.00	0.00
Senegal	203.36	3.46	408.11	0.00	54.75
South Africa	3449.25	84.42	6203.11	291.91	729.78
Tanzania	92.39	50.65	114.15	0.00	12.45

Source: Information available at World Bank (2020), Collated by Author.

governments of DR Congo, Ethiopia and Kenya should explore natural gas importation as an alternative to ease the burden on electricity and fossil fuel.

Regarding the consumption of nuclear power and renewable energy, South Africa is the only country with a record of nuclear power consumption, and the country with the highest consumption of renewable energy. Countries like Côte d'Ivoire, DR Congo and Nigeria are yet to start consuming renewable energy. Energy poverty is quite dominant in Sub-Saharan Africa, where the majority of the population lacks access to electricity and renewable energy despite the abundant resources in the continent to meet current and future needs.

In developed countries that are sensitive to environmental issues, all transport businesses are operated in such a way that they will be environmentally friendly, sustainable, and profitable, and must encourage a fair sort of innovation capable of permitting innovative approaches to complicated environmental concerns. Also, vehicle manufacturers comply with environmental standards particularly being conscious of renewable energy (Dogaru, 2017). Renewable energy refers to the process of lowering the environmental effect of economic operations, as well as the logical and sustainable use of natural resources. This is regarded as not just a key to competitiveness, but also a vital aspect in resolving natural resource challenges such the climate change and energy security.

STUDY IMPLICATIONS

Mobility and Urbanisation

Since 2018, the African urban population has increased by 260 million (+90%). Cities now account for more than 43% of the population, an increase of eight percentage points since this time last year. The fact that urban centres contribute a significant role in economic output is a crucial impetus for this shift; in sub-Saharan Africa, 143 cities create about $500 billion, or half the region's GDP. By 2040, 600 million people will be relocating to or being born in African cities. Although worldwide urbanisation tendencies have been noticed, the extent of the shift that is presently reshaping African demography has never been witnessed in any other part of the globe and is likely to be twice as great as India's projected urbanisation rate in the next 20 years.

The need for transportation in urban and rural regions is vastly different. The 6.5 million passenger automobiles in sub-Saharan Africa's cities (excluding South Africa) account for about 80% of the region's total car stock. In the Africa's case, this number rises at a rate of 6% per year, surpassing 23 million automobiles and raising the percentage of urban regions to 85% of total car stock by 2040. The same number rises at a rate of more than 7% per year, with goals for a more wealthy economy growing the urban automobile fleet to more than 30 million. Rural regions, on the other hand, account for 51% of the region's current stock of 15 million motorcycles and tricycles.

In the African case, the rural share of motorcycles and tricycles continues to account for a large 42% of total stocks of these light vehicles until 2040, before declining somewhat to meet the trend of fast-expanding urbanisation in both nations. Fuel efficiency improvements in the African case save 4.7 MTOE of energy consumption from automobiles in urban areas, which is much more than 0.8 MTOE saved in rural areas due to a larger number of cars in cities and poorer road conditions in rural and bucolic areas. Motorcycles and tricycle savings are less significant since their stocks grow faster than their fuel economy features improve.

CONCLUSIONS

The circumstances around better living have spurred living standards through numerous technical phases of progress. Despite the fact that these advances were necessary and helpful, it has come to our attention that natural resources must be protected via a collaborative effort. As a result, we must strive for long-term growth. Africa continues to have poor rates of energy access and security. Renewable energy can help address these issues while also safeguarding the environment.

Although there are numerous blind spots and uncertainties when it comes to estimating the African continent's future energy consumption, given the varying demands and stages of development of each country, the vast scope for expansion throughout the area is clear. This potential for expansion is especially significant in sub-Saharan Africa, where most nations, except for South Africa and Nigeria, are among the lowest energy users per capita. Modernisation of the transport industry has the potential to address many of sub-Saharan Africa's current social, economic, and environmental concerns.

Availability of safe, efficient, reliable and contemporary transportation may improve access to employment, education and healthcare, hence increasing societal production and well-being. Furthermore, transportation plays a significant role in promoting cross-border commerce, and economic losses incurred by inefficient transportation networks may be avoided with improved design and appropriate laws. Even though road travel consumes the majority of energy in Africa, the continent still has some of the world's lowest automotive ownership rates, including Ethiopia, Tanzania, Mozambique and DR Congo. Africa's industrialisation will become a priority, as envisioned in Agenda 2063, boosting the importance of freight transit, ports and railroads.

Aviation consumes the majority of the energy of any non-road mode of transportation and is expected to increase more as cities become more densely populated. There is a pressing need for the usage of biofuels in Africa. Biofuels account for less than 0.1% of transport energy use in Africa today, but there is an enormous possibility for growth from this small base. The market grew yearly by 5% between 2017 and 2018 and was led mostly by South Africa, which contributed to more than one-third of the growth, and Nigeria. It was revealed that many of the selected African nations have tremendous potential for advanced biofuel production due to the size of the continent's agricultural economy. Increasing biofuel production from agricultural waste is most sustainable when crop intensification is employed.

RECOMMENDATIONS

The usage of renewable energy enhances the potential to reduce the negative environmental impact of energy consumption, particularly its contribution to climate change. Nonetheless, the consumption of renewable energy has a significant detrimental impact on people and the environment. The financial consequences result from activity in the renewable energy usage and energy industry, though the electricity market has the technology for harnessing energy from renewable sources (de Dieu Uwisengeyimana, Teke, & Ibrikci, 2017). There is presently a tremendous push to improve the capacity of renewable energy electricity generation and to broaden the scope beyond electricity generation. Such expansion in scope and capacity will increase the demand for sparse solid minerals; this will have a detrimental impact on society, the environment and production dynamics (African Development Bank Group, 2020). Managing these repercussions would require a balanced policy strategy which is analytically based, environmentally sound, politically acceptable, socially credible, technologically based and sustainable, for realising the recycling of renewable energy products, controlling the supply of renewable energy products, and increasing the manufacture and usage of renewable energy vehicles.

Alternative vehicle types, such as hybrids, all-electric cars and vehicles fuelled by hydrogen or natural gas, increase our need on oil. Nonetheless, determining an ideal balance of vehicle types can be difficult, especially when it comes to selecting a cost-effective option (Jebli & Youssef, 2015). Different engines, accompanying technology and maintenance processes are used in vehicles suited for different fuels. Each one requires its own specific gasoline delivery mechanism. For example, hydrogen filling stations require unique technology and extensive implementation before hydrogen-powered automobiles become a viable option for most drivers (Acar & Dincer, 2019). To overcome perceived hurdles to ownership and use, potential mainstream users of plug-in cars require further encouragement, knowledge and incentives. This is also applicable to other renewable energy powered vehicles.

DECLARATION

Conflict of Interest: We declare that there is no conflict of interest.

REFERENCES

Abanda, F. H. (2020). Renewable energy sources in Cameroon: Potentials, benefits and enabling environment. *Renewable and Sustainable Energy Reviews, 16*, 4557–4562.

Abbasi, T., & Abbasi, S. (2020). *Renewable energy sources: Their impact on global warming and pollution.* New Delhi: PHI Learning Pvt. Ltd.

Abbasi, T., Premalatha, M., & Abbasi, S. (2019). The return to renewables: Will it help in global warming control? *Renewable and Sustainable Energy Reviews, 15*, 891–894.

Acar, C., & Dincer, I. (2019). Comparative assessment of hydrogen production methods from renewable and non-renewable sources. *International Journal of Hydrogen Energy, 39*(1), 1–12.

Africa-EU Renewable Energy Cooperation Programme. (2017a). Renewable energy potential, Cameroon. Retrieved from https://www.africaeu-renewables.org/market-information/cameroon/renewable-energy-potential/

Africa-EU Renewable Energy Cooperation Programme. (2017b). Renewable electricity potential, South Africa. Retrieved from https://www.africa-eu-renewables.org/market-information/south-africa/renewableelectricity-potential/

Africa-EU Renewable Energy Coorperation Programme. (2017). Renewable energy potential, Botswana. Retrieved from https://www.africa-eurenewables.org/market-information/botswana/renewable-energy-potential/

African Development Bank Group. (2015). "Renewable energy in Africa: TANZANIA country profile", Avenue Jean-Paul II 01 BP 1387, Abidjan 01, Côte d'Ivoire African Development Bank Group, Immeuble du Centre de commerce International d'Abidjan CCIA (p. 72).

African Development Bank Group. (2019). *Tracking Africa's progress in figures*.

African Development Bank Group. (2020). Renewable energy in Africa. Retrieved from https://www.afdb.org/en/blogs/afdbchampioning-inclusive-growth-across-africa/post/renewable-energy-in-africa-8829/

Ahmad, N., Du, L., Lu, J., Wang, J., Li, H. Z., & Hashmi, M. Z. (2017). Modelling the CO_2 emissions and economic growth in Croatia: Is there any environmental Kuznets curve? *Energy, 123*, 164–172.

Ajayi, O. O., & Ajanaku, K. O. (2016). Nigerian's energy challenge and power development: The way forward. *Bulletin of Science Association of Nigeria, 28*, 1–3.

Arthur, R., Baidoo, M. F., & Antwi, E. (2019). Biogas as a potential renewable energy source: A Ghanaian case study. *Renewable Energy, 36*, 1510–1516.

Bah, M. M., Abdulwakil, M. M., & Azam, M. (2019). Income heterogeneity and the environmental Kuznets curve hypothesis in sub-Saharan African countries. *Geojournal, 85*, 617–628.

Barrios, S., Bertinelli, L., & Strobl, E. (2016). Climatic change and rural–urban migration: The case of sub-Saharan Africa. *Journal of Urban Economics, 60*, 357–371.

Bertine, K., & Goldberg, E. D. (1971). Fossil fuel combustion and the major sedimentary cycle. *Science, 173*, 233–235.

Besada, H., Sewankambo, N., Lisk, F., Sage, I., Kabasa, J. D., & Willms, D. G. (2015). Climate change in Africa: Adaptation, mitigation and governance challenges. Retrieved from https://www.cigionline.org/publications/climate-change-africa-adaptation-mitigation-and-governance-challenges/

Bhusare, S. R. (2015). Renewable energy: An eco-friendly alternative? *Quest-The Journal of UGC-HRDC Nainital, 9*(2), 152–155.

Bloemen, S. (2019). Why electric mobility revolution should not bypass Africa's rural women. Retrieved from https://news.cgtn.com/news/3d3d674e3567444e32457a6333566d54/index.html

British Petroleum PLC. (2017). *Statistical review of world energy* (66th ed., p. 52). London.

Bugaje, I. (2016). Renewable energy for sustainable development in Africa: A review. *Renewable and Sustainable Energy Reviews, 10*, 603–612.

Chaabouni, S., & Saidi, K. (2017). The dynamic links between carbon dioxide (CO_2) emissions, health Spending and GDP growth: A case study for 51 countries. *Environmental Research, 158*, 137–144.

Challinor, A., Wheeler, T., Garforth, C., Craufurd, P., & Kassam, A. (2016). Assessing the vulnerability of food crop systems in Africa to climate change. *Climatic Change, 83*, 381–399.

Chambers, R., & Conway, G. R. (1991). *Sustainable rural livelihoods: Practical concepts for the 21st century*. Institute of Development Studies DP 296, 1991, Brighton: University of Sussex.

Chioma, Y. J. (2019). Recent trends and patterns of gasoline consumption in Nigeria. *Africa Development, XXXV*(3), 159–177.

Chukwu, P. U., Isa, A. H., Ojosu, J. O., & Olayande, J. S. (2015). Energy consumption in transport sector in Nigeria: Current situation and ways forward. *Journal of Energy Technologies and Policy, 5*(1), 75–83.

Collier, P., Conway, G., & Venables, T. (2015). Climate change and Africa. *Oxford Review of Economic Policy, 24*, 337–353.

Conteh, F., Takahashi, H., Hemeida, A. M., Krishnan, N., Mikhaylov, A., & Senjyu, T. (2021). Analysis of hybrid grid-connected renewable power generation for sustainable electricity supply in Sierra Leone. *Sustainability*, *13*, 11435. doi:10.3390/su132011435

De Arce, R., Mahía, R., Medina, E., & Escribano, G. (2020). A simulation of the economic impact of renewable energy development in Morocco. *Energy Policy*, *46*, 335–345.

de Dieu Uwisengeyimana, J., Teke, A., & Ibrikci, T. (2017). Current overview of renewable energy resources in Rwanda. *Journal of Energy and Natural Resources*, *5*, 92.

Dogaru, L. (2017). Environmental change and its effects. *Curentul Juridic*, *69*(2), 38–43.

Edenhofer, O., Pichs-Madruga, R., Sokona, Y., Seyboth, K., Kadner, S., & Zwickel, T. (2019). *"Renewable energy sources and climate change mitigation", Special report of the intergovernmental panel on climate change.* Cambridge: Cambridge University Press.

Edifon, A. I., Edwin, N. I., & Ben, I. A. (2016). Estimation and ranking of the photovoltaic energy potential for local government areas in Akwa Ibom State, Nigeria. *Science Journal of Energy Engineering*, *4*(6), 68–77. doi:10.11648/j.sjee.20160406.14

Edward, N. O. (2021). Potential of renewable energy utilization in Akwa Ibom State, Nigeria. *International Journal of Environmental Sciences*, *3*(2), 352–359.

EIA. (2015). Overview of egpyt energy analysis. Retrieved from https://www.eia.gov/beta/international/analysis.cfm?iso=EGY

Ellabban, O., Abu-Rub, H., & Blaabjerg, F. (2019). Renewable energy resources: Current status, prospects and their enabling technology. *Renewable and Sustainable Energy Reviews*, *39*, 748–764.

Energypedia. (2016). Burundi energy situation. Retrieved from https://energypedia.info/wiki/Burundi_Energy_Situation

EXIM Bank of India. (2018). Connecting Africa: Role of transport infrastructure. Retrieved from https://www.tralac.org/news/article/12896-connecting-africa-role-of-transport-infrastructure.html

Fagbenle, R. O. (2018). National renewable energy policy objectives and programmes in Botswana. *Renewable Energy*, *24*, 419–437.

Felix, B. D. (2019). *Clean energy investment in Nigeria: The domestic context, country case study completed for IISD's clean energy investment project.* Retreived from www.iisd.org

Fussler, C., & James, P. (1996). *Driving renewable energy: A breakthrough discipline for innovation and sustainability.* Boston, MA: Pitman Publishing.

Georgia, P. (2019). *Energy consumption in the transport sector.* Retrieved from www.ifp.fr

Geothermal Development Company-GDC. (2017). GDC's geothermal projects. Retrieved from https://www.gdc.co.ke/projects_intro.php

GIZ. (2017). Characteristics of the in-service vehicle fleet in Kenya. Retreived from http://www.changing-transport.org/publications/characteristics-of-the-in-service-vehicle-fleet in-kenya/

GNESD. (2016). Reaching the millennium development goals and beyond: Access to modern forms of energy as a pre-requisite. Retrieved from http://www.eng.uc.edu/reaching-the-millennium-development-goals-and-beyond-access-to-modern-forms-of-energy-as-a-pre-requisite/

Gyamfi, S., Modjinou, M., & Djordjevic, S. (2015). Improving electricity supply security in Ghana-the potential of renewable energy. *Renewable and Sustainable Energy Reviews*, *43*, 1035–1045.

Hellstrom, T. (2016). Dimensions of environmentally sustainable innovation: The structure of renewable energy concepts. *Sustainable Development, Ltd and ERP Environment*, *15*(3), 148–159.

Hochberg, M. (2017). Renewable energy growth in Morocco: An example for the region. Policy focus Series, Middle East Institute, 1761 N Street NW, Washington, DC 201762016. p. 13.

Hossain, M. S. (2019). Panel estimation for CO_2 emissions, energy consumption, economic growth, trade openness and urbanization of newly industrialized countries. *Energy Policy*, *39*, 6991–6999.

Hubbert, M. K. (1949). *Energy from fossil fuels.* Moses King.

International Energy Agency. (2015a). Benin: Renewables and waste for 2015. Retrieved from https://www.iea.org/statistics/statisticssearch/report/?country=Benin&product=RenewablesandWaste.

International Energy Agency. (2015b). Togo: Renewables and waste for 2015. Retrieved from https://www.iea.org/statistics/statisticssearch/report/?country=Togo&product&RenewablesandWaste

International Energy Agency. (2017a). Energy and CO2 emissions in the OECD. Retrieved from https://www.iea.org/media/statistics/energy_and_CO2_emissions_in_the_OECD.pdf

International Energy Agency. (2017b). Morocco. Retrieved from https://www.iea.org/countries/non-membercountries/morocco/

International Trade Administration (ITA). (2017). Mauritius – Energy: Overview. Retrieved from https://www.export.gov/article?id=MauritiusRenewable-Energy

Iwata, H., Okada, K., & Samreth, S. (2020). An empirical study on the determinants of CO_2 emissions: Evidence from OECD countries. *Applied Economics, 44*, 3513–3519.

Jalil, A., & Mahmud, S. F. (2015). Environment Kuznets curve for CO_2 emissions: A cointegration analysis for China. *Energy Policy, 37*, 5167–5172.

Jalloh, B. (2018). The energy sector in Sierra Leone (Ministry of Foreign Affairs). Retrieved from https://www.rvo.nl/sites/default/files/2018/07/sector-scan-the-energy-sector-in-sierra-leone.pdf

James, P. (1997). The sustainability circle: A new tool for product development and design. *Journal of Sustainable Product Design, 2*, 52–57.

Jebli, M. B., & Youssef, S. B. (2015). The environmental Kuznets curve, economic growth, renewable and non-renewable energy, and trade in Tunisia. *Renewable and Sustainable Energy Reviews, 47*, 173–185.

Kalogirou, S. A. (2021). *Solar energy engineering: Processes and systems*. London: Elsevier.

Kaygusuz, K. (2020). Energy for sustainable development: A case of developing countries. *Renewable and Sustainable Energy Reviews, 16*, 1116–1126.

Keeling, C. D. (1973). Industrial production of carbon dioxide from fossil fuels and limestone. *Tellus, 25*, 174–198.

Kenya Renewable Energy Association. (2016). Renewable sources. Retrieved from https://kerea.org/geothermal-energy/

Lacheheb, M., Rahim, A. S. A., & Sirag, A. (2015). Economic growth and CO_2 emissions: Investigating the environmental Kuznets curve hypothesis in Algeria. *International Journal of Energy Economics and Policy, 5*, 1125–1132.

Mathias-Gustavsson, O. B., Mark, H., & Karin, S. (2015). "Energy Report for Uganda: A 100% Renewable Energy Future by 2050", WWF Uganda Country Office, Plot No. 2, Sturrock Road, Kololo. P.O. Box 8758, Kampala, Uganda. (p. 87).

Mentis, D., Hermann, S., Howells, M., Welsch, M., & Siyal, S. H. (2015). Assessing the technical wind energy potential in Africa a GIS-based approach. *Renewable Energy, 83*, 110–125.

Merven, B., Stone, A., Hughes, A., & Cohen, B. (2020). Quantifying the energy needs of the transport sector for South Africa: A bottom-up model. Energy Research Centre, University of Cape Town.

Mirzaei, M., & Bekri, M. (2017). Energy consumption and CO2 emissions in Iran, 2025. *Environmental Research, 154*, 345–351.

Mohee, R., Surroop, D., & Jeeta, P. (2020). Renewable energy potential in Mauritius and technology transfer through the DIREKT project. In *Proceedings of International Conference on Agriculture, Chemical and Environmental Sciences (ICACES'2020)* (pp. 6–7).

Mui-Yin, C., Chin-Hong, P., Teo, C. L., & Joseph, J. (2018). The determinants of CO_2 emissions in Malaysia: A new aspect. *International Journal of Energy Economics and Policy, 8*, 190.

Multi News. (2019). Renewable energy in Burundi. Retrieved from https://fortuneofafrica.com/burundi/renewable-energy-in-burundi/

New and Renewable Energy Authority. (2017). Renewable energy. Retrieved from https://www.nrea.gov.eg/english1.html

Notter, B., Weber, F., & Fuessler, J. (2018). Greenhouse gas emissions from the transport sector: Mitigation options for Kenya. Retrieved from http://www.changing-transport.org/greenhouse-gas-emissions-from-the-transport-sector-mitigation-options-for-kenya

Nygaard, I., Rasmussen, K., Badger, J., Nielsen, T. T., Hansen, L. B., & Stisen, S. (2019). Using modeling, satellite images and existing global datasets for rapid preliminary 98 assessments of renewable energy resources: The case of Mali. *Renewable and Sustainable Energy Reviews, 14*, 2359–2371.

Ogunbodede, E. F., Ilesanmi, A. O., & Olurankinse, F. (2019). Petroleum motor Spirit (PMS) pricing crisis and the Nigerian public passenger transportation system. *The Social Sciences, 5*(2), 113–121.

Oxford Business Group. (2016). *The report: Tunisia.* Retrieved from https://www.oxfordbusinessgroup.com/tunisia-2016/energy

Oxford Business Group. (2017). Government promoting renewables in Tunisian energy sector. Retrieved from https://www.oxfordbusinessgroup.com/analysis/promoting-renewables-authoritiestake-steps-di

Palanichamy, C., Babu, N. S., & Nadarajan, C. (2017). Renewable energy investment opportunities in Mauritius-an investor's perspective. *Renewable Energy, 29*, 703–716.

Panwar, N., Kaushik, S., & Kothari, S. (2019). Role of renewable energy sources in environmental protection: A review. *Renewable and Sustainable Energy Reviews, 15*, 1513–1524.

Pata, U. K. (2018). The influence of coal and noncarbohydrate energy consumption on CO_2 emissions: Revisiting the environmental Kuznets curve hypothesis for Turkey. *Energy, 160*, 1115–1123.

Programme UND. (2016). *Sustainable development goals.* Retrieved from https://www.undp.org/content/undp/en/home/sustainabledevelopment-goals.html

Rennings, K. (2018). Redefining innovation – Renewable energy research and the contribution from ecological economics. *Ecological Economics Review, 32*(2), 319–332.

Sabaly, H. N., Basse, J., Diba, I., Sarr, A. B., & Camara, M. (2021). Analysis of wind distribution and potential wind energy in Senegal with focus on Basse Casamace. *International Journal of Physical Sciences, 16*(2), 52–67.

Saboori, B., Sulaiman, J., & Mohd, S. (2020). Economic growth and CO_2 emissions in Malaysia: A cointegration analysis of the environmental Kuznets curve. *Energy Policy, 51*, 184–191.

Sadikov, A., Kasimova, N., Isaeva, A., Khachaturov, A., & Salahodjaev, R. (2020). Pollution, energy and growth: Evidence from post communist countries. *International Journal of Energy Policy, 10*, 656–661.

Sambo, A. S. (2015). Renewable energy electricity in Nigeria, the way forward. In *Renewable Electricity Policy Conference*, Abuja, Nigeria (pp. 20–29).

Shahbaz, M., Hye, Q. M. A., Tiwari, A. K., & Leitão, N. C. (2021). Economic growth, energy consumption, financial development, international trade and CO_2 emissions in Indonesia. *Renewable Sustainable Energy Review, 25*, 109–121.

Shata, A. A., & Hanitsch, R. (2016). Evaluation of wind energy potential and electricity generation on the coast of Mediterranean Sea in Egypt. *Renewable Energy, 31*, 1183–1202.

Solarin, S. A. (2021). Tourist arrivals and macroeconomic determinants of CO_2 emissions in Malaysia. *Anatolia, 25*, 228–241.

Tambo Springs. (2019). *Tambo springs intermodal terminal.* Retrieved from https://www.tambosprings.co.za/home/tambo-springs-intermodal-terminal/

The World Bank. (2017). *World development indicators.* Retrieved from https://data.worldbank.org/data-catalog/world-development-indicators

Thomas, J. (2016). *Renewable energy policy of Sierra Leone.* Retrieved from https://www.energy.gov.sl/PR_Renewable%20Energy%20policy%20of%20SL_FINAL%20for%20Print.pdf

Thomson, K. S. (1998). Marginalia: 1798: Darwin and Malthus. *American Scientist, 86*, 226–229.

Twidell, J., & Weir, T. (2015). *Renewable energy resources.* London: Routledge.

UNECA. (2015). *The transport situation in Africa, Addis Ababa.*

UNEP. (2021). *Final report on pilot global fuel economy initiative study in Ethiopia.*

United Nations. (2015). *Financing Africa's infrastructure development.*

United States Department of Commerce. (2019). South Africa – Rail infrastructure. Retrieved from https://www.export.gov/article?id=SouthAfrica-rail-infrastructure

USAID. (2017a). Rwanda energy sector overview. Retrieved from https://www.usaid.gov/powerafrica/rwanda

USAID. (2017b). Togo: Power Africa fact sheet. Retrieved from https://www.usaid.gov/powerafrica/togo

USAID. (2017c). Guinea energy sector overview. Retrieved from https://www.usaid.gov/powerafrica/guinea

Word Bank. (2015). The welfare impact of rural electrification: A reassessment of the costs and benefits. Retrieved from https://openknowledge.worldbank.org/the-welfare-impact-of-rural-electrification-a-reassessment-of-the-costs-and-benefits/. ISBN: 13:9780821373675.

World Bank. (2019). *Africa's transport infrastructure: Mainstreaming maintenance and management.* Washington, DC.

World Bank. (2020). World development indicators. Retrieved from https://data.worldbank.org/data-catalog/world-development-indicators

World Bank. (2021). *Rail transport: Framework for improving railway sector performance in sub-Saharan Africa.* (Vol. 94, pp. 61–81). World Bank. IBRD-IDA.

World Economic Forum. (2019). Here's how to make Africa's aviation industry soar. Retrieved from https://www.weforum.org/agenda/2019/01/here-s-how-to-makeafrica-s-aviation-industry-soar/

Wuebbles, D. J., & Jain, A. K. (2018). Concerns about climate change and the role of fossil fuel use. *Fuel Processing Technology, 71,* 99–119.

Zalengera, C., Blanchard, R. E., Eames, P. C., Juma, A. M., Chitawo, M. L., & Gondwe, K. T. (2019). Overview of the Malawi energy situation and A PESTLE analysis for sustainable 99 development of renewable energy. *Renewable and Sustainable Energy Reviews, 38,* 335–347.

TAKING OFF FOR NET-ZERO AVIATION: SUSTAINABILITY POLICIES AND COLLABORATIVE INDUSTRY ACTIONS

Ferhan K. Sengur and Onder Altuntas

ABSTRACT

Aviation is not only one of the key contributors to the economy and social structure of the world but it is also an industry whose environmental impacts are being closely monitored. Aircraft efficiency and technological advancements have significantly reduced aviation noise and emissions in recent decades. Nevertheless, as the need for passenger and freight transportation grows, the aviation sector is becoming a primary source of environmental issues and a significant driver of global warming. This chapter focusses on environmentally sustainable aviation with a net-zero emission target. It also highlights sustainable aviation policies and collaborative initiatives in the aviation industry to meet the 2050 net-zero emission goal. While the industry's efforts have increased opportunities recently, the industry has also had to face several challenges to achieve the net-zero aviation target.

Keywords: Net zero; environmental impact of aviation; sustainable aviation; net-zero aviation; aviation emissions; aviation and climate change

INTRODUCTION

The air transportation industry serves the global economic and social system, paving the way for globalisation and the erasure of national boundaries (Kuyucak & Vasigh, 2012; Rhoades, 2016). In addition to its direct economic and social contributions like mobility, employment, contribution to regional and national development, and provision of aid materials in emergencies, it is also one

Achieving Net Zero
Developments in Corporate Governance and Responsibility, Volume 20, 233–250
Copyright © 2023 by Emerald Publishing Limited
All rights of reproduction in any form reserved
ISSN: 2043-0523/doi:10.1108/S2043-052320230000020010

of the most significant supporters of industries like tourism, education and health. Aviation connects markets and people, increasing regional competitiveness and fostering personal social and economic growth, which impacts the three pillars of sustainability – social, economic, and environmental (Dimitriou & Sartzetaki, 2018, 2020). The industry is constantly expanding, except for times of crisis like COVID-19. According to statistics before COVID-19, aviation supported \$3.5 trillion in the world economy and produced 87.7 million employment worldwide. The industry generates 87.7 million jobs worldwide and provides \$3.5 trillion to the global economy, according to data from pre-COVID-19 normal conditions (ATAG, 2020). Air travel accounts for more than 50% of all tourist movements worldwide. Air travel does, however, have unfavourable environmental externalities. Aviation's most significant environmental consequences are noise, emissions, air, water and light pollution. In reality, perceived noise has fallen by 75%, and CO_2 emissions per passenger seat kilometre have decreased by 80% since the introduction of the first jet aircraft in the 1950s (ATAG, 2008). However, the demand for air travel is constantly rising, except for crises, which effectively precludes the overall reduction of these negative impacts, which decline per seat-km or passenger with technical advancements.

In order to improve the quality of life, sustainability is seen as a notion for the future in which economic, social and environmental aspects are balanced. It is founded on guiding principles orientated on broad concepts like equality, social tolerance, eradicating poverty, preserving the environment, protecting natural resources and creating a just and peaceful society. Although sustainability has a long history in the human agenda, real progress has been challenging (Howes et al., 2017; Steffen et al., 2015). Today, climate change has become the most critical problem in front of human civilisation, and aviation is no exception. Climate change will impact aviation operations as we anticipate more extreme and frequent weather events, which might result in delays, route changes and possible airport infrastructure damage. The five primary ways that climate change is anticipated to impact aviation are changes in temperature, precipitation, storm patterns, sea level and wind patterns.

Aircraft performance, infrastructure and demand patterns are all impacted by temperature change. Changes in precipitation patterns may result in more cancellations and delays. There will likely be more severe storms, which will disrupt schedules more. The airport capacity may be reduced, and networks may be disrupted due to rising sea levels. Changes in wind patterns may result in more turbulence, longer travel times and interruption (CAPA, 2019).

Although many policies for mitigating climate change are already in operation on a global scale and have been incorporated into the larger agenda for policy-making, when it respects adverse environmental effects and externalities, aviation has lagged behind other industries for a very long period (Efthymiou & Papatheodorou, 2020). Particularly in recent years, intergovernmental organisations such as the International Civil Aviation Organization (ICAO), EURO-CONTROL (The European Organisation for the Safety of Air Navigation) and the International Air Transport Association (IATA) on a sectoral basis have worked to reduce the detrimental environmental effects of climate change and aviation. Associations, such as the Air Transport Action Group (ATAG), collaborate with other organisations in addition to sectoral organisations such as the IATA and Airports Council International (ACI). Concrete steps are being taken to reduce the negative environmental impacts of aviation, such as reducing net aviation carbon emissions to half of 2005 levels by 2050, sustainable use of aviation fuels and carbon trading. The main aim of this book chapter is to reveal developments in the air transport industry's sustainability, environment and climate change in policy development and implementation. Following the revealing of the developments of sustainability and sustainable development concepts with a historical view, the aviation industry's collaborative efforts and regulations, especially on environmental sustainability and climate change, will be discussed in detail in this chapter.

SUSTAINABILITY AND SUSTAINABLE DEVELOPMENT IN THE WORLD AGENDA

The origins of sustainability may be traced back to ancient times, even though the exact date of its inception is unknown. Some writers contend that this concept dates back to Ancient Greece. However, others claim that since these and similar related phenomena are already rooted in Eastern thought as a way of life, the term has a far deeper antiquity. The Latin *sustinere* is where the word sustainability first appeared (*tenere* means to hold, and *sus* means up) (Jeronen, 2020). The term 'sustainable' has been part of the human vocabulary for over three centuries (Fischler, 2014). Although the English word 'sustainability', which expresses supporting, maintaining and ensuring a particular issue, is the basis for the current usage of the term, it is also noted in the literature that the concept's roots concerning its current meaning can also be found in the German word 'nachhaltigkeit', which is mentioned in texts expressing the sustainability of forests (Grober, 2014). Regardless of where the idea came from, it gained popularity and began to be used with its current connotation after the latter part of the twentieth century.

The cornerstone of sustainability in the modern sense is the environment and environmental consciousness, even if it describes a comprehensive phenomenon. After the Second World War, there was an expansion in international interactions, economic growth and fast industrialisation. These developments were all influenced by the new climate of peace created globally. While technical advancements sped up manufacturing, they also cut costs, spurring an exponential output rise. Since scientific and technical advancements have helped people live longer by preventing diseases, this has also contributed to a significant increase in the human population. Particularly in industrialised nations, factors like the cessation of significant conflicts and the rise in welfare and disposable money have considerably raised birth rates and population growth. As a result, more resources are needed now than in the past to address the demands of this constantly growing population, including those related to health, transportation and nutrition. The availability of resources has forced nations, particularly industrialised ones, to look for resources outside their boundaries to offer the required production level to feed this population. Therefore, as production-based mobility has increased, transportation operations have broadened and become more straightforward. However, technological advancements have simplified and reduced the cost of transportation. The decrease in the barriers to international circulation and the increase in the mobility of people, capital and goods have revealed the concept of globalisation. Globalisation, on the other hand, has not only removed the national barriers to industrial production but has also become and continues to be the cause of critical social transformations such as the spread of tourism, the increase in educational opportunities and the spread of science and technology.

The fast depletion of natural resources was an issue that came along with the dizzying advances that dominated the twentieth century. The awareness of environmental issues emerged, together with the concept of sustainability. Various organisations and authors have voiced environmental problems loudly since the 1960s. Local and regional efforts, which started with the awareness of the ongoing environmental problems in the 1970s, are dominant. These efforts are generally focussed on pollution eradication and prevention. In the 1980s, these efforts gained a national dimension. However, with the environmental problems gaining weight, it has been realised that this situation must be handled globally. Additionally, the need for a holistic approach that should be addressed in a way that the problem is not only environmental but also includes its much more profound economic and social dimensions has gradually settled on the world agenda.

Starting from the UN Conference on the Human Environment, often known as the Stockholm Conference, environmental hazards and sustainability were brought to the worldwide agenda. The Common Future Report, prepared under the chairmanship of the Norwegian Prime Minister Gro Harlem Brundtland and presented to the United Nations General Assembly in 1987, declared that the only way out of humanity's environmental issues, which are becoming worse by the day, is to balance the relationship between the environment and economic development and to make development sustainable. The Brundtland Report was the first declaration of sustainability as a concept. The United Nations Conference on Environment and Development (UNCED) was held in Rio de Janeiro from 3 to June 14, 1992, and attended by delegates from 178 countries. The Conference was a significant step forward in terms of the adoption of a set of governance principles for states to adopt environmentally friendly management styles as well as the adoption of Agenda 21, an action plan. The Kyoto Protocol, signed in Kyoto, Japan, in 1997 and is a component of the United Nations Framework Convention on Climate Change, is one of the significant efforts to reduce global warming and GHG emissions. Although complete global adoption of the Protocol, which ended in 2020, was impossible due to developmental gaps and various needs across nations, the Protocol contributed to the escalation of international efforts on climate change.

Governments endorsed the Millennium Declaration and the Millennium Development Goals for 2015 during the United Nations Millennium Summit in

2000. The Millennium Development Goals outline eight targets for UN Member States to meet by 2015, ranging from poverty to hunger to the environment. The much broader Sustainable Development Goals (SDGs) later replaced these goals.

Following the termination of the Kyoto Protocol on December 12, 2015, to cover the period after 2020, the Paris Agreement was adopted in COP21 with the unanimous consent of the states that are party to the current; UN Framework Convention on Climate Change. With the Paris Convention, a new era in global efforts to combat climate change has begun. The act seeks to achieve net zero emissions by 2050 and a worldwide emissions reduction of at least 50% by 2030.

As a result of intergovernmental negotiations that lasted for three years, Sustainable Development Goals were decided as a continuation of the Millennium Development Goals. On September 27, 2015, 'Agenda 2030: UN Sustainable Development Goals (SDGs)' was adopted in New York. The SDGs Agenda of the United Nations consists of 17 goals, 169 targets and an initial set of 230 indicators. It is a comprehensive and ambitious plan to achieve sustainable development by 2030 (United Nations, 2015). In order to accomplish economic, social and environmental goals in line with the requirements of current and future generations, the SDG 2030 Agenda calls for global cooperation involving all countries and stakeholders in the public and private sectors (United Nations, 2023) United Nations SDGs can be seen in Fig. 1.

The SDGs set a new global development framework to reach targets by 2030. In addition to environmental issues such as sustainable cities, combating desertification and drought, climate change and protecting biodiversity, social issues such as combating poverty, gender equality and economic issues such as responsible production and consumption, innovation, and peace and governance

Fig. 1. United Nations Sustainable Development Goals. *Source:* United Nations (2023) (https://www.un.org/sustainabledevelopment/ Used permission with the UN 'The content of this publication has not been approved by the United Nations and does not reflect the views of the United Nations or its officials or Member States').

were included in the sustainable development agenda. The 17th aim emphasises the cooperation and partnerships between the stakeholders to implement the objectives. None of these goals is independent or focussed on a single subject, each related to the others. The exact purpose is in horizontal intersections with more than one subject.

GREENHOUSE GASES, CLIMATE CHANGE AND AIR TRANSPORT

Today, the planet is in existential danger due to climate change and the destruction of ecosystems. The Earth is warmed by the reflection of the sun's rays from the Earth. If there were no gases (such as carbon dioxide (CO_2), ozone (O_3), water vapour (H_2O), methane (CH_4) or nitrogen oxides (N_2O)), which are known as GHGs, in the atmosphere, the Earth's temperature would be approximately − 18°C. The greenhouse effect is essential to life on Earth. However, as the number of GHGs in the atmosphere increases, the greenhouse effect becomes more robust, and the temperature of the Earth continues to increase. This phenomenon is also called global warming. This increase in temperature also causes dreadful environmental problems. For this reason, actions have been put forward globally. The temperature has increased by 1.01°C since 1880. If the current situation does not change, the Earth's temperature is expected to increase by 1.5°C between 2030 and 2052. At the Paris Conference, which was held in Paris in 2015 with the participation of 195 countries, the participating countries committed to take the necessary measures to ensure that the average temperature would not increase by more than 1.5°C compared to the pre-industrial period. If the average temperature rises, according to the IPCC increases by 2°C instead of 1.5°C (Altuntas, 2019; IPCC, 2014; IPCC, 2018):

- 1.7 billion more people will be exposed to severe heat waves,
- The sea level will rise by an average of 10 cm,
- Hundreds of millions more will be exposed to poverty due to the risk of climate change
- Yields will decrease in cereal products,
- Coral reefs, which are important for all ecosystems, will disappear,
- There will be a severe decrease in the fish population in the seas,
- The risks of heavy rain events will increase,
- Areas affected by flood hazards will expand,
- Biodiversity and some species will be at risk of extinction and
- Due to the rising sea level, the threat of reduction of land areas and the fact that some cities might go under the sea.

About 25% of the European Union's (EU) total GHG emissions come from transportation, which has grown recently (EC, 2022a). According to 2017 EU reports, the amount of aviation related-CO_2 is 3.8% of total CO_2 emissions. Also, air transportation is only 13.9% of the total transportation activities in the EU

(EC, 2022a). GHGs released into the atmosphere due to the combustion of jet fuels in aviation activities, especially in aircraft operations, disrupt the radiative balance of the atmosphere. In aviation activities, it is crucial to examine emissions in two parts. First, emissions from the combustion of jet fuels in aircraft engines during aircraft operations (air-side). The second is emissions from energy use at airports that provide access to air transportation (land-side).

There are two ways to investigate global warming effects. The first one is the effects of aircraft operations and airports on climate change. The second is the harmful effects of global warming on aviation activities, as we know that global adverse effects (such as volcanos, COVID-19 etc.) directly affect flights.

INTERNATIONAL POLICIES AND COLLABORATIVE INDUSTRY ACTIONS FOR NET-ZERO AVIATION

Although sustainability and environmental issues have taken an important place on the world agenda in the last 30–40 years, it has become an inevitable task for all sectors to take concrete steps, especially climate change. Reducing GHG emissions caused by humans can assist in reducing global warming. Thirty-seven industrialised nations were given legally binding GHG reduction objectives, or limits, under the Kyoto Protocol, which was agreed upon in 1997. As a result, policy tools were required to fulfil the Kyoto initiatives (EU ETS Handbook, 2015). Although the aviation industry and emissions from air transport operations were excluded from the Kyoto binding scheme, achieving the net-zero target in the following years has become an industry target for aviation as well. The EU aims to reduce total GHGs by up to 55% by 2030 to reach net zero by 2050. By 2050, GHG emissions connected to transportation must be reduced by 90% and to achieve this target, a specific path must be followed (EC, 2022a).

ICAO, a specialised intergovernmental agency of the UN, is dedicated to developing safe and efficient international air transport for peaceful purposes and ensuring a reasonable opportunity for every state. The Organization was established in 1947 by the Convention on International Civil Aviation (1944), which 52 states in Chicago had signed. Since then, Chicago Convention has constituted the fundamentals of international aviation under the ICAO administration. One of the strategic objectives of the ICAO is environmental protection to 'minimise the adverse environmental effects of civil aviation activities'. This strategic objective supports ICAO's leadership in all aviation-related environmental operations and conforms to the ICAO and UN systems' environmental protection policies and standards. The ICAO Council convened a Committee on Aviation Environmental Protection (CAEP) as a technical body. CAEP declared that crucial results were achieved on the long-term aspirational goal (LTAG) for international aviation, new global standards and guidance to support the continuous implementation of ICAO's Carbon Offsetting and Reduction Scheme for International Aviation (CORSIA), and on technical aspects of the sustainability of aviation fuels at its 12th meeting in 2022 February. The Council will subsequently consider all the technical recommendations agreed upon by it for official approval.

Technological, operational and market-based measures are the main instruments to mitigate the impact of the expected growth on the aviation industry towards 2050 will bring along technological solutions (such as digitalisation and alternative fuels). In 2050, current technologies and processes will be able to reduce CO_2 emissions per passenger kilometre by 75% and NOx emissions by 90%. Also, it is aimed that aircraft noise will be reduced by 65% (Tsiropoulos, Nijs, Tarvydas, & Ruiz, 2020). Air traffic management (ATM) and other new operational procedure changes can also reduce GHG emissions. In the last decades, integrated ATM systems have been introduced to help aircraft operators adhere to preferred flight profiles and meet scheduled departure and arrival times while imposing the fewest possible restrictions on safety. In the satellite era, a new interoperable, integrated ATM method is described by the acronym CNS/ATM as a communication, navigation and surveillance system (IPCC, 1999; Sengur, 2022). It combines ground-based systems like radar and fixed navigational aids with voice, satellite and digital communications. The employment of the new systems is expected to result in the most significant prospects for fuel savings, including the use of more direct routes and more effective conditions such as optimal altitude and speed. New operational procedures such as Reduced Vertical Separation Minima (RVSM) have been evaluated as achieving a considerable reduction in yearly fuel costs and a decrease in annual carbon dioxide emissions. Thus, even though an integrated, worldwide ATM system arose from the need to satisfy increasing demand, the result will be improved operations, more efficiency and improved environmental performance, notably through decreased fuel use for a given level of demand.

In recent years, market-based measures such as emission trading and offsetting systems have been added to the technology and operational measures, which are essential in combating global warming and climate change in aviation. Numerous Emission Trading System (ETS) initiatives have been launched internationally due to the Kyoto Protocol obligations and operated worldwide (such as in Canada, the United States and Japan). Although the aviation industry was excluded from the Protocol, ETSs might be helpful instruments for all aviation companies (land-side or air-side) to measure and manage their emissions. Therefore, after the debates on voluntary or obligatory ETS implementations in aviation have been on the industry's agenda for years, implementations are on now. Currently, two primary emission-combatting systems are integrated into international air transportation. The first emission-trading scheme in aviation was the EU Emissions Trading Scheme (EU ETS), which built the main bracket for all EU's Climate Change policies. The aviation industry was included in the EU ETS framework in 2012. The other one is The ICAO Carbon Offsetting and Reduction Scheme for International Aviation (CORSIA) created by ICAO. First, have a greenhouse gas emission cap covering all economic sectors. Whereas offsetting schemes (e.g. CORSIA) compensates for emissions by reducing emissions in particular sectors but do not have an accompanying emissions cap. In the following section, this chapter will provide information on the EU ETS, CORSIA and other collaborative initiatives in the industry.

The EU ETS

The EU ETS is a cornerstone of the EU's climate change policy. It is the primary technique for lowering GHG emissions from energy generation and industry, such as carbon dioxide (CO_2). As a critical component of EU environmental law, The EU ETS has a legal foundation in the Single European Act (SEA), passed in 1986 and updated in the 1957 Treaty of Rome (EU ETS Handbook, 2015). As the world's first international ETS, which was established in 2005, the EU ETS is a classic 'cap-and-trade system' in which a limit (the cap) is imposed on the right to release specific pollutants across a geographical region, and enterprises can exchange emission rights within that area. The EU ETS makes it economically profitable for businesses and airlines to invest in environmentally friendly equipment (EU ETS, 2022). A distinctive aspect of the EU ETS, in addition to its size in terms of geographical reach, the number of resources and the amount of funding, is that it is implemented through the EU rather than a single state or national government (Ellerman, Marcantonini, & Zaklan, 2016).

The Direction of EU ETS was adopted in 2003, and the system went into effect on January 1, 2005. While all ranges and boundaries were drawn in the first three phases, The EU ETS is currently in its fourth phase (between 2021 and 2030). The EU adopted some legislative proposals in 2021 for the fourth phase, which includes interim targets for at least a 55% reduction in GHG emissions by 2030. These legislative studies aim to determine how to achieve the EU's climate-neutral target by 2050.

Instead, the EU also has a Fit for 55 that will cut its GHG emissions by 55% by 2030. The European Commission put out the plan in July 2021. The measures might become law in the following years if the parliamentary procedure is sped up (EC, 2022b).

CORSIA

The ICAO CORSIA is a programme to reduce the effects of aviation activities on climate change. Carbon offset is a financial tool aimed at reducing GHG emissions and is vital for the implementation of CORSIA. In 2018, the ICAO adopted the first edition of Annex 16, Volume IV, which includes Standards and Recommended Practices (SARP) that addresses the implementation of CORSIA. CORSIA SARPs became available for all State Aircraft Operators, and CORSIA began monitoring, reporting and verifying CO_2 emissions in 2019. All EU and EFTA (The European Free Trade Association) members (including four European states: Iceland, Liechtenstein, Norway and Switzerland) have volunteered to participate in the CORSIA offsetting trial phase beginning in 2021. By the end of 2022, 118 states have voluntarily participated in CORSIA. This number has risen to 107 in 2022, representing the vast majority of ICAO Member States.

CORSIA is primarily a carbon neutralisation/reduction programme that aims to offset emissions that technological advances, operational improvements and sustainable aviation fuels cannot reduce. All aircraft operators flying internationally in ICAO Member States must monitor, verify and report their CO_2 emissions. Therefore, the ICAO CORSIA programme includes regulations for monitoring, reporting and verifying CO_2 emissions from most international flights. On the other hand, some flights listed are not covered by CORSIA:

– Aircraft operators produce less than 10,000 metric tonnes of CO_2 per year,
– Aircraft which has less than 5700 kg MTOW (Maximum Take-off Weight),
– The humanitarian, medical and firefighting processes use aircraft emissions.

In addition to the CORSIA and the EU ETS, initiatives such as New Green Deal, Fit for 55, Flightpath 2050, Fly the Green Deal 2030–2050, Fly Net Zero, Perspectives for Aeronautical Research in Europe (PARE Project), and European Perceptions of Climate Change (EPCC) aim to create a flight path for net-zero aviation.

The *European Green Deal* is one of the primary initiatives taken at the supranational level. The Green Deal's primary objective, being the first continent to be carbon-neutral by 2050, calls for significant transportation improvements. The 'New Green Deal' aims for carbon-neutral aviation by 2050. The 'Fit for 55' targets a 55% reduction in CO_2 emissions by 2030. The European Aviation Research Advisory Council set forth by the (ACARE) initiative Flightpath 2050 sets out a European aviation vision by 2050 for sustainable, safe and efficient air transport with an innovative technology-led system. *Fly the Green Deal* indicates Europe's Vision for Sustainable Aviation for 2030–2050. Through the assistance of ACARE, the European Commission, its Member States, aviation research organisations, design and manufacturing industries, airlines, airports, and aviation energy and service providers have come together to envision a coordinated transformation path that will ensure that Europe can lead the rest of the world towards a competitive, climate-neutral and citizen-centred air mobility system. It defines the activities and participants required to achieve aviation's three primary strategic goals. It outlines three-time horizons and specifies the need for a pro-active and coordinated implementation framework, supported by the European Commission and EU Member States, that consists of both the initiating instruments (policies, regulations and incentives) as well as a system of measuring and impact monitoring to ensure the goals are achieved.

Fly Net Zero is an airline commitment to achieve net-zero carbon emissions by 2050, which was adopted by IATA member airlines during the 77th IATA Annual General Meeting in Boston, USA, on October 4, 2021. Aligning air travel with the Paris Agreement's goals of keeping global warming to 1.5°C, this resolution will need the concerted efforts of the whole sector (airlines, airports, air navigation service providers and manufacturers), as well as significant government assistance to be successful (IATA, 2022).

Another collaborative action, *PARE* (Perspectives for the Aeronautical Research in Europe overarching), is to encourage cooperation between European stakeholders to support the achievement of the Flightpath 2050 goals. To this end, PARE produces annual reports (and associated methodologies) that evaluate the progress, gaps and barriers, and suggest appropriate solutions to close the remaining gaps. The 'Perspectives for Aerospace Research in Europe' reports, which are produced by PARE three times a year, are its main products. They employ specific benchmarks to evaluate the gap between each of the 23 Flightpath goals and the progress made in achieving them.

EPCA (the European Partnership for Clean Aviation) initiative focusses on activities at TRL4 and beyond. The importance of a complete Life Cycle Assessment (LCA) includes design, testing, certification, production, operations and maintenance, as stated in this call for proposals.

The goals and objectives of the stakeholder initiatives in the aviation and the air transport industry are compiled below (ACARE, 2020; EC, 2019; EC, 2022a, 2022b; ICAO, 2019; NLR, 2021; PARE, 2020).

- SDGs put humans at the centre of all actions. It is essential to consider all the factors affecting people as a priority. Also, user-oriented transportation, which is the core of the EU transport policies, must support intermodality. By 2030, it aims for European citizens to make informed mobility choices and have affordable access to sustainable, reliable, fair, accessible, flexible, customer-oriented and seamless connectivity for passengers and freight. And then, in the long term (by 2050), it is desired that 90% of European passenger and freight transport activities can be completed in less than four hours. France has already moved to ban domestic flights on routes that can be reached in two and a half hours by train. High-speed rail lines might have eliminated the need for flying on the same routes. In this sense, the use of transport modes complementary becomes a rule of thumb.
- To combat climate change considering, education, training, research and innovation as a priority is essential. By 2030, research programmes and public–private partnerships will increase the research and innovation pipeline in climate-neutral aviation technologies by 50% compared to 2020. Research and activities on fuel (such as sustainable aviation fuel (SAF) or Hydrogen), emission and noise are essential. For example, EU action plans include creating, certifying and producing infrastructure for large, ultra-efficient hydrogen-powered aircraft between 2035 and 2040. Thus, an important step will be taken for emission and noise reduction.
- It is crucial to develop a complete system understanding of CO_2 and non-CO_2 impacts, minimise uncertainties, evaluate the impacts and risks arising from these uncertainties, and establish a priority environmental action plan and global environmental standards in the short term.
- People spend less time at airports and reduce the noise and emission values they are exposed. In the short term, all noise exposure is expected to be reduced in all airports. Land use management principles will be applied for each airport

zone in Europe with no population growth within the L_{den} = 65 dB (the mid-term) contour, followed by the L_{den} = 45 dB contour (by 2050) according to the 2019 baseline.

- The second action, to create a liveable zone in the EU, will be climate-neutral air mobility. The main aim is to find solutions for reducing aviation related-CO_2 emissions in the short term and then to solve (reach the net zero) them entirely in the long term. Compared to the 1990 baseline, to reduce net CO_2 emissions from all intra-EU flights departing the EU, by 55% (by 2030), to net zero (by 2050). Then, by 2030, plans are in place to set reduction targets in line with the latest scientific understanding and available mitigation solutions, where non-CO_2 climate impacts will be fully understood, managed and monitored. Also, non-CO_2 climate impacts aim to achieve a 30% reduction in all intra-EU flights departing the EU by 2035. By 2050, new technologies and operating procedures will cause 90% less NOx, non-volatile particulate matter (nvPM) and contrail by all intra-EU flights and departures from the EU compared to 2000.

- It is crucial to make improvements to the fuels used to reduce emissions. The energy policies determined by the Continentals are essential for directing energy in aviation. For example, European Aviation activities are fully integrated with the EU energy and fuel sector. The initial goal is to enable the use of SAF, which includes advanced biofuels and electrofuels. In the short term, standards are being established to ensure the composition and conformity of SAFs. SAFs are targeted to account for 10% of all aviation fuel consumed in Europe for inbound and outbound flights in the short term. The use of the ratio of SAF will be 20% in the mid-term and 80% in the long term. The use of SAFs has the opportunity to lower emissions from aircraft significantly. This promise is mainly unrealised, though, since these fuels account for just 0.05% of all fuel used in the aviation industry (EC, 2022a). Apart from air-side activities, fuel consumption is also essential on the land side. All aircraft and engines entering service after 2030 will be certified for 100% unmixed SAF or other low/zero carbon fuels (e.g. liquid hydrogen). By 2030, it is aimed to increase the use of energy sources other than conventional fuel in ground operations at EU airports. It provides all kinds of renewable fuel refuelling, fuel-cell charging, fuel-cell replacement and hydrogen refuelling for ground vehicles within or accessing the airport. By 2050, sustainable hydrogen as an aviation fuel will be available at all European airports. For example, with EU energy and transport policies, passengers can get on a hydrogen-powered bus to a hydrogen-powered airport and board a hydrogen-powered aeroplane. It also has been observed that many studies have been started on hybrid aircraft, especially in supporting green transportation in cargo transportation. It is seen that these are based on lower costs and more on environmentally friendly solutions (Manikandan & Pant, 2021). New power sources are critical for a sustainable future of aviation.

- Another goal is that to improve global leadership and competitiveness. By 2030, appropriate certification and regulatory frameworks will have been developed for the widespread use of sustainable zero-emissions vehicles. The start of deployment of zero-emission aircraft across Europe has been included in the medium-term targets. After the short and mid-term, it is seen that a 30% increase in the cost competitiveness of 'Made in Europe' aviation technology, products and services are targeted in the long term (until 2050). Simultaneously, it is aimed to reduce the cost of certification by 50% in the long term, owing to advanced digital capabilities and new standards.

- In the long term, all activities are intended to be ultimately carbon-neutral. According to sustainability parameters, airport and ATM operations will also improve. By 2030, 30% of airports and other aviation infrastructure are targeted to operate as climate-neutral. By 2050, airports and other aviation infrastructure will be organised to operate with zero emissions. For this, it is seen that shortening the flight trajectory and reducing the operation times on the ground will be an essential step. It is seen that detailed studies have been conducted in this context. All flights should be scheduled with the ability to dynamically reschedule along the route on climate-optimised routes that eliminate adverse environmental impacts and minimise social impacts such as emissions and noise. Recent expansions of global air traffic transport have been done with the scope of (i) conventional subsonic (ii) supersonic aircraft, (iii) EVTOls (electric vertical take-off and landing), or (iv) UAM (Urban Air Mobility).
- A digital transformation is an essential tool in this process that also brings some challenges, such as
  - Cyber security with data processing, sharing and access.
  - Cooperation between different stakeholders.
  - The relationship between the human and the machine.
  - Complex systems with non-deterministic emergent and learning behaviours.
  - Compliance with the standards and rules set forth despite innovations.
  - GDPR-compliant personal data exchange.
  - Management, including all aspects of the supply chain.
- In the short term, the abovementioned shortcomings should be identified and resolved. In the long term, all major aircraft parts must be certified, mainly through digital certification (so that paper-related pollution can be avoided). To minimise errors in the production processes, all routeing should be based on digitised 4D navigation. Real-time simulations should determine precise results, including CFD (Computational Fluid Dynamics) and FEA/FEM (Finite Element Analysis/Method). Therefore, it will be ensured that aircraft operations are maintained safely.
- Other necessary steps are enhancing safety, security and durability by 2030:
  - Safety Management System (SMS) risks arising from diseases, security threats and climate change must be considered.
  - Establishing a close link between aviation and international health organisations such as World Health Organization (WHO) and the European Medicines Agency (EMA), thereby developing systems to help prevent future pandemics.
  - Accommodating disruptive technologies such as artificial intelligence (AI), digital twins and interconnected systems to create an advanced manned-unmanned team for air transport safety management can bring opportunities and challenges.

- Developing specialised training devices, such as hybrid simulation tools, to qualify and/or certify air transport safety devices might also reveal opportunities and challenges.
- The security level is expected to double in the mid-term and five times in the long term. By 2050, the transportation system should be resilient to catastrophic events; it can automatically and dynamically reconfigure individual journeys within the network to meet passenger needs in the event of an outage, helping the system continue to operate at (acceptable) high-performance levels.

Airports, airline companies and other stakeholders are responsible for improving sustainable aviation. All industry actors must take their parts to reach sustainable aviation and the net-zero emission targets. Some exemplary implementations in terms of enterprises can be given. For example, Zurich Airport has reduced its CO_2 emissions by around 30% (by around a third) since 1991 and aims to reduce CO_2 emissions to zero by 2050. According to the airport's sustainability report (2021), process management has been made by considering all SDGs. According to the report, six SDGs (3, 8, 9, 11, 13 and 16) were prioritised while contributing to 15 targets (Zurich Airport, 2021).

Sustainable management and corporate social responsibility (CSR) are critical components for reducing climate change and reaching SDGs. The primary premise of CSR is to include all stakeholders and take them into account while making decisions (Seifi & Crowther, 2018). More and more businesses are embarking on environmental and social sustainability efforts to show that they consider all stakeholders in their decisions and are developing CSR reporting to make these efforts more visible (Sengur, 2021). In recent years the number of airlines that voluntarily publish their social, environmental and sustainability activities in their environmental or sustainability reports is increasing (Okumus, Sengur, Koseoglu, & Sengur, 2020), and many airlines have determined their priority on SDGs and continue to operate in this direction. For example, in the 2021 sustainability report of Turkish Airlines, it is seen that almost all 17 SDGs are in action and making improvements. The company's Sustainability Strategy and SDG distribution are listed as follows (Turkish Airlines, 2021):

- Management Fundamentals (Corp. Gov., Business. Eth., Legal Comp., Risk Man., Cust. Satis., Financial Perf.)
- Responsible Company (Climate C., Waste Man., Fleet Mod.)
- Reliable Operator (Flight Saf. Sec., Emp. Health Saf. Business Cont., Dig., Chang. in Cost. Exp. Behv.)
- Fair Employer (Talent Man.)

CHALLENGES, OPPORTUNITIES AND THE FUTURE OF NET ZERO AVIATION

Decarbonising aviation is not easily accessible, and there are several challenges in front of a zero-emission target. The industry will need to overcome several significant obstacles to become carbon-neutral. One of the main issues is the air transport industry's growth. Under normal conditions, the industry doubled in 15 years. While this is an opportunity for the survival and competitiveness of the industry, it also creates a barrier to environmental goals.

Moreover, the demand for air travel has not yet matured in Asia Pacific, South America, Africa and the Middle East. Those regions are expected to grow above the average in the following decades. Also, since transport is a fundamental human right, it is not easy to restrict it and, therefore, decreasing the demand or cutting the service will always have a public-service and human-right perspective challenge. In addition, the customer base of air transport is generally very privileged, and they will demand past services.

On the other hand, a crisis such as COVID-19 has several complicated impacts on the industry and economic and social life. During the pandemic, the demand for air travel dropped dramatically, decreasing the carbon emission for passenger transport very sharply; the need for intercontinental transportation of emergency and health supplies, vaccines and e-commerce products exploded cargo flights.

Renewing old aircraft and switching to new aircraft that consume less fuel and have lower environmental costs are an important opportunity for the sector. However, renewing fleets is not an easy task for airlines financially. Sustainable aviation fuels might be a sustainable alternative instead of renewing the whole fleet in the short term. However, SAFs also come with their challenges. Although the move to SAF is desirable, and they have the potential to reduce aviation emissions drastically, it does not appear realistic to implement it completely, at least in the near future. This promise has primarily gone unfulfilled because alternative fuels account for just 0.05% of the total fuel consumed in the aviation sector (EC, 2022a). It is inconceivable to create enough SAFs for the whole industry in the short term, and these fuels are also exceedingly expensive.

In fact, one of the biggest challenges might be slowing the progress rate on SDGs worldwide. According to the latest sustainability report prepared by Cambridge University, the globe is no longer progressing towards the SDGs for the second year. Especially goals related to climate change and biodiversity are moving too slowly, particularly in wealthy nations (Sachs, Kroll, Lafortune, Fuller, & Woelm, 2022). Despite constant demands for decarbonisation from all sectors, emissions in 2022 exceed historic levels, with carbon emissions from fossil fuels reaching record levels at 36.6 billion tonnes. The Conference of Parties, sometimes called COP, is the body that makes decisions about the supervision and evaluation of the application of the United Nations Framework Convention on Climate Change. Unfortunately, the COP27, held in Egypt in November 2022, failed to progress on promises or demonstrate that nations were taking meaningful action to reduce global emissions. Even though each COP is crucial to advancing the primary goal of keeping the increase in global temperature to below 1.5 degrees Celsius, COP27 was a missed opportunity and perhaps a step back. However, the crucial concerns for developing countries, such as climate adaptation and loss and damage, were highlighted, rebalancing the discussions and re-establishing the parties' trust in one another. Although the fund's details still need to be worked out, a revolutionary agreement to offer loss and damage financing for vulnerable nations severely affected by climate disasters was recognised as a success.

The UN SDGs are the main triangulation points for future sustainable aviation. While all SDGs are interconnected, they must also be governed holistically and in balance.

With this view, social, economic and ecological development are no longer considered distinct components of the sectorial strategy that is now in use. Aviation needs to implement this viewpoint as a basis for its sustainability strategy. While holding the environmental sustainability of aviation, economic and social goals must also be considered. Without a holistic approach, none of the SDGs will be able to reach.

While there are several challenges in front of net-zero aviation, the industry's commitment and collaborative actions might be promising for the future of aviation. Stakeholders in the aviation industry have started to work together on climate issues, and concrete steps are being taken to reduce the negative environmental impacts of aviation, such as reducing net aviation carbon emissions to half of the 2005 levels by 2050, using sustainable aviation fuels, and engaging in carbon trading. All these environmental efforts might take the future aviation industry in a more sustainable way that meets most of the SDGs.

CONCLUDING REMARKS

While aviation is an essential building block that serves humanity economically and socially, it is also responsible for reducing its environmental impacts. In this sense, sustainability and sustainable development are not only an obligation to reduce the adverse effects of air transportation but also an approach that will determine the sector's economic success.

The 'Agenda 2030: UN Sustainable Development Goals (SDGs)' was established on September 27, 2015, in New York, and they serve as the primary indicators that define the quantifiable objectives that will lead humankind on this road until 2030. By capitalising on the synergy produced by coordinated activities on a global scale, 17 objectives and 169 sub-indicators seek to advance the world towards a more sustainable state. These objectives are linked, and the objective stresses cooperation and working towards common objectives.

Climate change and the industry's environmental impacts are currently one of the most critical challenges facing air transport. Aviation industry stakeholders are involved in a number of collaborative industry actions that will decrease the amount of GHG emissions and mitigate the impact of climate change. The industry embodies its efforts together with all its stakeholders in order to minimise its adverse effects on the environment. Realising these efforts based on targets yearly is critical to reaching the targets set until 2050.

REFERENCES

ACARE. (2020). Time for change, the need to rethink Europe's FlightPath 2050. Advisory Council for Aviation Research and Innovation in Europe. Retrieved from https://www.acare4europe.org/wp-content/uploads/2022/02/Time_for_change_FlightPath_2050.pdf

Altuntas, H. (2019). Biodiversity management. In T. H. Karakoc, C. O. Colpan, O. Altuntas, & Y. Sohret (Eds.), *Sustainable aviation* (1st ed., pp. 81–96). Springer. doi:10.1007/978-3-030-14195-0

ATAG. (2008). The economic and social benefits of air transport 2008. Retrieved from http://www.atag.org/files/ATAG%20brochure-124015A.pdf

ATAG. (2020). Aviation: Benefits beyond borders. Retrieved from https://aviationbenefits.org/downloads/aviation-benefits-beyond-borders-2020/. Accessed on September 30, 2020.

CAPA – Centre for Aviation. (2019). *Climate change: Its impact on aviation. The time to plan is now.* Retrieved from https://centreforaviation.com/analysis/reports/climate-change-its-impact-on-aviation-the-time-to-plan-is-now-454475

Dimitriou, D., & Sartzetaki, M. (2018). Social dimension of air transport sustainable development, world academy of science, engineering and technology. *International Journal of Industrial and Business Engineering, 12*(4), 568–571.

Dimitriou, D. J., & Sartzetaki, M. F. (2020). Social dimensions of aviation on sustainable development. In *Sustainable aviation* (pp. 173–191). Cham: Palgrave Macmillan.

EC. (2019). *The European Green Deal.* Brussels: Communication from the Commission to the European Parliament, the European Council, the Council, the European Economic and Social Committee and the Committee of the Regions. Retrieved from https://ec.europa.eu/info/sites/info/files/european-green-deal-communication_en.pdf

EC. (2022a). *Fly the Green Deal, Europe's Vision for Sustainable Aviation, Report of the Advisory Council for Aviation Research and Innovation in Europe (ACARE).* Retrieved from https://open4aviation.at/resources/pdf/Fly_the_green_deal.pdf

EC. (2022b). Fit for 55. Retrieved from https://www.consilium.europa.eu/en/policies/green-deal/fit-for-55-the-eu-plan-for-a-green-transition/

Efthymiou, M., & Papatheodorou, A. (2020). Environmental policies in European aviation: A stakeholder management perspective. In *Sustainable aviation* (pp. 101–125). Cham: Palgrave Macmillan.

Ellerman, A. D., Marcantonini, C., & Zaklan, A. (2016). The European Union emissions trading system: Ten years and counting. *Review of Environmental Economics and Policy, 10*(1), 89–107.

EU Emission Trading System (EU ETS) Handbook. (2015). Retrieved from https://climate.ec.europa.eu/system/files/2017-03/ets_handbook_en.pdf

EU ETS. (2022). EU emissions trading system. Retrieved from https://climate.ec.europa.eu/eu-action/eu-emissions-trading-system-eu-ets_en

Fischler, F. (2014). Sustainability: The concept for modern society. In C. Weidinger, F. Fischler, & R. Schmidpeter (Eds.), *Sustainable entrepreneurship: Business success through sustainability* (pp. 13–21). Dordrecht: Springer.

Grober, U. (2014). The discovery of sustainability: The genealogy of a term. In *Theories of sustainable development* (pp. 6–15). London: Routledge.

Howes, M., Wortley, L., Potts, R., Dedekorkut-Howes, A., Serrao-Neumann, S., Davidson, J., & Nunn, P. (2017). Environmental sustainability: A case of policy implementation failure. *Sustainability, 9*(2), 165.

IATA - International Air Transport Asssociation. (2022). Our commitment to fly net zero by 2050. Retrieved from https://www.iata.org/en/programs/environment/flynetzero/

ICAO - International Civil Aviation Organization. (2019). *CORSIA eligible fuels.* CORSIA supporting document—Life cycle assessment methodology. Retrieved from https://www.icao.int/environmentalprotection/CORSIA/Documents/CORSIA%20Supporting%20Document_CORSIA%20Eligible%20Fuels_LCA%20Methodology.pdf

IPCC - Intergovernmental Panel on Climate Change. (1999). In J. E. Penner, D. H. Lister, D. J. Griggs, D. J. Dokken, & M. McFarland (Eds.), *Prepared in collaboration with the Scientific Assessment Panel to the Montreal Protocol on substances that deplete the ozone layer* (p. 373). Cambridge: Cambridge University Press.

IPCC - Intergovernmental Panel on Climate Change. (2014). In Core Writing Team, R. K. Pachauri, & L. A. Meyer (Eds.), *Climate change 2014: Synthesis Report. Contribution of Working Groups I, II and III to the Fifth Assessment Report of the Intergovernmental Panel on Climate Change* (p. 151). Geneva: IPCC.

IPCC - Intergovernmental Panel on Climate Change. (2018). *Global warming of 1.5°C. An IPCC Special Report on the impacts of global warming of 1.5°C above pre-industrial levels and related global greenhouse gas emission pathways, in the context of strengthening the global response to the threat of climate change.*

Jeronen, E. (2020). *Geography education promoting sustainability.* Basel: MDPI-Multidisciplinary Digital Publishing Institute.

Kuyucak, F., & Vasigh, B. (2012). Civil aviation. In H. K. Anheier & M. Juergensmeyer (Eds.), *Encyclopedia of global studies* (pp. 191–195). Thousand Oaks, CA: Sage Publications.

Manikandan, M., & Pant, R. S. (2021). Research and advancements in hybrid airships—A review. *Progress in Aerospace Sciences, 127,* 100741. doi:10.1016/j.paerosci.2021.100741

NLR. (2021). *Destination 2050 – A route to net zero European aviation.* Royal Netherlands Aerospace Centre, SEO Amsterdam Economics. Retrieved from https://www.destination2050.eu/wp-content/uploads/2021/03/Destination2050_Report.pdf

Okumus, F., Sengur, F. K., Koseoglu, M. A., & Sengur, Y. (2020). What do companies report for their corporate social responsibility practices on their corporate websites? Evidence from a global airline company. *Journal of Hospitality and Tourism Technology, 11*(3), 385–405.

PARE. (2020). *Perspectives for Aeronautical Research in Europe.* EU Horizon 2020 Project Report. Retrieved from https://www.pareproject.eu/_files/ugd/e00f26_cf9f0a53493748db85357 7a3ce11a12b.pdf

Rhoades, D. L. (2016). *Evolution of international aviation: Phoenix rising.* London: Routledge.

Sachs, J., Kroll, C., Lafortune, G., Fuller, G., & Woelm, F. (2022). *Sustainable Development Report 2022.* Cambridge University Press.

Seifi, S., & Crowther, D. (2018). The need to reconsider CSR: Introduction. In D. Crowther & S. Seifi (Eds.), *Redefining corporate social responsibility* (pp. 1–11). Bingley: Emerald Publishing Limited.

Sengur, F. (2021). Corporate social responsibility reporting: Evolution, institutionalization, and current state. In *The Palgrave handbook of corporate social responsibility* (pp. 1321–1345). Cham: Springer International Publishing.

Sengur, F. K. (2022). Air traffic management. In D. Buhalis (Ed.), *Encyclopaedia of tourism management and marketing* (pp. 117–119). Cheltenham: Edward Elgar Publishing.

Steffen, W., Richardson, K., Rockström, J., Cornell, S. E., Fetzer, I., Bennett, E. M., & Sörlin, S. (2015). Planetary boundaries: Guiding human development on a changing planet. *Science, 347*(6223), 1259855.

Tsiropoulos, I., Nijs, W., Tarvydas, D., & Ruiz, P. (2020). *Towards net-zero emissions in the EU energy system by 2050. Insights from scenarios in line with the 2030.*

Turkish Airlines. (2021). *Turkish Airlines Sustainability Report.* Retrieved from https://investor. turkishairlines.com/documents/sustainability/turkish-airlines-sustainability-report-2021.pdf. Accessed on November 20, 2022.

UN - United Nations. (2015). *Transforming our world: The 2030 Agenda for Sustainable Development.* A/RES/70/1, publication, New York, NY.

UN - United Nations. (2023). 17 goals to transform our world. Retrieved from https://www.un.org/ sustainabledevelopment/. Accessed on November 20, 2022.

Zurich Airport. (2021). *Zurich Airport Sustainability Annual Report.* Retrieved from file:///C:/Users/ Anadolu/Zotero/storage/5MR5DW6P/focus.html. Accessed on November 20, 2022.